MASS MEDIA

GARLAND REFERENCE LIBRARY
OF SOCIAL SCIENCE
(Vol. 310)

MASS MEDIA
A Chronological Encyclopedia
of Television, Radio, Motion Pictures,
Magazines, Newspapers, and Books
in the United States

Robert V. Hudson

GARLAND PUBLISHING, INC. · NEW YORK & LONDON
1987

Library of Congress Cataloging-in-Publication Data

Hudson, Robert V. (Robert Vernon), 1932–
Mass Media

(Garland Reference Library of Social Science;
vol. 310)
Bibliography: p.
Includes index.
1. Mass Media—United States—History—Chronology.
I. Title.   II. Series: Garland Reference Library of
Social Science; v. 310.

P92.U5H77   1987   001.51′0973   85-45153
ISBN 0-8240-8695-3 (alk. paper)

Cover design by Alison Lew

Printed on acid-free, 250-year-life paper
Manufactured in the United States of America

To
Edwin Emery

Contents

Contents

Contents

Sources and Acknowledgments

━━━━━━━━━━━━━━━ ‖●‖ ━━━━━━━━━━━━

When I was researching and writing my biography of Will Irwin, *The Writing Game*, I discovered the varied usefulness of Richard B. Morris's *Encyclopedia of American History*.[1] In one volume the encyclopedia provided correction, corroboration, or verification of details about many events Irwin wrote of in books, magazine articles, newspaper stories, and pamphlets and commented on in public lectures. In other instances it filled gaps among primary and secondary sources. At the same time, it provided context and background that could be woven into the narrative or used to enhance my understanding of the events Irwin reported and experienced. Oh, if there'd only been a similar quick reference source of the mass media while I was a student! And subsequently, as a researcher and teacher of mass media, I have often needed a quick reference for historical data. One can hardly avoid studying or teaching any aspect of mass media—and many other subjects, so much do those media permeate our society—without involving their past. To a large part, the mass media, their practitioners, and their practices are what they are because of what they were. But, alas, there existed no single, comprehensive, detailed quick-reference source specifically about this facet of American history. The closest document to it was *The Press and America: An Interpretive History of Mass Media* by Edwin Emery and Michael Emery.[2] However useful, it still didn't provide nearly enough of the kinds of information I wanted, especially dates. I was lamenting this gap in reference literature to colleague John Murray one day at lunch when he suggested why not fill the gap myself.

This volume could not have been created without mass media themselves—books, newspapers, magazines, motion pictures, radio, and television—and especially documentary media, the most preserved. A few sources were fleetingly live, from my experiences during thirty-five years as a participant in media and as an observer or consumer of them. Occasionally a phone call to an authority elicited an obscure fact, especially for the recent past. But, in addition to media themselves as primary sources, I mostly depended on three kinds of secondary sources: (1) general reference works, (2) cross-media reference works, and (3) single-medium reference works. (Histories and textbooks functioned as reference works for my purposes.) Many of those sources warrant further reading.

You can find mass media data in many general reference works (indicating the importance of media in society). Those include *Biography Almanac*[3] and *Webster's Biographical Dictionary*,[4] and many general and specialized "Who's Whos." General almanacs and yearbooks are loaded with media information. For the *Chronological Encyclopedia* I found historical encyclopedias more useful than general encyclopedias, which provide too few details of the past. Of the latter, the *Academic American Encyclopedia* ranks among the best.[5]

The most valuable single cross-media source, especially for information on journalistic aspects, is the readable but at times repetitious textbook *The Press and America*.[6] Another readable and valuable, though less timely, journalism history, mainly of newspapers, is Frank Luther Mott's *American Journalism*.[7] The crisply written textbook by Maurice R. Cullen, Jr., *Mass Media & the First Amendment*, aptly summarizes some recent issues and problems.[8] Garland allowed me to consult the galleys for William H. Taft's *Encyclopedia of Twentieth-Century Journalists*, a comprehensive volume of concise biographies of mostly contemporary practitioners, which should prove widely useful, particularly for dates and miscellaneous facts.[9]

Legal books fall under cross-media references because each contains cases and commentary on several mass media. Court reporters provide the full opinions, but readers and textbooks are handier in that they condense court opinions and explain them. Two of the most comprehensive commentaries are *Mass Media Law and Regulation* by William E. Francois[10] and *Law of Mass Communications* by Harold L. Nelson and Dwight L. Teeter Jr.;[11] Francois's volume would probably suit a lay reader better because it is slightly less technical. The law school textbook *Mass Communication Law* by Donald M. Gillmore and Jerome A. Barron emphasizes cases; it also includes helpful commentary.[12] *Bill of Rights Reader*, edited by Milton R. Konvitz, contains mostly cases, with brief background introductions.[13] An interesting interpretation of *Freedom of Speech and Press in Early American History* is a book with that title and the subtitle of *Legacy of Suppression* by Leonard W. Levy.[14] Cases and their contexts are often summed up in general media history textbooks.

For each media section in the chronology, I found a wide variety of other kinds of secondary sources invaluable, too. Biographies of media makers and histories of media organizations abound. Newspapers, notably the New York *Times*, cover all media, with sections of pages regularly devoted to books, motion pictures, radio, and television, as well as coverage of all media industries in the general news and business sections. Yesterday's contemporary report quickly becomes today's historical record. Many articles about media also appear in magazines of general circulation as well as trade journals. With new technology, television as well as radio reports on media—which have been increasing—become more accessible. Among media, only motion pictures rank as a virtually worthless secondary source.

Each medium's products, however, speak for themselves as primary sources.

For the book sections, for example, no source can better describe a work's content than the book itself. Reviewers in such periodicals as the *New York Times Book Review* contribute evaluations. For bibliographical and biographical data about writers, one of the best specialized sources is *Contemporary Authors*.[15] The *Bowker Annual of Library & Book Trade Information* provides abundant data about the book business.[16] Another must source for book trade information is *Publishers Weekly*. For a heavily researched panorama of U.S. book publishing, no source beats John Tebbel's impressively comprehensive *A History of Book Publishing in the United States*, which includes histories of publishing houses and takes readers to 1980 in four readable, detailed volumes.[17]

For newspapers specifically, I found *American Newspapers in the 1980s* by Ernest C. Hynds[18] the most useful single volume besides Mott and the Emerys. Title notwithstanding, Hynds's book is as much a history as a description of contemporary newspapers. For early developments, two classic sources are *History of Printing in America* by Isaiah Thomas and *Main Currents in the History of American Journalism* by Willard Grosvenor Bleyer.[19] A seminal book on the modern alternative press is *The Underground Press in America* by Robert J. Glessing.[20] For general circulation newspapers, developments are reported in the two leading trade journals, *Publishers' Auxiliary* for weeklies and *Editor & Publisher* for dailies; the latter's *International Yearbook* is an invaluable directory.[21] The annual *Ayer Directory of Publications* contains basic data on magazines as well as newspapers.[22]

For magazine sections specifically, three outstanding histories provide an abundance of information. By far the most detailed for magazines to mid-twentieth century is the Pulitzer Prize-winning *A History of American Magazines* by Frank Luther Mott,[23] the premier media historian before Edwin Emery. In five volumes Mott gives historical overviews as well as individual magazine histories. Overlapping and continuing from about where Mott left off is *Magazines in the Twentieth Century* by Theodore Peterson, the best one-volume history of consumer magazines.[24] Picking up where Peterson left off as well as drawing on him and Mott is *American Magazines for the 1980s* by William H. Taft,[25] the magazine counterpart of Hynds's book about newspapers. Containing much less detail but written in popular style is James Playsted Wood's *Magazines in the United States*,[26] perhaps the most readable of the broad consumer magazine histories. Among directories, *Ayer* provides brief, basic data; for editorial information, a bountiful but concise annual is *Writer's Market*.[27] For business data, the monthly trade journal *Folio:* and its annual *Folio:400* issue are extremely valuable. Standard Rate and Data Service's directories[28] emphasize advertising policies but contain current circulation, staff, and editorial information, too.

For motion pictures specifically, one of the most useful reference works is Leslie Halliwell's *Filmgoer's Companion*.[29] Two readable, well-illustrated histories effectively synthesize the development of motion pictures, internationally as well as nationally. *A Short History of the Movies* by Gerald Mast, which is far from short, emphasizes content and technique in the film as art, carrying into the late 1970s.[30] Taking history into the early 1980s is *A History of Film* by Jack C. Ellis; this volume provides a broader perspective, covering film as both art and business.[31] While Ellis and Mast necessarily overlap, each contains information and interpretation the other omits.

For radio and television specifically, the trade journal *Broadcasting* and its yearbook[32] are quite useful, but three books together provide an especially comprehensive look at those related media. Although subtitled *A Concise History of American Broadcasting, Stay Tuned* by Christopher H. Sterling and John M. Kittross is about as thorough a one-volume history of electronic mass media as you can find, except it ends in the late 1970s,[33] just about the time new technologies began to blossom. Sterling joined with Sydney W. Head to update Head's *Broadcasting in America*, whose fourth edition includes new technologies.[34] The authors devote one of four sections to the "Origin and Growth of Broadcasting," and the other parts contain some historical data. (Of course, as any contemporary work ages its historical nature grows.) Like *Stay Tuned* and *Broadcasting in America*, John R. Bittner's *Broadcasting and Telecommunication* is a textbook.[35] And like *Broadcasting in America*, it emphasizes contemporary technology and contains a historical section, one of five, "The History and Development of Telecommunication." Though panoramic, Bittner's coverage is the least detailed, most concise, and most up to date of the three, touching the mid-1980s.

Because the electronic media have been regulated more than any other mass medium, government documents are particularly important. A handy one-volume source is *Documents of American Broadcasting*, edited by Frank J. Kahn.[36] He has aptly selected a wide variety of material, including statutes, speeches, law cases, and Federal Communications Commission statements. *Documents* effectively supplements the historical information in the three textbooks.

In addition to the authors and editors of the hundreds of sources I used—cited and uncited—my thanks go to many individuals who helped in many ways. My son Drew R. Hudson processed some early rough draft. For the final manuscript Carol Smith took over as chief typist, assisted by Susan Hazard and proofreader George Smith. Jean C. Kast also assisted in the final stages of manuscript preparation. Terry P. Link, reference librarian at Michigan State University, provided valuable assistance, particularly in preparation of the index. Erik S. Lunde, author of *Horace Greeley*,[37] allowed me to bounce ideas off him. Editor Gary Kuris of Garland showed remarkable patience through my reconceptualizations and delays.

In later stages, I particularly appreciated Editor Phyllis Korper's encouragement and Copyeditor Shirley M. Cobert's innumerable improvements. Production Editor Robert Kowkabany adroitly shepherded the conversion from hard copy to page proofs, co-produced the index, and contributed in many other ways. Helping in a variety of other ways were Erwin P. Bettinghaus, Dorothy D. Hudson, Robert H. Hudson, Boyd L. Miller, Herbert J. Oyer, Todd Simon, Stanley I. Soffin, Linda W. Wagner-Martin, and innumerable reference librarians. Special thanks go to Professors J. Edward Gerald and Donald M. Gillmor, who introduced me to legal research, and, of course, to Professor Murray, who aided and abetted the original conception. My thanks also go, in memoriam, to Dr. Warren C. Price, who stimulated my interest in the history of mass media.

Last but foremost my gratitude goes to Professor Edwin Emery, who guided my initial immersion into researching the *histories* of mass media. Although retired from the University of Minnesota, Dr. Emery remains unchallenged as the leading contemporary historian of mass media. To him I dedicate this book.

Robert V. Hudson
Lansing, Michigan
March 1986

Notes

[1]*The Writing Game: A Biography of Will Irwin* (Ames: Iowa State University Press, 1982). The sixth edition of the *Encyclopedia of American History* (New York: Harper & Row, Publishers, Inc.), edited by Morris, was published in 1982.

[2]Englewood Cliffs, N.J.: Prentice Hall, Inc., 1954, 1962, 1972, 1978, 1984.

[3]Detroit: Gale Research Company, 1981, 1982, 1983.

[4]Most recently called *Webster's New Biographical Dictionary* (Springfield, Mass.: Merriam-Webster Inc., Publishers, 1983).

[5]Danbury, Conn.: Grolier Incorporated, 1985.

[6]*See note 2.

[7]Third edition (New York: The Macmillan Co., 1962).

[8]*Mass Media & the First Amendment: An Introduction to the Issues, Problems, and Practices* (Dubuque, Iowa: Wm. C. Brown Company Publishers, 1981).

[9]New York: Garland Publishing, Inc., 1986.

[10]Second edition (Columbus, Ohio: Grid Inc., 1978).

[11]*Law of Mass Communications: Freedom and Control of Print and Broadcast Media*, fourth edition (Mineola, N.Y.: The Foundation Press, 1982).

[12]*Mass Communication Law: Cases and Comment* (St. Paul, Minn.: West Publishing Co., 1969, 1974, 1979, 1984).

[13]*Bill of Rights Reader: Leading Constitutional Cases* (Ithaca, N.Y.: Cornell University Press, 1954, 1963, 1965, 1968, 1973).

[14]New York: Harper & Row, Publishers, 1963.

[15]Most recent was the bimonthly New Revision Series (Detroit: Gale Research Co., 1981–).

[16]Thirtieth edition (New York: R. R. Bowker Company, 1985).

[17]New York: R. R. Bowker Company, 1972, 1975, 1978, 1981.

[18]New York: Hastings House, Publishers, 1980.

[19]Two volumes, second edition (Albany, N.Y.: Joel Munsell, Printer, 1874); Boston: Houghton Mifflin Company, 1927.

[20]Bloomington: Indiana University Press, 1970.

[21]New York: The Editor & Publisher Co., Inc., 1985.

[22]Most recently called *The IMS Directory of Publications* (Fort Washington, Penn.: IMS Press, 1986).

[23]Cambridge: Belknap Press of Harvard University Press, 1930, 1938, 1957, 1968.

[24]Urbana: University of Illinois Press, 1964.

[25]New York: Hastings House, Publishers, 1982.

[26]Second edition (New York: Ronald Press, Inc., 1956).

[27]See note 22; Cincinnati: Writer's Digest Books, 1985.

[28]Published monthly are Business Publication Rates and Data and Consumer Magazine and Agri-Media Rates and Data.

[29]New York: Charles Scribner's Sons, 1965, 1967, 1970, 1974, 1976, 1977, 1980, 1984.

[30]Third edition (Indianapolis: Bobbs-Merrill Educational Publishing, 1981).

[31] Second edition (Englewood Cliffs, N.J.: Prentice-Hall, Inc., 1985).

[32]Broadcasting Cablecasting Yearbook 1985 (Washington, D.C.: Broadcasting Publications Inc., 1985).

[33]Belmont, Calif.: Wadsworth Publishing Company, 1978.

[34]Broadcasting in America: A Survey of Television, Radio, and New Technologies (Boston: Houghton Mifflin Company, 1982).

[35]Second edition (Englewood Cliffs, N.J.: Prentice-Hall, Inc., 1985).

[36]Fourth edition (Englewood Cliffs, N.J.: Prentice-Hall, Inc., 1984).

[37]Boston: Twayne Publishers, 1981.

How to Use This Encyclopedia

———————————— ||●|| ————————————

The purpose of this encyclopedia is to provide one handy, comprehensive reference for historical facts about the mass media in the United States of America. Beginning in 1638, when the first press was founded in the English colonies, to 1985, at the conclusion of this writing, this volume traces the origin and development of books, broadsides, pamphlets, newspapers, magazines, motion pictures, radio, and television. Emphasis is on achievements, dates, events, and people.

An introductory overview, "Trends in Mass Media History," precedes the Chronology. The Trends section highlights the changes that characterize the history of the American media, emphasizing the evolution of the only business expressly protected by the Constitution. This overview shows that the media system sanctioned by one brief, broad statement in the First Amendment has increased tremendously in size and complexity. That growth, whether or not progress, is also reflected in the increasing diversity and number of entries in the detailed Chronology.

The Chronology presents synopses of significant events—including founding of media and related organizations—in mass media history. All information applies to the United States unless otherwise specified. Although ethnic, geographical, and media diversity has been sought, selection emphasizes events of national import, with the major exception of newspapers, usually a local medium.

Events are arranged sequentially within periods reflecting American history. Each period is divided into sections by medium or interrelated media, beginning with the earliest mass media (Books, Broadsides, Pamphlets) and ending with the latest mass media (Radio and Television). Such media categories (sections) have been added to periods as the media arrived on the American scene. General or cross-media entries usually run under the medium most affected or under newspapers. Entries are by years to facilitate your consultation of individual items; where appropriate, parenthetical founding dates within entries provide leads to related entries. Lacking knowledge of the year, you can find an item through the detailed Index, which follows the Chronology. To highlight trends, statistical summaries of media, such as the number of foreign-language newspapers or of cable television systems, appear occasionally under the years in which they apply. With this structure you not only can easily find isolated facts, but also can read the entries sequentially as a detailed narrative.

Entries are usually structured chronologically, beginning with a statement of origin. Court cases begin with the citation and a statement of significance, then are summarized chronologically. Life dates for media, organizations, and prominent historical figures appear in parentheses after the names of primary entries. For example, in

1831. *The Liberator* (1 January–29 December 1865)

the first date (1 January) indicates the founding, or first issue, in 1831, and the second date (29 December 1865) indicates the discontinuance, or last issue. (Discontinuance dates are omitted within parentheses when given in the narrative description below [or when unavailable].)

Parenthetical life and death dates of principals appear in only the first mention of that person within a period. Their names usually appear in full on first mention and as popularly known (or by last only) thereafter. An organization commonly referred to by its initials (e.g., Federal Communications Commission) is usually so identified (FCC) after its first, full reference. Common technical abbreviations (e.g., VHF for very high frequency) are used throughout the Chronology after their introduction. In newspaper entries, the name of the home city or town is excluded from the title, whether or not it appeared in the nameplate. When the title pertains to a county, state, or region, however, the name of the area is included.

Trends in Mass Media History

————————— ‖●‖ —————————

In the history of what is now the United States of America, the major media of communication have served both general and narrow audiences with ideas, information, and entertainment. At different periods a medium may serve predominantly one vast audience with many diverse and similar interests or a vast variety of audiences, each having a common interest, or both. These characteristics are reflected in this overview, which broadly coincides with the periodization in the Chronology. The overview outlines the growth in size and complexity of the mass communication system.

During the first century of occupation of the New World by the English and continental Europeans, the indigenous communication system was simple. Ideas, information, and entertainment traveled by handwritten documents, by word of mouth, or by books, broadsides, and pamphlets. Development of products of the printing press, which the Puritans had introduced to North America (1638), was limited by local authorities and English government restrictions, notably the licensing act.

Domestic publications were usually sanctioned by theocrats, if not the crown. Most publications were religious, like the first book (*Bay Psalm Book*, 1640), or educational, for the Puritans' schools. The only newspapers came from Europe, mainly London. An attempt to publish a colonial newspaper, in Boston (1690), got as far as one issue, whose content rankled the authorities, before it succumbed to their censorship. Expiration of the licensing act (1694) opened the way for more publications, but English common law and local authorities still restrained printers.

In the eighteenth century colonists fought with increasing success against those restraints, as the authoritarian philosophy of control by government gradually gave way to the libertarian philosophy of control by marketplace. Crumbling restraints made it easier for printers and their backers to undertake new ventures. The foundation was laid, publication by publication, for an open-market system dominated by books, newspapers, and magazines.

The first continuous colonial newspaper (1704), the Boston *News-Letter*, was, however, "Published by Authority." The first printer flauntingly to break the custom of publishing with at least the tacit permission of the British or local authorities was James Franklin of Boston. He seems to have relished criticizing and defying them in his *New-England Courant* (1721), even though it landed him in jail.

If Franklin's contumacy was a street sign pointing the way toward ultimate freedom to publish criticism of the government, John Peter Zenger's seditiousness was a billboard. Zenger's *New-York Weekly Journal* (1733), backed by a political faction opposing the crown's local representatives, published criticism of his majesty's minions, who charged him with seditious libel. The jury took the law into its own hands and returned an illegal verdict of "not guilty." The case set no legal precedent but did reflect public opinion, and the crown abandoned the case. Apparently crown prosecutions for published criticism stopped. But colonial assemblies continued to cite for contempt and otherwise to harass obdurate printers.

By the Stamp Act (1765) foreign-language newspapers and colonial magazines had been added to the media mix, although they were few. Religious, literary, eclectic, and public affairs magazines were launched. A relatively new indigenous medium, magazines played a less important role in the American Revolution than newspapers and pamphlets.

All four media, however, often played interrelated roles. Both Whig John Dickinson's arguments for home rule (1767–1768) and patriot Thomas Paine's appeals for freedom (1776) appeared in pamphlets and newspapers. Paine also wrote for the *Pennsylvania Magazine* (1775) of Philadelphia. Book publisher Isaiah Thomas of Boston staunchly supported the patriot cause in his *Massachusetts Spy* newspaper and *Royal American Magazine*. Also each medium in its own way spread propaganda and information. The press was controlled by mobs who attacked publishers sympathetic to the royalist cause and by British occupation forces who sanctioned royalist newspapers.

With the war's end (1783) the media system began to grow again. The first indigenous fiction appeared in books. The first daily newspapers were printed. The western movement stimulated frontier newspapers. Magazines, increasing in popularity, often carried more original content, including literature and politics, in addition to traditionally purloined matter from foreign and domestic publications. In all three media, writers argued over the new constitution.

Ratification (1789) made freedom of the press official. The First

Amendment stipulated that "Congress shall make no law . . . abridging the freedom of . . . the press." For the first time anywhere a federal constitution sanctioned citizens' rights to write and publish without federal legislative restraints.

No model for free expression existed, and invective flourished, especially in partisan political papers. But the important new trend was the growth of the press north, south, and west. Postal acts (1792, 1794) facilitated the circulation of newspapers and magazines.

With war pending against the French in the late 1790s, the Federalist government, jarred by verbal lashes of its critics, many of them aliens, felt threatened. In an authoritarian move, Congress passed the alien and sedition acts (1798) to silence critics. Most victims were Antifederalists. Biased, unfair administration of the acts helped Antifederalist Thomas Jefferson win the turn-of-the-century election; as he took office the acts expired. Jefferson, who believed in prosecutions for libel under state civil laws, ushered in a new era of libertarianism that encouraged the expansion of book, newspaper, and magazine publishing.

In the growing free marketplace of the nineteenth century, the media system expanded numerically and geographically. Increasing literacy, immigration, urban growth, and westward movement created new and larger audiences. Technological advances of the Industrial Revolution helped publishers meet the increasing demands for faster, wider dissemination of ideas, information, and entertainment.

In the first third of the century the party press, which the Jacksonian democrats effectively used in the West, and the mercantile press, which aggressively gathered news to serve its commercial readers in the East, wielded most influence. Each kind of newspaper served its own audience, whose members could afford to subscribe at the high rate of about six cents a copy. Books and magazines also were too expensive or too narrow in appeal for the "common man." No mass medium existed.

In 1833 printer Benjamin Day took the first step in filling that gap when he founded the New York *Sun* to appeal to the lowest common denominator of readers. The *Sun* played up human interest and crime news. It sold on the street by the copy for only one cent. The necessary financial support came from the advertising that followed high circulation. The *Sun*'s success spawned imitators. To appeal to wide audiences, penny papers carried sensationalized news colored by no political affiliation, although an editor might independently make a political endorsement. The telegraph and railroad accelerated reporting. Faster presses and other new printing technologies enabled publishers to turn out greater numbers of thicker editions faster. As the penny press matured, its sensationalism diminished. Interpretation and opinion leadership were added to news coverage. Also added was a cent or two to the price. The increasing importance of advertising stimulated the founding of ad agencies. Competition for advertisers and readers became fierce in large urban markets. A mass medium, primarily local in this instance, was born.

Increasing emphasis on news led to cooperative efforts to share the rising costs of reporting. The Harbor News Association (1849) was the first of many news services founded in this and the next century. Feature syndicates would also follow.

With the growth of the mass press came the growth of the specialized press. Newspapers for Indians and blacks were founded. The foreign-language press expanded. Some newspapers and magazines were founded to agitate for abolition of slavery.

Before the Civil War the magazine medium was firmly established. Most magazines appealed to specialized interests, such as agriculture or religion. Some editors aimed for women or children, while others produced eclectics or miscellanies for families. Narrow appeal, high prices, and limited transportation kept circulation low.

Book publishing increased slowly in the first third of the century; only about a third of the volumes sold were published in the United States. That began to change in the second third of the century with the development of a steam press for books and the founding of publishing houses. But book (and magazine) publishers still freely purloined unprotected works by foreign writers, a custom that restricted the development of indigenous literature.

While the War Between the States slowed expansion of the media system, it also stimulated the growth or founding of some media. In the South a few new periodicals replaced northern publications that no longer circulated there. However, newspapers in particular suffered as paper and printers joined the war effort. South and North each had a press association. New York newspapers profited from circulation boosted by war coverage displayed in multideck, boldface headlines and multicolumn woodcut maps made possible by the new stereotype plate. Faster, higher capacity presses rapidly turned out thicker papers and extras. Erratic Union censorship diminished with trial and error. Illustrated magazines, foreshadowing photojournalism of the next century, reported war and politics in words and woodcuts. Military, commercial, and other specialized magazines were launched. A kind of wedding of the book and magazine was the popular dime novel, often published as a story paper.

As the nation healed and expanded, prewar trends intensified. Industrial advances aided all media but none more than daily newspapers, which depended on speed for timeliness. The modern newspaper looked brighter, livelier. Color comics and supplements became important ingredients of Sunday newspapers. Political and social unrest spurred crusades in the news and editorial columns, boosting circulation. Large, attention-grabbing headlines appeared. Stunt reporting and other promotions boosted circulation in fiercely competitive markets. Sometimes content was sensational, even irresponsible, but that was the price of freedom. The best papers were independent, beholden to no outsiders but their readers, although advertisers paid the bills. Big-city newspapers became big, departmentalized businesses whose managers founded trade associations.

In the 1880s and 1890s magazine publishers finally discovered the formula for mass circulation: low price and popular content. A mixture of articles and stories won vast national circulations—now possible with the transcontinental railroad and favorable postal laws—that drew profitable advertising. Some mass magazines, like some literary magazines, were published by men who also published books, which were also becoming a national mass medium.

Great publishing houses expanded or were founded. The rise of free public education, the spread of free public libraries, and the publishing of paperbacks stimulated public interest in reading books. An international copyright agreement curbed widespread pirating of foreign authors' works, expanding the market for U.S. authors.

By 1900, books, magazines, and newspapers appealed to wider audiences than ever before, although each medium still included many titles appealing to special interests. The nineteenth-century trend of growth generally continued into the twentieth century. Now a major new technological development stirred the mass media mix—the motion picture.

By World War I nickelodeons were community fixtures, exhibiting silent feature films and newsreels. Filmmakers cooperated in the government's propaganda efforts, as did most U.S. media. Those that might not or did not cooperate, notably the German and socialist press, were prosecuted under such laws as the Espionage (1917) and Sedition (1918) acts. The mass media covered the war in Europe, overcoming erratic foreign censorship.

After the war a new era of media growth began, large-city newspapers excepted. In many markets where several papers competed, some were discontinued or merged for economic reasons, continuing a practice that had begun earlier in the twentieth century. New tabloids partially filled the gaps. Many tabloids were smaller versions of broadsheets. But three in New York City, particularly (the *Daily News* [1919], *Daily Mirror* and *Evening Graphic* [1924]), gave the term "tabloid" a new sensational connotation by combining nineteenth-century yellow journalism with twentieth-century photojournalism. Circulations soared into record millions.

There were successful innovations in both mass and class magazines, too. The compact *Reader's Digest* (1922) aimed for a wide audience, while the sophisticated *New Yorker* (1925) aimed for a select readership. The increasing number of fan magazines cashed in on the popularity of movie stars.

Movie moguls established large studios in "Hollywood," which became the symbol, if not exactly the site, of the film industry. Some movie stars faded when talkies began to replace silents late in the decade. The industry, however, mushroomed, raking in wealth for the major film companies, which controlled movies from production to exhibition.

The book industry innovated in marketing techniques, which included major book clubs. Also, editors cultivated a new batch of novelists, some of whom would write modern American classics. F. Scott Fitzgerald and Ernest Hemingway were among the new literary "stars."

The rising media star of the fertile Jazz Age was radio. Experiments with this medium, concentrating on point-to-point communication, had taken place before World War I. The government took over radio during the war. Afterward, limited broadcasting resumed. Battles over patents and the formation of Radio Corporation of America (1919) reflected the economic importance of the new electronic technology, but few people in the industry viewed radio as a potential mass medium. At first broadcasting looked like an effective way to promote station owners' goods or services. Some stations were owned by churches, newspapers, or department stores (to sell crystal sets). Advertisers discovered radio's selling power, and by 1927 it was clear that advertising would become the principal source of revenue for broadcasters. To cash in, two major networks were founded (1926, 1927), setting the pattern for the broadcasting industry. As broadcasting developed without government regulation, the situation became chaotic. More stations created intolerable interference, and industry leaders asked the federal government to create order out of the chaos. The Radio Act (1927) set the pattern for broadcasting regulation. It solved the immediate problem of interference. More importantly, it provided a conceptual foundation based on the theory that the public owned the airwaves and on the reality that the number of frequencies was limited. The act allowed for the orderly growth of radio.

Of the five major mass media, broadcasting probably suffered least during the Great Depression. Advertisers and listeners, in their own ways, found radio an economical medium. Movies also provided inexpensive escape from economic woes, but some theaters closed and studio production dropped. Publishing houses survived with books on escape and social subjects; then as the country pulled out of the depression, one entrepreneur launched (1939) a new paperback book revolution, offering 25-cent classics to the masses. Outstanding special-interest and mass magazines were launched, including the pioneering photojournalism magazine *Life* (1936). The daily newspaper was the hardest hit medium, as economic conditions forced discontinuances and consolidations. There were two positive notes, however. The Supreme Court outlawed prior restraint under the First Amendment (1931), as the founding fathers had apparently intended; and more newspapers added specialists to their staffs and interpretation to their reporting, as the New Deal government grew in size and complexity. Competition between newspapers and radio for advertising dollars led to a temporary curtailing of news reporting on radio, but by the late 1930s radio came of age as a news medium by reporting the impending war in Europe. During the decade, however, the big story in the industry was regulatory.

The government strengthened its grip on the medium when it refined the Radio Act (1927) by passing the Communication Act (1934), which provided for a powerful Federal Communications Commission to administer the law. While the new act prohibited censorship, it withheld (as the previous law had) the full First Amendment protection accorded the print media. One did not need a license to publish a newspaper, magazine, or book or even to make a movie; but one still had to obtain a license to operate a broadcast station. FCC approval was necessary, for example, to begin operating commercial FM stations (1940) and commercial television stations (1941). Eventually the FCC would exercise its power to restrict monopoly growth, too. At the time, few newspaper publishers perceived a possible threat to freedom of the press by this modified libertarian system.

World War II tabled further development of television and FM radio, but books, newspapers, magazines, motion pictures, and AM radio developed talent and technology to cover the global conflict. The mass media cooperated in the war effort; few closings by the government were necessary. Paper-cover Armed Services Editions of books were distributed to military personnel. Military publications thrived. Photojournalists covered home and war fronts for newspapers, magazines, and newsreels. A record number of women correspondents reported from abroad. Movies and radio coated entertainment fare with propaganda. And radio reported the news with the drama of sound and immediacy (which would eventually kill the newspaper extra). Armed forces broadcasting and the new Voice of America (1942) contributed to the war effort, too. At home the biggest change in broadcasting was the FCC-forced sale of one of NBC's twin networks, which would become the American Broadcasting Company (1945).

After the war the mass media phenomenon was television, whose unprecedented competitive power would eventually force changes in the other mass media. The movie industry felt TV's impact first.

The competition could hardly have come at a worse time. The Supreme Court had just ended (1948) block booking and vertical control by the Hollywood giants, which broke up their monopolies, setting the stage for a decentralized industry. And a House of Representatives subcommittee had held hearings (1947) on Communist infiltration into the movie business, destroying some careers. TV competition added to the economic fear and uncertainty of blacklisting. Except for drive-ins sprouting across the country, the number of theaters decreased. To draw audiences, studios introduced wide-screen movies with stereo sound, three-dimensional films with thrills and chills, and other technological novelties that boosted attendance temporarily. Color became standard. Some filmmakers launched a campaign against the production code by which the industry self-regulated the moral content of its films to avert government interference. The strategy was to draw people to movies by delivering fare unavailable on pristine TV. To deflect regulation and criticism, the movie industry instituted a more flexible code that would permit rampant violence and sex on the wide screen. But all this was not enough to match the economic power of the upstart medium. Unable to defeat TV, Hollywood studios finally joined it—first by selling their own theater features to it, then by making films for it. Independent filmmakers took over the manufacture of most features for theaters.

TV was also changing the radio industry. As ABC, CBS, and NBC poured their money and talent into TV, network radio waned. Radio became primarily a local medium, consisting of AM and fledgling FM, boosted by FCC approval of stereo broadcasting. Stations replaced network programming with recorded music. Only public radio would have its own national program services in the fourth quarter of the twentieth century.

Less affected by TV than radio or motion pictures, print media changed slowly. Changes included more content about TV and improved visual appeal. *TV Guide* (1953) was the first major national magazine to tie in with the tremendous surge of public interest in the new medium. TV replaced most general, mass magazines (some founded in the nineteenth century) as the national mass medium, leaving the industry to special-interest periodicals. Book houses survived by selling paperback originals and by promoting their hard- and soft-cover wares on TV. They also discovered that promotional tie-ins with TV and movies were effective sales boosters. Mergers and buy-ups by conglomerates, endemic among mass media, further commercialized the literary marketplace.

The Commission on Freedom of the Press, which had studied the mass media just after the war, took the consolidation trend into paramount consideration. Fewer owners meant, the commissioners thought, limited public access to the free marketplace of ideas, which diminished the opportunity for truth to defeat error. Society could no longer tolerate irresponsibility as the price of freedom of the press.

Apparently influenced by the regulatory pattern of broadcasting, the commissioners called (1947) for more social responsibility in all mass media, even if the government had to enforce it. Better, the commissioners said, the media should regulate themselves. A recommendation between the two extremes was that the media and public cooperate in forming something like a National News Council to monitor media performance. Newspapers and other media resisted the proposal then, just as they did years later when a council was finally formed (1973). By the 1980s most of the commission's shocking suggestions had been implemented by the media themselves under public or government pressure.

A temporary increase in the diversity of voices occurred during the Vietnam war years with the spread of a youth counterculture whose soap boxes were alternative, or underground, papers that reported topics too radical or shocking for the commercial press. The youthful protesters relished criticizing and defying the "establishment," which included such traditional U.S. institutions as government and commercial newspapers. In the 1960s and early 1970s hundreds of counterculture publications were published. Most faded with the end of the Vietnam war.

Partly because alternative papers carried either unconventional (often sexually explicit) advertising or none and appealed to a different readership, they posed little threat to commercial metropolitan newspapers. The most serious immediate threat came from neighborhood and suburban newspapers, which had grown with cities after World War II. Increased use of color and a federal law (1970) permitting joint operating agreements between local newspapers if one was failing financially helped some metropolitan dailies. But operating costs kept rising. Chains, or groups, expanded their hold on the nation's newspapers, until by 1971 they owned about half the dailies and almost two-thirds the circulation. The trend continued.

Rising costs was only one problem newspapers shared with other media. The Pentagon Papers case (1971), in which the federal government temporarily got away with prior restraint against two newspapers, left open the possibility of future censorship. Court restrictions on pretrial and trial coverage, as well as development of a new, national law of libel (1964), involved all media but motion pictures (TV had killed newsreels). The same media also were affected negatively by court decisions that prohibited newspeople from concealing sources in criminal cases (1972) and positively by "sunshine" laws that opened some government meetings. The fluctuating legal definition of obscenity most affected books, magazines, and movies, which for a time were not allowed First Amendment protection. The government gradually reduced restrictions on radio and TV as part of a deregulation trend based on the premise that channels were no longer scarce.

The FCC had encouraged the reduction in channel scarcity in radio by curbing national (clear) channels and allowing expansion of FM stereo and in TV by providing for ultra high frequency (UHF) and lower power (LPTV) broadcasting. Commercial radio stations aimed for segments of the local audience, and public radio and TV served other special audiences. By the fourth quarter of the twentieth century, TV seemed to be following the direction of the radio and magazine industries.

Cable and satellite technology made it possible—and profitable—to serve segments of the mass video market. New specialized program services spread, distributed by satellite interconnections to cable companies. Satellite transmission directly to homes and businesses offered more opportunities for special services. Firms tested interactive circuits, which allowed viewers to "talk back" to their sets. For protection and profit, media corporations invested in the new technology.

In the twentieth century the prevailing trend of increasing size, complexity, and interrelationship in the mass media system has seemed paradoxical. While the electronic mass media added efficient new ways to reach both wider and narrower audiences, the tremendous growth of one-medium groups and cross-media conglomerates (many with nonmedia investments) diminished the diversity of sources for ideas and information. The trend of megaconsolidation seemed destined to continue through the twentieth century.

Selected Firsts in Mass Media

———————— ‖●‖ ————————

The game of "firsts" is one of the chanciest for a historian. Tomorrow a researcher may discover evidence that today's "first" is really a "second." The careful historian, therefore, expresses a first as specifically as possible, hedges with a qualifier, or does both—all the time regarding the first as an "earliest known." A reader would be wise to follow suit.

The firsts below reflect far-reaching earliest known achievements in the U.S. mass media. Brief descriptions appear in the Chronology, where they can be found on the page(s) indicated after each selection. More firsts, particularly those of less geographic impact, are omitted from the list but appear in the Chronology.

Selected Firsts in Mass Media

1950 first nonexperimental educational television station, 266

1951 first continuing documentary public affairs series on a (radio) network, 267–268

first motion picture studio to establish a television production division, 188

1952 first legal recognition of motion pictures as a medium for expression of ideas, 262–263

first television coverage nationally of a presidential campaign, 269

first wide-screen motion picture, 262

1953 first educational television channel on a reserved frequency, 269

first major motion picture to lack the Hollywood Production Code's seal of approval, 263

1954 first major congressional investigation of television's relation to juvenile delinquency, 286–287

1955 first major motion picture company to release old feature films to television, 189

first major newspaper to report without language taboos, 274–275

1956 first wide-screen system to use 70mm film, 283

1957 first time U.S. Supreme Court upheld constitutionality of obscenity laws, 272

1961 first live radio and television coverage of a presidential news conference, 291

1962 first metropolitan daily printed by offset in a competitive situation, 276

1963 first half-hour television network news program, 196, 293

first public telecast between Europe and the United States, 292

first videotape "instant replay" (sports coverage), 292–293

1965 first commercial communications satellite, 321

1967 first application of Fairness Doctrine to commercials, 323–324

1968 first "customized" radio networks, 243–244

1971 first statewide press council, 307

MASS MEDIA

1638–1764

Founding Period

━━━━━━━━━━■■●■■━━━━━━━━━━

Books, Broadsides, Pamphlets

1638. First press established in the colonies (Cambridge). Supervised by Harvard College authorities, the printers produced almanacs, broadsides, a catechism, law books, a psalter, sermons, and, after adding a second press, a Bible in an Indian language.

1639. *The Freeman's Oath*, the first printed matter in the colonies. It was followed in the same year by an almanac.

1640. *Bay Psalm Book: The Whole Book of Psalms Faithfully Translated into English Metre*, the first English-language book printed in the colonies. Authors were Puritan theologians Thomas Welde, or Weld (1595–1661), Richard Mather (1596–1669), and John Eliot (1604–1690). Twenty-seven editions were printed before 1750.

1648. *Survey of the Summe of Church Discipline*, by Thomas Hooker (c. 1586–1647). Postulating the principle of divine absolutism, Hooker, in this book and his sermons, intended to "fasten the nail of terror deep" into sinners' hearts.

1662. *Day of Doom*, a religious poem by colonial writer Michael Wigglesworth (1631–1705), a best seller.

1682. *Sovereignty and Goodness of God*, the most popular account of captivity; republished many times under its subtitle, *The Narrative of the Captivity and Restoration of Mrs. Mary Rowlandson*. The author (c. 1635–c. 1678) had been captured by the Indians in a raid on Lancaster in 1676.

c. 1683. *The New England Primer*, compiled and published by Benjamin Harris (fl. 1673–1716), a best seller. Over many years it sold an estimated 6 to 8 million copies.

c. **1689.** *The Present State of New-English Affairs,* a broadside, published with permission of the Massachusetts government. It gave news of Increase Mather's work in behalf of a new charter for Massachusetts. It looked like the front page of a contemporary English newspaper but contained no exact date or serial number.

1693. *Wonders of the Invisible World,* by the eminent congregational theologian Cotton Mather (1663–1728), an annal of Salem witchcraft events.

1699. *Journal, or God's Protecting Providence,* by Jonathan Dickinson (1663–1722), a best-selling account of his captivity in Florida.

1702. *Magnalia Christi Americana* or *The Ecclesiastical History of New England, 1620–98,* Cotton Mather's most important work. In it Mather expounded the splendor of government by God's elect, mixing fable and gross misrepresentation with accurate information. Mather was the most prolific colonial writer, with more than 400 published works.

1707–1741. Best sellers by colonial writers—*The Redeemed Captive* (1707) by John Williams (1664–1729); *Mother Goose's Melodies for Children* (1719); *Astronomical Diary and Almanack* (1725–1764) compiled by Nathaniel Ames; *Poor Richard's Almanack* (1732–1757) by Benjamin Franklin (1706–1790); *No Cross, No Crown* (1741) by William Penn (1644–1718). William Bradford (1663–1752) printed the first American *Book of Common Prayer* (1710).

1754. A *Careful and Strict Enquiry into the Modern Prevailing Notions of Freedom of the Will,* Jonathan Edwards's greatest intellectual effort. Edwards (1703–1758) expounded his understanding of Calvinist predestination. Pastor at Northampton, Massachusetts, and a leading writer on theological and moral questions, he was devoted to the revival of religious values during the Great Awakening.

1762. A *Vindication of the Conduct of the House of Representatives* (Massachusetts), the first political pamphlet of James Otis (1725–1783). In it the Boston lawyer affirmed the privileges of the colonies under British law. In response to the Sugar Act, he wrote *The Rights of the British Colonies Asserted and Proved* (July 1764), in which he raised the argument of no taxation without representation.

1764. First volume of *The History of the Colony of Massachusetts Bay,* by Thomas Hutchinson (1711–1780), covering 1628–1691. The second volume (1767) covered 1691–1750; the third volume (1828), 1750–1774. Hutchinson's *History* was the major historical work of the period.

Newspapers

1690. Boston *Publick Occurrences: Both Foreign and Domestick* (25

September), the first attempt at a continuous newspaper in the colonies. Published by Benjamin Harris, it was suppressed by the government after one issue for criticizing conduct of the war between England and France. Harris had violated the Massachusetts licensing act by publishing without government approval. *Publick Occurrences* was printed in newspaper format and contained foreign and local news.

1692. Intercolonial mail system authorized by the British government.

1704. Boston *News-Letter* (24 April–22 February 1776), the first continuous colonial newspaper. It contained both foreign and local news. It ran the first illustration in a colonial newspaper (19–26 January 1707/1708) and the first advertisement in a North American newspaper. Every issue was approved by the governor's office. Its highest circulation was about 300. Editor-Publisher-Postmaster John Campbell (1653–1728) printed the *News-Letter* "for a Publick Good, to give a true Account of all Foreign & Domestick Occurrences, and to prevent a great many false reports of the same." In 1723 printer Bartholomew Green (1666–1732) became publisher. Upon his death, his son-in-law, John Draper (1702–1762), took over. After 1762 the paper was run by Draper's son, Richard (1727–1774), who continued as the official printer for the governor and province council until his death, when his widow, Margaret (fl. 1750–1807) took over. John Howe briefly published it as a Tory organ, the only paper printed in Boston during British occupation. The *Massachusetts Gazette and Boston News-Letter*, as it had been known for some time, ceased publication a few weeks before the British evacuation of Boston.

1719. Boston *Gazette* (21 December–1741). For the first time colonial readers had a choice of a domestic newspaper, competing against the *News-Letter*. Editor-Publisher-Postmaster William Brooker (Campbell's successor as postmaster) had every issue approved by the government before publication, though formal licensing had expired. Five successive postmasters published the *Gazette* until its 1741 merger with the rival *New-England Weekly Journal*.

• Philadelphia *American Weekly Mercury* (22 December –c. 1746), the first newspaper outside of Boston. Editor-Publisher-Postmaster Andrew Bradford (1686–1742) defended James Franklin when he was jailed (1722) for criticizing authorities. Bradford reprinted the controversial "Cato Letters," arguments for civil and religious liberties, first published in London.

1721. Boston *New-England Courant* (7 August–1726), the first colonial newspaper continuously published without government approval and thus instrumental in establishing the tradition of editorial independence. The *Courant* was bold and literary. When Publisher James Franklin (1697–1735) was jailed for criticizing the local leaders, particularly the theocracy, it was issued by his younger half-brother and apprentice, Benjamin (1706–1790). The paper was the first to "crusade." Also it published Benjamin Franklin's "Silence Dogood" essays.

1725. New-York Gazette (8 November–1742), founded by William Bradford (1663–1752), the first newspaper in New York.

1727. Boston New-England Weekly Journal (20 March–1741), founded by Samuel Kneeland, the first newspaper to have correspondents in nearby communities to send in news of their neighbors, still a common weekly newspaper practice: merged (1741) with Boston Gazette.

• Annapolis Maryland Gazette (1727–1734; 1745–1839), founded by William Parks (c. 1698–1750), the first newspaper in Maryland. Jonas Green revived it in 1745.

1728. Philadelphia Universal Instructor in all Arts and Sciences: and Pennsylvania Gazette (December–1815) founded by Samuel Keimer and later purchased (2 October 1729) by Benjamin Franklin, who shortened the title to Pennsylvania Gazette. Hugh Meredith was co-publisher 1729–1732. Under Franklin the newspaper was one of the best in the colonies, with lively writing, profitable advertising, and large circulation. In 1766 David Hall succeeded Franklin as publisher. The paper was published during the Revolution by two sons of Hall and by William Sellers; publication was suspended during the British occupation of Philadelphia (1777–1778).

1731. Boston Weekly Rehearsal (1775) founded by Jeremy Gridley. Thomas Fleet took over about 1732 and later changed the name to the Evening-Post, which became one of the best and most popular papers in Boston. It followed a neutral course in the pre-Revolutionary period.

1732. Philadelphia Zeitung, published by Benjamin Franklin, the first foreign-language newspaper in the colonies. It expired after a few issues.

• Charleston South-Carolina Gazette (–1802), founded by Thomas Whitmarsh with the help of Benjamin Franklin, the first newspaper in South Carolina. Subsequent publishers included Louis Timothée; his widow, Elizabeth; and Mary Crouch. After the Revolution, the paper was published by Benjamin Franklin Timothy, grandson of Louis, as the South Carolina State Gazette.

• Newport Rhode-Island Gazette (27 September–1733), founded by James Franklin, Rhode Island's first newspaper. Franklin maintained his press there until his death, when his widow and children, all printers, carried on.

1733. New-York Weekly Journal (5 November–1751) founded by John Peter Zenger (1697–1746) with the support of a political faction opposing Governor Sir William Cosby. The paper was involved in a landmark seditious libel case (1734–1735). After Zenger's death his widow and son published the weekly.

1734. Boston *Weekly Post-Boy*, founded by Boston Postmaster Ellis Huske, a Tory organ in the pre-Revolutionary period; suspended about 1755.

1734–1735. Zenger case. John Peter Zenger was jailed 17 November 1734 on a charge of raising sedition; the case came to trial 4 August 1735. His *New-York Weekly Journal* (f. 1733) had consistently attacked the colonial administration of Governor Cosby. Defense attorney Andrew Hamilton argued that truth should be a defense and that the jury should have a new right to determine if the publication was seditious (the law) as well as its established right to determine if the defendant had published the allegedly seditious matter (the fact). The jury's verdict: not guilty. Zenger was freed. Although the verdict established no legal precedent, it enunciated the principle of the right to criticize government officials and discouraged other colonial court trials of printers for seditious libel; none is on record after 1735. Hamilton's arguments for truth as a defense and the right of the jury to determine both the law and the fact were later included in federal and state laws.

1736. Williamsburg *Virginia Gazette* (–1780), founded by William Parks, the first newspaper in the Virginia colony. William Hunter took over at Parks's death (1750). The *Gazette* was succeeded by four other weeklies of the same name and finally was published in Richmond. The paper was revived in the restoration of colonial Williamsburg.

1739. Germantown *Zeitung* (–1778), founded by Christopher Sower (1693–1758) near Philadelphia, one of the longest-lasting foreign-language newspapers in the colonies. The publication, which had a religious tone, went from a quarterly to a biweekly to a weekly. It was continued by Sower's son and Loyalist grandson.

1741. Boston *Gazette* (f. 1719) merged with Boston *New-England Weekly Journal* (f. 1727); the first American newspaper merger. The merged paper lasted ten years.

1742. Philadelphia *Pennsylvania Journal and Weekly Advertiser* (–1793), founded by William Bradford III (1722–1791); the first newspaper to print the original "Crisis" essay by Thomas Paine in 1776. During the British occupation of Philadelphia (1777–1778) publication was suspended.

1743. New York *Gazette, or Weekly Post-Boy* (–1752), founded by James Parker, a successor to the *New-York Gazette* (f. 1725). Independent and bold, it was the foremost newspaper in that colony for years. In 1753 Parker took in William Weyman as partner.

● Boston *Weekly Museum* founded by Gamaliel Rogers and John Fowle.

1744. New York *Evening-Post* (–1752) founded by Henry DeForest.

1748. Boston *Independent Advertiser* (–1749), founded by Gamaliel Rogers and John Fowle. It consisted mainly of radical political writings by Editor Samuel Adams (1722–1803) and his friends.

1750. Fourteen weekly newspapers published in the six most populous colonies. The first semiweekly and triweekly newspapers had already appeared.

1751. New Bern *North-Carolina Gazette*, founded by James Davis, the first newspaper in North Carolina. It continued with suspensions and title changes until the Revolution.

1752. New York *Mercury* founded by Hugh Gaine (1727–1807). In 1768 it absorbed the New York *Gazette* to become the *Gazette and Weekly Mercury*. On 21 September 1776 the paper was taken over from Gaine by Loyalists. On 30 September the British began printing it under Gaine's title, while Gaine published another edition in Newark, New Jersey. In November Gaine moved back to New York and resumed publication under the crown.

1754. First newspaper cartoon published (9 May), in the *Pennsylvania Gazette*, a divided snake with each of the eight sections identified as a colony. Captioned "Join, or Die," the cartoon was designed by Benjamin Franklin to foster united action by the colonies in the anticipated war against the French and Indians.

1755. First newspaper tax passed (8 January), by the Massachusetts General Assembly, for war purposes. The tax was a half-penny per paper printed after 29 April 1755. Printer-publishers complained and passed the cost on to their subscribers, who objected; the tax was usually paid during its two years in effect.

● New Haven *Connecticut Gazette* (–1768), founded by James Parker, the first newspaper in its colony and the first in New England to be firmly established outside of Boston. Parker managed the paper from New York. The paper was suspended for 15 months (1764–1765), revived for three years by Benjamin Mecom, a nephew of Benjamin Franklin, and then discontinued.

● Boston *Gazette*, founded by Benjamin Edes (1755–1803) and John Gill (1732–1785), a leading patriot organ, with such contributors as John Adams, Josiah Quincy, and Joseph Warren.

1756. Portsmouth *New-Hampshire Gazette* founded by Daniel Fowle (1715–1787).

1757. Tax on newspapers passed (1 December) by the New York General Assembly; lasted until 1760. It was similar to the Massachusetts tax (1755–1757).

1758. Free newspaper delivery ended by deputy postmasters general of the colonies Benjamin Franklin and William Hunter, who issued (10 March) notice of regulations for newspaper postage. The regulations required subscribers to pay postage of ninepence sterling a year for every 50 miles or less that a post rider carried a newspaper. Riders would collect both their own postage fee and publishers' subscription money; no fee was charged for carrying papers exchanged between publishers, indicating the importance of the exchanges.

● New London, Connecticut, *Summary* founded by Timothy Green, Jr. After Green's death, his son Timothy III changed the title to *Gazette*.

● Newport, Rhode Island, *Mercury* founded by James Franklin, son of Benjamin's older half-brother.

1759. New York *Gazette* founded by William Weyman. On 30 October 1760 the *Gazette* became the first North American newspaper to devote its entire front page to advertisements, running 15 ads in three columns. In 1768 the paper merged with the New York *Mercury* (f. 1752) to become the *Gazette and Weekly Mercury*.

1762. Rhode Island *Providence Gazette* (–1825) founded by William Goddard, his sister Mary Katherine, and their mother, Sarah.

● New York *American Chronicle* (–July 1762) founded by Samuel Farley.

● *Wöchentliche Philadelphische Staatsbote* (–1779), founded by Heinrich Miller; one of the longest-lasting foreign-language newspapers in the colonies.

1763. New York *Pacquet* (–August 1763) founded by Benjamin Mecom.

● Savannah *Georgia Gazette* founded by James Johnston. During the Revolution it was a Loyalist paper published under British occupation as the *Royal Georgia Gazette* (1779–1782).

1764. Hartford *Connecticut Courant* founded by Thomas Green (1735–1812), a son of Timothy Jr. It later became the Hartford *Courant*.

Magazines

1741. First two colonial magazines founded as monthlies in Philadelphia—*American Magazine, or a Monthly View of the Political State of the British Colonies* (dated January–March), issued on 13 February by Andrew Bradford (1686–1742) and *General Magazine, and Historical Chronicle, for All the British Plantations in America* (dated January–June) issued on 16 February by Benjamin Franklin (1706–1790).

1743. Three early magazines founded in Boston. *American Magazine and Historical Chronicle; for All the British Plantations* (March–December 1746), by Gamaliel Rogers and John Fowle, was modeled on the *London Magazine* and ran pieces mainly from English magazines. *Boston Weekly*

Magazine (March) ran three issues. *Christian History* (5 March–1745), the first religious magazine in the colonies, was a weekly that reported the Great Awakening.

1751–1755. Several weeklies founded in New York. *Independent Reflector* (30 November 1751–22 November 1753), by James Parker, was edited by William Livingston and contained exemplary essays. Its successors, *Occasional Reverberator* (7 September 1753–5 October 1753) and *John Englishman* (9 April 1755–5 July 1755), carried on the tradition of distinguished essays. Also published was *Instructor* (6 March 1755–8 May 1755).

1757. *American Magazine and Monthly Chronicle* (October–October 1758), founded in Philadelphia by William Bradford III (1722–1791), the most original and vital of the literary magazines published before the Revolution. It was edited by Reverend William Smith (1727–1803), provost of the College of Philadelphia, primarily to represent the culture and politics of the colonies to England. It had a substantial circulation of about 1,000.

1758. *New American Magazine* (January–March 1760) founded in Woodbridge, New Jersey, by James Parker.

1765–1783

The American Revolution

━━━━━━━━━━━━━━━ ‖●‖ ━━━━━━━━━━━━━━━

Books, Broadsides, Pamphlets

1765. *Considerations Upon the Rights of the Colonists to the Privileges of British Subjects*, by John Dickinson (1732–1808), a pamphlet prompted by the Stamp Act (1765).

1768. *Letters from a Farmer in Pennsylvania to the Inhabitants of the British Colonies*, by John Dickinson, a pamphlet widely distributed and reprinted in the colonies and Britain. The most significant statement of the legal basis for opposition to the Townshend Acts (1767), it conceded Parliament's authority to regulate trade but denied its right to tax it to raise revenue in America and declared the Townshend duties illegal. Dickinson's arguments had first appeared in the *Pennsylvania Chronicle* (5 November 1767–January 1768) as 14 essays under the same title.

● *A Dissertation of the Canon and Feudal Law*, by John Adams (1735–1826), a revised version of a series of articles prompted by the Stamp Act and originally published (1765) in the Boston *Gazette*.

1769. *To the Betrayed Inhabitants of the City and Colony of New York* (16 December), a broadside by Alexander McDougall (1732–1786) criticizing the assembly for appropriating money (15 December) for supplies for British soldiers quartered in New York. British soldiers and the patriot Sons of Liberty, of which McDougall was a leader, tried to prevent each other from posting broadsides. After a clash on Golden Hill between soldiers and citizens (19 January 1770) resulted in the serious wounding (no fatalities) of several men on both sides, McDougall was arrested (8 February) on a charge of writing the critical broadside of 16 December. Refusing to post bond, he remained in prison until 29 April, when he entered a plea of not guilty and was released on bail. The case never came to trial because the government's witness died. On 13 December, however, the New York Assembly sentenced McDougall for contempt, and he was jailed until 27 April 1771.

1775–1776. *McFingal*, by John Trumbull (1750–1831), a popular epic satire on the Tories (first complete edition published in 1782). Trumbull was also known for a Hudibrastic satire about education, *The Progress of Dullness* (1772–1773).

1776. *Common Sense* (10 January), by Thomas Paine (1737–1809), published in Philadelphia. The most influential of all Revolutionary pamphlets, it was the first clarion call for independence. Paine charged that the "Royal Brute" George III was mainly responsible for the obnoxious measures against the colonies, and he attacked government by monarch. His simple yet dynamic presentation converted thousands to the cause of independence.

• *The American Crisis* (–1783), by Paine, a series of 16 irregularly published essays designed to raise patriot morale. The first number began, "These are the times that try men's souls."

• "The Beauties of Santa Cruz" (1776, 1786), a notable lyric poem by Philip Freneau (1752–1832), the major poet of the period. His other efforts included "To the Memory of the Brave Americans," or "Eutaw Springs" (1781), an elegy to Revolutionary War heroes, and "The Indian Burying Ground" (1788), an idealization of the "Noble Savage." His sea poems included "The Battle of Lake Erie" and "The Memorable Victory of Paul Jones."

1778. "The Battle of the Kegs," a satire by Francis Hopkinson (1737–1791), one of the Revolution's most popular poems. Hopkinson also wrote satirical essays and composed music.

Newspapers

1765. Stamp Act, the first direct tax levied by Parliament upon America (22 March, effective 1 November). It placed a special tax on paper used in legal documents, books, broadsides, pamphlets, newspapers, etc. It was an effort by Parliament to make the colonies pay for England's expense in the war against the French and Indians fought on behalf of the colonists. The *Pennsylvania Gazette* and *Pennsylvania Journal*, in their last issues before the tax became effective, used heavy black rules, signifying mourning. After the tax became effective, some papers found ways around paying it and some suspended publication. After a great outcry by the press and public protesting this "taxation without representation," the act was repealed (March 1766).

1766. New York *Journal or General Advertiser* founded by John Holt (1721–1784). During the Revolution this patriot organ was published in Kingston and Poughkeepsie. In 1793 it merged with (Thomas) *Greenleaf's New York Journal* (f. 1787).

1767. Philadelphia *Pennsylvania Chronicle* (January) founded by William Goddard, who discontinued it on the eve of the Revolution.

● *Connecticut Journal*, founded by Thomas and Samuel Green, the first paper in New Haven.

● The Townshend Acts (approved 29 June, effective 20 November), Parliament's next attempt to control colonial trade, taxed glass, lead, paint, paper, tea, etc. With support from newspapers, many colonies entered into nonimportation and nonuse agreements against English goods. On 12 April 1770 duties were limited to tea.

● "Letters from a Farmer in Pennsylvania to the Inhabitants of the British Colonies" (5 November–January 1768), by John Dickinson, first published in the *Pennsylvania Chronicle*. A Whig, Dickinson opposed the Townshend Acts; he considered Parliament's taxation an invasion of the rights of Englishmen, but he opposed independence. His 14 essays were widely reprinted in colonial papers and in Britain.

1768. Salem, Massachusetts, *Essex Gazette* founded. In 1775 the paper moved to Cambridge as the *North East Chronicle* and in 1776 to Boston as the *Independent Chronicle*. From 1840 to 1876 it continued publication as the *Semi-Weekly Advertiser*.

1769. *New York Chronicle* (–1770) founded by James Robertson.

1770. Boston *Massachusetts Spy* (–1904), founded by Isaiah Thomas (1749–1831) and Zechariah Fowle, as a nonpartisan paper but later staunchly patriot. The *Spy* was noted for its apparent eyewitness account of the Battle of Lexington and Concord (19 April 1775). The paper moved to Worcester 3 May 1775 and became the *Gazette* in 1781.

1771. Philadelphia *Pennsylvania Packet and the General Advertiser* (–1790), founded by John Dunlap (1747–1812), emphasized commercial interests rather than politics. Published in Lancaster during British occupation of Philadelphia (1777–1778), the paper was a weekly, semiweekly, and triweekly before becoming a daily (21 September 1784), published by Dunlap and David C. Claypoole.

1772. Committees of Correspondence, organized by Samuel Adams (1722–1803), a primitive but efficient news service. Local agents reported news of important meetings to Adams's central committee, which processed it for dissemination in behalf of the patriot cause.

1773. *Rivington's New-York Gazetteer; or the Connecticut, New-Jersey, Hudson's-River, and Quebec Weekly Advertiser* founded by James Rivington (1724–1802). Despite his Tory sympathies, Rivington presented all sides in the *Gazetteer* until the Battle of Lexington and

Concord. He discontinued the paper in 1775, then resumed it in 1777 as the Loyalist *Royal Gazette* (–1783).

1775. Philadelphia *Pennsylvania Evening Post* (January–1784), founded by Benjamin Towne. At first the *Evening Post* took the patriot side and was the first paper to print (6 July 1776) the Declaration of Independence. When the British took Philadelphia (1777) and other publishers fled or had their newspapers suspended, Towne remained and turned Tory. When the British evacuated (1778), Towne stayed, changing colors again, and was allowed to continue publishing. On 30 May 1783 the *Evening Post* became the first daily newspaper in America.

• Philadelphia *Pennsylvania Ledger* (January–1778) founded by James Humphreys, a Tory who suspended publication (November 1776) and fled the city before the British occupation. He resumed publishing (26 September 1777) during the occupation, then fled when the British evacuated (1778).

• At the time of the Battle of Lexington and Concord (19 April 1775) 37 newspapers existed in the colonies; only 20 would survive the war, many of these having suffered suspensions. Most papers were weeklies, although attempts had been made to issue semiweeklies and triweeklies.

1776. New York *Packet* (4 January–1792) founded by Samuel Loudon (1727–1813) despite a paper shortage (most printing supplies and equipment had been imported from England). In January 1777 the *Packet* was moved to Fishkill; in 1783 the weekly returned to New York, where it became a daily.

• *Common Sense* (15 January), the influential pamphlet by Thomas Paine advocating independence, reprinted in many patriot newspapers.

1777. Burlington *New-Jersey Gazette* (5 December–1786) founded by government printer Isaac Collins (1746–1817), with the endorsement of Governor William Livingston and a subsidy by the legislature.

• *Royal Pennsylvania Gazette* (–1778) published by James Robertson during the British occupation of Philadelphia.

1782. *New-York Evening-Post* (–1792) founded by Christopher Sower (1693–1758) and partners. In 1783 it became the semiweekly *Morning Post*, published by Samuel Horner and William Morton, who on 23 February 1785 made it the city's first daily, the New York *Morning Post and Daily Advertiser*.

• New York *Independent Journal* (–1795) founded as a semiweekly, the first newspaper to publish "The Federalist" essays (27 October 1787–2 April 1788). Later it became the *Daily Gazette*.

Magazines

1774. *Royal American Magazine* (January–March 1775), founded in Boston by Isaiah Thomas, the first magazine of distinction in America. It carried the *Massachusetts Spy*'s patriot propaganda and a wide selection of other domestic material, including essays, as well as the usual items from English magazines. After six months, Thomas relinquished editorial direction to Joseph Greenleaf, who made it less militant. Greenleaf printed the first important engravings, including some on copper, by Paul Revere (1735–1818), holding British oppression up to obloquy. Other distinctive content included the words and music of a song and confessional, sentimental love stories.

1775. *Pennsylvania Magazine* (January–July 1776), published in Philadelphia by Robert Aitken, an outstanding magazine of the century. Edited by Thomas Paine, the periodical contained a wide variety of material, much of it original. Paine wrote for the magazine in prose and verse about marriage, mechanics, and politics. Notable contributors included Dr. Benjamin Rush and David Rittenhouse. The last issue contained the Declaration of Independence.

1779. *United States Magazine* (January–December 1779) founded in Philadelphia; edited by Hugh Henry Brackenridge (1748–1816). It carried a lampoon of James Rivington by John Witherspoon (1723–1794), president of the College of New Jersey.

1783–1799

The New Nation

========||●||========

Books, Pamphlets

1783. *A Grammatical Institute of the English Language*, by Noah Webster (1785–1843), designed for schoolchildren, and with a grammar (1784) and a reader (1785), influenced the standardization of spelling and pronunciation. By 1837 the *Spelling Book*, or *Blue-Backed Speller* as the book came to be known, had a printing estimated at 15 million copies, by 1890, more than 70 million.

1788. *The Federalist* (March, May), the most influential work supporting ratification of the Constitution, published in book form. The original 77 essays, signed by "Publius," had appeared as pamphlets and in New York newspapers (27 October 1787–2 April 1788) as part of the propaganda by advocates (Federalists) and opponents (Antifederalists) of the Constitution. The two-volume *Federalist* included 6 additional essays. Alexander Hamilton (1757–1804) wrote 50 of the essays, James Madison (1751–1836) 28, and John Jay (1745–1829) 5. They stressed the inadequacy of the Confederation and the need for a strong central government.

1789. *The Power of Sympathy*, by William Hill Brown (1765–1793), the first American novel.

1790. *Journal*, or *History of New England*, by John Winthrop (1588–1649), a diary recorded from March 1630 to 1649. It was revised twice (1825, 1929–1931). The *Journal* contained the Massachusetts Bay Colony governor's General Court speech (1645) on the nature of liberty, which Winthrop argued must be under authority and restraint, and accounts of Massachusetts authorities' relations with such major critics as Anne Hutchinson and Roger Williams.

17

1791. *Charlotte Temple,* by Susanna Haswell Rowson (c. 1762–1824), a popular sentimental novel.

1792. *Modern Chivalry,* by Hugh Henry Brackenridge (1748–1816), a best-selling satire that depicted frontier conditions. It reflected the influence of Cervantes.

1794. *Autobiography,* by Benjamin Franklin (1706–1790), a best seller that became an American classic. It was written between 1771 and 1789 and covered Franklin's life to the end of 1759. In 1791 it appeared in part in France; in 1867 it was published in complete form in the United States. In it Franklin exemplified the Yankee-Puritan spirit.

● Part I of *The Age of Reason,* by Thomas Paine (1737–1809), published. Part II of this deistic work came out in 1796.

1798. *Wieland,* by Charles Brockden Brown (1771–1810), a Gothic romance attacking superstition; and *Alcuin,* by Brown, a treatise on women's rights, the first feminist work. His other novels included *Ormond* and *Edgar Huntly* (1799); *Arthur Mervyn* (1799–1800); *Clara Howard* and *Jane Talbot* (1801). Brown was the first U.S. novelist to attain an international reputation.

Newspapers

1783. Charleston *South-Carolina Weekly Gazette* founded, a descendant of the *South-Carolina Gazette,* which Benjamin Franklin had helped to establish (1732). Run by Benjamin Franklin Timothy and partners, it later was called the *South-Carolina State Gazette;* in 1786 it became a daily.

1784. Boston *Massachusetts Centinel* (–1840) founded by Benjamin Russell (1761–1845) and William Warden. As the *Columbian Centinel,* it was a leading Federalist paper, beginning in 1790.

1785. *Daily Advertiser* (–1809), founded by Francis Childs, the first New York newspaper to begin as a daily.

1786. Pittsburgh *Gazette,* founded by John Scull and Joseph Hall, the first newspaper west of the Alleghenies. It supported the Federalists. The paper continued as the *Gazette* until a 1927 merger, when it became the *Post-Gazette.*

1787. Lexington *Kentucky Gazette* (11 April–1848) founded by John Bradford (who was indirectly related to the renowned Philadelphia publishing family) primarily to promote statehood.

1789. Reporters were granted access to the House of Representatives (8 April), two days after it was established.

● New York *Gazette of the United States* (15 April), founded by John

Fenno (1751–1798) with Federalist backing, the first paper to be an avowed organ of the government. Alexander Hamilton (1755–1804) was a supporter and contributor. Fenno began publishing in Philadelphia (3 November 1790) when that city became the national capital. He suspended semiweekly publication for about three months in 1793 because of financial losses, then resumed the paper as a daily. It was known as the *United States Gazette* 1804–1818.

1790. There were 92 newspapers: 8 published daily, 70 weekly, 14 semiweekly or at other intervals.

● Philadelphia *General Advertiser* (1 October–1835), founded by Benjamin Franklin Bache (1769–1798), grandson of Benjamin Franklin, the first Antifederalist newspaper. Extremely partisan, it often carried personal attacks against Federalists. Known as *Aurora*, it was later edited by William Duane (1760–1835).

● Pennsylvania enacted the first state criminal (seditious) libel law to recognize truth as a defense and the jury's right to determine both the law and the fact.

1791. Philadelphia *National Gazette* (31 October–26 October 1793), founded by Philip Freneau (1752–1832), the leading Republican, or Antifederalist, newspaper, strongly supporting Thomas Jefferson. The semiweekly often battled Fenno's *Gazette of the United States*. It was discontinued for lack of financial support, leaving *Aurora* the leading Republican paper.

1792. Postal Act fixed postage on newspapers at one cent to 100 miles, one and one-half cents over 100 miles; exchanges between editors were still carried free.

1793. New York *American Minerva* (9 December–) founded as a daily by Noah Webster; supported Federalists. In 1794 it was named the *American Minerva and the New York Evening Advertiser*, and in 1797 the *Commercial Advertiser*, which became one of the best and most prosperous mercantile dailies. In 1821 Federalist William L. Stone became editor. The paper became antislavery Republican. Later Collis Potter Huntington (1821–1900) purchased the evening *Commercial Advertiser* and in 1891 added a *Morning Advertiser*, formerly the New York *Star*. In 1905 H. J. Wright consolidated the *Commercial Advertiser* with his *Evening Globe* (f. 1904), creating the *Globe and Commercial Advertiser*, an independent liberal newspaper. In 1923 Frank Andrew Munsey (1854–1925) merged it into his New York *Sun*.

● Philadelphia *American Daily Advertiser* founded by John Dunlap (1747–1812) and David C. Claypoole. In 1800 it became *Poulson's American Daily Advertiser* and in 1839 was absorbed by the Philadelphia *North American*.

● Boston *Massachusetts Mercury* founded; from 1803 to 1814 known as the *North East Palladium*.

• Cincinnati *Centinel of the North-Western Territory*, founded by William Maxwell, the first newspaper in Ohio. Maxwell advocated opening the Mississippi River to navigation.

• Walpole *New Hampshire Journal* (–1810) founded. Joseph Dennie (1768–1812) edited the paper 1796–1799. From 1797 it was best known as *The Farmer's Weekly Museum*.

1795. New York *Argus*, founded by Thomas Greenleaf, the leading Republican paper of New York. A commercial and political daily, it excoriated President Adams. In 1798 Greenleaf died, and his widow carried on. In 1800 the *Argus* was sold and the name changed to *American Citizen*. Under Editor James Cheetham it was a leading Jeffersonian paper until 1807, when Cheetham rejected Jefferson's Embargo Act and the paper rapidly lost influence.

1796. Baltimore *Federal Gazette* (–1825) founded.

1797. Philadelphia *Porcupine's Gazette and United States Advertiser* (4 March–26 October 1799), a daily founded by William Cobbett (1763–1835). It was the most vituperative Federalist paper. As Peter Porcupine, Cobbett viciously attacked the Republicans.

1798. Naturalization, alien, and sedition acts, passed by a predominantly Federalist Congress. These laws were attempts to repress political opposition and to control the Antifederalist press. Several Antifederalist (Republican) leaders were refugees from Europe. Threat of war against France heightened hostility toward aliens. The Naturalization Act (18 June–) authorized the president to deport aliens regarded as dangerous to the country or suspected of "secret" or "treasonable" tendencies. It expired in 1802. The Alien Enemies Act (6 July–) authorized the president, during declared war, to banish or imprison aliens from an enemy country. The Sedition Act (14 July–3 March 1801) declared that "any false, scandalous and malicious writing" bringing into disrepute the government or its officials was punishable by a maximum fine of $2,000 and maximum imprisonment of two years. Under the act a defendant could plead truth as a defense and the jury had the right to determine both the law and the fact (arguments in the Zenger case, 1734–1735). Of the 25 persons prosecuted, all Republicans—among them several editors or printers—10 were convicted.

• Frankfort, Kentucky, *Palladium* (–c. 1817) founded.

1799. Cincinnati *Western Spy* (–1822) founded.

• Raleigh, North Carolina, *Register* founded by Joseph Gales (1761–1841). For a short time his son-in-law, William Winston Seaton (1785–1866), was his partner; in 1832 Gales transferred his paper to his son Weston Raleigh Gales.

• Baltimore *American* founded; became a strong Union organ in the Civil War. In 1921 Frank A. Munsey bought the paper, and in 1923 he sold it to William Randolph Hearst (1863–1951), who in 1928 made it a Sunday only paper.

• Alexandria, Virginia, *Times*, George Washington's home paper, carried the first news (16 December) of his death (14 December).

Magazines

1783. *Boston Magazine* (October–October 1786) published by John Eliot, James Freeman, and George R. Minot.

1784. *Gentleman and Lady's Town and Country Magazine* (May–December 1784) founded in Boston.

1786. *Columbian Magazine* (–1792), founded in Philadelphia by Mathew Carey (1760–1839) and partners, one of the most attractive periodicals of the century, carrying elaborate illustrations, including copperplate engravings. In 1790 it merged with *Universal Asylum*, and during the latter half of its life was known as the *Universal Asylum, and Columbian Magazine*. It was one of the four longest-lived magazines in the century.

• *New Haven Gazette and the Connecticut Magazine* (16 February–18 June 1789) founded by Josiah Meigs and Eleutheros Dana.

• *Worchester* (Massachusetts) *Magazine* (April–March 1788) founded by Isaiah Thomas (1749–1831).

1787. *American Museum* (January–December 1792) founded and edited in Philadelphia by Mathew Carey for educated readers. Invaluable for studying the economics, politics, and society of its day, it was one of four longest-lived magazines of the century.

• *American Magazine* (December–November 1788), founded by Noah Webster, New York City's first monthly. It devoted space to political topics and current events, including vigorous discussion of the new Constitution.

1789. *Massachusetts Magazine* (January–December 1796), founded in Boston by Isaiah Thomas, one of the most respected publications of the time, mainly for its writing and wide variety of content. It was one of the four longest-lived magazines of the century.

1790. *New–York Magazine* (January–December 1797), one of the four longest-lived magazines of the century. It carried a variety of interesting miscellany.

1794. Postal Act amended to provide mail service for magazines. They were no longer distributed at the whim of postmasters, few of whom had much regard for the medium. Postage, paid by subscribers, ran high: 48 cents–96 cents, depending on distance.

1795. *Theological Magazine* (July–February 1799) founded in New York.

1799. *Monthly Magazine and American Review* (April–December 1800) founded in New York; edited by Charles Brockden Brown.

● *National Magazine* (June–1800) founded in Richmond, Virginia.

1800–1829

The Expanding Nation

Books

1800. *Life of George Washington*, by Mason Locke Weems (1759–1825), a best-selling biography.

1809. *A History of New York . . . by Diedrich Knickerbocker*, by Washington Irving (1783–1859), a best seller. The first edition was reprinted in 1927. New York's Knickerbocker school of writers (which included Irving, William Cullen Bryant, and James Fenimore Cooper) took its name from this satire. Irving's *Sketch Book* (1819), a long-time best seller, included such stories as "Rip Van Winkle" and "The Legend of Sleepy Hollow." It was produced in England. In continental Europe, Washington wrote *Bracebridge Hall* (1822), *The Life and Voyages of Columbus* (1828), *The Conquest of Granada* and *Tales of a Traveler* (1829), and *The Alhambra* (1832). Returning to the United States (1832), he continued his popularity with *A Tour on the Prairies* (1835), *Astoria* (1836), and *The Adventures of Captain Bonneville* (1837). Of his later works, most important was *Life of Washington* (1855–1859).

1817. J. & J. Harper, publishing house, founded in New York by brothers James Harper (1795–1869) and John Harper (1797–1875); became Harper & Bros. in 1833. The firm achieved more effective distribution in 1830 by adopting stereotyping plates for "omnibus editions" of English reprints. In the 1840s it increased its profits by issuing 25-cent English novels.

1821. *The Spy*, James Fenimore Cooper's first best seller and the first of his works using an American theme and setting. In the novel Cooper (1789–1851) displayed his ability to depict forest life and create authentic North American characters. Other best sellers by Cooper included *The Pilot* (1823), a sea story, and the Leatherstocking Tales, which emphasized conflicts between primitive and civilized values on the frontier. These tales consisted of *The Pioneers* (1823), the first; *The Last of the Mohicans* (1826); *The Prairie* (1827), last in narrative order; *The Pathfinder* (1840); and *The Deerslayer* (1841). Cooper established the North American historical romance.

1824. *The Life of Mrs. Jemison,* by James Everett Seaver, a best-selling story of Indian captivity.

1825. *Journal,* by Sarah Kemble Knight (1666–1727), a vivid account of a horseback journey alone to New York (1704–1705), with humorous sidelights on rural manners and speech.

1827. *Northwood, or Life North and South,* by Sarah Josepha Hale (1788–1879), probably the first novel on an antislavery theme.

• *Peter Parley* published for juveniles. Samuel Griswold Goodrich (1893–1860) employed writers to mass produce these moralistic stories; they sold about 7 million copies 1827–1860. The growth of the middle class, establishment of subscription libraries, extension of free public education, and the lyceum movement influenced book publishing and literary standards, creating a mass audience that expanded the market for books of practical instruction and morally uplifting sentimental novels. Popular sellers included etiquette books and juveniles.

1829. Carey & Hart, publishing house, founded in Philadelphia by Edward Carey and Abraham Hart; a leader in distribution methods.

Newspapers

1800. Washington, D.C., *National Intelligencer* (31 October–c. 1865), founded by Samuel Harrison Smith as a triweekly (with his Philadelphia *Universal Gazette* as its weekly edition); became daily 1 January 1813. Although the triweekly was an unofficial organ of the Jefferson administration, it reported Congressional proceedings without bias. During 26 years of patronage the *National Intelligencer* had $1 million in government printing contracts; it held the House of Representatives printing contract 1801–1805. The paper was displaced as the administration organ during the Jacksonian years, and it represented the Whig party through the 1840s. In 1810 Joseph Gales, Jr. (1786–1860), purchased the *Intelligencer,* and from 1812 to 1860 it was published by Gales and William W. Seaton (1785–1866).

• Georgetown *Washington Federalist* (25 September–1809), founded as a Federalist triweekly; scurrilously attacked President Jefferson.

• Charleston, South Carolina, *Times* founded.

1801. There were 202 newspapers (1 January); about a dozen of the many papers born in the Revolutionary period were still being published.

● New York *Evening Post* (16 November–) founded by Alexander Hamilton (1757–1804) and others, with William Coleman as editor; influential Federal organ. For 1829–1878 William Cullen Bryant (1794–1879) was editor in chief; he veered from Federalist tradition and supported the Democratic Party. Sold in 1881 to Henry Villard (1835–1900). Edwin Lawrence Godkin (1831–1902) was editor in chief 1883–1899, Horace White (1834–1916) 1899–1903. In 1900 Oswald Garrison Villard (1872–1949), Henry's son, became publisher and continued the paper as a liberal newspaper; it was pacifist during World War I. In 1939 Dorothy Schiff (1903–) bought the *Post*; she made it a tabloid, departmentalized news, and added features and columns, including columnist Max Lerner. Editors were Ted O. Thackrey, then James W. Wechsler. Beginning in 1952, the *Post* backed Democratic presidential nominees. In 1967 the paper became the only afternoon daily in New York City, increasing its circulation by two-thirds. In 1977 Australian Rupert Murdoch (1931–) bought the *Post* and sensationalized it. Advertising increased and circulation rose. The *Post* was the city's oldest surviving daily in the mid-1980s, when daily circulation was about 930,000, sixth largest nationally.

1803. Charleston, South Carolina, *Courier* (10 January–) founded by Aaron Smith Willington, Stephen Cullen Carpenter, and Lorring Andrews. It became Charleston's leading mercantile paper and showed enterprise in gathering news by meeting incoming ships. Later, as the *News and Courier*, it was Unionist during the Nullification crisis in South Carolina.

1804. Richmond, Virginia, *Enquirer* (9 May–1877) founded as a semiweekly by Thomas Ritchie (1778–1854) with Alexander Hamilton's help; successor to Meriwether Jones's *Examiner* (1798–1804). Under Ritchie the *Enquirer* became a powerful paper in the South and a leading voice of the Democratic Party in the nation.

● Vincennes *Indiana Gazette* founded by Elihu Stout, who had been promised a territorial legal printing contract. In 1807 it became the *Western Sun* and in 1879 the *Sun-Commercial*.

● Croswell libel case, the most celebrated press case in this period. Harry Croswell published in his Hudson, New York, *Wasp*, a Federalist weekly, an exchange from Alexander Hamilton's New York *Evening Post* reporting that President Jefferson had paid Richmond editor James Callender to spread the word that George Washington had been a perjurer, robber, and traitor and that other Federalists were equally reprehensible. This was a serious charge against Jefferson and the office of the president. Prosecution was brought under state law. The *Wasp*, rather than the *Evening Post*, was prosecuted because the *Wasp* was the kind of scandal sheet that Jefferson had in mind when he suggested punishing the worst Federalist editors under state laws. New York law still adhered to the old British common law of seditious libel, "the greater the truth, the greater the libel," which was based on the assumption that truthful criticism of officials was more likely than lies to lead to violence threatening the stability of the government. After Croswell was convicted of criminally libeling President Jefferson, he appealed. Croswell's attorney, Alexander Hamilton, pleaded a defense drawing on Andrew Hamilton's arguments in the Zenger case (1735) that the jury had the right to determine both the law and the fact, and that truth was a defense, when (Alexander H. added) published with "good motives" and "justifiable ends." (Only in Pennsylvania [1790] were truth and the jury's two rights recognized.) A divided court denied a motion for a new trial, and the prosecution was dropped.

1805. New York libel law (6 April) enacted, adopting Alexander Hamilton's arguments in the Croswell libel case (1804). (The bill had been introduced in the legislature before the judges had announced their decision.) Provisions incorporated in constitutions of 1821 and 1846. The law was the model for guarantees of press freedom in many state constitutions.

1806. Frankfort, Kentucky, *Western World* (–1810) founded; exposed the "conspiracy" in which Aaron Burr organized an expedition supposedly for separating the western states from the United States (1806–1807).

1807. Philadelphia *Democratic Press* (–1829) founded.

1808. Frankfort, Kentucky, *Argus of Western America* (–c. 1838) founded by William Gerard. Under the editorship of Amos Kendall (1789–1869), the *Argus* became the Democratic voice of the region and supported Andrew Jackson for president. After Kendall went to Washington (1829), Francis P. Blair (1791–1876) became editor.

• Baltimore *Federal Republican* (–1834) published by Alexander Hanson and Jacob Wagner. For its opposition to the War of 1812, a mob destroyed its plant. The paper was then printed in Georgetown, where a mob killed several men defending its offices. Publication was suspended; it was resumed in 1816.

• St. Louis *Missouri Gazette* (12 July–) founded by Joseph Charless as the first newspaper (weekly, later daily) in what is now Missouri. Later as the Democratic *Missouri Republican*, the paper had wide influence, especially through its weekly edition. In 1888 Charles H. Jones took over, making it the morning *Republic*. In 1893 David R. Francis bought it. In 1919 it was absorbed into its morning rival, the *Globe-Democrat* (f. 1852).

1809. Detroit *Michigan Essay* briefly published under the patronage of Father Gabriel Richard, a Catholic missionary; only the 31 August issue definitely known.

• Concord *New Hampshire Patriot* (–1921), a Democratic paper, published by Isaac Hill (1789–1851).

1811. Fort Stoddert *Mobile Centinel* (23 May–1812), founded by John B. Hood and Samuel Miller, the first newspaper in what is now Alabama. Mobile was situated in territory that was still Spanish, and the paper was published at the fort about 20 miles north.

• Columbus *Ohio State Journal* (–1959) founded as a weekly; in 1837 a daily. In the early 1900s Robert F. Wolfe and Harry P. Wole bought it.

1812. New York *National Advocate* (–1829) founded by Tammany Hall, the New York City political club that controlled the local Democratic Party. Editors at various times included Henry Wheaton, Mordecai Manuel Noah (1785–1851), and James Gordon Bennett (1795–1872).

1813. Albany, New York, *Argus* (–1920) founded as a weekly edited by Jesse Buel. Edwin Croswell served as editor 1824–1840. The *Argus* became daily in 1824. In the second third of the century it became the organ of the "Albany Regency," an influential Democratic clique in national politics. When the Democrats were in power in New York, the *Argus* grew fat on state printing. The paper was an extreme sympathizer with the South during the Civil War.

• Boston *Daily Advertiser*, founded by Nathan Hale (1784–1863), the first successful daily in New England. It was a Whig mercantile paper noted for its cultural reporting and one of the first papers to feature editorials. In 1840 a semiweekly edition was formed out of four papers: *Centinel, Commercial Gazette* (f. 1795 as *Price-Current*), *Independent Chronicle and Boston Patriot* (formed in 1817 merger), and *New-England Palladium* (f. 1793 as *Massachusetts Mercury*). In 1884 the *Record* was founded as the evening edition of the morning *Daily Advertiser*. In 1917 William Randolph Hearst (1863–1951) bought the *Daily Advertiser* and in 1920 merged the morning and evening editions. The merged daily was first known as the *Advertiser*, then in tabloid format as the *Record*, with the *Advertiser* name preserved in a Sunday edition.

1814. Congressional act requiring that all new federal laws be printed in two newspapers (1818, increased to three) in each state or territory; contributed to the support of many newspapers in new communities, especially in the West.

• Kaskaskia *Illinois Herald*, founded by Matthew Duncan, the first newspaper in the Illinois territory; later moved to the new capital at Vandalia and named the *Illinois Intelligencer*. The paper depended largely on revenue from public printing.

1815. Cincinnati *Daily Gazette* founded as a weekly and became a daily in 1827, a leading Whig paper. In 1883 it consolidated with the Cincinnati *Commercial* (f. 1843) to form the *Commercial Gazette*.

• St. Louis *Western Journal* (May–) founded as a weekly by Joshua

Norvell, who was backed by local Republicans. Norvell sold out about 1816. In May 1817 the paper became the *Emigrant and Western Advertiser* and then in 1819 the *St. Louis Enquirer*. Thomas Hart Benton (1782–1858), an early editor, advocated Missouri's admission to the Union with a constitution that did not forbid slavery.

1816. Philadelphia *American Centinel* (–1846) founded; predecessor of the *Bulletin*.

• Columbus *Ohio Monitor* founded, a Democratic paper. In 1838 it became the *Ohio Statesman*, edited by Samuel Medary. In later years, the paper had various titles, ending in 1907 as the Columbus *News*.

1817. *Detroit Gazette* (25 July–22 April 1830), founded by Editor John Pitts Sheldon and Ebenezer Reed, the first regularly published newspaper in what became Michigan.

1819. Arkansas Post *Arkansas Gazette* (20 November–) founded by William W. Woodruff. In 1821 it moved to Little Rock, the territorial capital.

• Nacogdoches *Texas Republican*, edited by Horatio Biglow, the first English-language paper in Texas.

1820. Philadelphia *National Gazette* (–1841) founded by William Fry and Editor Robert Walsh (1784–1859), a Federalist turned liberal and Abolitionist. The *Gazette* became Philadelphia's most quoted political paper.

1821. St. Augustine *Florida Gazette*, founded by Richard W. Edes (grandson of the patriot editor of the Boston *Gazette*), the first paper published after Florida came under United States control (1821). Edes died of yellow fever shortly after the *Gazette* started.

• Mobile, Alabama, *Register* founded.

1822. Charleston, South Carolina, *Mercury* (–c. 1868) founded, with Henry Larens Pinckney editor 1823–1832. It became the virtual mouthpiece of Robert Barnwell Rhett, who helped make it the leading advocate of secession. During the Civil War it was owned and edited by Robert Barnwell Rhett, Jr.

• Washington, D.C., *National Journal* (August–1842) founded to support the presidential candidacy of John Quincy Adams; edited by Thomas L. McKinney, later Peter Force. In 1824 it turned daily at the beginning of the political campaign and then became the administration organ. When Jackson became president, the *National Journal* became an opposition paper.

1824. Boston *Courier* (–1864) founded by Joseph T. Buckingham (1779–1861).

• Springfield, Massachusetts, *Republican* (8 September–) founded as a Whig weekly by Samuel Bowles II (1797–1851). On 27 March 1844 it became the first Massachusetts daily outside Boston. The paper had already established an outstanding regional reputation when Samuel

Bowles III (1826–1878) took full control in 1851 and began to build its national reputation. A pioneer in independent journalism, the *Republican* attacked Abolitionists and approved the Fugitive Slave law, fearing agitation over slavery would destroy the nation. In 1854, after the passing of the Kansas-Nebraska bill and the death of the Whig Party, the *Republican* supported the new Republican Party. It exerted its greatest influence in the late 1850s and in the 1860s, mostly through a weekly edition, which had a geographically broad circulation of 12,000 by 1860. During the Civil War the *Republican* supported Lincoln. In 1878 Samuel Bowles IV (1851–1915) took over.

• Richmond, Virginia, *Whig* (–1888) founded by John H. Pleasants (1797–1846), who was killed in a duel by a journalistic rival, a son of the founder of the Richmond *Enquirer* (f. 1804).

1825. Detroit *Michigan Herald* founded.

1826. New York *Enquirer* founded and edited by Mordecai M. Noah. In the 1829 merger with the *Morning Courier* (f. 1827) the paper became the *Courier and Enquirer*.

• Washington, D.C., *United States Telegraph* (–1837) founded by Duff Green (1791–1875). Shortly after Andrew Jackson became president, the paper became an administration organ, but around 1830 Green switched allegiance to Jackson's party rival, John Calhoun.

1827. Continuous coverage of Congress began (December). Correspondents involved were James Gordon Bennett, New York *Enquirer*; Joseph T. Buckingham, Boston *Courier*; and Samuel L. Knapp, Charleston *Courier*.

• New York *Freedom's Journal* (16 March–1830), founded by John B. Russwurm and the Reverend Samuel E. Cornish, the first black newspaper. After Russwurm left (1828), the name was changed to *Rights for All*. The editors agitated against slavery.

• New York *Journal of Commerce* founded by Arthur Tappan (1786–1865) as a commercial paper with a strong religious tone. The *Journal* was soon taken over by Gerard Hallock (1800–1866) and David Hale. They became the most enterprising news gatherers in New York, meeting incoming ships for foreign news, covering Wall Street, starting Pony Express service between New York and Washington, and helping form the first cooperative news-gathering agency (Harbor News Association, 1848–1849). The *Journal* was Democratic and pro-slavery. In midcentury the paper defended secession of the cotton states, and the postmaster general briefly banned it from the mails, leading to Hallock's retirement; the paper became less aggressive but continued to oppose the administration. In May 1864 the *Journal of Commerce* was one of the two New York papers (also the *World*) banned for two days by the federal government for printing a forged presidential proclamation purporting to order a draft of 400,000, news that could cause riots. In the late 1890s the paper condemned the sensational jingoism of the yellow press and supported President McKinley's efforts to avoid intervention in Cuba. In 1927 the sons of Publisher Herman Ridder bought the paper and merged it with the *Commercial*. In 1951 the *Wall Street Journal* bought the paper.

● Philadelphia *Journeyman Mechanic's Advocate*, the first labor paper. Although it lasted only a year, it showed that labor was ready to express itself.

● New York *Morning Courier*, a mercantile paper; in the same year purchased by James Watson Webb (1802–1884). In 1829 Webb bought the *Enquirer* and merged the two papers. In 1833 the *Courier and Enquirer* claimed the largest U.S. daily circulation (4,500). The paper was unusually bright and aggressive for the mercantile press and showed enterprise in news gathering. Under Webb the paper went from being in the Jacksonian camp to becoming a leading Whig organ. In 1861 the *Courier and Enquirer* was absorbed into the New York *World* (f. 1860).

● Baltimore *Republican* (–1863) founded; backed the Democrats.

1828. New Echota, Georgia, *Cherokee Phoenix* (–1834), an Indian paper printed in characters invented by Sequoyah (1770?–1865).

● Philadelphia *Mechanics' Free Press* (–c. 1837), the first successful labor paper. It had a substantial average weekly circulation of about 1,500. The paper counteracted prejudices against workingmen and offered them information and inspiration.

1829. Two labor papers founded in New York City—*Working Man's Advocate* (–1851), by George Henry Adams (1805–1856), a strong supporter of labor's movement to organize; and *Free Enquirer*, by Frances Wright (1795–1852), supporting the cause of labor and dealing with social issues.

● Boston *Appeal* issued by David Walker. It advocated the elimination of slavery through force.

● Portland, Maine, *Daily Courier*, founded by Seba Smith (1792–1868), the first daily north of Boston and one of the lower-priced papers ($4 a year) appearing before 1830. As Major Jack Downing (pseudonym), Smith humorously satirized politics.

● Philadelphia *Pennsylvania Inquirer* founded; in 1860 became the *Philadelphia Inquirer*. In 1830 the Curtis-Martin Newspapers purchased it. In 1933 the *Public Ledger* (f. 1836) was merged into the *Inquirer* and an evening edition begun (–1942). In 1970 John S. Knight (1895–1981) bought the *Inquirer*, and in 1974 it became part of Knight-Ridder when Knight merged his 16 dailies with Ridder Publications' 19 dailies. In 1982 the *Inquirer* ranked among the top 15 dailies, and in 1983 it ranked eleventh in daily circulation with 544,777. In 1985 this morning paper had 525,569 circulation.

Magazines

1800. *Connecticut Evangelical Magazine* (July–December 1815) founded in Hartford.

• *Philadelphia Repository and Weekly Register* (15 November–5 April 1806) founded; in 1805 became *Repository and Ladies' Weekly Museum.*

1801. *Port Folio* (3 January–December 1827) founded in Philadelphia by Joseph Dennie (1768–1812), a staunch Federalist. An 1803 series declaring that democracy was a failure and that Jefferson's election doomed the new nation led to a seditious libel indictment of Dennie, acquitted in 1805. In 1808 he gave up ownership, and the magazine soon became nonpartisan. Contributors such as John Quincy Adams and Charles Brockden Brown added to its reputation as a literary monthly. One of the most important magazines of 1794–1825, it attained a circulation of 2,000.

1802. *Balance and Columbian Repository* (5 January–27 December 1808) founded in Hudson, New York, as a weekly miscellany.

1803. *Massachusetts Baptist Missionary Magazine* (September–December 1909) founded in Boston by Reverend Thomas Baldwin, editor 1803–1825, as a national denominational semiannual; eventually (1825) became a monthly. It was named *American Baptist Magazine and Missionary Intelligencer* in 1817; variations followed. It was the *Baptist Missionary Magazine* (1836–) at its discontinuance.

• *Literary Magazine and American Register* (October 1807) founded in Philadelphia as a semiannual by Charles Brockden Brown (1771–1810), who wrote much of the content.

1804. *Philadelphia Medical Museum* (17 September–1811) founded.

1805. *Panoplist* (June–) founded in Boston as a Unitarian theological monthly. In 1808 it absorbed the *Massachusetts Missionary Magazine* (f. 1803) and became the *Panoplist and Missionary Magazine,* whose last issue was December 1820. In 1821 it became the *Missionary Herald.*

1807. *Tickler* (16 September–17 November 1813) founded in Philadelphia by Henry K. Helmbold as a comic, satirical periodical.

1808. *American Law Journal* (–1817), founded in Philadelphia by John E. Hall, probably the first lawyer's magazine.

1810. *Eclectic Repertory* (October–) founded in Philadelphia as a medical quarterly. In 1820 it was continued by the *Journal of Foreign Medical Science and Literature* (January 1821–October 1824), which in 1824 merged into the *American Medical Recorder* (f. 1818), which in 1929 merged into the *American Journal of Medical Sciences.*

1811. *The American Review of History and Politics* (–1812), founded by Editor Robert Walsh (1784–1859), the first quarterly.

• *Niles Weekly Register* (–1849), founded by Hezekiah Niles (1777–1839), a precursor of the modern news magazine. Although Niles was a Whig, his periodical won national influence for its factual, unbiased reporting.

1812. *New England Journal of Medicine and Surgery* (January–) founded in Boston. In 1827 it became the *New England Medical Review and Journal*, which in 1829 was united with the *Boston Medical Intelligencer* (f. 1823) to form the *Boston Medical and Surgical Journal*. In 1928 it became the *New England Journal of Medicine*. In the 1980s circulation of this prestigious medical journal exceeded 200,000.

1813. *The Analectic Magazine* (January–29 December 1821) founded in Philadelphia by Moses Thomas as a monthly successor to *Select Reviews and the Spirit of the Foreign Magazines* (January 1809–December 1812), which he had purchased in 1812. *Select Reviews* had been an eclectic monthly with mainly British content. *Analectic's* editor 1813–1815 was Washington Irving. In 1819, when the magazine was purchased by James Maxwell, it had become noted for its illustrations. In 1821 the title was changed to the *Literary Gazette* and the frequency to weekly.

● *Religious Remembrancer* (4 September–) founded in Philadelphia by John W. Scott as a Presbyterian religious weekly. By August 1861 it had become the *Free Christian Commonwealth*, published in Louisville, Kentucky. During its lifetime it absorbed eight similar periodicals.

1814. *New-York Weekly Museum, or Polite Repository of Amusement and Instruction* (May–October 1817) founded in New York City as a continuation of a newspaper that had borne the first part of the periodical's name.

1815. *North American Review* (–1939) founded in Boston as a quarterly, edited by William Tudor (1779–1830). Other early editors who helped make it an influential intellectual periodical included Edward Everett (1794–1865) and Jared Sparks (1789–1866). In September 1817 William Cullen Bryant's "Thanatopsis" made its first U.S. appearance in the magazine. About 1876 the *Review* was purchased by Allen Thorndike Rice and became a bimonthly; in 1879 it became a monthly. In 1891 circulation hit a peak of 76,000 (at $5 per year). In 1899 George Briton McClellan Harvey (1864–1928) bought controlling interest and became editor. In 1926 William Butler Mahony bought it. In the 1930s it became a quarterly again and was sold twice, finally to an agent of the Japanese government for propaganda purposes.

1816. *Portico* (January–1818) founded in Baltimore by Dr. Tobias Watkins and Stephen Simpson; a monthly noted for its literary criticism.

● *Cobbett's American Political Register* (6 January–January 1818) founded in New York by William Cobbett (1763–1835); American edition of an English magazine.

1817. *Atheneum, or Spirit of the English Magazines* (January–

December 1832) founded in Boston as a weekly offering the best from foreign periodicals.

1818. *Methodist Magazine* (January–) founded in New York by the Methodist Episcopal Church; became the *Methodist Quarterly Review,* then the *Methodist Review.* After the Civil War it was an outstanding church monthly, edited by Daniel D. Whedon.

1819. *American Farmer* (2 April–) founded in Baltimore by John S. Skinner; suspended during the Civil War, resumed 1866. It became an influential farm periodical that was variously published weekly, semi-monthly, and monthly under several titles.

• *Universalist Magazine* (3 July–) founded in Boston as a religious weekly. During the nineteenth century it absorbed many other Universalist periodicals. About 1821 it became the *Trumpet and Universalist Magazine;* in 1862 the *Universalist;* in 1926 the *Universalist Leader,* after a merger with the *Christian Leader.*

1821. *The Genius of Universal Emancipation* (January–) founded in Mount Pleasant, Ohio, as a monthly by Benjamin Lundy (1789–1839), the first notable antislavery magazine. The *Genius* called for gradual abolition and for colonization. In 1822 it moved to Greenville, Tennessee, and in 1824 to Baltimore, where in 1826 it became a weekly. It became a monthly again and moved (c. 1830) to Washington. Lundy moved shortly before his death to Lowell, Illinois. After his death the periodical was continued in Lowell as the *Genius of Liberty* (December 1840–April 1842), then in Chicago as the *Western Citizen* (1842–1853) and *Free West* (1853–July 1855).

• *Saturday Evening Post* (4 August–) founded in Philadelphia by Charles Alexander and Samuel Coate Atkinson. In 1829 it became *Atkinson's Evening Post, and Philadelphia News.* In 1840 Atkinson sold it to the firm of Dusolle and Graham, which a short time later sold it to Edmund Deacon and Henry Peterson (1818–1891), later H. Peterson & Company, which in 1873 changed its name to The Saturday Evening Post Company and restored the magazine's original title. Peterson was editor 1846–1874. In 1897 Cyrus Hermann Kotzschmar Curtis (1850–1933) rescued the lagging periodical from Publisher Andrew Smythe, and on 10 June 1899 appointed George Horace Lorimer (1868–1937) editor in chief. Under Lorimer the low-cost weekly reflected middle-class America to itself and was the magazine leader in circulation and advertising for many years, particularly after World War I. Lorimer retired at the end of 1936. Succeeding editors included Ben Hibbs (1901–1975), who took over in 1942 and made the *Saturday Evening Post* the giant of the magazine world by 1947. After Hibbs resigned in 1962, the magazine declined, partly due to large losses in libel suits. In November 1964 the weekly became a biweekly, then with the 8 February 1969 issue was discontinued. Smythe had originated and

Curtis had promoted the fiction that the *Saturday Evening Post* was a descendant of Benjamin Franklin's *Pennsylvania Gazette* (f. 1728); actually, the magazine had only taken over (1821) the printing plant where the newspaper had been last printed six years previously. In May 1970 Beurt R. SerVaas of Indianapolis bought control of Curtis Publishing Company and in June 1971 revived the *Saturday Evening Post* as a quarterly edited by Cory SerVaas. In 1973 it was published six times a year and in 1977 became predominantly a monthly. The SerVaases continued the magazine into the 1980s in much the Lorimer-Hibbs traditions. In the mid-1980s circulation was about 700,000.

1822. *United States Catholic Miscellany* (5 June–1832) founded in Charleston, South Carolina, as a weekly by Bishop John England (1786–1842). It was the first strictly religious magazine established in the United States to defend Catholic doctrine.

● *New England Farmer* (3 August–24 June 1846) founded in Boston by Thomas W. Shepard and Thomas Green Fessenden (1771–1837), the editor to 1837. John B. Russell gained control in 1824; his successors were George C. Barrett, then Joseph Breck. The *Farmer* was one of the most influential agricultural journals.

1823. *Zion's Herald* (19 January–) founded in Boston as a weekly. The unofficial Methodist organ opposed slavery and advocated temperance and women's rights.

● *New York Mirror* (2 August–c. 1857) founded by George Pope Morris (1802–1864) and Samuel Woodworth; a weekly commenting on manners and morals of the times under various owners and titles.

1824. *The Christian and Theological Review* (January–) founded in Boston as a successor to *The Christian Disciple* (f. May 1813 by Unitarians). After 1828 titles varied. In January 1844 the *Monthly Miscellany of Religion and Literature* (f. 1839) merged into the *Christian Examiner*. In 1857 Thomas B. Fox bought the magazine, which then became more liberal. In November 1869 it was merged with the *Old and New*. The bimonthly was one of the most important religious reviews because of its literary criticism and its comment on educational, philosophical, and social problems.

1825. *Biblical Repertory* (January–) founded in Princeton, New Jersey, by prominent Presbyterians. Variations in titles included *The Presbyterian Quarterly* (1872–) and *Princeton Review* (1878–), a bimonthly. After the December 1884 issue, publication lapsed for a year. A. C. Armstrong & Son revived the periodical in 1886 as *The New Princeton Review*, which in 1888 was purchased by Ginn and Company; after the December 1888 issue, the *Review* was merged into Ginn's *Political Science Quarterly*.

● *New-Harmony Gazette* (1 October–) founded by Robert Owen's New Harmony, Indiana, association to interpret the socialistic community experiment to the world. From 29 October 1828 to 25 February 1829 it was published as *The New Harmony and Nashoba Gazette, or the Free Enquirer*; 4 March 1829–2 June 1835, published in New York City as *The Free Enquirer*. The weekly advocated agnosticism, feminism, socialism, and other "liberal" causes.

1826. *American Journal of Education* (January–December 1839), founded in Boston by Thomas B. Wait, the first magazine of major importance in education. In 1831 William Channing Woodbridge purchased controlling interest, and during 1832–1837 the monthly was known as the *American Annals of Education*.

• *Casket* (January–), founded in Philadelphia by Samuel C. Atkinson and Charles Alexander, subtitled *Flowers of Literature, Wit and Sentiment*. In 1839 George Rex Graham (1813–1894) bought the monthly, and after the December 1840 issue combined it with *Gentlemen's Magazine*, making them *Graham's Magazine*, which he edited to 1853.

• *Franklin Journal* (January–) founded in Philadelphia by the Franklin Institute for Promotion of Mechanic Arts (1824). The monthly later became the *Journal of the Franklin Institute*.

• *Christian Advocate* (9 September–) founded in New York by Nathan Bangs; the national weekly of the Methodist Church.

1827. *American Quarterly Review* (March–December 1837) founded in Philadelphia by Robert Walsh as a Whig quarterly.

• *The Youth's Companion* (16 April–) founded in Boston by Asa Rand and Nathaniel Willis, editor to 1857. In 1857 the weekly was sold to John W. Olmstead and Daniel Sharp Ford, who after the Civil War made it one of the best and most popular children's magazines of all time. Instructive and entertaining, the content appealed to the entire family. Beginning in the late 1860s, *The Youth's Companion* was the first magazine successfully to give premiums for annual subscriptions. By 1898 circulation passed a half million. In 1925 the Atlantic Monthly Company purchased the magazine, edited it strictly for boys and girls, then in 1928 made it a monthly. After the September 1919 issue, it was absorbed by *American Boy* (f. 1899).

1828. *Ladies Magazine* (January–December 1836) founded in Boston by Sarah Josepha Hale (1788–1879), who advocated female education and women's rights. In 1837 Hale sold her magazine to her chief rival, *Godey's Lady's Book* (f. 1830) of Philadelphia. She became second in command to Louis Antoine Godey (1804–1878), although she actually edited the magazine, making it the best woman's magazine before the Civil War. She retired in 1877.

• *Southern Agriculturist* (January–December 1846) founded in Charleston, South Carolina; in 1840 changed to *Southern Cabinet of Agriculture*.

• *Southern Review* (February–February 1832) founded in Charleston, South Carolina, as a quarterly by Hugh S. Legaré (1797–1843).

1829. *American Jurist and Law Magazine* (January–January 1843) founded in Boston as a quarterly, the most important legal journal of its time. In 1843 it was moved to Philadelphia and its title changed to *American Law Magazine* (–1846).

1830–1860

The Antebellum Period

━━━━━━━━━━ ‖●‖ ━━━━━━━━━━

Books

1830. Steam press for books developed by Isaac Adams of Boston; widely used for many years.

1831. D. Appleton & Co., publishing house, founded in New York City by Daniel Appleton (1785–1849) and William Henry Appleton (1814–1899).

1832. *The Young Christian,* by Reverend Jacob Abbott (1803–1879), a best seller. A northern author of novels for juveniles, Abbott was later renowned for his 28-volume Rollo series, including *Rollo at Play, Rollo Learning to Read,* and *Rollo's Travels.*

1834. *Guy Rivers,* by William Gilmore Simms (1806–1870), the first of the author's best works and one of his Border romances. His two other best works were *The Partisan* (1835), a Revolutionary romance, and *The Yemassee* (1835), a colonial romance. Simms was the most prolific Southern writer of the time.

● *History of the United States* (volume 1), by George Bancroft (1800–1891), published. This patriotic history eventually ran to eleven volumes, concluding with the establishment of the national government. Bancroft's works were known for their scholarship, including the use of primary sources.

1836. J. B. Lippincott & Co., publishing house, founded in Philadelphia by Joshua Ballinger Lippincott (1813–1886).

● *The Slave: Or, Memoirs of Archy Moore,* by Richard Hildreth, (1807–1865), perhaps the second novel based on an antislavery theme.

● *Awful Disclosures,* by Maria Monk (1817?–1850), a best seller in which an escaped novice revealed shocking practices in a Montreal nunnery. In 1836 the exposé was exposed as a fraud.

1837. Charles C. Little & Co. (also Charles C. Little & James Brown or C. C. Little & J. Brown) founded in Boston by Charles Coffin Little (1799–1869) and James Brown (1800–1855); became Little, Brown & Co. (1847).

● *Three Experiments of Living*, by Hannah Farnham Lee (1780–1865), a best seller. Lee also wrote biographical works.

● *Nick of the Woods*, by Robert Montgomery Bird (1806–54), a forerunner of dime-novel thrillers and a best seller.

1839. *Voices of the Night*, by Henry Wadsworth Longfellow (1807–1882), a best seller. Longfellow's popularity was based on *Voices* and such other poems as *Evangeline* (1847), *The Song of Hiawatha* (1855), and the *Courtship of Miles Standish* (1858).

● *The Green Mountain Boys*, by Daniel Pierce Thompson (1795–1868), a best seller.

1840. *Two Years Before the Mast*, by Richard Henry Dana, Jr. (1815–1882), a best seller that became an American classic. The exciting adventures, based on Dana's experiences as a sailor (1834–1836), were described by a sensitive man with the humanitarian aim of stopping the cruel practice of flogging.

1841. The first two *Essays*, by Ralph Waldo Emerson (1803–1882), a best seller. With the second collection (1844), the *Essays* established Emerson's reputation in the United States and Europe. Together the two volumes constituted a statement of the Transcendental philosophy, a revolt against orthodoxy that involved a search for reality through spiritual intuition. Emerson's other works included *Nature* (1836), a comprehensive exposition of Transcendental doctrines; *Poems* (1847); *Representative Men* (1850); *English Traits* (1856); and *The Conduct of Life* (1860).

1842. *The Poets and Poetry of America*, edited by Rufus Wilmot Griswold (1815–1857), a best-selling anthology.

1843. *The Wonders of the World*, by Robert Sears, a best seller.

● *History of the Conquest of Mexico* (three volumes), by William Hickling Prescott (1796–1859), a best seller. Specializing in Spain and Spanish conquest, Prescott also wrote *History of the Reign of Ferdinand and Isabella* (three volumes, 1837), *History of the Conquest of Peru* (two volumes, 1847), and *History of the Reign of Philip the Second, King of Spain* (three volumes, 1855–1859). His other works included *Biographical and Critical Miscellanies* (1845) and *History of the Reign of Charles V* (1857). Prescott's emphasis on narrative and literary form popularized the reading of history by North Americans.

1844. *The Monks of Monk Hall*, by George Lippard, a best seller; printed in 1845 as *The Quaker City*.

1845. *The Raven and Other Poems*, by Edgar Allan Poe (1809–1849), a best seller. Poe was a skillful metrist who strived for poetic unity of emotion or mood. He also was a critic and fiction writer. He has been called the father of the U.S. short story and the detective story. Among his other works was *Tales of the Grotesque and Arabesque* (1840). During this period, Poe was the greatest literary figure produced by the South, but his work was independent of geography and history. He spent his most productive years in Philadelphia and New York.

1846. Baker & Scribner, publishing house, founded in Boston by Isaac D. Baker and Charles Scribner (1821–1871); became Charles Scribner's Sons in 1878.

• *Napoleon and His Marshals* (two volumes), by Joel Tyler Headley (1813–1897), a best seller.

1848. *The Vision of Sir Launfall, A Fable for Critics,* and *Biglow Papers, First Series,* all by James Russell Lowell (1819–1891), published. The plot of *Vision* was based on Malory, and the work was prized for its descriptions of nature and its emphasis on narrative. *Fable,* published anonymously, characterized contemporary authors. *Biglow Papers* originally consisted of nine satirical numbers published separately beginning 17 June 1846 in the Boston *Courier* and four subsequently in the *National Anti-Slavery Standard:* in them Lowell opposed the war with Mexico and the annexation of Texas. In the second series of *Biglow Papers* (1867) he attacked slavery. The *Papers* were exemplary poetic, regional, and comic satire and are regarded as Lowell's best work.

1849. *Poems,* by John Greenleaf Whittier (1807–1892), a best seller. Another popular work was his antislavery *Poems Written During the Progress of the Abolition Question* (1838). As well as agitating against slavery, Whittier wrote ballads and narrative poems based on New England culture. His two most important works were the prose *Leaves from Margaret Smith's Journal* (1848), a semifictional romance of colonial times, and the poem *Snow-Bound* (1865, 1866) a regional, period portrait that became a school classic by the 1880s.

• *The California and Oregon Trail,* by Francis Parkman (1823–1893), a famous account of a journey by the author to the Far West in 1846. With publication of the *History of the Conspiracy of Pontiac* in 1851, Parkman began a nine-volume scholarly epic of France and England in North America to 1763. He wrote most of his works after the Civil War and despite poor vision and a nervous disorder became the leading American historian of his time.

1850. *The Scarlet Letter,* by Nathaniel Hawthorne (1804–1864), a best-selling novel that became a classic. The Puritan tale concerned the struggle of individual conscience and the effects of concealed sin. Hawthorne's *Twice-Told Tales* (1837) and *The House of Seven Gables* (1851) were also best sellers. His other major works included *The Blithedale Romance* (1852) and *The Marble Faun* (1860).

• *The Wide, Wide World,* by Susan Bogert Warner (1819–1885), and

Reveries of a Bachelor, a Book of the Heart, by Ik Marvel, best sellers. Warner was one of several leading women authors in the 1850s who were responsible for the decade being called the "Feminine Fifties." Other works of Marvel, pseudonym for Donald Grant Mitchell (1822–1908), included *Dream Life* (1851), *Doctor Johns* (1866), *English Lands, Letters and Kings* (four volumes, 1889–1897), and *American Lands and Letters* (two volumes, 1897–1899).

1851. *Moby-Dick; or, The Whale*, by Herman Melville (1819–1891), eventually a best seller and American classic. In this philosophical allegory, man's will was pitted against the white whale, symbol of infinite evil. Melville had been a sailor, and he set his romances against the background of the sea. His other major works included *Typee: A Peep at Polynesian Life* (1846), *Omoo: A Narrative of Adventures in the South Seas* (1847), *Mardi: And a Voyage Thither* (1849), *White-Jacket: or, The World in a Man-of-War* (1850), *Pierre; or, The Ambiguities* (1852), and *Billy Budd* (written 1881–1891 and discovered after Melville died, not published until 1924).

1852. E. P. Dutton & Co., publishing house, founded in Boston by Edward Payson Dutton (1841–1912). In 1869 Dutton moved to New York City.

● *Uncle Tom's Cabin*, by Harriet Beecher Stowe (1811–1896), a best-selling antislavery novel. Publication coincided with the national antislavery crusade, and sales were enormous. Melodramatic and sentimental, the novel was based on personal experience and acquaintance and conveyed a powerful emotional appeal. The book has been credited with helping to galvanize antislavery feeling in the North. Stowe's second antislavery novel was *Dred, A Tale of the Great Dismal Swamp* (1856).

● *The Curse of Clifton*, by Mrs. Emma Dorothy Eliza Nevitte Southworth (1819–1899), a best-selling novel. Other Southworth best sellers included *The Hidden Hand* (1859), *The Fatal Marriage* (1863), and *Ishmael* (1864).

1854. Best sellers—*Struggles and Triumphs*, by Phineas Taylor Barnum (1810–1891); *Tempest and Sunshine*, by Mary Jane Holmes (1825–1907); *The Lamplighter*, by Maria Susanna Cummins (1827–1866), and *Ten Nights in a Bar-Room and What I Saw There*, by Timothy Shay Arthur (1809–1885). Arthur, a temperance advocate, published about 100 tracts and stories; a million copies were printed by 1860.

● *Walden; or, Life in the Woods*, by Henry David Thoreau (1817–1862), first published; later became a best seller and American classic. Mixed with this narrative of the two years that Thoreau lived close to nature at Walden Pond (4 July 1845–6 September 1847) were philosophical observations that reflected his Transcendental individualism and his belief that man could live better away from society's complex institutions. *Walden* fared little better than his first book, *A Week on the Concord and Merrimack Rivers* (1849), which was coldly received until after his death.

1855. *The Prince of the House of David*, by Joseph Holt Ingraham (1809–1860), a best seller. Other religious romances by Ingraham, a Protestant Episcopal priest, were *The Pillar of Fire* (1859) and *The Throne of David* (1860).

● *Leaves of Grass*, by Walter Whitman (1819–1892), later a best seller in successive editions with many additions and revisions to 1892. Initially, Walt Whitman's *Leaves of Grass*, 12 poems and a preface, was privately printed. The public as well as the reviewers criticized it as immoral. Additions that enlarged the second edition (1856) to 32 poems were often found objectionable, too. Extensive revisions in later editions reduced some offensiveness and improved the writing. Whitman's poems reflected his faith in democracy and presented a new indigenous approach to U.S. poetry. His major prose works were *Democratic Vistas* (1871) and *Specimen Days and Collect* (1882).

1856. *Lena Rivers*, by Mary Jane Holmes (1825–1907), a best seller.

● *History of the Plimouth Plantation*, William Bradford's major historical work, first published in full; written about 1630–1650. Bradford (c. 1588–1657), a Pilgrim on the Mayflower, eloquently described the sentiments of disembarking settlers.

1858. *The Autocrat of the Breakfast-Table*, a collection of witty essays by Oliver Wendell Holmes (1809–1894), published. They had run in *North East Magazine* (1831–1832) and as an installment in the *Atlantic Monthly* (1857). Holmes also wrote two notable similar collections of essays, *The Professor at the Breakfast-Table* (1860) and *The Poet at the Breakfast Table* (1872), and three novels, *Elsie Venner* (1861), *The Guardian Angel* (1867), and *A Mortal Antipathy* (1885), as well as poetry, including "Old Ironsides" (1830).

1859. *Beulah*, by Augusta Jane Evans (1835–1909), a best-selling novel that involved an inquiry into religious doubt. Her *St. Elmo* (1867) was a best-selling novel, too.

1860. *Malaeska, The Indian Wife of the White Hunter*, by Ann Sophia Stephens (1813–1886), a best-selling melodrama and first of the Beadle Dime Novels. Stephens had been a magazine editor and serial writer as well as author of two popular books, *Fashion and Famine* (1854) and *The Old Homestead* (1855).

● *Seth Jones, or the Captive on the Frontier*, by Edward Sylvester Ellis (1840–1916), also a best-selling dime novel.

● *Rutledge*, by Miriam Coles Harris (but published anonymously), a best seller about a heroine whose troubles were supposed to teach readers lessons about the proper deportment of young women. The book was reprinted more than 28 times and sold well for more than 50 years.

Newspapers

1830. Boston *Evening Transcript* (–1941) founded by L. M. Walter; cultural organ.

● Albany, New York, *Evening Journal* (–1925) founded by Thurlow Weed (1797–1882) with funding by the Anti-Masonic Party. Under Weed's editorship, 1831–1863, the paper became a semiofficial organ of the Whigs. When the Whig Party dissolved, the paper became Republican.

● Washington *Globe* (fall–1845) founded by Francis P. Blair (1791–1876) to succeed the *United States Telegraph* (f. 1826) as the Jackson administration organ. The paper received $500,000 in government printing contracts. Much of this favoritism continued through the succeeding Van Buren administration, but when the Whig Harrison became president, he chose the *National Intelligencer* (f. 1800) as the chief administration organ.

1831. Detroit *Democratic Free Press and Michigan Intelligencer* (5 May–) founded by local leaders as a political weekly; first publisher Sheldon McKnight, first editor John Pitts Sheldon. In 1835 the morning paper became a semiweekly (June), then the first daily (28 September) in the Michigan territory, changing its name to the *Detroit Daily Free Press*. The paper later (1 February 1836) was sold to John S. Bagg and L. LeGrand Morse, then (1840) to Asahel Bagg, etc. In 1853 Wilbur Fisk Storey (1819–1884) bought controlling interest, and on 2 February began editing the paper (–1861); on October 1853 he published the first Michigan newspaper distributed on Sunday morning. A London edition, *The Weekly Detroit Free Press*, was first published in 1881. In 1940 John S. Knight (1895–1981) bought the *Free Press*, and in 1974 his newspaper chain was merged with Ridder Publications, another chain. In 1985 the *Free Press* had the eleventh largest daily newspaper circulation in the United States (647,130).

● Louisville, Kentucky, *Journal* founded by George D. Prentice (1802–1870) as a Whig paper. In 1867 Henry Watterson (1840–1921) joined the *Journal* as editor and part owner. In 1868 he became editor of the *Courier-Journal*, formed in a merger with the *Democrat* (f. 1843) and the *Courier* (f. 1844).

● Boston *Morning Post* (–1956) founded by Charles G. Greene as a spicy inexpensive ($4 a year) daily; later became the *Post*.

1832. Boston *Atlas* (–1861) founded; the leading Whig paper in New England in the 1840s.

● Philadelphia *Pennsylvanian* (–1861) founded; the leading Democratic newspaper in Pennsylvania. During its life span there were numerous owners. For many years it was edited by part-owner John W. Forney (1817–1881).

1833. Navarino, Wisconsin, *Intelligencer* (–c. 1836), founded in what became Green Bay, the first paper in the Wisconsin territory. Published irregularly, it later merged with the *Wisconsin Free Press* to become the *Democrat*.

● Boston *Mercantile Journal*, founded by John S. Sleeper, sold for $4 a year (by subscription), a forerunner of the penny press. In 1845 the daily became the Whig *Evening Journal* and later a morning paper. In October 1902 the *Journal* was purchased by Frank Andrew Munsey (1854–1925), who sold it in 1913. Finally, it was absorbed by the Boston *Herald* in 1917.

● New York *Sun* (3 September–), founded by Benjamin Henry Day (1810–1889), the first successful penny daily, marking the beginning of mass communication and of modern newspaper journalism. The morning *Sun's* success started a trend away from expensive papers (often 6 cents) appealing to political or commercial interests toward inexpensive papers appealing to the masses. The *Sun* was hawked on the street by the copy, rather than sold through the mail by subscription, and emphasized local news of human interest and crime, including police court reports. The small daily was independent, sensational, and readable. In six months it had the highest circulation in New York City. In 1835 circulation rose with publication of the "Moon Hoax," a series purporting to describe life on the moon. That year the *Sun* was the first paper to install the new steam-powered press to keep up with reader demand; other penny papers would soon follow the *Sun's* lead. In 1838 Day sold to Moses Yale Beach (1800–1868), who printed more kinds of news (local, national, international) and more editorials. Beach also used the latest communication and transportation technology to be first with the news. In 1848 Beach's sons, Moses Sperry (1822–1892) and Alfred Ely (1826–1896), took over. In 1868 Charles Anderson Dana (1819–1897) and his backers bought the *Sun*. During Dana's 29 years as editor, the *Sun* became known as a "newspaperman's newspaper" of peerless literary quality, and its social and political policies grew conservative. In March 1887 Dana began the *Evening Sun*. Edward P. Mitchell succeeded Dana. In 1897 Business Manager William M. Laffan organized a bureau to gather news for the *Sun* and client papers. In 1916 the *Suns* passed to Frank A. Munsey, who combined the *Press* with the morning edition and discontinued the Laffan News Bureau. In 1920 the famous morning edition was absorbed into Munsey's *Herald* (f. 1835), and in 1950 the surviving *Sun*, which had absorbed the *Globe* (f. 1904), was purchased by Scripps-Howard and absorbed into its *World-Telegram* (f. 1931). In 1966 the *World-Telegram and Sun* was combined with the *Journal* and *Herald Tribune* to form the *World Journal Tribune* (–1967).

• Chicago *Weekly Democrat*, founded by John Calhoun, the city's first paper. About 1836 it was bought by John Wentworth, who in 1840 made it a daily and in 1857 made it Republican. In July 1861 the *Daily Democrat* was absorbed by the *Tribune* (f. 1847).

• White Pigeon *Michigan Statesman* founded by Henry Gilbert and Albert Chandler as a weekly. It was moved to Kalamazoo in 1835 and became the Kalamazoo *Gazette* in 1837. The paper was Democratic.

1834. Three notable papers founded in New York City. *Evening Transcript* (–1839), founded by Dr. Asa Green, was sensational like the *Sun* but raunchier and emphasized sports; later it was published as a morning daily. *Man* (–1835) was founded by George Henry Evans as a labor paper. *New Yorker Staats-Zeitung* was founded by Jacob Uhl as a German-language weekly. It became a triweekly in 1842 and a daily in 1848. During the Civil War it had strong southern sympathies. In 1880, under the proprietorship of Mr. and Mrs. Oswald Ottendorfer, it claimed the largest German-language circulation (50,000) of any newspaper in the world. In 1890 Herman Ridder (1851–1915) became manager and in 1907 president. In 1892 an evening edition, the *Abendblatt*, was founded. Ridder's three sons took over in 1915. The Ridder newspaper chain began with the *Staats-Zeitung*.

• Santa Fe *El Crepusculo de la Libertad*, founded by Antonio Barreiro, the first paper in New Mexico and the first effort to publish a newspaper for the large Spanish-speaking population of the Southwest and California. The paper lasted for only a few issues.

1835. Regular Pony Express service established between New York City and Philadelphia by Postmaster General Amos Kendall (1789–1869), taking over a route from the New York *Courier and Enquirer*, which had found the cost of maintenance too high. By 1836 this express service was extended along main routes, reducing delivery time between New York and New Orleans to less than seven days. Express riders carried proof sheets ("slips") of full newspapers. This system enabled papers around the country to work out cooperative exchange systems for beating rivals to big news. In the 1840s the railroads gradually replaced pony services.

• Toledo, Ohio, *Blade* founded as a weekly; later a daily with a weekly edition of wide circulation. It was noted for the humorous and satirical articles by writer David Ross Locke (1833–1888), who wrote under the pen name of Petroleum V. Nasby.

• New York *Morning Herald* (6 May–) founded and edited by James Gordon Bennett, Sr. (1795–1872), as the second major penny daily in the city; priced at 2 cents in 1836. Bennett perfected some techniques of the *Sun*, his chief rival, and innovated other techniques. He extensively covered financial, society, and sports news; sent correspondents to cover Congress; assigned reporters to cover the Mexican and Civil wars; early recognized the journalistic importance of the telegraph; and initiated a readers' letters column. In 1835 and 1838 attempts to publish the first Sunday edition of a New York daily failed after a few issues, but in 1841 an attempt succeeded. Bennett initiated new advertising policies, including requiring advertisers to pay in advance and to change copy often to enhance the news value of advertisements; the *Herald* became the city's advertising leader (until 1884). By 1860 it had 77,000 circulation, perhaps the world's largest; during the Civil War, circulation soared to more than 100,000 as the *Herald* became the most popular U.S. newspaper. Politically independent, Bennett opposed the Abolitionist movement and during the Civil War was soft toward the South, grudgingly supporting President Lincoln. In 1869 James Gordon Bennett, Jr. (1841–1918), took over. He founded a Paris edition in 1887. In 1918 the *Herald*s were sold to Frank A. Munsey, who in 1924 sold them to Ogden Mills Reid (1882–1947) and Helen Rogers Reid (1882–1970), publishers of the *Tribune* (f. 1841), which became the *Herald Tribune*. In 1966 that paper became part of the new *World Journal Tribune* (–1967).

• Two Abolitionist newspapers founded, later attacked by mobs, in the Midwest. Despite attacks, James Gillespie Birney (1792–1857) continued to dedicate his Cincinnati *Philanthropist* to the elimination of slavery and to the promotion of press freedom. For expressing antislavery views, Reverend Elijah Lovejoy (1802–1837) was forced to move his strident St. Louis *Observer* to Alton, Illinois, where he was killed 7 November 1837 by a mob attacking his office. Lovejoy became the first great martyr of the antislavery cause. Several persons were indicted but found not guilty.

• *Shawnee Sun*, printed at the Baptist Mission in what is now Kansas, a missionary paper in Indian language.

• Two papers founded in Texas. San Felipe *Telegraph and Texas Register* (–1877) was the official organ of the provisional revolutionary government; it later became the *Telegraph*, the first Houston paper. Nashville *Union* (–1875) supported Polk's candidacy.

1836. Boston *Daily Times* (16 February–23 April 1857) published by George Roberts and William H. Garfield. This evening daily was the first successful penny paper in Boston.

• Philadelphia *Public Ledger* (March–) founded by William M. Swain, Arunah S. Abell, and Azariah H. Simmons as a sensational penny paper. This morning paper became a leading daily, making use of the latest developments in news coverage techniques and technological advancements, including the rotary press (installed 1847). In 1838 the *Public Ledger* absorbed its rival, the *Transcript*, and in 1864 it was purchased from the Swain family by George William Childs

(1829–1894); co-owner was Anthony J. Drexel. In 1902 the *Public Ledger* was sold to Adolph Simon Ochs (1858–1933), who consolidated it with the Philadelphia *Times*. In 1913 it was sold to Cyrus Hermann Kotzschmar Curtis (1850–1933), who in 1914 added an evening edition (–1942) and in 1933 merged the morning edition into the *Inquirer*.

• Cincinnati *Volksblatt* founded as a German-language paper.

1837. New Orleans *Picayune*, founded by George Wilkins Kendall (1809–1867) and Francis Asbury Lumsden, originally sold for a picayune, a Spanish half reel equivalent to 6-1/2 cents (newspaper prices were generally higher in New Orleans than in New York). The morning daily won a reputation as an aggressive news gatherer, especially for Editor-Publisher Kendall's coverage of the Mexican War. In 1838 a weekly edition was launched for distribution to outlying regions. The *Picayune* was later sold; after the new publisher's death his widow, Eliza Holbrook, ran the paper. In 1914 the *Picayune* and *Times-Democrat* merged to become the morning *Times-Picayune*, owned by L. K. Nicholson. In 1933 Nicholson bought Robert Ewing's *States* for an evening edition. Samuel Irving Newhouse (1895–1979) bought the papers in 1962.

• Milwaukee *Sentinel* (27 June–) founded as a weekly by Solomon Laurent Juneau (1793–1856). John O'Rourke was its first editor. In May 1843 the paper became triweekly and in December 1844 became the first daily (morning) in Wisconsin. Ownership changed several times in the 1800s. In the 1890s the *Sentinel* opposed the Spanish-American War but reported it sensationally. The paper early opposed U.S. involvement in the European War of 1914. In 1924 William Randolph Hearst (1863–1951) bought the *Sentinel*'s morning and evening editions, then discontinued the latter. In July 1962 the Milwaukee Journal Company bought the *Sentinel*.

• Baltimore *Sun* (17 May–) founded as a penny paper by Arunah S. Abell with the backing of William M. Swain and Azariah H. Simmons. In the daily's first year, Abell established a Washington bureau that came to be relied on by many western papers for accurate, complete.coverage of national news. The *Sun* also was noted for enterprise and for technological progress, including pioneering the development of telegraph news. In 1910 the paper took over the *Evening World* and made it the *Evening Sun*. The *Sun* continued to be highly regarded as a regional newspaper and noted for excellence in foreign and Washington correspondence.

1838. Pontiac, Michigan, *Jacksonian* founded (24 March–).

1839. Philadelphia *North American* (3 March–1925) founded by Morton McMichael; became a major Whig newspaper. It soon acquired several smaller Philadelphia papers. Robert T. Conrad was one of its editors. In 1847 the *North American* purchased its most respected Whig rival, the *United States Gazette*. When the Whig Party dissolved in the 1850s, the paper turned Republican.

1840. Cincinnati *Spirit of the Times* founded by Calvin W. Starbuck and others. Its title was later shortened to the *Times*. In 1879 it was purchased by Charles Phelps Taft (1843–1929), who in 1880 merged it with the *Star* (f. 1872), another afternoon paper. The *Times-Star* was high-tariff Republican. In 1958 E. W. Scripps Company bought the paper and merged it with the *Post*.

1841. First advertising agency founded, in Philadelphia, by Volney B. Palmer, as a liaison between newspapers and businesses. Shortly thereafter offices were established in other cities.

• Cincinnati *Enquirer* (April–) founded by John and Charles Brough as a Democratic evening paper; became a morning daily in 1843. In the 1850s James J. Faran and Washington McLean bought it. Under Faran's editorship the paper became strongly anti-Lincoln. In 1870 John R. McLean took over management and in 1881 ownership. Under him the *Enquirer* was sensational and still Democratic though less of a political organ and more of a newspaper. In the late 1800s a weekly edition had more than 100,000 circulation. In 1914 the *Enquirer* opposed U.S. intervention in the European war. In 1930 the paper absorbed the *Commercial Tribune* (f. 1896). In 1952 the *Enquirer* was purchased by its employees, and in 1956 by E. W. Scripps Co. Threatened by government antitrust action, Scripps, which controlled the Cincinnati dailies, was forced to sell the *Enquirer*. In the mid-1980s it was owned by Gannett Company, Inc., and its circulation was 194,700 daily and 305,000 Sunday.

• New York *Tribune* (10 April–) founded by Horace Greeley (1811–1872) as a morning penny paper. Less sensational than the *Sun* and *Herald*, it represented the maturing penny press. Although Whig-Republican, Greeley was an independent thinker and supported abolition, labor, and prohibition. On 2 September 1841 Greeley first published the *Weekly Tribune*, which absorbed the *New Yorker* (f. 1834) and the *Log Cabin* (f. 1840). With wide circulation in northern and midwestern rural areas, the *Weekly Tribune* established Greeley's reputation as the most influential editor of his time. By 1852 the weekly's popularity accounted for most of the *Tribune*'s circulation of more than 100,000 (the daily would always trail the *Sun* and *Herald*). Upon Greeley's death, Whitelaw Reid (1837–1912) became editor. He was succeeded by Ogden Mills Reid and Helen Rogers Reid, husband and wife. In 1924 the Reids bought the New York and Paris *Heralds* from Frank A. Munsey, forming the *Herald Tribune*, which became known for its foreign and Washington correspondence, cultural news, and quality writing. Upon Ogden's death his sons, Ogden R. and Whitelaw, joined their mother in running the paper. In 1958 the Reids sold the *Herald Tribune* to John Hay Whitney, and the paper adopted a magazine style appearance. The last issue of the *Herald Tribune* was 24 April 1966. In Sept. 1966 it became part of the evening and Sunday *World Journal Tribune* (–1967).

1842. Cleveland *Plain Dealer* founded by Joseph William Gray as a

Democratic weekly; became a daily in 1845. After Gray's death in 1862, the owners bought the *Herald*'s morning and evening editions. In 1884 the *Plain Dealer* was sold to Liberty E. Holden and associates. In 1892 the *Evening Plain Dealer* was named the *Evening Post* to make it distinctive from the morning *Plain Dealer*. In the early 1900s the paper opposed U.S. involvement in the European war. In 1917 the *Plain Dealer* absorbed the *Leader* (f. 1854). Later the paper was published by Forest City Publishing Co. with the *News*. In 1960 the *Press* (f. 1878) bought the *Plain Dealer* and the *News*. In 1967 Samuel I. Newhouse bought the *Plain Dealer*. In the mid-1980s morning circulation was about 482,500.

1843. Cincinnati *Commercial* founded. In 1865 Murat Halstead, an active Republican, took control; he became editor, then publisher. In 1883 the *Commercial* and *Gazette* (f. 1815) were consolidated. In 1890 Halstead sold the *Commercial Gazette*. In 1896 it was merged with the *Tribune* (f. 1893) to form the *Commercial Tribune*, which in 1930 was merged into the *Enquirer* (f. 1841).

• Pittsburgh *The Mystery*, the oldest black religious weekly, founded by Dr. Martin R. Delany in response to the refusal of regular dailies to publish contributions by blacks. In 1848 *The Mystery* was purchased by the African Methodist Episcopal Church and named the *Christian Herald*, which in 1852 was moved to Philadelphia and renamed the *Christian Recorder*.

1844. First telegraphic transmission of news (24 May)—sent in the afternoon from Washington, D.C., by Samuel Finley Breese Morse (1791–1872) to the *Baltimore Patriot*. Message: "One o'clock—There has just been made a motion in the House to go into committee of the whole on the Oregon question. Rejected—ayes, 79; nays, 86."

• Grand Rapids, Michigan, *Eagle* (25 December–) founded by Aaron B. Turner as a Whig weekly.

1845. New Orleans *Delta* (–1863) founded.

• Battle Creek, Michigan, *Western Citizen* (–1846) founded by Leonard Stillson.

1846. Boston *Herald* (–1972) founded as a lively penny daily by printers from the Boston *Daily Times* (f. 1836), which it absorbed in 1857. In the 1890s the *Herald* opposed the Spanish-American War but reported it sensationally. In 1912 the publishers bought the *Traveler* for an evening edition and in 1917 absorbed Frank A. Munsey's *Journal*. In 1967 both morning and evening editions were merged into the *Herald Traveler*.

• Two notable papers published on the Pacific coast. Oregon City *Oregon Spectator* (–1846), founded as a semimonthly by an association of local promoters to encourage settlement and sale of land, was the first newspaper on the coast. Monterey *Californian* (15 August–), founded as a weekly by Reverend Walter Colton (1797–1851) and Robert Semple, was the first newspaper in California. Half was printed in English, half in Spanish. In May 1847 the paper moved to Yerba Buena (San Francisco). In 1849 the new *Alta California* absorbed it.

1847. Rotary press, invented by Richard March Hoe (1812–1886), first used by Philadelphia *Public Ledger*. It accelerated the processing of news. Printing from a revolving surface, this revolutionary press produced 8,000 sheets an hour on one side; thus more copies of thicker papers could be run off faster.

● San Francisco *California Star* (7 January–), founded by Samuel Brannan (1819–1899), the first newspaper in San Francisco. The weekly was subsidized to print legal notices in Spanish. In 1849 it was absorbed by the new *Alta California*.

● *Cummings' Evening Telegraphic Bulletin* founded by Alexander Cummings, the first successful evening paper in Philadelphia; later named the *Evening Bulletin*, then the *Bulletin*. During the Civil War, Gibson Peacock edited the staunchly Republican daily. When William Lippard McLean (1852–1931) bought the *Evening Bulletin* in 1895 it had an Associated Press franchise and about 6,000 circulation. McLean supported reforms, emphasized local news, lowered the price to 1 cent, added equipment, and developed new circulation techniques, boosting circulation to about 220,000 in ten years. "In Philadelphia Nearly Everyone Reads the *Bulletin*," the city's circulation leader advertised itself. William L. McLean, Jr., and Robert McLean took over upon their father's death. In 1968 the *Bulletin* had 671,525 circulation daily, 728,276 Sunday. In the 1970s the emphasis on local news continued, with zone editions. William L. McLean III was editor, publisher, and president. By the end of the decade circulation had slipped to 462,137 Monday through Friday, 445,638 Saturday, and 542,924 Sunday. Faced with rising deficits, McLean discontinued publication in 1982.

● Chicago *Daily Tribune* (10 June–) founded. In 1855 Joseph Medill (1823–1899) and partners purchased the paper. It became a leading daily, opposing slavery and in 1856 and 1860 supporting Lincoln. In 1861 it absorbed the *Daily Democrat* (f. 1833). Horace White (1834–1916) served as editor 1866–1874. In 1874 Medill gained full control; he was a conservative, crusading, nationalistic editor. In 1914 Joseph Medill Patterson (1879–1946) and Robert Rutherford McCormick (1880–1955) published the morning *Tribune*, the ultraconservative McCormick eventually dominating it. McCormick was known for slanting the news to support isolationism, to oppose the New Deal, etc. A turning point in policy came in 1969 when Clayton Kirkpatrick (1915–) became editor; he balanced news coverage and modernized makeup. In 1977 McCormick's legend, "World's Greatest Newspaper," was dropped, and in 1982 the paper printed lavishly in color. That year the *Tribune* climbed to fifth in a poll of the nation's best newspapers; in 1985 it was seventh among U.S. dailies in circulation

(776,348). The McCormick-Patterson family still controlled the *Tribune* in the middle 1980s.

● Richmond, Virginia, *Examiner* founded and edited by John Moncure Daniel (1825–1865), secessionist and severe critic of Jefferson Davis. In 1867 the paper merged with the *Enquirer*.

● Santa Fe *Republican* (September–1849), the first successful newspaper in present New Mexico. The weekly was subsidized to print legal notices in Spanish. Two pages were printed in Spanish, two in English.

● Rochester, New York, the *North Star* (3 December–) founded by Frederick Douglass (c. 1817–1895); co-edited by Douglass and Martin R. Delany until Delany left in 1848. The Abolitionist weekly became the first black newspaper with both foreign and domestic circulation. Douglass had his own printing plant, the first ever owned by a black person in the United States. On 26 June 1851 the *North Star* was named *Frederick Douglass' Paper*, which in 1860 was merged with *Douglass' Monthly* (f. 1858).

1848. New Orleans *Crescent* (–1869) founded.

● Lansing, Michigan, *Free Press* (January 11–) founded, first newspaper printed in the new state capital. The name was soon changed to the *Michigan State Journal*. Publication was suspended in 1861 or 1862, then resumed by John W. Higgs in 1866 as the *State Democrat*.

1849. Harbor News Association (11 January 1849), formed by six New York dailies (*Courier and Enquirer, Express, Herald, Journal of Commerce, Sun, Tribune*), a precursor of the modern Associated Press. In May 1848 the six papers had made an informal arrangement for acquiring the telegraph news. Now they formally arranged to operate two boats to gather news from ships arriving in the New York harbor, to share the costs, and to sell news to papers outside the city. In 1851 the partners, with a seventh member (New York *Times*), signed a new agreement forming the Telegraphic and General News Association. In 1856 members adopted Regulations of the General News Association of the City of New York, soon called the New York Associated Press.

● San Francisco *Alta California* (4 January–1891), founded as a weekly; in 1850 became the first daily in California. It gained wide recognition because of the writings of Bret Harte and Mark Twain.

● Des Moines *Iowa Star* founded; in 1870 named *Iowa State Leader*. In 1902 it was combined with the new *Iowa State Register* to form the *Register and Leader*.

● St. Paul *Minnesota Pioneer*, founded as a weekly, the first newspaper in Minnesota. In 1854 the title was changed to the *Daily Pioneer* and in 1875 to the morning *Pioneer-Press*, which later became part of the Ridder chain.

● Jackson, Michigan, *American Citizen* (15 August–) founded by Albert A. Dorrance as a weekly Whig paper.

1850. Railroads expanded to 9,000 miles of track, from 23 miles in 1830, serving newspapers as a fast way to transmit long messages, such as copies of presidential speeches, and as a fast method of distribution.

● Salt Lake City *Deseret News* founded by the Church of Jesus Christ of Latter-Day Saints. By 1867 the paper achieved the distinction of being the first successful religious daily in the English language.

● Portland *Weekly Oregonian* (4 December–) founded by Thomas J. Dryer, Portland's first newspaper. On 4 February 1861 the name was changed to the *Morning Oregonian*, and the paper was issued as a daily. In 1877 Editor Harvey W. Scott (1838–1910) became co-owner with Henry L. Pittock, who had acquired the paper from Dryer. Scott gained a national reputation as an editorial writer. After the co-owners' deaths, their heirs ran the paper. In 1933–1946 Palmer Hoyt was editor. In 1950 Samuel I. Newhouse bought the paper, which in 1982 absorbed the *Oregon Journal* (f. 1902), purchased by Newhouse in 1961. *Oregonian* circulation in the mid-1980s was about 290,300.

1851. Los Angeles *Star* founded by John E. Lewis and E. Gould Buffum; subsidized to print legal notices in Spanish.

● New York *Daily Times* (18 September–) founded by Henry Jarvis Raymond (1820–1869) and George Jones (1811–1891) as a penny paper. In 1857 the name was changed to *The New York Times*. Editor Raymond steered a middle course in news coverage between the sensationalism of the *Sun* and *Herald* and the conservatism of the *Tribune*. Though deeply involved in Whig and Republican politics, Raymond established a *Times* tradition of fair, thorough news reporting and excellent coverage of European events. After Raymond's death, Jones went from business manager to publisher. In 1893 Editor-in-Chief Charles Ransom Miller (1849–1922) and other staff members purchased the paper. In August 1896 Adolph S. Ochs bought it. He emphasized solid news coverage, thoughtful editorial opinion, and a politically conservative Democratic tone. In 1904 Carr Van Anda (1864–1945) became managing editor and ran an outstanding news department. In 1935 Arthur Hayes Sulzberger (1891–1968), Ochs's son-in-law, became publisher. In 1961 Orvil E. Dryfoos (1912–1963), Sulzberger's son-in-law, became publisher. In 1962 the *Times* began a western edition (–1964) printed in Los Angeles. In 1963 Arthur Ochs (Punch) Sulzberger (1926–) became publisher. In 1980 the *Times* began a national edition, printed by satellite transmission in California, Chicago, and Florida. By 1983 the *Times* had won a record 53 Pulitzer prizes. The *Times* was consistently first in polls of the nation's best newspapers because of its reputation for completeness and integrity. Among U.S. dailies in the mid-1980s it was fifth in daily circulation (934,616).

1852. Cleveland *Alienated American* (–1856), published by W. H. Day, a black religious weekly advocating abolition.

● Olympia *Columbian* (–1861), the first newspaper in what is now Washington state; later *Washington Pioneer*, noted for announcements of new discoveries of gold.

● St. Louis, Missouri, *Democrat* founded; a Republican daily. In 1875 it merged with the *Globe* to become the *Globe-Democrat*, which rose to prominence under Joseph B. McCullagh. In 1919 the paper bought its morning rival, the *Republic* (f. 1808). In 1925 E. Lansing Ray became publisher, and in 1955 Samuel I. Newhouse purchased the *Globe-Democrat*.

1854. Three notable papers founded in the Midwest. Belleview *Nebraska Palladium* (June–) was the first newspaper published in the Nebraska territory (first number was issued in Iowa). Leavenworth *Kansas Weekly Herald* (15 September–1861) was the first English-language newspaper in Kansas. It became a daily in 1859. The Chicago *Times* under Publisher-Editor Wilbur F. Storey became a sensational Copperhead sheet that was suspended by military authorities for three days. In 1895 the paper was consolidated with the *Herald* (f. 1881) to become the *Times-Herald*, a successful Democratic morning paper. Later that year, after Publisher James W. Scott's death, the *Times-Herald* and its evening edition, the *Evening Post*, were purchased by Herman Kohlsaat. In 1908 the *Record* (f. 1881) bought the *Times-Herald*, forming the *Record-Herald*.

1855. San Francisco *Bulletin* (5 October–) founded by James King as a radical, crusading evening paper. King was killed the next year for opposing corrupt government and lawlessness. Fremont Older (1856–1935) later carried on the crusading tradition, fighting the political machine. In 1859 C. O. Gerberding purchased the paper, and in 1919 it was bought by William Randolph Hearst, who merged it with the *Call* (f. 1856) to form the *Call-Bulletin*.

● New York *Daily News* (–1906) founded by W. Drake Parsons as a penny pro-slavery Tammany organ. For open hostility to the Civil War the morning paper lost its postal privilege in August 1861; in September it suspended publication. It resumed 18 months later as an evening paper. About 1862 Benjamin Wood bought it and made it a more radical pro-slavery Tammany organ, opposing force against the Confederacy and attacking Lincoln. When the cost of paper dropped in 1867, Wood lowered the price of the *Daily News*, which had risen to 4 cents, back to 1 cent, and by 1870 it had a circulation of 100,000. For many of the next 30 years, it led U.S. dailies, circulation going as high as 175,000. The cheap, sensational content was avidly read by immigrants who crowded New York tenements. In November 1901 Frank A. Munsey bought the paper from Wood's widow, then made changes that diminished its appeal to tenement dwellers, and lost money. He sold the paper to an employee in 1904.

● Lawrence *Kansas Free State* founded; Free-Soil paper.

● Two significant Michigan newspapers founded—Grand Rapids *Herald* and Lansing *State Republican* (28 April–). The *Herald*, founded by A. E. Gordon, was the first daily in Grand Rapids. In the middle 1860s the title was changed to the *Democrat*. The *State Republican* was founded by Henry Barnes as a weekly Republican voice in the state capital.

1856. Fifty-six German-language newspapers being printed.

● San Francisco *Call* founded as a morning newspaper. About 1900 John D. Spreckles acquired it. In 1913 William Randolph Hearst purchased it, combining it with the *Evening Post* to create an evening companion for his morning *Examiner* (f. 1865). Conservative, the *Call* early opposed U.S. entry into the European war. In 1929 Hearst bought the *Bulletin* (f. 1855) to form the *Call-Bulletin*, which in 1959 was combined with the Scripps-Howard *News* to form the *News-Call Bulletin*. Scripps-Howard withdrew in 1962 and the paper was discontinued in 1965.

● Des Moines *Iowa State Register* founded as a Free-Soil paper. In 1860 its name was shortened to the *Register*, and in 1902 the paper was combined with the *Iowa State Leader* (f. 1849) to form the *Register and Leader*, purchased in 1903 by Gardner Cowles, Sr.

● New Orleans *Daily Creole*, the first black-owned daily in the South.

1858. Sioux Falls, South Dakota, *Democrat* (–1862) founded; in 1859 renamed the *Northwestern Independent*.

● Genoa *Territorial Enterprise* (November–1916), the first newspaper published in Nevada; later moved to Carson City, later (1860) to Virginia City. As city editor and reporter in the early 1960s, Mark Twain helped make the paper famous.

1859. Tubac *Weekly Arizonian* (March–1871), the first newspaper in the Arizona area; moved to Tucson in 1860. Suspended temporarily about 1861, the paper ultimately became the *Citizen*.

1860. In the United States 3,725 newspapers in operation, including 387 dailies, 3,173 weeklies, 79 semiweeklies, and 86 triweeklies.

● Government Printing Office established by President Abraham Lincoln (1809–1865) to eliminate both the government's need to patronize individual newspapers and political favoritism in awarding printing contracts. This action, the emergence of the penny press, and the dissolution of the Whig Party contributed to the decline of partisan reporting.

● New York *World* (14 June–) founded by Alexander Cummings as a morning Democratic penny paper with moral, religious overtones; in

November raised to 2 cents. In 1861 the *Courier and Enquirer* was absorbed. On 1 July 1861, August Belmont and Fernando Wood purchased the *World*; Manton Marble (1835–1917) became editor (to 1867). At first the *World* supported Lincoln, but after Emancipation the paper was openly hostile. In May 1864 the government suspended publication of the *World* (and New York *Journal of Commerce*) for two days for printing a forged presidential proclamation purporting to order another draft of 400,000 men, a hoax that could cause rioting. Later the paper was acquired by Jay Gould (1836–1892), then on 9 May 1883 by Joseph Pulitzer (1847–1911), who made it a sensational liberal paper with strong news coverage and a quality editorial page. Under John Cockerill, managing editor then editor in charge, the paper gained fame for its crusades, promotions, and stunts. In 1884 the *World* passed the *Herald* in advertising. In 1887 the Sunday edition, built up by Editor Morrill Goddard (1865–1937), had the largest U.S. newspaper circulation (250,000). That year an *Evening World* was established; it soon achieved greater popular appeal than the morning edition but never its distinction for journalistic brilliance and public responsibility. In 1886 Pulitzer resumed publishing the *World Almanac*, previously issued 1868–1876. In the twentieth century two notable figures directed the paper's editorial policy: Frank Irving Cobb (1869–1923), editor in chief 1911–1923, and Walter Lippmann (1889–1974), editorial page director 1924–1931. In 1931 the *Worlds* were purchased by Roy Wilson Howard (1883–1964), who discontinued the morning edition and merged the evening edition with the Scripps-Howard *Telegram*. On 4 January 1950 the *World-Telegram* absorbed the New York *Sun*. The *World-Telegram and The Sun* in September 1966 became part of the new *World Journal Tribune* (–1967).

Magazines

1830. *The Lady's Book* (July–), founded in Philadelphia by Louis Antoine Godey (1804–1878) and Charles Alexander, the first major women's periodical. In 1837 the monthly absorbed Sarah Josepha Hale's *Ladies' Magazine* (f. 1828). Hale (1788–1879) co-edited with Godey the combined periodical, which from 1840 was titled *Godey's Lady's Book and Ladies' American Magazine*. During 1837–1850 *Godey's Lady's Book* published all the popular writers. Noted for its sentimental content and hand-colored engravings of women's fashions, *Godey's* made other magazines aware of the importance of the female market and was widely imitated. Most important of the early women's magazines, it set a circulation record of 150,000 before the Civil War. Later it became an unprosperous general magazine. In 1883 it was purchased by J. H. Haulenbeck and in August 1898 by Frank Andrew Munsey (1854–1925), who merged it into the *Puritan* (1897–1901).

1831. Two important specialized periodicals founded in Massachusetts. *The Liberator* (1 January–29 December 1865), founded and edited in Boston by William Lloyd Garrison (1805–1879), was a militant organ of the abolition movement. Garrison demanded immediate and complete emancipation of the slaves. Massachusetts imposed sanctions against exporting the *Liberator*, and Postmaster General Amos Kendall (1789–1869) allowed it and other papers favoring abolition to be rifled from U.S. mail sacks in the South. Of the antislavery papers, the *Liberator* was the most eloquent and effective. *Biblical Repository* (January–December 1850), founded in Andover by Bela B. Edwards, was a learned and weighty religious periodical. In 1834 Edwards's *American Quarterly Observer* (f. 1833) was combined with the *Biblical Repository*. During 1837–1844 the periodical was known as the *American Biblical Repository*.

● *Genesee Farmer* (January–) founded in Rochester, New York, by Luther Tucker (1802–1873). In 1839 it was merged into the regional *Cultivator* (f. 1834) of Albany. In 1853 the *Country Gentleman* was begun as a weekly edition of the *Cultivator & Country Gentleman*. In 1911 Cyrus Hermann Kotzschmar Curtis (1850–1933) bought the periodical, moving it to Philadelphia and making it a national weekly with broader interests to rural audiences. In 1925 it was issued as a monthly. In 1955 it became *Better Farming*, and that June Curtis sold it to the *Farm Journal* (f. 1877), the largest and most important national farm periodical.

● *Spirit of the Times* (10 December–22 June 1861), founded in New York by William T. Porter, the first general sports magazine. A high-class periodical, it covered baseball, cricket, horse racing, etc. In 1832 C. J. B. Fisher purchased it and merged it with the *Traveller* to form the *Traveller and Spirit of the Times*. In 1835 Porter repurchased the magazine, restored its original name, and varied the content with humorous sketches, stories, and theatrical coverage, as well as sports. In 1856 Porter withdrew from *Spirit of the Times* to found *Porter's Spirit of the Times*. In 1868 he dropped his own name from the title of the second magazine and in 1873 adopted numbering to conform to his claim that it was the original *Spirit of the Times*.

1832. *American Railroad Journal* (2 January–), founded and edited in New York by D. Kimball Minor to encourage railroad growth, the first successful magazine for railroads. In May 1837 the *Mechanics Magazine and Journal of the Mechanics' Institute* (f. 1833) was combined with the *American Railroad Journal*; in 1846–1847 the journal relocated in Philadelphia. In 1849 John H. Schultz bought it. During the magazine's long life it went from weekly to semimonthly to monthly publication, with many variations of titles, including *Railway Locomotive and Cars*, *American Engineer and Railroad Journal*, *Railway Mechanical Engineer*, and *Railway Age, Mechanical Edition*.

1833. Two major magazines founded in New York City. *Knickerbocker Magazine* (January–October 1865) was the first popular monthly. After 1834 it was edited by Lewis Gaylord Clark (1808–1873), who strengthened the magazine with contributions by William Cullen Bryant, James Fenimore Cooper, Washington Irving, Henry Wadsworth Longfellow, and other noted writers. *Knickerbocker* changed from a gently satiric review of New York life to a rabid Copperhead periodical. *Parley's Magazine* (March–December 1844) was founded by Samuel Griswold Goodrich (1793–1860), known as children's writer Peter Parley, and edited for children. It was first published biweekly, then semimonthly, then monthly. In 1834 Goodrich sold to Charles S. Francis. In 1845 *Parley's* was merged into *Robert Merry's Museum* (f. 1841).

1834. *New-Yorker* (22 March–11 September 1841), founded by Horace Greeley (1811–1872) in partnership with Jonas Winchester, a literary weekly. In 1841 it was absorbed into the weekly edition of the *New York Tribune* (f. 1841).

• *The Southern Literary Messenger* (August–June 1864) founded in Richmond, Virginia, by Thomas Willys White, a leading southern magazine. The monthly was proslavery and mostly devoted to literature by southern writers. Editors and contributors included Matthew Fountain Maury, Edgar Allan Poe, and William Gilmore Simms. In July 1843 Benjamin Blake Minor bought the *Messenger*. In December 1845 Minor bought the *Southern and Western Monthly Magazine* (f. 1845) of Charleston from Simms and combined it with the *Messenger* to form *The Southern and Western Literary Messenger and Review*. In autumn 1847 Minor sold to John Reuben Thompson (1823–1873), who in 1853 sold to Macfarlane & Ferguson (the magazine's printers), which in December 1863 sold to Wedderburn & Alfriend.

1835. *Army and Navy Chronicle* (3 January–21 May 1842) founded in Washington as a weekly; later merged with *Military and Naval Magazine* (f. 1833).

• *Southern Literary Journal* (September–December 1838) founded in Charleston, South Carolina, by Daniel K. Whitaker as a monthly review with regional appeal. A leading contributor was William Gilmore Simms. The magazine was discontinued August 1837 but revived by Bartholomew Rivers Carroll in January 1838.

1837. *United States Magazine and Democratic Review* (October–October 1859) founded in Washington, by John L. O'Sullivan (editor) and Samuel D. Langtree; later moved to New York City. It began as a monthly, then was issued as a weekly, and finally as a quarterly. It absorbed the *Boston Quarterly Review* in November 1842. The *United States Magazine* was expansionist and in 1845 contained the earliest known appearance of the term Manifest Destiny in an unsigned opinion piece, later attributed to O'Sullivan. The United States had, he believed, a manifest destiny to annex Texas and otherwise spread over the continent. In July–August 1845 the periodical became known as the *Democratic Review*; subsequently known under other titles with various publishers. In 1856 *United States Review* merged with it. In the first half of 1857, it was published as a newspaper.

1838. *Boston Quarterly Review* (January–1875) founded by Orestes Augustus Brownson (1803–1876). In 1842 it merged with *United States Democratic Review* (New York), which in 1844 became *Brownson's Quarterly Review* (Boston). The *Review* was not published from January 1865 until October 1872, at which time it resumed for three years.

● *Pennsylvania Freeman* (January–1854) founded in Philadelphia by the Pennsylvania Anti-Slavery Society. The offices were sacked and burned in 1838. Editors included John Greenleaf Whittier (1807–1892) and James Russell Lowell (1819–1891).

● *Jeffersonian* (17 February–9 February 1839) founded in Albany, New York, by William Henry Seward (1801–1872) and Thurlow Weed (1797–1882), with Horace Greeley (1811–1872) as editor, to promote Whig presidential and vice-presidential candidates.

● *Connecticut Common School Journal* (August–December 1866) founded in Hartford by Henry Barnard (1811–1900); published irregularly. In January 1854 State Teachers' Association of Connecticut took it over.

● *Common School Journal* (November–December 1852) founded in Boston as a semimonthly by Horace Mann (1796–1859).

1839. Two notable magazines founded in July in New York City. *Brother Jonathan* (–c. 1845), founded by Park Benjamin (1809–1864) and Rufus Wilmot Griswold (1815–1857), was a cheap fiction weekly (10 cents) that printed mostly serials pirated from English publishers. Wilson and Company bought it in 1840. *Merchants' Magazine and Commercial Review* (–1870), founded by Freeman Hunt, was an encyclopedic monthly of commercial subjects. During the decade 1850–1860 it was known as *Hunt's Merchants' Magazine*.

1840. *New World* (6 June–10 May 1845), founded in New York by Park Benjamin, Rufus Wilmot Griswold, and Jonas Winchester, a weekly specializing in pirated fiction from England. The publishers put out monthly serial supplements and a daily edition, the *Signal*.

● *Log Cabin* (2 May–) founded in New York City and Albany by H. Greeley & Co. (Horace Greeley, William Henry Seward, Thurlow Weed) to promote Whig presidential candidates. In 1841 Greeley's new *Weekly Tribune* absorbed it.

- *The Dial* (July–April 1844) founded in Boston by the Transcendental Club. Editors included Margaret Fuller (1810–1850), Ralph Waldo Emerson (1803–1882), and George Ripley (1802–1880). An avant-garde, individualistic Transcendentalist organ, the *Dial* became the most famous quarterly of its time.
- *Lowell Offering* (October–1845) founded in Lowell, Massachusetts, as a literary magazine edited and published by young women mill workers; most prominent of the magazines edited by factory employees.
- *Graham's Lady's and Gentleman's Magazine* (December–December 1858) founded in Philadelphia by combining the *Casket* (f. 1826) and *Burton's Gentleman's Magazine* (f. 1837). The innovative editor and publisher, George Rex Graham (1813–1894), demonstrated that a magazine could increase its circulation by paying top rates that would lure such well-known writers as William Cullen Bryant, James Fenimore Cooper, Henry Wadsworth Longfellow, and James Russell Lowell. Edgar Allan Poe (1809–1849) served as literary editor 1841–1842. Also renowned for its lavish use of original copper and steel engravings, the monthly became the leading U.S. magazine. In 1848 Graham sold to Samuel D. Patterson & Co., then in 1850 regained control. About three years later *Graham's Magazine* was sold again.

1841. *Robert Merry's Museum* (February–June 1872) founded in Boston by Samuel Griswold Goodrich (1793–1860). *Parley's Magazine* (f. 1833) merged with it in 1841. There were many variations on the monthly's original title. The most important content was the moral and didactic tales of Peter Parley (Goodrich's pen name). In 1855 John N. Stearns purchased the periodical. In 1866 Horace B. Fuller took over. In 1867 Louisa May Alcott (1832–1888) became editor (to 1870).

1842. *Ladies National Magazine* (January–April 1898), founded in Philadelphia by Charles J. Peterson, a successful imitator of *Godey's Lady's Book* (f. 1830), eventually surpassing it in circulation. The longest lasting of the monthly's several titles was *Peterson's Magazine* (1855–1892). Ann S. Stephens co-edited the periodical, which was noted for its combination of light literature and women's fashions, illustrated with hand-colored engravings. Upon Peterson's death in 1887, his widow took over; in 1892 she sold to a stock company headed by Roderic Penfield, who abandoned fashions for art, literature, and the theater and changed the title to *The New Peterson Magazine*. In 1894 the title was changed to *Peterson Magazine of Illustrated Literature*, and in 1895 the periodical was again sold.

- *Pennsylvania Law Journal* (January–1852) founded in Philadelphia as a weekly; later a monthly. In 1848 it was named the *American Law Journal*.
- *American Agriculturist* (April–) founded in New York City by A. B.

Allen and R. L. Allen, the longest living farm journal. It went from a monthly to a weekly (1894). A leading farm journal, it absorbed many competitive publications, including the *Rural New Yorker* (f. 1849) and the *American Farmer* (f. 1819). In the mid-1890s it was published monthly by American Agriculturist, Inc., mainly for farmers in New York State and New England.

1843. *The New Englander* (January–) founded in New Haven, Connecticut, by Edward Royall Tyler as a religious quarterly; became bimonthly in 1878, monthly in 1885. During 1885–1892 it was known as *The New Englander and Yale Review* with enhanced appeal to Yale University alumni.

1844. *Littell's Living Age* (11 May–1941) founded in Boston by Eliakim Littell (1797–1870); contained mostly reprints from English and other foreign periodicals. In 1897 the title was shortened to *The Living Age* and in 1898 the magazine was consolidated with *Eclectic Magazine* (f. 1844). It changed hands several times until 1919, when it was purchased by the Atlantic Monthly Company. A propaganda agent for the Japanese government, Joseph Hilton Smyth, bought it in 1938.

1845. *The American Review* (January–December 1852) founded in New York as a monthly to support Whig candidates. (A preliminary issue had been published in autumn 1844.) Edgar Allan Poe's "The Raven" appeared in it for the first time. In May 1850 it was named *The American Whig Review*.

● *The Harbinger* (14 June–February 1849) founded at Brook Farm, West Roxbury, Massachusetts, by the Brook Farm Phalanx, with George Ripley editor. It was a Fourierist weekly. In October 1847 it became affiliated with the American Union of Associationists, New York City.

● *Scientific American* (28 August–), founded in New York by Rufus Porter. From the beginning it has emphasized scientific discovery. In 1846 Porter sold it to Orson Munn and Alfred Beach. In 1921 the periodical went from a weekly to a monthly. In the mid-1980s Scientific American, Inc., published it, running articles only by professional scientists.

● *The National Police Gazette* (13 September–), founded in New York by Enoch E. Camp and George Wilkes, with crime as its focus. In 1866 the weekly was sold to Wilkes's erstwhile enemy, Police Chief George W. Matsell of New York, who sensationalized the content with sex scandals and added more pictures and sporting items. In lieu of an unpaid bill for woodcuts, Matsell's engravers, Mooney & Lederer, took over in 1874. Richard K. Fox took over in 1877 and made the periodical lurid with more sex. In 1890 content consisted chiefly of crime, sex, theater, and lots of sports. In February 1932 the *Police Gazette* was sold and discontinued. Revived in 1933, it became a semimonthly in 1934; it was sold to Harold H. Roswell and became a monthly in 1935.

1846. *Commercial Review of the South and West* (January–June 1880) founded in New Orleans by James Dunwoody Brownson De Bow (1820–1867); outstanding for its economic coverage of the antebellum South. In 1853 it became *De Bow's Review*. Strongly proslavery and secessionist, it was one of the South's leading periodicals. There were offices in Washington, D.C.; New Orleans; and then both in Richmond (editorial) and Charleston (publication). The monthly was suspended August 1862–January 1866 (except for the July 1864 issue), then resumed in Nashville. After De Bow's death, his widow continued the magazine. In March 1868 William MacCreary Burwell bought the *Review*, moving it back to New Orleans, and became editor. *De Bow's New Orleans Monthly Review*, as it was then known, suspended publication in July 1870. In 1879 it was revived by L. Graham & Company for four issues.

● *Horticulturist and Journal of Rural Art and Rural Taste* (July–) founded in Albany, New York, by Luther Tucker (1802–1873), who edited it until 1852. In 1853 it was purchased by James Vick of Rochester, New York; in 1855 by Robert Pearsall Smith of Philadelphia; in 1858 by C. M. Saxton of New York City. Its last issue was December 1875, when it was absorbed by a Philadelphia periodical, *Gardener's Monthly and Horticultural Adviser* (f. 1859), which became *Gardener's Monthly and Horticulturist*, which in 1888 was absorbed into *American Garden* (f. in 1872 as *Flower Garden*).

● *Dry Goods Reporter and Commercial Glance* founded in New York by W. B. Burroughs, Jr., to cover the textile trade. Later it became the *United States Economist and Dry Goods Reporter*.

1847. *National Era* (January–1859) founded in Washington by Gamaliel Bailey (1807–1859) as an abolition journal. It gained a wide reputation for publishing works by Nathaniel Hawthorne and for serializing *Uncle Tom's Cabin*.

● *The Merchant's Ledger* (20 January–December 1903) founded in New York by D. Anson Pratt as a mercantile weekly. In 1850 it was sold to Robert Bonner (1824–1899), who added essays, fiction, and verse to make it a general family periodical. It became *The New York Ledger* in 1855, when Bonner eliminated the mercantile content. Using name writers and advertising extensively, Bonner aimed for a mass readership. By 1860 circulation was 400,000. In 1898 the cheap literary miscellany became *The Ledger Monthly*. In 1902 it was sold to a stock company.

1848. *The Independent* (7 December–13 October 1928) founded in New York by a group of Congregationalists, including Henry C. Bowen (c. 1814–1896), to further their cause and to fight slavery. Initially, the *Independent* was a weekly "religious newspaper," a type of periodical that flourished from the 1820s into the 1880s, but opinion and miscellany were more important than denominational news, and it reached a more general audience than most such publications. Under the editorship of Henry Ward Beecher (1813–1887) the publication became less religious and more political. When slavery was no longer an issue, the *Independent* espoused women's suffrage. In 1872 a magazinelike format came with expanding literary content and renewed religious fervor. After Bowen's death the *Independent* dropped its religious emphasis and concentrated on public affairs, fiction, and some illustration. In 1913 the magazine was sold to a new company headed by Hamilton Holt (1872–1951), a grandson of Bowen, who increased illustrations and added articles by prominent statesmen and officials, including ex-President Taft. In these years it absorbed the *Chautauquan* (1 June 1914), *Harper's Weekly* (22 May 1916), and *Countryside* (2 January 1917). During this time the *Independent* espoused the League of Nations. In 1919 a printers' strike caused the magazine to miss several issues. In October 1921 it was sold to Fabian Franklin (1853–1939) and Harold DeWolf Fuller, editors and publishers of the *Weekly Review*, who consolidated the publications; that year they missed some issues due to financial problems. In May 1922 frequency was changed from weekly to biweekly. In February 1924 the *Independent* was sold to Richard Ely Danielson and Christian A. Herter, who in April moved it to Boston. In October 1928 it merged with the *Outlook* (f. 1870 as the *Christian Union*) to form the *Outlook and Independent*.

● *New England Farmer* (9 December–December 1871) founded in Boston as a semimonthly; suspended five months in 1864.

1849. *Mercersburg Review* (January–October 1926) founded in Mercersburg, Pennsylvania, by alumni of Marshall College as the journal of the German Reformed Church. In 1853 it went from a bimonthly to quarterly; publication was suspended 1862–1866. In 1879 it was titled the *Reformed Quarterly Review* and in 1897 the *Reformed Church Review*.

1850. *Harper's New Monthly Magazine* (June–) founded in New York by the House of Harper to promote its books. At first *Harper's* surveyed contemporary English literature; later it published the best U.S. and English authors. It became one of the most successful magazines, by 1861 achieving a circulation of 200,000. William Dean Howells (1837–1920) was editor 1885–1891. In 1900 *New* was dropped from the title. From the late nineteenth century to 1925 the magazine was heavily illustrated. In the 1920s the periodical's emphasis changed from literature to public affairs, and in 1925 the title was further shortened to *Harper's Magazine*. In 1965 John Cowles, Jr., bought half interest from Harper & Row, and in July 1980 his Minneapolis Star and Tribune Co. sold the magazine to the John D. and Catherine T. MacArthur Foundation. In the mid-1980s *Harper's* was published by the Harper's Magazine Foundation and circulation was about 152,000.

• *Waverley Magazine* (–1908) founded in Boston by Moses A. Dow as a weekly for amateur (unpaid) writers.

1851. *Gleason's Pictorial Drawing-Room Companion* (3 May–24 December 1859), founded in Boston by Frederick Gleason, the first major copiously illustrated magazine. In November 1854 the weekly was sold to Maturin M. Ballou.

1852. *American Law Register and Review* founded in Philadelphia. In 1897 it became the *University of Pennsylvania Law Review and American Law Register*.

1853. *Putnam's Monthly Magazine* (January–) founded in New York by Charles F. Briggs and George Palmer Putnam (1814–1872) of F. P. Putnam & Company. The monthly's content was political and literary, including such authors as James Fenimore Cooper, Henry Wadsworth Longfellow, James Russell Lowell, Herman Melville, and Henry David Thoreau. In late 1857 it merged with *Emerson's United States Magazine* (f. 1854) to form *Emerson's Magazine and Putnam's Monthly*, which in December 1870 was absorbed by the new *Scribner's Monthly*. In 1906 *Putnam's* was revived as *Putnam's Monthly and the Critic* (*Critic* f. 1881), an illustrated general magazine of varied contents. In 1907 *Critic* was dropped from the title, and in March 1908 the original title was restored. In April 1910 *Putnam's* was merged into *Atlantic Monthly* (f. 1857).

1854. *Herald of Freedom* (–1860) founded in Wakarusa, Kansas, by Dr. George W. Brown as a Free Soil periodical; after the first number, published in Lawrence, Kansas (1855–).

1855. *The American Journal of Education and College Review* (August–1882) founded in New York by Henry Barnard (1811–1900) and Reverend Absalom Peters; encyclopedic work on education of the time. In March 1856 the title was shortened to *The American Journal of Education*.

• *Frank Leslie's Illustrated Newspaper* (15 December–24 June 1922) founded in New York by Henry Carter (1821–1880), whose pseudonym was Frank Leslie (legally adopted in 1857). The illustrated weekly presented a lively and vivid picture of the American scene, including picture and text coverage of the Civil War. Fiction eventually was added. In 1880 Leslie's widow became editor and publisher; in 1889 she sold the magazine to W. J. Arkell and Russell B. Harrison. In 1898 John A. Schleicher purchased the magazine, then known as *Leslie's Weekly*.

• *Squatter Sovereign* (–1909) founded in Atchison, Kansas, by Dr. J. H. Stringfellow and Robert Skelly to oppose Free Soilers. Later owners in 1857 made it a free-state periodical under the title *Freedom's Champion*; in 1868 named *Atchison Champion*.

1856. *Journal of Agriculture* (–1921) founded in St. Louis.

1857. *Harper's Weekly* (3 January–13 May 1916) founded in New York by Fletcher Harper (1806–1877) of the Harper Brothers book publishers, as a news weekly. Content included essays, fiction, and many illustrations. It was noted for its outstanding coverage of the Civil War, including woodcuts of Mathew Brady's photographs, and for the illustrations of Thomas Nast, particularly his political cartoons in the 1870s. The weekly was sold to Samuel Sidney McClure (1857–1949) in 1913 and then absorbed by the *Independent* (f. 1848) on 22 May 1916.

• *The Atlantic Monthly* (November–) founded in Boston by Francis H. Underwood and Moses Dresser Phillips of Phillips, Sampson & Company, book publishers, as a national literary periodical with a New England emphasis. Contributors included Ralph Waldo Emerson, Henry Wadsworth Longfellow, and Henry David Thoreau. In 1859 *Atlantic Monthly* was purchased by Ticknor & Fields; by 1909 the periodical was published by the Atlantic Monthly Co. Noted editors included James Russell Lowell (1819–1891) 1857–1861; William Dean Howells, 1872–1881; Walter Hines Page (1855–1918) 1898–1899; and Ellery Sedgwick (1872–1960) 1908–1938. Sedgwick broadened content to reflect economic, political, and social changes in contemporary life; but he and his successors continued to publish leading literary writers, including Saul Bellow, Lillian Hellman, Ernest Hemingway, and Edwin O'Connor. In the 1960s *Atlantic* editors emphasized public affairs. In the mid-1980s the *Atlantic* was edited by William Whitworth for an academic and professional audience interested in arts, politics, and science; circulation exceeded 433,000.

1858. *Douglass' Monthly* (–1863) founded in Rochester, New York, by Frederick Douglass (c. 1817–1895) to raise funds in the British Isles for abolition in the United States. In 1860 the magazine, one of the first published by a black person, absorbed *Frederick Douglass' Paper* (f. as *The North Star* in 1847). The monthly later ran into severe financial problems.

• *Pacific Medical Journal* (–1917) founded in San Francisco.

1859. *Spirit of the Times and Sportsman* (10 September–) founded in New York by George Wilkes as a turf weekly. After the Civil War it became a leading general sports periodical, covering field sports and theater as well as racing. It ran until 13 December 1902, when it merged into the *Horseman* (f. 1881). A successor was *Sports of the Times* (1902–1912).

1860. About 40 agricultural periodicals published.

• *Mining and Scientific Press* (–1922) founded in San Francisco as a semiannual.

1861–1877

Civil War and Reconstruction

Books

1862. *Parson Brownlow's Book,* by William Gannaway Brownlow (1805–1877), a best seller.

1863. *Faith Gartney's Girlhood,* by Mrs. Adeline Dutton Train Whitney (1824–1906), a best seller.

1864. Hurd & Houghton, publishing house, founded in Boston by Henry Oscar Houghton (1823–1895) and Melancthon Montgomery Hurd. By the end of the war, the firm was known in Cambridge and Boston as H. O. Houghton & Co. and in New York as Hurd & Houghton. In 1872 George Harrison Mifflin (1845–1921) joined the firm. In 1878, with the addition of James R. Osgood, Hurd & Houghton became Houghton, Osgood & Co. In 1880, with Osgood's retirement, the imprint became Houghton Mifflin & Co.

1865. *Hans Brinker, or the Silver Skates,* by Mary Elizabeth Mapes Dodge (1831–1905), a best seller this year and later.

1866. Leypoldt & Holt, publishing house, founded in New York by Henry Holt (1840–1926) and Frederick Leypoldt (1835–1884). In 1870, with the addition of Ralph O. Williams, the firm became Leypoldt, Holt & Williams. In 1871, with Leypoldt's retirement, the name was changed to Holt & Williams. In 1873, with Williams's retirement, the firm became Henry Holt & Co. In 1928 family control ended and Holt became a public corporation. Holt acquired Rinehart & Co. (f. 1929) and John C. Winston Co. (f. 1884) in 1959 to become Holt, Rinehart & Winston, Inc. The transaction was the first in a long series of major mergers among publishers. In 1967 Holt, Rinehart & Winston was acquired by the Columbia Broadcasting System.

1867. *Miss Ravenel's Conversion from Secession to Loyalty*, by John William De Forest (1826–1906), a Civil War novel. In 1872 De Forest, an early realist, published *Kate Beaumont*, the story of a feud in South Carolina. Both books were candid accounts of seamy aspects of life.

• Two best sellers—*St. Elmo*, by Augusta Jane Evans Wilson (1835–1909), and *Ragged Dick*, by Horatio Alger, Jr. (1832–1899); latter also a later best seller. Alger wrote more than 100 extremely popular books for boys, including *Luck and Pluck* (1869) and *Tattered Tom* (1871).

1868. Two best sellers this year and later—*The Gates Ajar*, by Elizabeth Stuart Phelps Ward (1844–1911), and *Little Women*, by Louisa May Alcott (1832–1888). A second volume of *Little Women* followed in 1869. Alcott's other works included *An Old Fashioned Girl* (1870), *Jo's Boys* (1886), and the best-selling *Little Men* (1871). Her juveniles were popular until World War I. Ward followed *Gates Ajar* with *Beyond the Gates* (1883), *The Gates Between* (1887), and *Within the Gates* (1901). Ward's novels *Hedged In* (1870) and *The Silent Partner* (1871) grew out of her interest in the plight of working women, especially in the mills, and were based on government reports. *Doctor Zay* (1882) reflected Ward's interest in problems of professional women.

1869. Macmillan Co., publishing house, founded in New York by George Edward Brett as a branch of Macmillan & Co., London. In 1896 the branch became a U.S. corporation. In 1936 it issued the landmark best seller *Gone With the Wind*.

• *Innocents Abroad*, the first best seller of Samuel Langhorne Clemens (1835–1910), whose pseudonym was Mark Twain. The first of several travel books by Twain, *Innocents Abroad* displayed the author's frontier irreverence for Old World culture. His other best sellers in this and later periods included *Roughing It* (1872), which depicted his experience on the far western frontier; *The Adventures of Tom Sawyer* (1876) and *Huckleberry Finn* (1885), picaresque portrayals of regional character and the frontier experience; and *Life on the Mississippi* (1883), an autobiographical work with huge sales in the 1940s in pocket books. Twain's first novel was *The Gilded Age* (1873), written with Charles Dudley Warner (1829–1900); like his other novels, it was marked by episodic improvisation.

1870. Dodd & Mead, publishing house, founded in New York, by Frank Howard Dodd (1844–1916) and Edward S. Mead, upon the retirement of Moses Woodruff Dodd (1813–1899) from his own publishing business. In 1876, with the addition of Bleecker Van Wagenen, the firm became Dodd, Mead & Co.

• *The Luck of Roaring Camp*, by Francis Brett Harte (1836–1902), a best seller this year and later; one of the first local color stories of the West. In stories like *Luck* and *Mrs. Skaggs's Husbands* (1873), Bret Harte used stock characters and plots to create romantic legends of California. He extended this view in such poems as "Plain Language from Truthful James" (1870), a satiric comic ballad popularly known as "The Heathen Chinee."

1871. *The Hoosier Schoolmaster*, by Edward Eggleston (1837–1902), a best seller this year and later. Eggleston founded the "Hoosier school" with his middle-border novels, which also included *The Circuit Rider* (1874), *Roxy* (1878), and *The Graysons* (1888). He also wrote pioneer historical works on U.S. cultural history, notably *The Transit of Civilization* (1901).

• *The Pike County Ballads*, by John Milton Hay (1838–1905); helped establish a vogue for vernacular western poetry. Hay's prose works included *Castilian Days* (1871), an attack on the Catholic Church; *The Bread-Winners* (1883), an antilabor novel; and *Abraham Lincoln: A History* (1890), a ten-volume biography written with John George Nicolay (1832–1901).

1872. *Barriers Burned Away*, by Edward Payson Roe (1838–1888), a best seller. Roe's other works included the best seller *Opening a Chestnut Burr* (1874), *From Jest to Earnest* (1875), *Without a Home* (1881), and *He Fell in Love with His Wife* (1886).

1873. Notable works by two balladists of the West—*Farm Ballads*, by Will Carleton (1845–1912), including the poem "Over the Hills to the Poor House," and *Life Amongst the Modocs*, by Cincinnatus Hiner (or Heine) Miller (1839–1913), whose pseudonym was Joaquin Miller. The latter—the prose counterpart of Miller's *Songs of the Sierras* (1871), which had won acclaim in England—romanticized some of his early experiences in the Far West. Miller also published in 1873 *Songs of the Sunlands*. His *Songs of the Soul* (1896) included his better known "Columbus" and "The Passing of Tennyson."

1876. *Helen's Babies*, by John Habberton (1842–1921), a best seller this year and later. Other stories by Habberton included *Other People's Children* (1877), a sequel to *Helen's Babies*, and *Budge & Toddie, or, Helen's Babies at Play* (1908).

• *Roderick Hudson*, the first major novel by Henry James (1843–1916), a story of an American sculptor residing abroad. James's other major works included *The American* (1877), *The Portrait of a Lady* (1881), *What Maisie Knew* (1897), *The Wings of the Dove* (1902), *The Ambassadors* (1903), and *The Golden Bowl* (1904). Through sensitive interpretation of subtle characters, James contrasted American and European cultures and moral standards. He was a leader in psychological realism and master of a complex style. He was also distinguished as a writer of short stories, such as "The Turn of the Screw" (1898), and of criticism, such as prefaces to his revised collected works (1907–1909).

1877. *Deephaven*, the first novel by Sarah Orne Jewett

(1849–1909). It revealed social and psychological problems in declining Maine seaport settlements. Her series culminated in *The Country of the Pointed Firs* (1896). Jewett's works exemplified New England regional fiction.

Newspapers

1861. R. Hoe & Company manufactured a newspaper press using stereotype plates (solid plates produced from type forms and curved to fit press cylinders). The plates had been used for years in book printing. Now newspaper makeup no longer was limited by column rules, which held type in the press cylinder, and production speed was greatly increased because publishers could use as many plates from a single type form as a press was equipped to employ. Within a few years all large newspapers were using stereotype plates.

• Censorship began in the North. Early in the War Between the States, General George Brinton McClellan (1826–1885) exacted from eastern correspondents promises as to what war activities they would refrain from reporting; this informal censorship was moderately effective. In April all telegraph lines from Washington were placed under State Department censors, and transmission of information about army activities was strictly limited. The House Judiciary Committee investigated inconsistencies in enforcing the rules and reported on 20 March 1862 that wholesome criticism and discussion were being restrained. Censorship was taken over by the War Department and an assistant secretary appointed military superintendent of all U.S. telegraphic offices and lines. In August 1861, meanwhile, the War Department had issued a General Order calling attention to the 57th Article of War, which provided court martial, with possible death sentence, for directly or indirectly giving military information to the enemy. The order also forbade printing any news of camps, troops, and army or navy movements, except by express permission of the officer in command. Correspondents usually disregarded the order, but the better reporters concealed information of value to the enemy. In 1861 General William Tecumseh Sherman (1820–1891) banished all correspondents from his army; he later allowed some to return. In May 1862 General Henry Wager Halleck (1815–1872) expelled all newspapermen from his army. Other generals were almost as strict.

1862. Censorship began in the South. In January all correspondents were banished from the Army of the Potomac, and the Confederate Congress made it a crime to publish any news of the destination, disposition, movements, or numbers of southern land or naval forces. Confederate censorship was stricter, more consistent, and more effective than northern censorship.

● Western Associated Press informally organized by midwestern newspapers in protest against the dictatorial methods of the New York Associated Press, which had a virtual monopoly of wire news, sold under contracts to newspapers outside New York City. In 1866 the Western AP was strong enough to defy the New York AP and threatened to set up a competitive news-gathering agency. Cooperation was restored with regional reports and equitable charges. Other sectional associations soon demanded and received similar concessions.

● On 1 August a 3 percent tax levied by the federal government on newspaper advertising in effect. Publishers' complaints led to occasional allowances and exemptions, the most important being one of 1864 that relieved from the tax all newspapers whose average circulation was 2,000 or less. Tax repealed 2 March 1867.

● Lewiston *Golden Age* published, the first newspaper in Idaho.

1863. First web-perfecting press, made by William Bullock for Philadelphia *Inquirer*. This press accelerated production by printing both sides of a continuous sheet automatically fed from a roll. In 1871 R. Hoe & Company brought out a superior web-perfecting press.

● Press Association of the Confederate States of America (J. S. Thatcher, superintendent) established. It served 43 dailies in the South with news in 1863–1864.

● Fort Bridger *Daily Telegram*, the first newspaper in Wyoming, the only state to have a daily for its first paper.

● Boise, Idaho, *News* founded to serve the Boise Basin; later the Idaho City *News*.

1864. St. Louis, Missouri, *Dispatch* founded. On 9 December 1878 the paper, with its valuable Associated Press franchise, was acquired by Joseph Pulitzer (1847–1911), who on 12 December 1878 combined it with the St. Louis *Post* (f. 1875).

● Fort Union *Frontier Scout*, North Dakota's first newspaper.

● Virginia City *Montana Post*, the first newspaper in Montana. In 1868 it moved to Helena, where it soon perished as result of a fire that had swept the community.

1865. Three newspapers founded in San Francisco. *Dramatic Chronicle* (16 January–) founded by Michel Harry de Young (1849–1925) and Charles de Young (1847–1880), was a free theater-program tabloid. In 1868 it became a regular, standard-size newspaper, the *Daily Morning Chronicle*, advocating parks, boosting California, exposing land-grant frauds, and opposing other political corruption. By 1875 it had the largest circulation of any newspaper west of the Mississippi. Mark Twain and Bret Harte were contributors. Charles de Young was fatally shot in connection with the paper's fight against the Workingmen's Party, and Michel took over entirely, making the Chronicle a high-protection organ; he supervised it until his death. In 1907 the paper carried the first regular daily cartoon strip, "Mutt and Jeff" by H. C. (Bud) Fisher. In the 1930s and 1940s the Chronicle was known for its comprehensive national and foreign news coverage. In the 1950s it began emphasizing columnists and features, increasing circulation. In 1965 management entered into a joint business arrangement with its long-time arch rival, the Examiner, to share a plant and co-publish a Sunday edition. In 1982 the Chronicle had the twelfth largest U.S. daily circulation (535,050) and was listed in a poll as one of the better U.S. dailies (below the top 15). Morning circulation in the mid-1980s was about 535,800, thirteenth among dailies. The Elevator (–1899), a weekly founded by Phillip A. Bell. It had an unusually long life for a black paper. Evening Examiner founded by William Moss. It passed through several ownerships before George Hearst (1820–1891) bought it in 1880 and made it a morning paper, the Daily Examiner, which became the leading Democratic organ in California. Circulation increased from 4,000 to about 20,000 in 1887, when Hearst's son, William Randolph (1863–1951), took over. The younger Hearst made the Daily Examiner the most enterprising and sensational paper in San Francisco, hiring a large, talented staff that included Arthur McEwen as editor, Samuel S. Chamberlain as news editor, Ambrose Bierce as a columnist, and Winifred Black Bonfils ("Annie Laurie") as a reporter. In a year circulation doubled and by 1893 had passed the Chronicle with almost 60,000. A crusading, jingoistic paper, it continued to grow after Hearst went to New York in 1895. In 1908 circulation reached 100,000, and for many year the Examiner remained one of the few consistently profitable papers in the Hearst chain. In 1965 management entered into a joint business arrangement with its long-time arch rival, the Chronicle, to share a plant and co-publish a Sunday edition. An evening paper in the mid-1980s, its circulation was about 148,000.

● A. N. Kellogg Newspaper Company, founded in Chicago by Ansell N. Kellogg, the first major newspaper syndicate. It provided a readyprint service for local papers, relieving editors of clipping column material, fiction, poetry, and other entertainment features from newspaper and magazine exchanges. One side of the newsprint sheets was blank for local news and advertisements. Readyprints contributed to the growth of small-town weeklies.

● G. P. Rowell & Company, founded in Boston by George Presbury Rowell (1838–1908), the first of many advertising agencies begun after the Civil War. In 1867 it moved to New York and expanded, eventually becoming a leading agency. George P. Rowell devised the "advertising list" method, by which space in many newspapers was offered to advertisers for a lump sum. Like other agents, Rowell bought his space low and sold it high, making 25 to 75 percent commission. By guaranteeing payment, he won the confidence of publishers accustomed to large losses on collections. In 1868 he founded the *Advertiser's Gazette* as a company promotion; in 1871 it became the *American Newspaper Reporter and Advertiser's Gazette*, the first important business paper for publishers. In 1869 he founded the first annual directory of periodicals, the *American Newspaper Directory*, which listed 5,411 U.S. and 367 Canadian publications with their systematically calculated circulation; the directory helped businesses place ads. In 1888 Rowell launched *Printer's Ink*, a weekly trade journal for advertisers.

1866. Successful operation of the Atlantic cable; brought European events closer to Americans.

● Detroit *Daily Post* founded by Republican Party radicals in Michigan. Editor in chief for the first year was Carl Shurz.

1868. Mrs. Emily Verdery Bettey hired by the *Sun*, probably the first woman to work as a general reporter on a New York daily, illustrating the increasing importance of women in newspaper journalism.

● Atlanta, Georgia, *Constitution* founded by W. A. Hemphill. In 1876 Evan P. Howell bought half interest and became editor, making the *Constitution* not only one of the six largest dailies south of Baltimore and Louisville and east of New Orleans, but also a model newspaper of the South. In 1880 Henry Woodfin Grady (1851–1889) bought a quarter interest and became editor, increasing circulation by aggressive news gathering. In 1889 the weekly edition achieved 140,000 circulation, making it the largest such edition in the United States. That year Clark Howell (1863–1936) succeeded Grady and was an owner and the editor until 1936. In 1938 Ralph Emerson McGill (1891–1969) became editor, opposing the Ku Klux Klan and the Talmadge political machine in Georgia; in 1959 he won a Pulitzer Prize for editorial writing. In 1960 he became publisher. In 1950 James M. Cox, owner of the Atlanta *Journal*, brought the *Constitution* into his chain, but the newspapers maintained separate editorial policies. In 1982 a poll listed the *Constitution* as one of the better U.S. dailies (below top 15). A morning daily, it had about 227,750 circulation in the mid-1980s.

1869. First step toward college education for journalism. General Robert Edward Lee (1807–1870), president of Washington College (later Washington and Lee University), on 30 March recommended to the board of trustees a plan whereby young men intending to enter journalism could work out their tuition in the printing trade while taking the college's classical course; six students were admitted. The program was ridiculed by many newspaper journalists. The courses were dropped in 1878. Education for journalism was finally established at the university in 1926.

● N. W. Ayer & Son, an advertising agency, founded by Francis Wayland Ayer. The firm, named after the founder's father, soon gained high standing. In 1879 it conducted the first marketing survey, testing ads in selected local publications. In 1880 it began an annual *Ayer Directory of Publications* (still published in the 1980s but by IMS Press, Fort Washington, Pennsylvania). In the 1960s the agency became a leader in public relations counseling.

1870. About 4,500 daily, triweekly, semiweekly, and weekly newspapers of general circulation being published, a one-third increase over the 1860s. The United States had about three times as many newspapers as the United Kingdom and more than one third of all the newspapers in the world.

● Philadelphia *Public Record* founded by William J. Swain to challenge the *Public Ledger*, which his father had co-founded. In 1877 the *Public Record* was purchased by William M. Singerly, who reduced the price from 2 cents to 1 cent, improved news coverage, strengthened the business pages, and crusaded for better parks and roads and against grave robbing and selling medical diplomas. With 120,000 circulation the *Public Record* soon passed the *Public Ledger*. In 1902 the *Public Record* was sold to Thomas Wanamaker.

1872. Western Newspaper Union founded in Des Moines, Iowa, to supply weeklies with already printed pages that gave newspapers with poorly equipped plants greater variety of content. After 1890 WNU was run by George A. Joslyn, who refined the "patented-insides" business, offering editors alternative preprinted material. In 1905 WNU devised an individual service that gave newspaper editors greater control of readyprint pages. Joslyn eliminated competition by acquiring WNU's rivals, including A. N. Kellogg Newspaper Company in 1906, Andrew J. Aikens's feature service in 1910, and American Press Association plate and mat business in 1917. The acquisitions gave WNU control of distribution of readyprints and stereotype plate and mats to weeklies. In 1938 John H. Perry gained control of WNU, and in the 1940s he acquired ownership of more than one-eighth of Florida's newspapers, including nine dailies, as well as newspapers in Kentucky and six radio stations. He also owned newsprint companies and two trade publications, *Publisher's Auxiliary* and *American Press*. In 1949 Perry sold American Press Association, by then an advertising agency, to its publisher stockholders. In 1952 WNU's readyprint service was discontinued because of declining demand, reflecting the decreasing importance of old-style country papers. At its peak WNU had supplied about 7,000 weeklies with its readyprint service.

● Lord & Thomas advertising agency founded. In 1898 it employed ad writer Albert Lasker, who became president and dominated it until 1952.

• Boston *Daily Globe* founded by Maturin Murray Ballou (1820–1895). In 1873 Charles H. Taylor (1846–1921) became publisher and in 1880 also editor (the paper remained in the Taylor family for more than 100 years). Taylor ran a semisensational paper with large headlines, emphasis on local news, and editorial support for the Democratic Party. In 1877 he added an evening edition, and by 1890 the *Globes* had a combined circulation of 150,000, among the ten largest dailies; in 1979 the two editions were merged into an all-day paper. In May 1967 the *Globe* became one of the first dailies to oppose the Vietnam war. In 1971 it joined the New York *Times* and Washington *Post* in publishing the Pentagon Papers, until stopped by court order. In 1968 and 1972 the *Globe* opposed Nixon's presidential candidacies, and in October 1973 it became the first major daily to call for President Nixon's impeachment. In the 1970s and 1980s the *Globe* was ranked among the top 15 dailies. In the early 1980s the *Globe* won four Pulitzer Prizes (three in 1980, one in 1983). In the mid-1980s it ranked fifteenth in daily circulation with about 520,000.

• Atlanta, Georgia, *Herald* (–1876) founded; a newsy, lively paper. In the first year Henry Grady became one-third owner.

• Cincinnati *Star* founded. In 1880 Charles Phelps Taft (1843–1929) merged it with the evening *Times* (f. 1840) to form the *Times-Star*, a conservative Republican paper. E. W. Scripps Company bought it in 1958.

1873. New York *Daily Graphic* (–1889), founded by a Canadian engraving firm, forerunner of the modern tabloid, but not sensational. Copiously illustrated, the *Daily Graphic*, a Republican paper, was the leading newspaper in the 1870s and 1880s, relying mainly on picture appeal. Initially pictures were printed from electroplates made by a photolithographic process. Then Art Editor Stephen Henry Horgan (1854–1941) invented a halftone engraving process that made possible the reproduction of photographs, and the tabloid ran his early experiments, including the first half-tone published in a U.S. newspaper, an 1880 engraving of good quality called "Shantytown." In the 1880s ownership changed frequently.

• Detroit *Evening News* founded by James Edmund Scripps (1835–1906). In the 1870s James's sister, Ellen Browning Scripps (1836–1932), and half-brother, Edward Wyllis Scripps (1854–1926), helped make the paper a success; in the 1880s it emerged as the city's afternoon circulation leader. In 1891 J. E. Scripps bought the *Tribune*. In 1920 the *News* operated the first newspaper-owned broadcast radio station, experimental 8MK. In October 1921 it was commercially licensed as WWJ, one of the first stations to broadcast news regularly. In

1960 the *News* absorbed the *Times*. In the mid-1980s the *News* had a daily circulation of about 656,300, the ninth largest.

1875. St. Louis *Post* founded by John A. Dillon. On 12 December 1878 Joseph Pulitzer merged it with the *Dispatch* (f. 1864) to form the *Post-Dispatch*, an afternoon daily that became noted for its news coverage; its independent, liberal editorial voice; and its crusading for cleaning and repairing streets and other worthy projects in the public interest. It also campaigned against gambling, lotteries, and tax dodging. In 1880 John A. Cockerill became managing editor, in 1908 Oliver K. Bovard. In 1912 Joseph Pulitzer, Jr. (1885–1955) took over, and in the late 1940s Joseph Pulitzer III began assuming control. In 1951 the *Post-Dispatch* absorbed the *Star-Times*. In 1959 the *Post-Dispatch* and *Globe-Democrat* combined their mechanical operations while remaining competitive; on 1 January 1961 the two papers began sharing profits. In 1960–1961 polls the *Post-Dispatch* ranked among the top six dailies; in 1970 it ranked third (tied with Louisville *Courier-Journal* and Washington *Post*); but in 1982, though still one of the better dailies, its ranking dropped below the top 15. A morning paper in the mid-1980s, it had circulation of about 264,700.

• San Francisco *Wah Kee* (–1879), the first Chinese newspaper in the United States. Unable to import the large type font necessary, Editor Yee Jenn produced the *Wah Kee* ("Oriental") by a primitive lithographic process. He claimed 1,000 weekly circulation.

1876. Chicago *Daily News* (3 January–4 March 1978) founded by Melville Elijah Stone (1848–1929), after publishing a trial issue 25 December 1875 with William Dougherty. The afternoon paper was noted for its aggressive editorial page policies, its political and financial independence, and its sensational news presentation. Stone personally liked newspaper detection of criminals. He built a talented staff including columnists Eugene Field and Finley Peter Dunne (Mr. Dooley). The paper became a "graduate school" for young reporters (e.g., Ben Hecht and Carl Sandburg) who often went on to other kinds of writing. In 1876 Victor Freemont Lawson (1850–1925) gained two-thirds interest. In 1878 the *Daily News* purchased the *Post and Mail*, obtaining its Associated Press franchise. In 1881 a morning edition, eventually named the *Record*, was founded; ten years later it absorbed the *Times-Herald*. In 1885 combined circulation of the morning and afternoon editions passed 100,000; in three years that doubled. In 1888 Stone sold his one-third interest to Lawson, who that year began building a distinguished foreign service (discontinued 1977). After Lawson died, Walter A. Strong was publisher until his death in 1931, when William Franklin Knox (1874–1944) took over. Upon Knox's death John S. Knight (1895–1981) purchased the paper. In 1959

Knight sold to Marshall Field IV, and in 1969 Marshall Field V took over.

1877. Transmission by telephone (invented in 1875 by Alexander Graham Bell [1847–1922]) of a lecture from Bell's laboratory in Salem, Massachusetts, to the offices of newspapers in that city. Within a few years some large newspapers were using telephones. In the 1880s specialization developed, with "leg men" on the scene phoning in reports to "rewrite men" in newspaper offices. However, telephones were not widely used by newspapers until the twentieth century.

● Washington *Post* founded by Stilson Hutchins as a Democratic morning paper. In 1888 it absorbed the *National Republican* (f. 1860) and became politically independent. In 1889 the *Post* was purchased by Frank Hatton (1846–1894) and Beriah Wilkins, whose heirs in 1905 sold it to John R. McLean. In 1933 Eugene Meyer (1875–1959) rescued the *Post* from receivership and began developing an intelligent editorial page, interpretive coverage of national news, and extensive coverage of foreign news. The *Post* became the most independent paper in the nation's capital. In 1954 Meyer bought Robert R. McCormick's *Times-Herald*, the morning competition. The suicide of Philip L. Graham (1915–1963) publisher since 1946, gave control of the Washington Post Company, which included *Newsweek* (purchased 1961) and broadcast stations, to his widow, Katharine (1917–). She appointed Benjamin C. Bradlee (1921–) managing editor in 1966, executive editor in 1968. In the late 1960s the company became a joint owner of the *International Herald Tribune*, successor to the Paris *Herald*. By 1970 the *Post* was one of the most influential liberal-intellectual papers, with a circulation of more than 500,000. In 1971 the *Post* won national attention by joining the New York *Times* in publishing the Pentagon Papers (also published by the Boston *Globe*), until stopped by court order. The *Post* won a Pulitzer Prize for leadership in exposing the 1972 Watergate scandal, which climaxed with President Nixon's resignation. In the 1970s the paper was cited as having one of the most integrated newspaper staffs, with several blacks. In 1979 Donald Edward Graham (1945–) became publisher; his mother continued to head company operations. An episode involving a Pulitzer Prize-winning article that proved fictitious slightly tarnished the paper's reputation in 1981. A 1982 poll ranked the *Post* as the third best daily; a 1983 poll ranked the *Post* as among the top four. In its circulation area the *Post* had 60 percent daily and 70 percent Sunday penetration (1983), best in United States; it had the seventh largest daily circulation (747,676). Late in 1983 the *Post* launched a tabloid weekly with a goal of 30,000 readers. In the mid-1980s the *Post's* daily morning circulation dropped to about 728,850, eighth in the nation.

Magazines

1861. *American Bee Journal* founded in Philadelphia by Samuel Wagner. Suspended 1862–1872, it resumed publication in Washington, D.C., 1866–1872; later it moved to Chicago, then Hamilton, Illinois, where the beekeeping monthly was published in the 1980s by Dadant and Sons, Inc.

• *American Churchman* (–1871) founded in Chicago as a Protestant Episcopal weekly.

• *Camp Kettle* (–1862) published by officers of the Roundhead Regiment at camps of the 100th Pennsylvania Infantry, one of several periodicals issued irregularly by Union army units when a printer could obtain a press.

1862. *American Spirit and Wine Trade Review* (–1886) founded in Chicago; later called *Western Spirit*, then *Wine and Spirit Review*.

• *Boston Commonwealth* (–1896) founded by Moncure D. Conway and Franklin Benjamin Sanborn (1823–1917), editor 1863–1867, primarily as an antislavery journal. It had many literary and religious affiliations in its long life.

• *Harry Hazel's Yankee Blade* (–1894) founded in Boston as a Saturday story paper. In the early 1880s *Harry Hazel's* was dropped from the title. Cora Stuart Wheeler was editor for several years.

• Two literary weeklies founded in Richmond, Virginia—*Magnolia* (27 September–1865), by Charles Bailie, and *Southern Illustrated News* (13 September–25 March 1865), by the firm of Ayres & Wade. Both reviewed dramatic productions in southern cities during the War Between the States; leading southern writers contributed to the two periodicals. In March 1863 *Magnolia* was purchased by Oakley P. Haines and William A. J. Smith and the name changed to *Magnolia Weekly*. This was at least the fourth *Magnolia*; others were published at Charleston (1840–1843), Richmond (1851), and Hudson, New York. There were also later *Magnolias*. The *Southern Illustrated News*, the second periodical with this title, was intended to take the place of popular northern periodicals removed from competition by the war.

• *The Old Guard* (June–December 1870) founded in New York by Reverend C. Chauncey Burr, its editor 1863–1869. The first issue was a pamphlet. The only consistently anti-Lincoln magazine published in the North during the Civil War, it defended slavery and the right of secession and urged cessation of the war. In the first year three issues were published under warning of the postmaster general against treasonable utterances; freer times came in 1863. Even after the war, Burr continued to attack the memory of Lincoln and to defend the Confederacy. The monthly published works by such leading southern writers as William Gilmore Simms.

• *Western Rural* (–1901) founded in Chicago with H. N. F. Lewis its editor. It became a well-known farm periodical. Its name was changed to *Western Rural and American Stockman* in 1884, to *Western Rural and Live Stock Weekly* in 1895, and to *National Rural and American Family Magazine* in 1899.

1863. *Army and Navy Journal* (29 August–) founded in New York by William Conant Church (1836–1917), editor to 1917, and Francis Pharcellus Church to oppose antimilitary propaganda and to maintain the U.S. military and naval establishments. As the military's weekly unofficial voice, the *Journal* published announcements, casualty lists, information about stations, official orders, personal news of officers, and advertisements. In 1899 it absorbed the *Army and Navy Gazette* of Washington and in the early 1900s the *Army and Navy Gazette* of Philadelphia. In 1921 Franklin Coe bought the *Journal*. In 1925 John Callan O'Laughlin bought the periodical and moved it to Washington. The *Journal* consistently advocated expansion of air, land, and sea forces.

• *Chicago Journal of Commerce* (–1906) founded; later in 1863 retitled, *Iron and Steel*. It reflected the great progress in U.S. manufacturing during this era. In 1902 it merged with *Age of Steel* of St. Louis (f. 1857), and the joint venture became *Iron and Machinery World*.

• Two periodicals founded in New York by Frank Leslie (originally Henry Carter [1821–1880]). *Frank Leslie's Boys of America* (–1878) was a juvenile magazine; in 1867 it became *Frank Leslie's Boys' and Girls' Weekly*. *Frank Leslie's Ten-Cent Monthly* (August–1896) soon gave place to *Frank Leslie's Pleasant Hours*, a 15-cent illustrated monthly devoted to light entertaining literature; the name changed in June 1865 to *Frank Leslie's New Monthly*.

• *Herald of Life* (–1931) founded in New York for Adventists; later moved to Springfield, Massachusetts; then Hartford, Connecticut; then New Haven.

• *Mirror and Farmer* (–1918) founded in Manchester, New Hampshire, as an agricultural magazine from combined *Dollar Weekly Mirror* (f. 1851) and *New Hampshire Journal of Agriculture* (f. 1857).

1864. *Herald of Truth* (–1908) founded in Elkhart, Indiana, for Mennonites.

• *Maryland Farmer* (–1902) founded in Baltimore; after 1877 known as the *Farmer's and Planter's Guide*.

• *Philadelphia Photographer* (–1923) founded; became a leading photographic journal. In 1885 it moved to New York. In 1889 it became [Edward L.] *Wilson's Photograph Magazine* and in 1915 the *Photographic Journal of America*.

• Two notable specialized weeklies established in New York—the *Telegrapher* (–1877), a union journal; and *Watson's Weekly Art Journal* (–1905), founded by Henry C. Watson, devoted mainly to musical criticism and trade news. In 1891 the *Art Journal* merged with *American Musician* (f. 1884).

1865. Three notable periodicals published in New York. *The Catholic World* (April–), founded by Father Isaac Thomas Hecker (1819–1888), the first editor, was a general monthly for Catholics. *Frank Leslie's Chimney Corner* (–1885), founded by Frank Leslie, as a copiously illustrated story paper, proved to be very successful until the later 1870s. In December 1884 the *Chimney Corner* was succeeded by *Frank Leslie's Fact and Fiction for the Chimney Corner*, which for six months tried adulterating the familiar formula of fiction with more serious matters—an unsuccessful venture. *The Nation* (6 July–), founded by Edwin Lawrence Godkin (1831–1902), the first editor, with the backing of Frederick Law Olmsted (1822–1903) and others, was a weekly journal of opinion created to discuss current affairs, report on conditions in southern states, and criticize books and works of art. It supported freedmen in reconstruction and displayed a passion for social justice. Notable contributors or staff members included Heywood Broun, William James, H. L. Mencken, Reinhold Niebuhr, Francis Parkman, George Seldes, Norman Thomas, Dorothy Thompson, Harold Clurman, and Dan Wakefield. The *Nation's* influence came not from the number of readers, since circulation in the first 50 years never exceeded 12,000, but from the readers' influential positions and the frequency with which the magazine was quoted. In June 1881 Godkin sold the *Nation* to Henry Villard (originally Ferdinand Heinrich Gustav Hilgard [1835–1900]), and for the next 33 years the periodical was issued as the weekly edition of Villard's New York *Evening Post*. The post-Godkin *Nation* opposed censorship and racial discrimination and supported labor and collectivism. In World War I it staunchly defended civil liberties. For more than 50 years it followed the liberal, pacifist course of Henry then Oswald Garrison Villard (1872–1949), who took over in 1918 and separated the magazine from the newspaper. Under the Villards the *Nation* became more internationally oriented. In 1934 Maurice Wertheim's Civic Aid Foundation bought the periodical. In June 1937 it was sold to Freda Kirchwey, who in 1943 transferred ownership to Nation Associates, Inc., a nonprofit organization. Kirchwey was editor to 1955, when George C. Kirstein became publisher and Carey McWilliams (1905–1980) editor; the latter was succeeded in 1976 by Blair Clark. In 1977 a group of 30 investors, led by Hamilton Fish, acquired the *Nation*; in 1978 Victor Saul Navasky (1932–) became editor. In the mid-1980s circulation was about 60,000.

● *New England Farmer* (–1915) founded in Boston as a weekly. In 1867 it became a monthly. The third periodical to carry this title, the weekly was a resumption of the *New England Farmer* of 1822–1846; both editions were published by R. P. Eaton & Company. In 1885 the third

New England Farmer was purchased by George M. Whitaker, who consolidated it with two or three other journals. In 1903 the magazine moved to Brattleboro, Vermont.

● *Western Watchman* (–1934) founded in St. Louis for Catholics.

1866. *Boston Journal of Chemistry* (July–December 1902) founded by Dr. James R. Nichols and William J. Rolfe as a monthly devoted to agriculture, the arts, the home, and medicine. Later it moved to New York, where it was owned by Benjamin Lillard, and the name was changed to *Popular Science.* In 1883 it became *Popular Science News.*

● *The Galaxy* (1 May–January 1878) founded in New York by William Conant Church and Francis Pharcellus Church as a literary semimonthly; became a monthly in May 1867. The Church brothers were editors throughout the *Galaxy*'s history. In 1868 Sheldon & Company became publishers and joint proprietors. Between May 1870 and April 1871 Mark Twain was an editor and wrote a department, "Memoranda." Noted contributors included Henry James. Although most space was devoted to fiction and criticism, articles on history, science, and politics also appeared. Illustrations were mediocre at best. The *Galaxy* touched popular life more than most other important magazines had to that time.

● *Harvard Advocate* founded in Cambridge, Massachusetts, as a fortnightly literary periodical.

● Two notable typographical journals founded. *Printer's Circular* (–1890), founded in Philadelphia by R. S. Menamin, was one of the best typographical journals begun soon after the Civil War. *Printing Gazette* (–1875) was published in Cleveland.

1867 Three notable specialized periodicals founded in New York. *Book Buyer* (–1918), founded by Scribner's, began as a monthly announcement for the publishing firm's books but grew to become "A Summary of American and Foreign Literature" (subtitle). In 1903 it became the *Lamp*; in 1905 it returned to its original title and its original policy as an advertising organ. *Church Union* (–June 1935) was founded by Henry E. Childs. Reverend Crammond Kennedy, owner and editor in 1869, gave the periodical, with its debts and 2,000 subscribers, to J.B. Ford & Company, which took over in September and in October changed the title to the *Christian Union* to broaden the appeal. From 1870 to 1881 the editor was Henry Ward Beecher (1813–1887). The weekly gradually changed from a religious journal into a family magazine with a variety of content. Early fictional serials were contributed by such noted authors as Louisa May Alcott, Edward Eggleston, and Harriet Beecher Stowe. In 1875 the Ford company went bankrupt, and in the following reorganization, the *Christian Union* became more a journal of opinion. Another reorganization occurred in 1881. In July 1893 it was renamed *The Outlook*, reflecting the broadened emphasis from religious news and comment to arts and letters and public affairs. In March 1909 former President Theodore Roosevelt (1858–1919) actively became editor. In 1927 controlling interest was purchased by Francis Rufus Bellamy, who became editor and publisher. A 1928 merger with the *Independent* resulted in the *Outlook and Independent*. In March 1932 it became a monthly. After a four-month suspension, it was purchased in September 1932 by Frank A. Tichenor, who changed the title to *New Outlook*. *Harper's Bazar* (2 November–), founded by Fletcher Harper (1806–1877) of Harper & Brothers, was a weekly women's magazine edited by Mary L. Booth until 1889. More than a fashion magazine, it was a woman's *Harper's Weekly*, with fiction, poetry, articles on gardening, the household, and other items of interest to women. It contained excellent art work, including cartoons by Thomas Nast and engravings by the *Harper's Weekly* group. Works by such writers as William Dean Howells and Mary E. Wilkens appeared. In May 1901 it became a monthly. In 1913 William Randolph Hearst's International Magazine Company bought it and made it a more sophisticated, "smart" journal. It became mainly an upper-class fashion magazine, with belles-lettres, fiction, and articles on beauty. In the 1980s it was geared for women in their late twenties or older, with at least a middle income and two years of college, who were "sophisticated and aware." Most readers "combined" families, professions, and travel, and often owned more than one home, and were active in the arts, their communities, or world affairs. Monthly circulation in the mid-1980s was 737,000.

● *Journal of Speculative Philosophy* (January–December 1893), founded in St. Louis by William Torrey Harris (1835–1909), editor for 20 years, as a quarterly; later published in New York. The *Journal* presented the earliest philosophical writings of some of the greatest modern U.S. thinkers. Critical essays offered the first systematic study of German philosophy to appear in North America. Among contributors were J. Elliot Cabot, William Ellery Channing, G. Stanley Hall, and John Weiss.

● *Loomis' Musical and Masonic Journal* (–1900) founded in New Haven, Connecticut, as a musical journal.

● *The Southern Review* (January–October 1879) founded in Baltimore by Albert Taylor Bledsoe and William Hand Brown as a quarterly; second periodical to have this title. It was originally intended as a southern apologia and as a representative of southern literary cultivation and scholarship. Its purpose was not religious until 1871, when it was taken over by the Methodist Church South, which substituted religious for political controversies. It did remain strong literarily. After Bledsoe's death in 1877 his daughter, Sophia Bledsoe Herrick, ran the *Review*.

● *Standard* (–1920) founded in Chicago as the result of the merger of several midwestern Baptist papers; became the leading journal of the Baptist denomination in the Northwest.

1868. *American Journal of Education* (–1920) founded in St. Louis by J. B. Merwin, editor for 25 years, as a monthly with circulation in the Midwest.

● *Communist* (–1917) founded in Buffalo, Missouri, by Alcander Longley, an adherent to the Social-Labor Party who engaged in several Utopian projects. From 1872 to 1877 the *Communist* was published at Friendship Community, near Buffalo. In 1885 the periodical was taken over by the Altruist Community of St. Louis and became the *Altruist*.

● *Lippincott's Magazine of Literature, Science and Education* (January–April 1916) founded in Philadelphia by J. B. Lippincott & Company as a literary monthly edited by John Foster Kirk (1824–1904) to 1884. It was one of the nation's best periodicals. The conservative content included fiction and travel articles. *Lippincott's* published such authors as Rebecca Harding Davis, Henry James, Brander Matthews, and William Gilmore Simms. In the 1870s it did more to encourage southern writers than any other magazine. In 1881 content was lightened, and more interest in social and political questions was shown. In 1915 the periodical was moved to New York as *McBride's Magazine*, which in 1916 was merged with *Scribner's Magazine*.

● *Literary Bulletin* (December–1872) founded in New York by Frederick Leypoldt (1835–1884), editor, as a monthly imprint circular for booksellers, modeled on Brockhaus's German bulletin. In September 1869 the *Literary Bulletin* was superseded by *Monthly Book Trade Circular*, a predecessor of *Publishers Weekly* (1872–) and the *Literary News* (1875–1904).

● *The Overland Monthly* (July–July 1935) founded in San Francisco by Anton Roman to boost California and offer a medium for young local writers. Bret Harte (1836–1902) was editor 1868–1870. *Overland* included works (early) by Miss Ina Coolbrith, Harte, and Mark Twain as well as (later) by Gertrude Atherton, Willa Cather, James Hopper, Edward Markham, and George Sterling. Publication was suspended in 1876 and resumed January 1883. In 1923 *Overland Monthly* absorbed *Out West Magazine* of Los Angeles and combined the titles. In 1931 it moved to Los Angeles.

● *Railway Review* (–1926) founded in Chicago for the railroad industry.

● *The Revolution* (8 January–17 February 1872) founded in New York by Susan Brownell Anthony (1820–1906) and George Francis Train as a women's rights weekly. Anthony ran the magazine; she was succeeded in May 1870 by Laura Curtis Bullard, who was succeeded in October 1871 by J. N. Hallock. The *Revolution* was readable, lively, belligerent. It contained detailed reports of woman-suffrage meetings, correspondence from home and abroad telling of progress in the cause, literary miscellany about the cause, editorials, a financial department, and advertisements. In 1872 it merged with the *Liberal Christian*.

● *Sunday School Journal* (–1926) founded in Philadelphia as a Methodist monthly for teachers.

1869. *American Bookseller's Guide* (–1875) founded in New York; published by the American News Company and distributed free to book and periodical trade. The *American Bookseller* (1876–1893) succeeded the *Guide*.

● *Appleton's Journal* (3 April–December 1881) founded in New York by Edward Livingston Youmans (1821–1887) of D. Appleton & Company, editor to 1870, as a literary weekly. It became a monthly in July 1876. Succeeding editors were Robert Carter, 1870–1872; Oliver Bell Bunce and Charles Henry Jones, 1872–1881. Of the periodicals published shortly after the Civil War, few provided a better picture of the times than did the weekly *Appleton's Journal*. Content was characterized by wide variety; short, readable articles; and current ideas and topics. Emphasis was on New York City. After 1878 the magazine became almost an eclectic, losing most of its original distinction.

● *Life and Light for Heathen Women* (–1922) founded in Boston as a Congregational missionary quarterly. It became a monthly including home missions and without *Heathen* in the title.

● *New National Era* (–1875) founded in Washington for freedmen.

● *Publisher's Auxiliary* founded in Chicago by Ansell N. Kellogg as a monthly; later a weekly. It combined the functions of a trade journal and a house organ. Western Newspaper Union took it over when buying out Kellogg in 1906.

1870. *Keepapitchinin* (–1871) founded in New York as a humorous magazine devoted to "cents, scents, sense, and nonsense"—and puns.

● *Petroleum Monthly* (–1882) founded in Oil City, Pennsylvania, as a trade journal for the new industry exploiting the state's oil fields; in 1872 succeeded by *Monthly Petroleum Trade Report*.

● *Plantation* (–1873) founded in Atlanta by T. C. Howard and R. A. Alston as an agricultural and life insurance quarterly. In 1871 Ben C. Yancey and others took it over, and in 1872 they changed it to a monthly.

● *Scribner's Monthly* (November–Spring 1930) founded in New York by Josiah Gilbert Holland (1819–1881), editor to 1881, Roswell Smith (1829–1892), and Charles Scribner (1821–1871) as a literary monthly; a quarterly in autumn 1929. In December 1870 it absorbed *Putnam's* and *Riverside Magazine*, a Boston juvenile; in 1875 it absorbed *Old and New*. Contributors included Hans Christian Andersen, Frances Hodgson Burnett, Rebecca Harding Davis, Edward Everett Hale, Bret Harte, Helen Hunt, and Charles Dudley Warner. *Scribner's*, significant for its study of life of that time, was characterized by high aesthetic and moral ideals and a force for social and political reform. In 1881 Scribner left, leaving ownership control to Smith, and *Scribner's* became *Century Illustrated Monthly Magazine*. The new periodical published works by such notables as William Dean Howells, Henry James, and George Kennan. In 1930 *Century* was absorbed by *The Forum* (f. 1886).

● *Women's Journal* (–1931) founded in Boston by Lucy Stone (1818–1893) and E. D. Draper. Stone served as editor with her husband, Henry Brown Blackwell (1825–1909). The periodical identified with the principles and interests of the American Women Suffrage Association. Not as belligerent as *The Revolution*. In 1870 the journal absorbed the *Agitator* of Chicago (f. 1869). In 1917 the journal moved to New York, became the *Woman Citizen*, and later resumed its original name.

1871. *Dry Goods Reporter* (–1919) founded in Chicago, a leading trade journal.

● *Nautical Gazette* founded in New York as a weekly for the shipping industry. Its motto was "American ships for American commerce." Alex R. Smith edited it through the 1890s. In 1888–1898 known as *Seaboard*.

● *Once a Week, the Young Lady's Own Journal* (4 March–1881) founded in New York as a weekly for young women. After three months the term *Young* was dropped; five months later the magazine became a weekly associate of the monthly *Frank Leslie's Ladies' Journal*, featuring hand-colored fashion plates and large woodcuts, and in time was recognized as the leading fashion periodical of the Leslie house.

● *Printers' Guide* (–1890) founded in San Francisco as an advertising sheet.

● *Sunnyside* (–1924) founded in New York by H. E. Taylor, a casket manufacturer, as a free-distribution miscellany of anecdotes and jokes. A few years later Frank H. Chase bought it and made it into the leading undertakers' trade journal. In 1925 *Sunnyside* was consolidated with *Casket* (f. 1876).

1872. *American Journalist* (–1877) founded in Philadelphia by the Coe, Weatherill & Company advertising agency as a monthly review of American journalism; in 1876 *and Advertiser's Index* added to title.

● *Chicago Ledger* founded by Samuel H. William, editor, as a weekly story paper. Initially, the *Ledger* was filled with "plate" designed as newspaper miscellany. Later it became a mail-order paper. In 1891 it passed into the control of W. D. Boyce and then gained large circulation as a sensational, cheap story paper. In 1919, after Boyce's death, George W. Weatherby and others purchased the periodical. In 1924 it was merged into the weekly *Toledo Blade* (f. 1847), which became the *Blade and Ledger*.

● *Flower Garden* (–1904) founded in Brooklyn, New York. In 1873 it was acquired by Beach, Son & Company and named *American Garden*.

In 1882 R. K. Bliss & Sons changed it from a quarterly to a monthly. In 1887 it absorbed the *Ladies' Floral Cabinet* (f. 1872), and in 1888 the *Gardener's Monthly and Horticulturist* (f. 1859). In 1892 it was named *American Gardening*.

• *Gleason's Monthly Companion* (–1887) founded in Boston by Frederick Gleason.

• *Grocer* (–1893) founded in Cincinnati; one of many grocers' trade journals.

• *North East* (–1889) founded in Portland, Maine.

• *Paper Trade Journal* founded in New York for paper manufacturers.

• *The Popular Science Monthly* (May–) founded in New York by Edward Livingston Youmans of D. Appleton & Company as an eclectic journal containing articles on the natural and social sciences, few illustrations, and no entertainment features. Most contributors were scientists. From May 1877 to February 1879 Appleton published a *Supplement to the Popular Science Monthly*, which ran the same kind of material as the parent periodical but without illustrations and with fewer pages. In 1900 Appleton sold *Popular Science* to McClure, Phillips & Company; in 1901 Science Press became publisher. In 1915 the name was sold to Modern Publishing Company, proprietor of *World's Advance*, a popular periodical devoted mainly to mechanical devices and developments. Modern Publishing adopted the name and numbering of *Popular Science*. The new periodical presented scientific information in a popular fashion and included many illustrations, aiming at hobbyists interested in mechanics or science. In 1967 the magazine became part of the Times-Mirror chain. In the 1970s the monthly gained a circulation of 1.8 million by "exploring and explaining to a nontechnical but knowledgeable readership [mostly men, many of them home workshoppers] the technical world around." In the 1980s the content covering science, technology, and new products was aimed at well-educated adults. *Popular Science*'s circulation in the mid-1980s exceeded 1.8 million.

• *Publishers' and Stationers' Weekly Trade Circular* (18 January–) founded in New York by Frederick Leypoldt, its editor until 1879. In January 1872 Leypoldt bought the *American Literary Gazette and Publishers' Circular* of Philadelphia (f. 1851) and merged the two periodicals; the next year he named the combined book-trade journal *Publishers Weekly*. Its most important content was publishers' announcements, and a cumulation was published beginning in 1876. In financial trouble, the magazine was taken over in 1879 by R. R. Bowker, still the publisher in the 1980s. The trade journal continued as the bible of the book industry, with reports on best sellers, new books, promotions, and trends, including electronic publishing.

• *Woman's Campaign* (–1872) published in New York by Mrs. Helen Barnard during the presidential canvass as a women's rights journal.

1873. *American Stationer* (–1928) founded in Brooklyn, New York.

● *The Delineator* (January–April 1937) founded in New York by E. Butterick & Co. as a fashion monthly. In the first half of its life it was one of the most popular fashion periodicals, giving secondary attention to household help; in the second half it was responsive to popular moods and tastes of readers. In 1899 it was sold to the sons of Jones W. Wilder and their associates, all of whom had been affiliated with Butterick. Theodore Dreiser (1871–1945) was editor 1907–1910. At first he edited conservatively, but eventually he innovated, adding coverage of current problems and such big-name contributors as Oscar Hammerstein, Julia Ward Howe, Jacob Riis, and Woodrow Wilson. Subsequent editors included George Barr Baker, 1911–1914, and Marie Mattingly (Mrs. William Brown Meloney), 1921–1926. In 1926 the *Delineator* became sophisticated, "smart"; in 1928 it absorbed its sister Butterick periodical, the *Designer*. In May 1937 the *Delineator*, then ranked fifth among big-circulation women's magazines, was merged into the fourth-ranking women's magazine, William Randolph Hearst's *Pictorial Review*.

● *Insurance Age* (–1936) founded in Boston. In 1924, after absorbing the *Insurance Journal* of Hartford (f. 1873), it was called the *Insurance Age-Journal*.

● *Medical Brief* (–1929) founded in St. Louis by Dr. J. J. Lawrence, editor for more than 30 years. In the 1880s the monthly had the highest circulation among medical periodicals: over 10,000 before 1885.

● *St. Nicholas* (–1940) founded in New York by Roswell Smith for Scribner & Company; a beautifully printed children's monthly. Mrs. Mary Elizabeth Mapes Dodge was editor 1873–1905. *St. Nicholas's* roster of authors included Louisa May Alcott, Walter Camp, Rudyard Kipling, Theodore Roosevelt, Robert Louis Stevenson, and Mark Twain. In 1881 Scribner withdrew and Century Company took over. In 1930 the magazine was purchased by American Education Press of Columbus, Ohio, and at the end of 1934 by Roy Walker, who moved the offices back to New York.

● *The Queen* (September?–) founded in New York by James McCall & Company as a fashion sheet to promote its pattern business. The first editors were James McCall and probably his wife. The publication, subtitled *Illustrating McCall's Bazar Glove-Fitting Patterns*, consisted mostly of woodcut pictures of clothes from patterns. *Queen* was published ten times a year. Eventually page size was reduced and fashion news added. After McCall died, in 1884, his widow became president and turned over the editing to other women. In 1891 the McCall Publishing Company, as the firm was now called, changed the title to *The Queen of Fashion*. In 1892 the firm of Page & Ringot bought the company. Circulation, after rising above 12,000, declined, and in 1893 James Henry Ottley took over management. Changes included more pages, better appearance, wider editorial variety (including fiction), and a new title (1897): *McCall's Magazine*. In 1908 circulation hit 1 million, one of the highest among women's periodicals. In 1917 an increase in single copy price from 5 cents to 10 cents removed *McCall's Magazine* from the cheap household periodical class. Despite articles by such name authors as Albert Bigelow Paine and Mary Heaton Vorse during World War I, circulation declined. Immediately after the war advertising dropped. In 1921 Harry Payne Burton became editor (–1927). He published such popular writers as Dorothy Canfield, James Oliver Curwood, Zane Gray, Kathleen Norris, Mary Roberts Rinehart, and Booth Tarkington. Color was widely used. By 1927 circulation exceeded 2 million, advertising revenue $6 million. Burton aimed for middle-class Americans nationally. In 1928 a new editor, Otis Lee Wiese, initiated more improvements. He published such by-lines as Faith Baldwin, F. Scott Fitzgerald, Wallace Irwin, J. P. Marquand, and Alice Duer Miller. During 1932–1950 Wiese organized the periodical as three magazines in one, each with its own cover page and distinctive content. Some advertising was moved from the back of the book to the front. Wiese's innovation influenced all women's magazines and others. Through the Depression circulation remained healthy, partly due to readership research, and hit 3 million by 1940. During World War II service matter was adapted to women's needs in wartime. After the war management emphasized community and social problems. Eleanor Roosevelt became a regular contributor. Circulation, advertising, and cover price rose. In the 1950s *McCall's* included child care, dressmaking, food, and fashions. Articles, fiction, and service were balanced for pacing. The periodical was more attractive than ever before. But circulation declined. In 1956, with circulation around 4,750,000, *McCall's* launched its "togetherness" promotion to engage entire families as readers. Eventually, with brighter writing and inks as well as striking layouts, circulation resumed climbing. Following a trend, management in 1971 reduced both format and circulation, from 8.5 million to 7.5 million. In the 1970s *McCall's* still included traditional fare, but some content reflected women's changing roles in society. In 1980 circulation of about 6,237,000 rated *McCall's* seventh among monthlies and tenth among consumer magazines. Circulation held up into the mid-1980s, when Robert Stein edited the monthly in New York. Content included nonfiction about ethical, material, physical, and social problems; short fiction; and poetry. High demography regional sections emphasized service, including decorating, home entertainment, and travel.

1874. *Central Law Journal* (–1927) founded in St. Louis. It had one of the largest circulations among legal periodicals.

• *The Home* (–January 1957) founded in Cleveland, Ohio, by S. L. and Frederick Thorpe. It consisted mostly of advertisements for mail-order products. In 1878, after Frederick's death (1877), S. L. bought another Cleveland monthly, *Little Ones at Home*, and consolidated the two as *Home Companion: A Monthly for Young People*. In 1880 monthly and semimonthly editions were issued; the monthly was soon dropped. In 1881 *Home Companion* was sold to E. B. Harvey and Frank S. Finn and became little more than an advertising paper. In 1883 Mast, Crowell & Kirkpatrick Co. of Springfield, Ohio, merged it and *Youth's Home Library* (f. 1877) into *Our Young People* (f. 1882), an illustrated semimonthly; the title was soon changed to *Home Companion*. Several months after absorbing *Young Folks' Circle* early in 1886, the title was changed to *Ladies' Home Companion*. In 1888 more space was devoted to fashions, foods, serial fiction, illustrations, and advertising. In 1890 *Ladies' Home Companion* was a leader in its category with 100,000 circulation. It carried many practical articles, fashion features, travel articles, serial fiction, and short stories. Contributors included Eugene Field, Helen Hunt Jackson, James Whitcomb Riley, and Ella Wheeler Wilcox. In March 1896 it became a monthly, and in January 1897 its title was changed to *Woman's Home Companion*. In 1901 editorial offices were moved to New York. In the 1900s editors emphasized the short story; early contributors included Hamlin Garland, Bret Harte, Sarah Orne Jewett, Jack London, and Rafael Sabatini. Later fiction was contributed by such popular writers as Faith Baldwin, Kay Boyle, Taylor Caldwell, and Mary Roberts Rinehart. In 1901–1939 the periodical was published by Crowell Publishing Co., and thereafter by Crowell-Collier Publishing Co. At midcentury, *Woman's Home Companion* emphasized service to the modern home with an inviting, colorful layout.

● *Metal Worker, Plumber and Steam Fitter* (–1931) founded in New York; later known as *Plumber's Trade Journal* (1881), *Sanitary Plumber* (1882), *Sanitary and Heating Engineering* (1921), and *Sanitary and Heating Age* (1929).

● *Novelist* (–1881) founded in Chicago as an illustrated weekly story paper. George E. Blakely was editor until 1881.

● *Pythian Journal* (–1933) founded in Indianapolis by the Knights of Pythias. It attained the largest circulation of the secret society's organs.

● *Ye Giglampz* (21 June–August 1874) founded in Cincinnati by Patricio Lafcadio Tessima Carlos Hearn (1850–1904) as a humor magazine. "Published daily except week days." Lafcadio Hearn issued only nine weekly numbers.

1875. *Baptist Flag* (–1925) founded in Fulton, Kentucky, for Southern Baptists.

● *Connecticut Farmer* (–1927) founded in New Haven, Connecticut; after 1915 named *New England Farms*.

● *Fabrics, Fancy Goods and Notions* (–1920) founded in New York. Titles subsequently varied.

● *Horse Shoers' Journal* (–1930) founded in Detroit for the carriage industry; later published in Chicago, then Indianapolis.

● *Literary News* (–1904) founded in New York as a monthly for general readers. It furnished reliable information about book publication.

● *Philatelic Monthly* (–1899) founded in New York for amateur collectors of stamps.

1876. *American Library Journal* (September 1876–) founded in New York by Frederick Leypoldt, editor to 1884, and others; chronicled the modern library movement.

● *Casket* founded in Rochester, New York, by Albert H. Nirdlinger for undertakers. After Nirdlinger's death his widow and then stepson Simeon Wile continued the periodical. In 1914 it was moved to New York and put under the same editorship as *Sunnyside* (f. 1871). In 1925 the two magazines were merged into one semimonthly entitled *Casket and Sunnyside*.

● *Frank Leslie's Popular Monthly* (January–1956) founded in New York by Frank Leslie as the ninth in his family of periodicals. The miscellany was lavishly illustrated by wood engravings and color lithographs. After Leslie died, his widow, Miriam Florence Follin (or Folline) Leslie (1836?–1914) took over. In 1881 she merged *Frank Leslie's Ladies' Journal* into the *Lady's Magazine*, and in 1882 she combined the latter with *Frank Leslie's Popular Monthly*, the leading Leslie monthly. (In 1882 she legally changed her name to Frank Leslie.) In 1895 she leased the monthly to a group headed by Frederick L. Colver; in 1898 she resumed control. In 1900 she again turned it over to Colver (she held an interest to 1903). Ellery Sedgwick (1872–1960) became editor and paid closer attention to public affairs but did not muckrake. Contributors included Stephen Crane, Burton J. Hendrick, Marietta Holley, and Stewart Edward White. In 1904 the title was shortened to *Leslie's Monthly*; in 1905 it was changed to *American Illustrated Magazine*, and a few months later *Illustrated* was dropped. In 1906 a group headed by John S. Phillips acquired the *American Magazine* and changed the title to *The American*, which became renowned as a muckraking periodical. Phillips's group included Ray Stannard Baker, Finley Peter Dunne, Lincoln Steffens, Ida M. Tarbell, and William Allen White. In 1915 the Phillips Publishing Company sold *The American* to Crowell Company of Springfield, Ohio, which aimed the magazine at the average family. In 1929 the magazine became more sophisticated. Its final issue was August 1956.

● *Railway Age* (17 June–) founded in Chicago by E. H. Talbott. On 5 June 1908 *Railway Age* merged with *Railroad Gazette* of New York (f. 1857), where the new *Railroad Age–Gazette* was published. *Gazette* was dropped from the title in 1918.

● *Y.M.C.A. Watchman* (–1932) founded in Chicago; later published in Cleveland, then New York. It became known as the *Association Men*, later *Young Men*.

1877. *American Cricketer* (–1933) founded in Philadelphia to rouse more U.S. interest in the game of cricket.

● *Farm Journal* (March–) founded in Philadelphia by Wilmer Atkinson, editor for 40 years. The monthly had a variety of content sparked by dry wit, homeliness, and many practical farming tips. Circulation grew to 500,000 by 1905. Atkinson was a pioneer in the protection of readers against advertising swindles, and in 1880 began to guarantee the *Farm Journal*'s advertising. Only a select class of advertisements was accepted. The publisher promised to make good any losses his subscribers sustained by trusting *Farm Journal* advertisers who proved to be deliberate swindlers. In 1935 the magazine was purchased by Graham C. Patterson, who revitalized it, emphasizing agricultural news. In 1939 the periodical absorbed *The Farmer's Wife* of St. Paul, and the titles were combined from May to 1945. By the mid-1950s the *Farm Journal* had become one of the largest and most important national farm magazines, with a peak circulation of almost 4 million. In June 1955 the journal bought *Better Farming* (f. 1955), and in 1956 published several regional editions. In 1968 the *Farm Journal* published 29 editions, with a total circulation of 3 million. In August 1969 the influential farm magazine began a "Top Operator" edition for mailing to subscriber-farmers grossing at least $20,000 annually. In 1984 the *Farm Journal* led farm periodicals in total revenue ($34,406,000) and in advertising revenue ($26,600,000). Circulation was 925,515, highest among business magazines. "The business magazine of American agriculture" published fourteen times a year hundreds of editions reflecting demographic, economic, and geographic sectors of the farm market, covering the basic commodities of beef, corn, cotton, dairy, hogs, milo, soybeans, and wheat.

● *Granite Monthly* (April–December 1930) founded in Concord, New Hampshire, by H. H. Metcalf, editor for many years, as a state periodical devoted to biography, history, literature, and progress. In 1894 it was owned by the Republican Press Association; later it was sold to the Rumford Printing Company. In 1919 its name was changed to *New Hampshire: the Granite State Monthly*; in 1930 it reverted to its original title. In its last years it was a booster magazine.

● *Magazine of American History* founded in New York. In 1883 Mrs. Martha J. Lamb bought the periodical from A. S. Barnes & Company. Under her editorship it became an unusually varied and elaborate historical journal, with lavish illustrations, published documents, biographical and historical articles, news of historical societies, and book reviews. After Lamb's death in January 1893, the *Magazine of American History* survived only until October. Alvah P. French resumed its publication in December 1901. The periodical was being published at Port Chester, New York, when it was discontinued in 1917, a war casualty.

● *Pennsylvania Magazine of History and Biography* founded in Philadelphia as a quarterly of Pennsylvania history, although it was not strictly limited to historical content. Contributors included Thomas Wentworth Higginson, Mark Twain, and Constance Fenimore Woolson. In the 1980s the magazine was published by the state historical society.

● *Puck* (14 March–September 1918) founded in New York by Joseph Keppler (1838–1894) and A. Schwarzmann, founders of a German-language *Puck* (September 1876), as a humorous weekly. The periodical contained Keppler's cartoons, verse, Swiftian satire, light wit, and comments on labor, politics, religion, and social topics. The English-language edition soon eclipsed the German edition (published for about 15 years). In 1917 William Randolph Hearst's International Magazine Company purchased the English-language *Puck* and published it as a fortnightly 20 June–5 February 1918 and as a monthly from March 1918.

● *Retail Grocers' Advocate* (–1934) founded in New York as a grocers' trade journal.

1878–1899

Expansion and Big Business

========= ||●|| =========

Books

1878. *The Leavenworth Case,* by Anna Katharine Green (1846–1935), a best-selling mystery novel this year and later.

1878–1882. *Diary of Samuel Sewall, 1674–1729,* by Samuel Sewall (1652–1730), published by the Massachusetts Historical Society; fullest diary of the period, with a gap 1677–1685. The diary attacked wearing of wigs, gave details of his courtships, reported daily events, and summarized sermons. It also showed the emergence of eighteenth-century secularism from the Reformation.

1879. *Old Creole Days,* by George Washington Cable (1844–1925), published; collection of short stories. A southern local colorist, Cable also wrote novels of Creole life: *The Grandissimes* (1880), *Dr. Sevier* (1885), and *Bonaventure* (1888).

● *Progress and Poverty,* by Henry George (1839–1897), a best seller this year and later; subtitled *An Inquiry Into the Cause of Industrial Depressions and of Increase of Want With Increase of Wealth.* The book was a comprehensive, logical inquiry into the fundamental cause of poverty and industrial turmoil, explaining why tycoons and paupers both increased and what was the remedy to that man-made condition. Two other important works by George were *Our Land and Land Policy, National and State* (1871), his first thorough attempt to provide a solution to "advancing poverty and advancing wealth," and *Protection of Free Trade* (1885), an examination of tariffs' effects on labor and a persuasive attack upon the fallacies of free trade.

1880. *Ben Hur: A Tale of Christ,* by Lewis Wallace (1827–1905), a best-selling romantic novel this year and later. It was translated into several European and Oriental languages, transcribed in braille, and dramatized (1899). Other novels by Wallace included *The Fair God* (1873), a historical work that won him recognition, and *The Prince of India* (1893), based on the story of the Wandering Jew. His two-volume *Lew Wallace: An Autobiography* (1906) was probably completed by his widow, Susan Elston Wallace.

• *Five Little Peppers and How They Grew*, by Mrs. Harriet Mulford Stone Lothrop (1844–1924), pseudonym Margaret Sidney, a best-selling juvenile, popular for more than 50 years. Other Lothrop juveniles included "Five Little Peppers" sequels and *A Little Maid of Concord Town* (1898).

• *Uncle Remus*, by Joel Chandler Harris (1848–1908), this year and later a best-selling collection of humorous animal legends reflecting Negro folk life. A southern local colorist, Harris provided an authentic picture of the "poor white," as in *Mingo and Other Sketches in Black and White* (1884), and of the Georgia black under slavery and Reconstruction, as in *Free Joe and Other Georgian Sketches* (1887).

1883. *The Old Swimmin'-Hole and 'Leven More Poems*, by James Whitcomb Riley (1849–1916), a best seller this year and later. "The Old Swimmin'-Hole" was a representative dialect poem of the Indiana poet, who also wrote nondialect poems. Other representative volumes, often of mingled prose and verse, were *Afterwhiles* (1887), *Pipes o'Pan at Zekesbury* (1888), *Rhymes of Childhood* (1890), *Green Fields and Running Brooks* (1892), *Poems Here at Home* (1893) and *Books of Joyous Children* (1902).

1885. *Personal Memoirs*, by Ulysses Simpson Grant (1822–1885), a best seller.

• *The Rise of Silas Lapham*, by William Dean Howells (1837–1920), a sympathetic study of the nouveaux riches. In his novels Howells presented a penetrating analysis of the post–Civil War economy. His many other books included *A Hazard of New Fortune* (1890), a social protest novel, and *Criticism and Fiction* (1891), a summary of his critical theories championing realism. The latter contributed to the acceptance of realism in novels.

1886. *Little Lord Fauntleroy*, by Frances Eliza Hodgson Burnett (1849–1924), a best seller this year and later. Popular among children and read by adults, *Little Lord Fauntleroy* was the Anglo-American writer's most famous novel. Burnett's other books included *That Lass o'Lowrie's* (1877), *Esmeralda* (1881), *A Lady of Quality* (1896), *The Shuttle* (1907), *A Fair Barbarian* (1881), *The Secret Garden* (1911), and *White People* (1917).

1887. *A Humble Romance and Other Stories*, by Mary Eleanor Wilkins Freeman (1852–1930), published. *A Humble Romance* and *A New England Nun and Other Stories* (1891), both collections of short stories, represented the most important work of this New England local colorist. Freeman's major novel was *Pembroke* (1894).

1888. *Looking Backward, or 2000–1887,* by Edward Bellamy (1850–1898), and *Mr. Barnes of New York,* by Archibald Clavering Gunter (1847–1907), best sellers this year and later. *Looking Backward,* Bellamy's most important work, was a Utopian romance that outlined a socialism achieved by gradual, orderly democratic steps. A sequel was *Equality* (1897). Other books by Bellamy included *The Duke of Stockbridge* (1900) and *Dr. Heidenhoff's Process* (1880). Gunter's action-packed, melodramatic *Mr. Barnes* was his first and most famous novel. His *Mr. Potter of Texas* was popular in 1889. Gunter also wrote the novels *That Frenchman* (1889), *Miss Nobody of Nowhere* (1890), and *A Prince in the Garret* (1905).

1890. American Book Company, a textbook publisher, formed by the amalgamation of A. S. Barnes & Co.; D. Appleton & Co.; Ivison, Blakeman & Co.; and Van Antwerp, Bragg & Co. On 17 May, American Book was incorporated under New Jersey law with offices in New York (headquarters), Chicago, and Cincinnati. On 1 January 1908 it was reconstituted as a New York corporation to avoid trust accusations.

1891. International Copyright Law enacted (3 March), effective 1 July; prevented pirating works of foreign authors.

● *Main-Travelled Roads,* by Hamlin Garland (1860–1940), the author's major work, published. It consisted of stories about the burdens of farm life. During 1887–1894 Garland wrote propaganda novels about agrarian conditions and prairie life. *Crumbling Idols* (1894) was an example of the honest realism, or "veritism," that he advocated. His autobiography, *A Son of the Middle Border* (1917), depicted the daily life of a group of migrating families to the plains and prairies in 1840–1895.

1894. *Coin's Financial School,* by William Hope Harvey (1851–1936), a best seller. Harvey argued for free silver and helped to focus public attention on bimetallism.

● *A Kentucky Cardinal,* by James Lane Allen (1849–1925), published. The novels of Allen, a southern local colorist, were set in the central Kentucky plateaus around his native Lexington. They included *Summer in Arcady* (1896), *The Choir Invisible* (1897), and *The Reign of Law* (1900).

● *Songs from Vagabondia,* by Richard Hovey (1864–1900), published. Hovey's poetry reveled in the joys of the open road. His other works included *More Songs from Vagabondia* (1896) and *Last Songs from Vagabondia* (1901). All three volumes were written in collaboration with Canadian-born poet William Bliss Carman (1861–1929).

1895. *The Red Badge of Courage,* by Stephen Crane (1871–1900), a best seller this year and later. Crane's masterpiece was a novel of Civil War cowardice and courage. His novelette *Maggie: A Girl of the Streets*

(1893) was an impressionistic study of New York slum life. Among his most successful short stories were "The Open Boat" and "Blue Hotel." Crane was a fiction writer of the naturalism school.

1896. Among the best sellers, *The Damnation of Theron Ware*, by Harold Frederic (1856–1898), and *The Jucklins*, by Opie Read (1852–1939). Frederic's romantic novel, his most important work, was about English life and an unsophisticated Methodist preacher. Frederic wrote other novels, which were historical, pseudorealistic, and romantic, including *The Lawton Girl* (1890), *The Copperhead* (1893), *Gloria Mundi* (1898), and *The Market Place* (1899). *The Jucklins*, a story of a Carolina backwoods community, was Read's major success; a sequel, *Old Lim Jucklin* (1906), was comparatively unsuccessful, with most early sales in cheap paperbacks. Read's other adventure stories included *A Tennessee Judge* (1893), *The Starbucks* (1902), and *Gold Gauze Veil* (1927).

1897. *In His Steps*, by Charles Monroe Sheldon (1857–1946), a best seller this year and later. Individual sales reached about 8 million and distribution, much of it free by religious groups, about 22 million. It was said that only the Bible and Shakespeare's works were more widely distributed. *In His Steps* was the story of a modern minister who lived his life according to what Jesus would do. Sheldon's three dozen books included *Richard Bruce* (1891), *The Narrow Gate* (1902), *All the World* (1918), and *In His Steps Today* (1921).

1898. *David Harum*, by Edward Noyes Westcott (1846–1898), a best seller this year and later. The novel, published six months after the author's death, was subtitled *A Story of an American Life*. Later it was adapted for stage and motion picture.

• *Red Rock*, by Thomas Nelson Page (1853–1922), published. A southern local colorist, Page idealized antebellum Tidewater Virginia in this study of the black problem. Page wrote short stories, poems, novels, and nonfiction, including *The Negro: The Southerner's Problem* (1904) and *Italy and the World War* (1920).

1899. Best sellers included *Janice Meredith*, by Paul Leicester Ford (1865–1902); *A Message to Garcia*, by Elbert Hubbard (1856–1915); *Richard Carvel*, by Winston Churchill (1871–1947), and *When Knighthood Was in Flower*, by Charles Major (1856–1913), pseudonym Sir Edwin Caskoden. *Janice Meredith* was a sentimental romance with authentic colonial atmosphere. Other Ford novels included *The Honorable Peter Stirling* (1894) and *The Story of an Untold Love* (1897). Historical works edited or written by Ford included *The Writings of Thomas Jefferson* (ten volumes, 1892–1894) and *The True George Washington* (1896). Ford also compiled bibliographies. *A Message to Garcia*, also a later best seller, was Hubbard's best-known work, a brief homily with sales of about 40 million. His best work was *Little Journeys*, a series of 170 essays about his pilgrimages to the homes of great men, begun in 1894 and continuing for 14 years. *Richard Carvel* was a historical romance, as was Churchill's *The Crisis* (1910). A middle-class progressive, Churchill also wrote the economic and political novels *Coniston* (1900), *Mr. Crewe's Career* (1908), *A Far Country* (1915), and *The Dwelling Place of Light* (1917). *When Knighthood Was in Flower* was a historical romance. Major's other works included *Dorothy Vernon of Haddon Hall* (1902), and *A Gentle Knight of Old Brandenburg* (1909).

● *The Man with the Hoe and Other Poems,* by Edwin Markham (1852–1940) published. "The Man with the Hoe," Markham's most popular poem, was inspired by Jean Francois Millet's painting. Other volumes by Markham included *Lincoln and Other Poems* (1901).

● *McTeague,* by Benjamin Franklin Norris (1870–1902), a major naturalistic novel of character disintegration under economic pressure. Other novels by Frank Norris included the first and second volumes of his "Epic of the Wheat" trilogy: *The Octopus* (1901), about the struggle between wheat growers and the Southern Pacific Railroad, and *The Pit* (1903), about the Chicago grain market. The third novel, *The Wolf,* was not completed.

Newspapers

1878. Cleveland *Penny Press* (–1982) founded by Edward Wyllis Scripps (1854–1926), with the help of his sister, Ellen Browning Scripps (1836–1932), and brothers James Edmund Scripps (1835–1906) and George H. Scripps. The low-priced, tightly edited afternoon daily appealed to the working people with human-interest articles, independent editorial opinion, and local crusades. The name was later shortened to the *Press.* Eventually it became a parent paper (with the Cincinnati *Post*) of the Scripps-McRae League of Newspapers (f. 1889).

1880. Foreign-language press included 641 German papers (80 dailies, 466 weeklies, 95 other periodicals), 49 Scandinavian, 41 French, 26 Spanish, 13 Bohemian, 5 Welsh, 4 Italian.

● Albion, Illinois, *American Sentinel* (–1882) founded by Benjamin Orange Flower (1858–1918) as a family weekly.

● Kansas City *Evening Star* founded by William Rockhill Nelson (1841–1915) as a small, 2-cent daily emphasizing news and entertainment. Nelson crusaded for efficient and low-cost public transportation, for boulevards and parks, and against gamblers and crooked politicians; his paper helped start the commission form of government in Kansas City. A training ground for many young writers, the *Star* became known for its human-interest content, intensive area coverage, literary qualities, and low price. In 1902 Nelson bought the morning *Times* (f. 1868). Before his death the daily *Star* reached 170,000 circulation and a weekly edition reached 150,000 (at 25 cents per year). During World War I Theodore Roosevelt wrote editorials for the *Star* criticizing the administration in Washington. In the 1920s it was one of the early newspapers to establish a radio station. In 1926 the staff bought controlling stock for $11 million. In 1929 the paper sent Theodore C. Alford to Washington, D.C., as one of the first specialists in agricultural correspondence. In 1947 Roy A. Roberts, who had been a Washington correspondent and managing editor, was elected president of the *Star* and *Times*. In 1955 the *Star* and its advertising manager were convicted of monopolizing dissemination of advertising and news in the Kansas City area. The *Star*, with its morning *Times* and broadcasting stations, WDAF and WDAF-TV, accounted for 85 percent of the mass media advertising income in the metropolitan area. The federal government charged that forced and tied-in sales of advertising and subscriptions had killed the competing *Journal-Post* in 1942. In 1957 the U.S. Supreme Court declined to review the case (*Kansas City Star Co. v. United States; Emil A. Sees v. United States* [8th Circuit] 240 Fed. 2d 643 [1957]). The *Star* agreed to end its combination sales and to sell the two stations. In 1977 *Star* employees sold their stock to Capital City Communications for $125 million. Both papers were well known regionally in the 1980s, but the *Times* was rated better than its more famous partner and rival.

1881. Typewriters becoming popular in newspaper offices. Christopher Latham Sholes (1819–1890), former editor of the Milwaukee *Sentinel*, had built the earliest practical typewriter in the 1860s. In 1873 he sold his rights to E. Remington & Sons, arms manufacturers, and in 1876 its Model 1 went on the market. In 1881 it was equipped to print both capital and lower-case letters. In 1885 the Associated Press adopted typewriters, and by 1890 typewriters saved composition costs on many large newspapers. Some newspapers and some veteran journalists adhered to handwritten copy into the twentieth century.

• Los Angeles *Times* founded by local printers. In 1882 Harrison Gray Otis (1837–1917) joined the company, and by 1886 he had full control of the 7,000-circulation morning daily. In 1890 Otis locked out printers in a dispute with the International Typographical Union over a closed shop and rules for resetting advertising mats. In 1894 he formed an employers' group in Los Angeles to oppose unions. By 1900 the *Times* had the largest advertising linage in the nation. On 1 October 1910 a bomb exploded in the *Times* building, killing 20 printers; in 1911 the McNamara brothers confessed to the crime. In 1914 Otis turned over the newspaper to his daughter and son-in-law, Marian and Harry Chandler (1864–1944). In 1941 the *Times* was fined for contempt of court for commenting on pending litigation in a series of editorials published in

1937–1938. The U.S. Supreme Court (in *Times Mirror Co. v. Superior Court*, 314 U.S. 252 [1941]) declared the contempt citation unconstitutional, applying the "clear and present danger" test. The decision expanded the right of the press to comment on pending cases, limiting it only when a judge could hold that comment created so great an immediate danger that the court could not function. (State courts, however, resisted the trend.) The *Times* won a Pulitzer Prize for fighting the contempt charge. In 1944 the Chandlers' son Norman (1899–1975), who was less conservative than Otis, became publisher. In 1958 he brought in Nick B. Williams as editor to revitalize the newspaper. In 1960 the Chandlers' grandson Otis became publisher; he expanded the paper with two new Sunday sections, two Sunday magazines, and significant foreign and national news. With Philip L. Graham (1915–1963), publisher of the Washington *Post*, Otis Chandler founded the Los Angeles Times–Washington Post News Service. Part of the *Times*'s new look was Paul Conrad, a liberal editorial cartoonist hired in 1964. During the 1960s the *Times* became a major force among newspapers, leading U.S. dailies in advertising linage and in space allotted to editorial material. In 1971 William F. Thomas replaced Williams as editor. That year the *Times* called on President Nixon to withdraw troops immediately from Vietnam. In 1972 the *Times* supported Nixon for reelection, but after Jack Nelson of the Washington bureau and others uncovered the Watergate scandal, the paper called for impeachment. Management, embarrassed by its earlier position, began a policy of not endorsing candidates for president or other high office, indicating a shift from staunch Republican to open-mindedness and independence. In 1977 Tom Johnson became *Times* president and chief operating officer. In the 1970s circulation reached 1 million, and the paper became known for giving reporters time to develop lengthy in-depth features. When Johnson became publisher in 1980, Chandler became editor in chief of the Times Mirror Corporation and Donald F. Wright became *Times* publisher. In the mid-1980s the paper was the fourth largest U.S. daily, with 1,046,965 circulation. The paper operated 7 national, 20 foreign, and 5 California bureaus; expanded suburban zone coverage with a printing facility at Northridge, and published editions for Orange County and San Diego. It also ran a feature syndicate with more than 1,300 clients and, with the Washington *Post*, the largest supplementary news service in the world, with about 500 newspaper, magazine, and broadcasting clients. The *Times* was frequently fourth in polls of the top 10 U.S. dailies.

    1882. United Press (–March 1897) founded in New York, with Walter Polk Phillips as general manager. Rebels of the New York Associated Press had been trying to form a rival news service since 1869. In 1891 the AP and UP executive committees secretly agreed for the two associations to exchange news, virtually ending competition and reaping financial rewards for insiders. Exposure brought about new conflict in AP, and in 1892 the New York *Sun* and *Tribune* bolted to UP. Late that year the Associated Press of Illinois was chartered, leading to a shift in AP control to the Midwest, and in 1893 the rest of the New York AP members bolted to UP. AP's acquisition of exclusive news exchange contracts with Havas in France, Reuters in Britain, and Wolff in Germany cut off UP's sources for foreign news, long enjoyed by its New York members, and a four-year struggle ensued, ending when all New York dailies except the *Sun* and *Journal* were admitted to AP. UP went into bankruptcy.

• New York *Morning Journal* (–1937) founded by Albert Pulitzer as a 1-cent daily. After Pulitzer raised the price to 2 cents, circulation dropped, and in 1894 he sold the paper to John R. McLean. In 1895 William Randolph Hearst (1863–1951) purchased it. Hearst moved some of his best employees from the San Francisco *Examiner* and hired other talented artists, critics, editors, and reporters, including Stephen Crane, Homer Davenport, Dorothy Dix, Alfred Henry Lewis, and Julian Ralph. Hearst raided Joseph Pulitzer's New York papers of Arthur Brisbane (1864–1936), Morrill Goddard (1865–1937), and Richard Felton Outcault (1863–1928), who drew the "Yellow Kid" comic that came to symbolize Hearst's brand of sensational "Yellow Journalism." For the Sunday paper Hearst added large color presses and "The American Humorist" 8-page comic section, soon replaced by "The Sunday American Magazine" 16-page color supplement, which became the *American Weekly*. On 28 September 1896 he founded his first afternoon daily, the *Evening Journal*, and appointed Brisbane editor. Using crusades, self-promotion, and sensationalism, Hearst battled J. Pulitzer's *World* for circulation. Hearst's papers bragged that they not only crusaded but also acted, such as obtaining a court injunction against granting a city franchise to a gas company. In 1897 Hearst's Sunday circulation caught up with Pulitzer's. Both publishers' papers were milking the conflict between Cuba and Spain. Striving to lead the competition, Hearst's papers manufactured stories about the Cuban insurrection and sent reporters Richard Harding Davis and James Creelman and artist Frederic Remington to Cuba. In 1896–1897 Hearst papers openly advocated war, exaggerated several minor incidents, and generally led the press in jingoism. They advocated annexation of Hawaii and the Philippines and development of military bases in the Caribbean. Hearst led a staff of 20 men and women artists, photographers (including a cinematographer), and reporters to Cuba, spent lavishly on coverage, and exploited the news. Domestically, in 1899 Hearst's editorial platform, radical even among liberal papers, called for election of U.S. senators by popular vote (rather than by state legislatures), improvement in the public school systems at all levels, public ownership of public franchises, and destruction of criminal trusts; it also encouraged labor unions. In the early 1900s Hearst used his *Journals* to advance his ambitions for public office, making heavy play for support of laborers, small-business owners, and other "ordinary people." The morning daily viciously criticized President McKinley, and after the anarchist who assassinated him was found to have a copy of the *Journal* in his pocket, the verbal assaults were recalled. Public criticism of Hearst and the *Morning Journal* led to changing the paper's name to the *American and Journal*; soon after, the title was divided, making the morning paper the *American*. In 1914 the *Evening Journal* achieved the largest U.S. daily circulation (c. 800,000), and the Sunday *American* achieved the largest U.S. Sunday circulation (c. 750,000). In 1921 the daily *American* added a tabloid section, but it was ineffective. On 24 June 1937 the *American* was combined with the *Journal* to form the *Journal-American*, which after World War II sold about 700,000 copies each evening and about 1.3 million on Sunday. In 1966 the *Journal-American* merged with the *World-Telegram and Sun* and *Herald Tribune* to form the *World Journal Tribune* (–1967).

1883. First general syndicate for literary material founded in New York by Irving Bacheller (1859–1950) to supply articles, news, short stories, etc. to large dailies.

1884. McClure Newspaper Syndicate founded in New York by Samuel Sidney McClure (1857–1949). The syndicate made such authors as Conan Doyle, Rider Haggard, William Dean Howells, Rudyard Kipling, Jack London, George Meredith, and Robert Louis Stevenson available even to small papers for a few dollars a column. Other material supplied included features, recipes, and a "Youth Department." By 1887 the syndicate was providing 50,000 words of serialized novels, short stories, and special features to editors weekly. By 1891 it grossed $100,000 annually, but its expenses almost matched that; so *McClure's Magazine* was established (1893) to use the best syndicate material.

● Pittsburgh, Pennsylvania, *Evening Penny Press* founded by Thomas J. Keenen; name condensed to *Press*. The paper actively undertook civic improvement campaigns. In a 1923 deal that killed the Pittsburgh *Dispatch* and *Leader*, the *Press* was purchased by Scripps-Howard, giving the chain its first Sunday edition.

● Philadelphia *Weekly Tribune* (c. November 25–) founded by Christopher James Perry, Sr., as a black paper to crusade against racial discrimination and corrupt officials. After Perry's death in 1921, his widow and two daughters continued the *Tribune*. A son-in-law, E. Washington Rhodes, became editor and publisher, serving until his death in 1970. The paper criticized affluent blacks for not doing enough to help poor blacks, and it organized charities and scholarship programs. By 1984 the staff had grown from 1 (Perry) to 60, and the paper was published thrice weekly. Expanding circulation, which on some days reached 92,000, encouraged management, including executive editor Garland L. Thompson, to start a $1 million improvement program that included computers and a modern press. When the *Tribune* celebrated its centennial, it had the distinction of being the oldest continuously published black newspaper in the nation.

1885. National Editorial Association organized by B. B. Herbert for weeklies and small dailies.

● Washington Gridiron Club formed by Ben Perley Poore (1820–1887).

● Dallas *Morning News* (1 October–) founded by Alfred H. Belo. A conservatively Democratic paper, the *News* campaigned for good roads for farmers. On Belo's death in 1901 his namesake son took over; he died within five years, and George B. Dealey became vice president and general manager of the Dallas *News* and Galveston *News* (f. 1842). His mother was titular president until her death in 1912. In 1922 the Dallas daily was one of the first newspapers to establish a radio station. In 1926 Dealey became official head of the firm; he bought controlling interest in the Dallas paper from Belo's heirs and campaigned for civic improvements. In 1950 the *News* founded a television station in Dallas. That year G. B. Dealey became chairman of the board and his son, E. M. (Ted) Dealey, became president. The *News* became an arch conservative voice in Republican Dallas. In the 1950s and 1960s *News* circulation steadily increased, in 1968 reaching 226,804 daily and 164,344 Sunday. In the mid-1980s the paper was highly regarded regionally and had a circulation of 360,340.

1886. Slug-casting Linotype first used in newspaper manufacture, by the New York *Tribune*. By July 1884 Ottmar Mergenthaler (1854–1899) had successfully incorporated stamping and casting type metal in the same machine, creating the first direct-casting Linotype. He patented it 26 August 1884 and that year, with James O. Clephane, founded the National Typographic Company of West Virginia for its manufacture. In 1885 a subsidiary, the Mergenthaler Printing Company, was established. The time-saving machine, which set a line of type as one slug (strip of lead), especially helped large afternoon dailies, under pressure to cover more news close to deadline. The Linotype furthered mass production of newspapers.

1887. American Newspaper Publishers Association founded as a trade association for daily newspapers, indicating the increasing importance of business problems. The ANPA was organized at the call of William Brearly, advertising manager of the Detroit *Evening News*, and others who wanted a daily newspaper trade association to help obtain national advertising. Soon the ANPA became involved in the problems of government mail rates, labor relations, mechanical developments, and newsprint supply. Most participants in association affairs were managers or publishers. Early presidents included publishers Charles W. Knapp of the St. Louis *Republic*, Herman Ridder of the *New Yorker Staats-Zeitung*, and James W. Scott of the Chicago *Herald*. Other leaders included John Norris, business manager of the New York *Times*, and Don C. Seitz, manager of the New York *World*, who represented their publishers, Adolph S. Ochs and Joseph Pulitzer, respectively. After 1900 the ANPA supported voluntary arbitration with printing unions. Because many members owned radio stations, the ANPA sought to solve the problem of broadcast interference by a new federal law, leading to the Radio Act of 1927. That year the association's radio committee reported that 48 newspapers owned stations, 69 sponsored programs on unowned stations, and 97 presented news programs on the air. Committee members believed that radio news stimulated newspaper sales. In December 1932 the board of directors recommended that press associations not supply news to radio before publication, that news broadcasting be limited to brief bulletins to encourage newspaper readership, and that radio logs be treated as paid advertising. This position led to a futile two-year effort to eliminate radio news competition. In the early 1930s the ANPA committee on press freedom, chaired by publisher Robert Rutherford McCormick of the Chicago *Tribune*, helped two newspapers win U.S. Supreme Court cases (*Near v. Minnesota ex rel. Olson*, 283 U.S. 697 [1931]; *Grosjean v. American Press Co.*, 297 U.S. 233 [1936]). In the 1930s membership reached 850. Manager Lincoln B. Palmer and counsel Elisha Hanson opposed major legislation of the New Deal; when reform bills came before Congress, the ANPA asked for exemptions for newspapers. When Cranston Williams became general manager in 1939, the uncompromising conservative stance began to change. In 1954 the ANPA added emphasis to its research activities, which included studying printing processes and newspaper readership, opening a research center in Easton, Pennsylvania, and incorporating a Research Institute. An annual mechanical conference for members emphasized computerized editing and typesetting, offset printing, photocomposition, run-of-paper color printing, and other technological advances. By 1960 the ANPA had become a progressive trade association; membership rose to 1,200 dailies. In 1960 it established the Newspaper Information Service to work with educators, students, the public, and other media. The ANPA's most important legislative victory came in 1970, after three years of debate in Congress, with the Newspaper Preservation Act, which exempted from antitrust suits the joint printing operations of 44 newspapers in 22 cities, overturning a U.S. Supreme Court decision dissolving a pooled business operation in Tucson. In other developments the association elected its first woman president, publisher Katharine Graham (1917–) of the Washington *Post*.

1889. Scripps-McRae League of Newspapers, first formal newspaper chain, founded by E. W. Scripps and Milton Alexander McRae (1858–1930). They planned to publish low-cost, tightly edited afternoon dailies mostly in small but growing industrial cities. They would start a paper with a few thousand dollars and a young, ambitious editor and business manager, the two of whom could receive up to 49 percent of the stock if they succeeded; if they did not, they were replaced. If a newspaper failed to make a profit within ten years, it was abandoned. Surviving newspapers had many employee stockholders, who were low paid, except for advertising salesmen. In 1890 Scripps, the policymaker, withdrew to a California ranch. E. W., who had general editorial control, and his brother George H. each held 40 percent of the stock; McRae, who managed the newspapers, held 20 percent. To serve their papers, in 1897 they organized the Scripps-McRae Press Association, a forerunner of United Press Association (f. 1907). In 1911 the chain included 18 newspapers in Colorado, Indiana, Iowa, Ohio, Oklahoma, Tennessee, and Texas. In 1914, a dispute forced McRae out; that year the chain published 23 newspapers. After a dispute between E. W. and his son James G., the latter in 1920 took with him five Pacific Coast papers, which after his death in 1921 were organized by his widow into the Scripps-Canfield chain, later the Scripps League. (Sale of the Seattle *Star* in 1942 left that chain with four newspapers in the Northwest managed by two grandsons of E. W.; another grandson headed the John P. Scripps chain in California.) James was replaced by Roy Wilson Howard (1883–1964). In 1922 E. W. retired, turning over his newspapers to his son Robert Paine (1895–1938), who gave Howard equal power, and the chain became known as Scripps-Howard. Howard made the papers less liberal, including reducing support for organized labor. In the 1920s and 1930s Scripps-Howard properties were strengthened by eliminating competition, and between 1923-1934 the chain was responsible for closing 15 newspapers. After World War II Charles E. Scripps became chairman; eventually editorial leadership went to Edward W. Scripps II, but Howard remained powerful as head of the New York *World-Telegram and Sun*. Later Howard's son Jack Rohe Howard (1910–) became president and general manager of the Scripps-Howard Newspapers and president of the parent E. W. Scripps Company, which controlled broadcasting and syndicate interests and United Press International. In 1980 B. J. Culter became editor in chief of the Scripps-Howard chain. In 1982 it was the seventh largest newspaper group, with 16 dailies and 6 Sundays, having a total circulation of 1,545,000 (2.5 percent of U.S. daily circulation).

● New York *Wall Street Journal* founded as an afternoon financial newspaper by Charles H. Dow (1851–1902). The newspaper evolved from a newsletter published by Dow Jones & Co. (f. 1882 with Edward

T. Jones), a financial service for individuals. In 1898 Dow began a morning edition of the *Journal*. In 1902 Clarence Walker Barron (1855–1925) became owner of Dow Jones & Co. The afternoon edition was discontinued in 1934. When Bernard Kilgore (1908–1967) became managing editor in 1940, the paper had about 30,000 circulation. Kilgore broadened the definition of business news to include virtually anything related to making a living. He widened coverage to include comprehensive features interpreting business trends as well as summaries of significant national and international events. As circulation rose, so did Kilgore in Dow Jones, becoming president in 1945. In 1955 circulation was 360,000; by 1960 it had passed 700,000. The *Journal* expanded to eight printing plants nationally, linking them to New York headquarters by electronic typesetting equipment. In a 1961 poll of journalism teachers the *Journal* ranked third among dailies, having showed the greatest improvement in the previous decade. Part of that improvement was reflected in its pioneering of new technology, part in the Pulitzer Prizes its writers won. By Kilgore's retirement in 1966 the *Journal* had become a national newspaper circulating more than 1 million copies daily, Monday through Friday. In a 1970 poll newspaper publishers ranked the paper ninth among dailies. That year Pulitzer-winner Edward R. Conny became executive editor. In the 1970s the *Journal* continued winning Pulitzers. Editors broke up the gray vertical makeup with an occasional line drawing, and increased coverage of arts and leisure. By 1976 circulation had risen to 1,450,000, second nationally to the New York *Daily News*. In the latter 1970s Dow Jones began providing facsimiles of full-size pages to its regional plants by communication satellite; by decade's end the *Journal* was printing by offset (cold type) in 8 of its 12 plants. The company also pioneered in use of private delivery systems for early morning delivery and postal cost savings; by 1978 systems had been set up in about 60 cities. In January 1979 Robert L. Barley became editor. By decade's end the paper had 1.6 million circulation in four U.S. editions (East, Midwest, Pacific Coast, Southwest) and in Asian daily and weekly editions. Climbing to first in daily circulation, the national business paper passed 2 million in the early 1980s, before declining slightly to 1,959,873 in 1985. The *Journal* was printed in 17 U.S. plants and in European and Asian plants. It had 25 news bureaus, including 11 abroad. In the 1980s polls ranked the *Wall Street Journal* among the best four U.S. dailies.

1890. Emporia, Kansas, *Gazette* founded; acquired in 1895 by William Allen White (1868–1944). The *Gazette* gained national attention for White's editorials, especially "What's the Matter with Kansas?" (1896). In the early 1900s the paper called for abolition of child labor, conservation of national resources, direct primaries, the initiative and referendum, railroad rate control, and workers' compensation. After World War I it supported the League of Nations.

• New York *Age* founded as a newspaper for blacks; successor to New York *Globe* (founded as *Rumor*). T. Thomas Fortune's editorials were widely quoted in the U.S. press. Booker T. Washington (1856–1915) selected the *Age* as the national voice for blacks and subsidized it. In 1952 the *Age* was sold to the Defender chain.

1891. Illustrations for newspapers and magazines supplied by about 1,000 artists; more newspapers hiring their own artists and installing engraving equipment. Photoengraving would soon turn the boom for artists into a bust. Within a short time after Stephen Henry Horgan (1854–1941) perfected a method of running halftone reproductions of photographs on rotary presses for the New York *Tribune* (1897), other large newspapers began running halftones frequently.

1892. First four-color press in operation (April); built for Chicago *Inter Ocean* by Walter Scott & Company. Scott installed a five-color press at the New York *World* in 1893.

• Baltimore *Afro-American* founded by Reverend William M. Alexander as a religious paper for blacks. John H. Murphy soon gained control, and before 1920 his paper had won a national reputation. The *Afro-American* fought to eliminate slums and to provide jobs for all; it sought to stay out of politics except to expose corruption and to condemn compromise, injustice, and race prejudice. In 1945 the *Afro-American* was one of the three largest black newspapers, with a national circulation of 137,000. The paper became moderate in tone, was occasionally crusading, and developed strong coverage of local news, sports, and women's news. In 1983 John H. Murphy III headed the *Afro-American* newspapers, which had a combined circulation of about 50,000. The largest unit was its semiweekly Baltimore edition with 10,000 circulation. Editions were also published in Richmond, Washington, and New Jersey. A national edition was published weekly. The group's vice president was Mrs. Elizabeth Murphy Moss, noted reporter and war correspondent.

1897. Rural free delivery initiated by the federal postal service, still the primary means of communication.

• Laffan News Bureau (–1916) organized by William Mackay Laffan (1848–1909), when the United Press went bankrupt. LNB not only served Laffan's New York *Sun* but also other clients, operating as an independent news agency. In 1906 Will Irwin "covered" the San Francisco earthquake and fire from the newspaper's local room, a feat that enabled the news bureau to compete successfully on the story against the much larger Associated Press. When Frank Andrew Munsey (1854–1925) bought the *Sun*, combining it with the *Press*, which had an AP franchise, the Laffan News Bureau was discontinued.

● New York *Jewish Daily Forward (Vorwärts)* founded by the Jewish Socialist Press Federation as a Yiddish-language Socialist paper. Under the editorship of Abraham Cahan (1860–1951) the *Daily Forward* carried analyses and reviews with a Socialist slant; it later mellowed. By 1923 it had daily editions in 11 cities; in 1924 circulation peaked at 220,000. In the 1960s the *Daily Forward* was the last Yiddish daily in North America and staunchly liberal. By 1982 circulation had declined to 35,000.

● Publishers Press Association founded by a group of newspaper owners as a wire service mainly for New York and Pennsylvania papers, soon joined by other eastern papers. In 1904 sold to Scripps-McRae Press Association (f. 1897).

Magazines

1878. *Christian Herald* founded in New York as an edition of a London journal issued mainly to promulgate sermons by Charles Haddon Spurgeon (1834–1892). It also published sermons by others, anecdotes, religious fiction, and miscellany. The *Herald* soon gained a reputation for a freshness of religious experience. Contents in the 1980s included stories emphasizing religious living in the family and church; the monthly was aimed at church-going families and published in Chappaqua, New York.

● *Iowa Farmer* (1892) founded in Cedar Rapids; became a well-known regional farm journal. The paper was edited for some years by James Wilson (1836–1920), later U.S. secretary of agriculture.

1879. Postal Act passed, clearly defining second-class matter. In 1885 Congress provided a 1 cent per pound rate for magazines and newspapers. These two actions opened the way for low-cost delivery of publications.

1880. *The Dial* (May–July 1929) founded in Chicago by Francis F. Brown, editor 1880–1913. It was published monthly to April 1892 and 1920–1929, semimonthly September 1892–February 1915, and fortnightly March 1915–November 1919. *The Dial* went through three periods: (1) as a conservative journal of literary criticism to 1916, when it moved to New York; (2) as a radical journal of opinion to 1920; and (3) as an artistic, critical, literary organ of modernism. It was a leading "little magazine." Contributors included Conrad Aiken, Sherwood Anderson, Van Wyck Brooks, e. e. cummings, T. S. Eliot, Waldo Frank, Anatole France, D. H. Lawrence, Amy Lowell, Edna St. Vincent Millay, Ezra Pound, George Santayana, Gertrude Stein, and William Butler Yeats.

1881. Two notable periodicals founded in New York—*The Critic* and *The Judge*. *The Critic* (15 January–September 1906) was founded by Jeannette Leonard Gilder (1849–1916), editor 1881–1906, and Joseph B. Gilder, co-editor 1881–1901, as a biweekly literary review. It was a weekly 1883–June 1898, except for the combination July-August 1898 issue, and then a monthly from 1898. Book reviewing was the most important content. Contributors included Julia Ward Howe and Walt Whitman. In 1884 *The Critic* absorbed *Good Literature*, briefly adding that name to its title. In 1898 G. Putnam & Company bought it, and ran longer articles; contributors included Gelett Burgess and Rupert Hughes. In 1905 *The Critic* absorbed *Literary World*, adding that name to its title. In October 1906 it merged with a revival of *Putnam's Monthly*, called *Putnam's Monthly and the Critic*. *The Judge* (29 October–1939) was founded as a comic weekly by James Albert Wales and other artists or authors who had defected from *Puck*. Artists contributing after 1900 included James Montgomery Flagg, Richard F. Outcault, and Art Young. In 1922 *Leslie's Weekly* merged with *Judge*, which was departmentalized and ran contributions by Heywood Broun, Ruth Hale, George Jean Nathan, S. J. Perelman, William Allen White, etc.

1882. Five significant periodicals founded in New York. *American Metal Market*, which converted from a weekly to a daily in 1902, was an iron and steel journal. *American Press*, founded as a house weekly to advertise boiler plate, carried news and hints for country weeklies. *Beadle's Weekly* (–1897) was founded by Beadle & Adams; in 1886 it became *Banner Weekly*, a famous thriller magazine. *The Golden Argosy, Freighted With Treasures for Boys and Girls* (December–) was founded as a children's weekly by Frank Andrew Munsey (1854–1925), editor 1882–1925. The first issues of *Golden Argosy* contained a serial by Horatio Alger, Jr., a puzzle department, and other miscellany. Munsey wrote fiction for the magazine and promoted it heavily. He dropped the subtitle with the 13 March 1886 issue, and *Golden* with the 1 December 1888 issue. The *Argosy* soon became an adult adventure magazine. In April 1894 it became a monthly. In 1896 Munsey made *Argosy* the first of the "pulps": an all-fiction magazine printed on coarse, pulp paper and appealing to boys and men with action, adventure, and mystery stories without illustrations. Contributors included Ellis Parker Butler, James Branch Cabell, Susan Glaspell, William Sidney Porter, Mary Roberts Rinehart, Upton Sinclair, and Albert Payson Terhune. From 1907 circulation declined, and in October 1917 Munsey made *Argosy* a weekly again, with the same format. In 1920 he merged it with another one of his periodicals under the title of *Argosy All-Story Weekly*, which absorbed several other magazines, including *Peterson's*. Contributors included Max Brand and Zane Grey. After Munsey's death, William T. Dewart bought this and other Munsey magazines, and it declined. In 1929

Argosy separated from *All-Story*. Contributors to *Argosy* included C. S. Forester, Erle Stanley Gardner, and Luke Short. At the end of 1941 the Munsey publications were sold to Popular Publications, a New York pulp group; and the March–July 1942 *New Argosy* emphasized features linked to world news and the war as well as true and melodramatic adventure. Photographs were added, as the periodical gradually became "slick." In July 1942 the postmaster general banned it from the mails for "obscenity." In 1942 *Argosy* appeared as an all-fiction slick. Immediately after World War II it became known as *Argosy—The Complete Men's Magazine* with striking four-color layouts, more humor, and higher paid contributors. In 1951 circulation soared to 1 million; in 1953 the magazine guaranteed a circulation of 1,250,000. Its successful formula included articles of strange and tough adventure, science, sports, and crime; its "Court of Last Resort" worked to free unjustly imprisoned persons. *War Cry* was the principal periodical of the Salvation Army and sold on the streets by its uniformed members to disseminate the gospel of helpfulness to urban derelicts. In this period the Salvation Army also published in New York other periodicals, including *Conqueror* (1892–1897) and *Harbor Lights* (1898–1900). *War Cry* was later published in various U.S. editions as well as worldwide in 30 languages. In the 1980s "The Official Organ of the Salvation Army" was published weekly in Verona, New Jersey, for people of evangelical Christian background, members and friends of the Salvation Army, and the "man in the street." Its circulation was around 280,000.

• *Printer and Publisher* founded in Indianapolis. In 1888 it merged with *National Journalist* (f. 1884), changing title to *National Editorial Journalist: Printer and Publisher*. In 1890 it became *National Journalist for Editors*, which in 1893 became the *National Printer-Journalist*. The latter was an organ of the National Editorial Association, which was dominated by weeklies and small-city dailies.

1883. *American Agriculturist* (–1895) founded in Wenham, Massachusetts.

• *American Journalist* (–1885) founded in St. Louis; edited by R. P. Yorkston.

• *Etude* (–1957) founded in Lynchburg, Virginia, by Theodore Presser (1848–1925) for pianists and music teachers. After it moved to Philadelphia in 1884, coverage was expanded to serve piano students and a voice department was added. Circulation grew with an elaborate offering of premiums and it became the leading monthly for independent music teachers.

• *Life* (4 January–November 1936) founded in New York by John Ames Mitchell (1845–1918) and his partners, Edward Sanford Martin (1856–1939) and Andrew Miller, as a humor weekly. Under Mitchell's editorship (–1918), the clever and satirical periodical kept up with current events and developments in drama, literature, manners, morals, and politics. Contributors included Wallace Irwin ("Hashimura Togo"), James Montgomery Flagg, and Charles Dana Gibson ("Gibson Girl"), who bought the magazine in 1920. That year Martin became editor (–1922); Robert Emmet Sherwood (1896–1955) served 1924–1928. Contributors in the 1920s included F. P. Adams, Corey Ford, Dorothy Parker, and Will Rogers. In that decade *Life* had more variety than earlier but lost its distinctiveness. Advertising decreased in the depression, and in 1932 *Life* became monthly. Late in 1936 the title was acquired by Time, Inc., for a planned picture magazine.

• *Science* (9 February–) founded in Cambridge, Massachusetts, by Alexander Graham Bell (1847–1922), Gardiner Greene Hubbard (1822–1897), and other prominent scientists as a weekly with a broad scope, including the new sciences of sociology, psychology, and public health. Operations moved to New York City in 1885. Leading U.S. scientists contributed. In March 1894 *Science* suspended publication, and on 4 January 1895 a new series began. In 1900 *Science* became the official organ of the American Association for the Advancement of Science. The journal continued to have articles by leading U.S. scientists.

• *Journal of the American Medical Association* (14 July–) founded in New York by the American Medical Association; became the most quoted AMA periodical. The weekly ran medical papers, news of state and local associations, advertisements, and other items of interest to the medical profession. The first editor (–December 1888) was Dr. Nathan Smith Davis (1817–1904), an AMA founder. Longest serving editor (1925–1949) was Dr. Morris Fishbein (1889–1976), who attacked frauds and quacks. In the 1980s the goal of JAMA was to educate physicians in clinical medicine, medical research, and other professional developments; circulation was about 239,000, with editions in French, Japanese, Portuguese, and Spanish.

• *The Ladies' Home Journal* (December–) founded in Philadelphia by Cyrus Hermann Kotzschmar Curtis (1850–1933) as a supplement to Curtis's *Tribune and Farmer* (f. 1879). It evolved from a women's department, edited by Mrs. Louisa Knapp Curtis. Originally, the *Journal* was a cheap household-hints paper with fiction. In October 1884 Curtis separated the *Ladies' Home Journal* from the *Tribune and Farmer*, promoting the former heavily, and circulation boomed. About 1890 Curtis began a modest British edition. On 20 October 1889 Mrs. Curtis relinquished the editorship to Edward William Bok (1863–1930), who would serve until 1920. Bok established the *Journal* as a leading periodical for middle-class homes, emphasizing intimacy. Advertising often appealed to men as well as women. Bok improved the *Journal*'s appearance, and the magazine became possibly the first to change its cover design monthly. He published musical compositions, including John Philip Sousa's marches, and began (1895) publication of house plans. He recruited such writers as Julia Ward Howe, William Dean Howells, Rudyard Kipling, James Whitcomb Riley, Margaret E. Sangster, and Ella Wheeler Wilcox; other contributors included Conan Doyle, Hamlin Garland, Joel Chandler Harris, Bret Harte, Sarah Orne Jewett, Dwight L. Moody, Mark Twain, President Theodore Roosevelt, and former presidents. Bok, who believed women belonged in the home, ran mild crusades against the pseudocultural activities of women's clubs and for sex education; a campaign for American rather than Paris styles failed. Subscribers looked upon the service magazine as a friend and counselor in the home. In 1903 the Ladies' Home Journal became the first major magazine to achieve 1 million circulation. In 1910 the Journal began its Curtis Advertising Code, designed to eliminate extravagant claims, fraud, and immoral and suggestive copy; the magazine banned advertising of alcoholic liquors, playing cards, and tobacco. During World War I emphasis was on supporting the home front. President Wilson, Herbert Hoover, and Franklin Delano Roosevelt contributed. The magazine was popular among soldiers. After the war the post-Bok magazine was edited less for a special class of noble but somewhat intellectually backward women, and its appeal to men was recognized. Circulation for some issues surpassed 2.5 million. In the 1930s the magazine discussed public questions, featured service activities, and ran regular portraits of "typical" families, health articles, moral essays, and serial fiction. In 1937 Eleanor Roosevelt and Dorothy Thompson became contributors. In 1942 circulation passed 4 million; in 1953, 5.2 million. In the 1950s the Ladies' Home Journal was known for its attractive layout and typography, generous use of color, skillful art work, and clever editing. The Curtis-Bok formula emphasizing known writers, reputable advertising, and service was continued; but women were no longer held on pedestals, and some appeal was made to their intellect, although as late as 1957 editors viewed women as uneasy about committing their lives to a career. In the 1960s the Journal ran relatively few articles on careers for women. That changed after Mrs. Lenore G. Hershey became the first woman editor (1973–1981) since Mrs. Curtis. As the 1970s ended the Journal focused more on beauty and fashion pieces for working women and on personality sketches, often of celebrities; there were some pieces about sex. In 1980 the Ladies' Home Journal was the eighth largest monthly, and in 1981 it offered an advertising rate base of 5.5 million. In 1983 it was published in New York by Charter Corp., a media group, and in 1985 by Family Media Inc. Mid-1980s circulation was slightly more than 5 million.

    1884. *Christian Oracle* founded in Chicago. In 1900 it became *The Christian Century*, the organ of the Disciples of Christ. In 1908 it was bought by Charles Clayton Morrison, who made it a liberal nondenominational periodical applying Christian principles to contemporary affairs. Under Morrison's editorship *Christian Century* became a leading religious periodical. His successors included Dr. Paul Hutchison and Harold E. Fey. In the early 1980s James M. Wall was editor, and the ecumenical weekly was published for progressive clergy and lay church people.

• *The Journalist* (–1907) founded in New York by Allan Forman, who managed it most of its life; Charles A. Byrne; and Leander Richardson. The newsy weekly, one of the first professional magazines for journalists, was suspended for the period 1895–1897. In 1906 it became a monthly, and in 1907 it was merged into *Editor and Publisher* (f. 1901).

1886. *Cosmopolitan Magazine* (March 1886–) founded in Rochester, New York, by Paul J. Schlicht as a hybrid of a conservative family monthly and a general literary periodical. In 1887 it moved to New York City and became a popular magazine. In March 1888 the publishers, Schlicht & Field, failed and *Cosmopolitan* passed into the hands of Ulysses S. Grant, Jr. It was soon purchased by Joseph Newton Hallock, who improved it, introducing new departments and features, experimenting with color illustrations, and increasing the number of pages. In 1889 John Brisben Walker (1847–1931) purchased it, and as editor (1889–1905) introduced timeliness and dignified sensationalism and made it an individualistic, functional periodical. It became a profitable part of the mass magazine revolution of the 1890s. By 1892 *Cosmopolitan* had become a leading illustrated magazine, with works by such artists as Charles Dana Gibson and Frederic Remington; it also ran a wide variety of fiction, including serials and short stories, as well as articles on the arts, public affairs, transportation, and travel. Contributors under Walker included Gertrude Atherton, Arthur Brisbane, Rudyard Kipling, Jack London, Robert Louis Stevenson, and Mark Twain. In 1892 William Dean Howells (1837–1920) briefly became co-editor, raising the periodical's literary prestige. He not only contributed but also published such writers as Hamlin Garland, Henry James, Sarah Orne Jewett, James Russell Lowell, Brander Matthews, and Theodore Roosevelt. When the price was cut from 15 cents to 10 cents in 1895, circulation climbed. More than 100 pages of advertising ran in each issue. Advertising manager Henry D. Wilson in 1894 had succeeded Eugene W. Spaulding. *Cosmopolitan* rose to its greatest height as one of the brilliant 10-cent illustrated monthlies of the latter 1890s. (Throughout the decade a large edition was also printed in London.) By 1900 the periodical's circulation was runner-up with *McClure's* to *Munsey's*; their formulas consisted of copious illustrations, general articles, and popular fiction. In the early 1900s Walker's *Cosmopolitan* tentatively entered the muckraking movement but carried articles sympathetic to business, as well as short stories. In 1905 Walker sold the magazine to William Randolph Hearst (1863–1951), who was making his first incursion into general magazine ownership. A succession of editors included Bailey Millard, 1905–1907; S. S. Chamberlain, 1907–1908, and Edgar Grant Sisson, 1914–1917. The magazine became more sensational and plunged into muckraking, with articles by such versatile writers as Alfred Henry Lewis, David Graham Phillips, and Charles Edward Russell. By 1909 Wilson made *Cosmopolitan* the advertising leader of general circulation magazines with more than 100 pages of advertising (at $448 per page) each issue. In 1912 the magazine stopped muckraking and relied mainly on fiction for its appeal, with serials or short stories by such contributors as Rex Beach, Elinor Glyn, Gouverneur Morris, and Booth Tarkington. Later contributors included Michael Arlen, Louis Bromfield, Irvin Cobb, Theodore Dreiser, Edna Ferber, Edgar A. Guest, Fannie Hurst, Ring Lardner, Sinclair Lewis, Somerset Maugham, O. O. McIntyre, Kathleen Norris, and H. G. Wells. In 1914 circulation reached 1 million. After World War I the magazine became comparatively risqué, with more sex than substance. In 1925 Hearst merged *Cosmopolitan* with another one of his magazines to form an expanded *Hearst's International with Cosmopolitan*, a title that lasted until 1952, when it reverted to *Cosmopolitan*. During the depression the magazine ran many notable serial stories by Hervey Allen, Faith Baldwin, Pearl Buck, A. J. Cronin, Joseph Hergesheimer, S. S. Van Dine, Rebecca West, and others, as well as novels by Sinclair Lewis. Other contributors of fiction included Agatha Christie, C. S. Forester, Clarence Budington Kelland, and Ellery Queen. Nonfiction contributors included Albert Einstein, President-elect Roosevelt, Bernard Shaw, and Ida M. Tarbell. In the 1940s editors ran some material about World War II by Bob Considine and others, increased color, and offered skillful layout and illustrations—appealing to entertainment seekers and the moderately sophisticated, mainly women. Through the 1950s the magazine was entertaining and striking, with abundant and varied content. Emphasis on fiction declined, although editors did publish Ernest Hemingway, John Hersey, John P. Marquand, and H. Allen Smith. Editors increased articles, cartoon sequences, features, picture essays, and service departments, with such writers as Dorothy Kilgallen and Louella O. Parsons. To meet the large cost increases of 1953–1955, the publisher cut circulation by about 50 percent and reduced advertising rates, creating savings that more than offset losses. In 1955 the magazine was making money on a circulation of slightly more than 1 million. In 1965, with circulation around 800,000, Helen Gurley Brown (1922–) became editor, and within a few years built circulation to 2.5 million, much of it on newsstands, by adding sex appeal for young married or single women. In 1980 the Hearst Corp. launched a spinoff, *Cosmo Living*, and by 1981 was publishing 15 editions on four continents. In the 1980s Brown edited *Cosmopolitan* for career women ages 18–34. In the mid-1980s circulation exceeded 2.8 million.

1887. *Scribner's Magazine* (January–May 1939) founded in New York by Charles Scribner's Sons as a quality literary monthly. The first editor (–1914), Edward Livermore Burlingame, presented popular topics with literary treatment and quality illustrations. The magazine was strong in autobiographical and biographical material; in articles on commercial, economic, social, and travel topics; in criticism of the arts and literature; in essays; and in poetry. Contributors in the nineteenth century included Stephen Crane, Richard Harding Davis, Joel Chandler Harris, Bret Harte, Robert Herrick, William Dean Howells, Henry James, William James, Sarah Orne Jewett, Rudyard Kipling, Edwin Markham, Julian Ralph, Jacob A. Riis, Theodore Roosevelt, Edith Wharton, and William Allen White. By 1890 *Scribner's* had added Australian and English editions. In 1909–1911 the U.S. edition was running more than 100 pages of advertising a month and circulation peaked at more than 200,000. In 1912 advertising and circulation began to drop. Around World War I the magazine still published articles by notable contributors, including John Galsworthy, Franklin D. Roosevelt, Henry L. Stimson, and Oswald Garrison Villard. After the war the quality of color, illustrations, and paper declined, but the quality of many contributions did not. In 1927 *Scribner's* began running detective mysteries, starting with S. S. Van Dine's *The Canary Murder Case* serial, eventually influencing other general magazines. In 1927 the periodical ran Thomas Wolfe's first published story, "An Angel on the Porch," and serialized Ernest Hemingway's *A Farewell to Arms*. During 1930–1936 Editor Alfred S. Dashiell attracted new authors, including Sherwood Anderson, Erskine Caldwell, William Faulkner, F. Scott Fitzgerald, D. H. Lawrence, and William Saroyan. Dashiell aimed much content at young intellectuals; old faithful subscribers dropped away, and new ones did not replace them fast enough. During 1936–1939 Editor Harlan De Baun Logan lowered the price, designed a new cover in full color, improved paper stock, fully illustrated the magazine, retained some departments, and changed others. Late in 1937 Harlan Logan Associates took over financial management. Circulation improved; losses dwindled. In the summer of 1939 *Scribner's* sold its list of 80,000 subscribers to *Esquire* (f. 1933) and its name to the *Commentator* (f. 1937), which in November became *Scribner's Commentator*, with *Commentator* serial numbering.

1888. *Collier's Once a Week* (28 April–4 January 1957) founded in New York by Peter Fenelon Collier (1849–1909), with Nugent Robinson as editor (–1890). In 1889 the title was changed to *Once a Week, an Illustrated Weekly Newspaper*. Fiction predominated until 1892. The title again changed, to *Collier's Weekly, an Illustrated Journal*, in

1895. It still ran fiction but emphasized news and public affairs and became a leading user of halftone news pictures. In 1898 the publisher's son, Robert Joseph Collier (1876–1918), became editor (–1902). He published news photographs by James H. Hare and illustrations by Art Young, Frederic Remington, James Montgomery Flagg, Charles Dana Gibson, and John T. McCutcheon as well as paintings by Maxfield Parrish. *Collier's* became a leader in the new era of colored illustrations. Collier also ran editorials and "Mr. Dooley" essays by Peter Finley Dunne; Spanish-American War correspondence by Frederick Palmer; sports by Walter Camp; poetry by James Whitcomb Riley, and fiction by Hall Caine, Rudyard Kipling, and Frank Norris; plus other features. Norman Hapgood (1868–1937) became editor in 1902, the year circulation reached 250,000, among the top for weeklies. Hapgood's formula included fiction by Rex Beach, Winston Churchill, O. Henry, Jack London, Booth Tarkington, Edith Wharton, and Owen Wister; poetry by Edwin Markham; and humor by George Ade, Wallace Irwin, and "Mr. Dooley." Richard Harding Davis, Jimmy Hare, Frederick Palmer, and Frederic Remington covered the Russo-Japanese War. By 1909 the importance of fiction had been replaced by comment on public affairs and muckraking that made *Collier's* distinctive. Hapgood wrote editorials and published works by Samuel Hopkins Adams, C. P. Connolly, Will Irwin, and Theodore Roosevelt. *Collier's*, since 1905 subtitled *The National Weekly*, campaigned for such reforms as direct election of senators, child labor laws, an income tax, railroad rate regulation, settlement houses, slum clearance, and woman suffrage. In 1912–1913 Rob Collier, who had become the magazine's president (1909), served as editor between Hapgood and Mark Sullivan (1874–1952). Under Sullivan, *Collier's* covered the European war in pieces by such noted war correspondents as James Hopper, Will Irwin, and Frederick Palmer, and supported President Wilson in articles by Ray Stannard Baker and Ida M. Tarbell. In 1917 Finley Peter Dunne (1867–1936) succeeded Sullivan, who continued to write for the magazine. During World War I *Collier's* ran fiction by Arnold Bennett, H. G. Wells, and Jesse Lynch Williams. In September 1919 Rob Collier's widow sold the magazine to Crowell Publishing Company of Springfield, Ohio, and New York, which changed the policy from liberalism to "normalcy" (less government). In the 1920s cartoons were contributed by Jay Darling, correspondence by William G. Shepherd, and articles defending the League of Nations by Will Irwin. The magazine campaigned for repeal of Prohibition, but into the 1930s fiction was the backbone, with serials by the leading writers of the day, such as Willa Cather, Sinclair Lewis, Kathleen Norris, and Sax Rohmer ("Fu Manchu"), and short stories by Samuel Hopkins Adams, Stephen Vincent Benét, James B. Connolly, Rupert Hughes, John P. Marquand, Mary Roberts Rinehart, and other well-known authors.

Humor by Don Marquis and nonfiction by Bruce Barton, George Creel, and William Allen White were popular. *Collier's* was financially strong enough to withstand the depression and continued its successful formula, with old contributors and new ones, such as Elmer Davis, Dashiell Hammett, Ernest Haycox, and William Saroyan; a new star was British journalist and statesman Winston Spencer Churchill. During World War II editors stressed war articles from abroad and home. Fiction, although deemphasized, was still important; contributors included Faith Baldwin, Pearl S. Buck, Agatha Christie, C. S. Forester, and Damon Runyon. Among 1940s contributors of articles were Bob Considine, John Gunther, Ernest Hemingway, Harold L. Ickes, André Maurois, Edward P. Morgan, Quentin Reynolds, and Wendell Willkie. More color photographs were used. In the late 1940s exposé articles were prominent. The average circulation stagnated at 3 million and advertising linage decreased. In the 1950s the magazine still displayed an imposing lineup of writers, including A. J. Cronin, Peter Kalischer, and Lowell Thomas, but the contents became sensational and violent as well as sexier—as if the publisher was desperately trying to boost circulation. In August 1953 *Collier's* became a fortnightly. In 1954 Paul Clifford Smith became its last chief editor.

• *The National Geographic Magazine* (October 1888–) founded in Washington, D.C., by Gardiner Greene Hubbard (1822–1897) as the organ of the nonprofit National Geographic Society, which aimed to diffuse and increase geographical knowledge. The periodical was published irregularly (second issue, April 1889) until it became a monthly in 1896. From the beginning the *National Geographic* carried charts and maps; early articles were scientific and technical, with limited appeal. In 1903 Gilbert Hovey Grosvenor (1875–1966) became editor (to 1954) and began broadening appeal by tempering hard geographical facts with human interest. In 1905 the *National Geographic* began its rise as a pioneering photojournalism magazine with publication in one issue of 11 pages of photos revealing mysterious Lhasa, Tibet. Within four years more than half of the space was devoted to pictures. In 1910 the first color photos (Autochrome) depicted people and scenes of China and Korea. The use of color in the next decade transformed *National Geographic* into a new kind of magazine. It became known for many photographic breakthroughs, among them the first picture to show the earth's curvature, the first aerial color pictures, and the first undersea pictures in natural color. In 1910 Grosvenor added a buff border to the original reddish-brown cover. The cover later was made yellow. By the 1960s the widely recognized border had been narrowed, as more photos had appeared on the cover, and in 1979 the border was eliminated. In 1935 circulation had reached one million. It continued to grow, stimulated by increased public interest in photography and travel. In

1957 Melville Bell Grosvenor became editor and *National Geographic* created a book service. In 1967 Frederick G. Vosburgh became editor. In the 1970s and 1980s the *National Geographic* continued to provide armchair travelers with journeys to near and remote parts of the world. The periodical was renowned for its photojournalism, mixing in-depth articles and high-quality photography. Families retained copies of the magazine for many years. In the 1980s Wilbur E. Garrett was editor. He ran first-person and general-interest articles as well as lavishly illustrated pieces on exploration, geography, natural history, and science. Circulation in the mid-1980s was more than 10.2 million, ranking *National Geographic* sixth among consumer magazines. Advertising revenue (taxed under the 1968 Tax Reform Act) totaled more than $30 million, overall revenue more than $183.4 million. The society also published the *National Geographic World* (f. 1975), for readers aged 8–13, which in the mid-1980s had about 1.2 million circulation.

1889. *The Arena* (December–August 1909) founded in Boston by Benjamin Orange Flower (1858–1918) as a monthly review emphasizing social reform and religion. *The American Spectator* (f. in 1886 by Flower and his brother Dr. Richard G. Flower) was merged into the *Arena*. (*American Spectator* was revived 1890–1891.) Flower, the editor, was a zealous reformer. He thought literature should be didactic, with a social purpose, and ran fiction by Hamlin Garland and others who shared his philosophy. Other contributors included Henry George and Joseph F. Smith. Flower ran some book reviews, literary criticism, and poetry. His *Arena*, however, was best known as a multiple-crusade magazine of general circulation, a new kind of periodical. Its biggest crusades were for agrarian reform, the initiative and referendum, primary elections, and the single tax, as well as against liquor traffic and the trusts. Women were important as contributors, editors, and subject matter, which included divorce, dress reform, education of women, female labor in factories, rights of women in marriage, and suffrage. Crusades were supplemented by clubs, pamphlets, and paper-covered books. In 1896 the *Arena* was the only magazine of national importance to support William Jennings Bryan, a contributor, and free silver, one of the magazine's major causes. The *Arena* had carried some advertising, but it was a minor source of support, and in the 1890s the Arena Publishing Company suffered financial problems, resulting in receivership at the end of 1896, when it was purchased by John D. McIntyre. Under John Clark Ridpath (1840–1900), editor 1897–1898, it continued to be radical. In 1897 the *American Magazine of Civics* (f. 1892 as *American Journal of Politics*) was merged into the *Arena*. In the latter 1890s the *Arena* also absorbed the *Coming Light* (f. 1896), *Journal of Practical Metaphysics* (f. 1896), *New Time* (f. 1897), and *The Temple* (f. 1897). In 1899 Charles A. Montgomery bought the *Arena*. Less than six months later he sold it to Albert Brandt, who installed Flower as editor, added pictures, and made the *Arena* attractive. Contributors included poets (e.g., Edwin Markham, Joaquin Miller), publicists, scholars, and statesmen. During the magazine's last five years Flower wrote editorials, book reviews, and philosophic, literary, and economic essays. In 1905–1906 the *Arena* moved from protest to elaborate factual exposé, joining the muckraking movement at about its midpoint. In fall 1909 Brandt filed for bankruptcy, making the *Arena* the first major muckraking magazine to collapse.

• *Munsey's Weekly* (2 February–October 1929) founded in New York by Frank A. Munsey, editor to 1925, as an imitation of the satirical weekly *Life* with a bit of *Harper's Weekly*. *Munsey's*, which included serial stories by Munsey, lost money. In 1891 Munsey overhauled the magazine, changing its frequency to monthly and it title to *Munsey's Magazine* and running articles, departments, fiction, and theatrical reviews. Its best-known writer was Horatio Alger, Jr. The magazine did not become popular until Munsey lowered the price from 25 cents to 10 cents in October 1893, precursing a trend toward cheap mass magazines. Munsey's own company distributed it. Advertising and editorial matter was abundant. Contributions included articles by Chauncey M. Depew, Conan Doyle, Theodore Dreiser, Bret Harte, William Dean Howells, and Theodore Roosevelt; fiction serials by Hall Caine and Munsey; and poems by Ella Wheeler Wilcox. Writers and photographers covered the Spanish-American War. The many illustrations included seminude females, a sex appeal that eventually decreased. In 1897 Munsey claimed his flagship magazine had a circulation higher than any other monthly's except the *Ladies' Home Journal's*, which it almost equalled. In 1899 a London edition was begun. In the early 1900s Munsey's roll of authors included fiction writers Dorothy Canfield, Susan Keating Glaspell, O. Henry, and Clarence B. Kelland, and poet John Kendrick Bangs. Munsey ran articles on public affairs but did not muckrake. He added some color illustrations. During World War I he occasionally increased the pages to 260 and ran rotogravure photographs, military articles, and fiction by Arnold Bennett, Joseph Conrad, Rupert Hughes, and P. G. Wodehouse. To increase advertising, in July 1921 *Munsey*—the title since 1918—was made an illustrated all-fiction monthly printed on wood pulp paper. Contributors included such leading pulp writers as Max Brand, Edgar Rice Burroughs, Ellis Parker Butler, Elisabeth Sanxay Holding, and T. S. Stribling. After October 1919 *Munsey* was merged with *Argosy All-Story* to form the *All-Story Combined with Munsey's*; *Argosy* resumed as a separate periodical. *Munsey's* soon was dropped as *All-Story* continued.

1890. *The Literary Digest* (1 March–19 February 1938) founded in New York by Isaac Kauffman Funk (1839–1912), editor to 1895, as an eclectic weekly without illustrations. Half the content consisted of condensations of articles on a wide variety of subjects from Canadian, English, French, German, Italian, and U.S. periodicals. In December 1893 the *Literary Digest* was improved with better departmental arrangement, layout, and typography as well as the addition of some illustrations and of introductions to quoted newspaper editorials. As editor during 1895–1905, Edward Jewitt Wheeler (1859–1922) gave the magazine the form and quality for which it became famous. He skillfully selected and presented material that would interest as well as inform, increasing the literary tone as well as the number of illustrations and enlivening the arrangement, content, and typography. The magazine covered the top four to five U.S. events with a news summary leading into exact quotations from parts of a document, an interview, or a news story, or a combination of those; there followed reprints of related newspaper editorials in large part or whole. Wheeler provided skillful introductions and transitions. The 1906 merger of *Public Opinion* with *Literary Digest* led to an extensive advertising campaign that eventually helped boost magazine circulation to 1.5 million. During World War I the magazine published elaborate annual résumés, ran maps in color, and collected for relief—all of which helped establish it as a high-ranking U.S. magazine. In the 1920s it carried abundant advertising and color reproductions of quality paintings, expanded old departments, and added new ones. It was known for its impartiality, high moral tone, and election polls, famous into the 1930s. During the depression the magazine suffered heavy loss of advertising, and editorial comment was reduced; it briefly carried articles on current topics by such well-known writers as Edward Price Bell and Silas Bent. The last straw was an erroneous 1936 poll that showed Alfred M. Landon victor by a landslide in the presidential election. In July 1937 the Review of Reviews Corporation acquired the *Literary Digest* from Funk and Wagnalls. The monthly *Review of Reviews* (f. 1891) and the weekly *Literary Digest* were combined into a news weekly entitled *The Digest: Review of Reviews Incorporating the Literary Digest*, and a new numbering system was adopted. In October 1937 George F. Havell and associates bought the *Digest*, which on 13 November was retitled the *Literary Digest*. In February 1938 the *Literary Digest* was suspended; three months later *Time* took over the unexpired subscriptions.

• *Smart Set* (March–July 1930) founded in New York by William D'Alton Mann as an amusing monthly accenting high society. With a light satirical touch, the periodical explored social intrigue, love without benefit of clergy, and irony at the expense of convention. In *Smart Set*'s first nine years most contributors were unpublished amateurs, but there were also such name writers as Mary Austin, Ambrose Bierce, James Branch Cabell, Theodore Dreiser, Robert Herrick, and Jack London. For years one-act plays, poems, and short stories appeared in French; plays in

French and English became a regular feature. In spring 1911 the magazine was purchased by John Adams Thayer, who built up advertising, revived a London edition, and hired James Montgomery Flagg to modernize the cover. Into the teens the magazine published works by Witter Bynner, Floyd Dell, Frank Harris, Joyce Kilmer, D. H. Lawrence, Richard Le Gallienne, Henry Louis Mencken, Harriet Monroe, George Jean Nathan, George Sterling, Sara Teasdale, Albert Payson Terhune, Louis Untermeyer, W. B. Yeats, and other noted writers. In 1914, with financial problems plaguing the periodical, Thayer toned down the satire, then sold out to Eugene F. Warner, who took over as owner and publisher after the September issue. That year Mencken (1880–1956) and Nathan (1882–1958) became co-editors and introduced a skeptical tone. The Smart Set Company branched out into cheap magazines, launching *Parisienne* in 1915 and *Saucy Stories* in 1916, and began making a profit. Playing down World War I, Mencken and Nathan discovered such new talents as Maxwell Anderson, F. Scott Fitzgerald, and Eugene O'Neill, but most newcomers were duds. At first the two editors published mostly hack nonfiction. But old and new name contributors kept the content appealing; new ones included Stephen Vincent Benét, Willa Cather, Ben Hecht, Sinclair Lewis, Somerset Maugham, and Hugh Walpole. Also notable were poems by Maxwell Bodenheim, works by James Joyce, and monthly critical pieces by the editors. In the 1920s Mencken stepped up his attack on the "booboisie," but the December 1923 issue was his and Nathan's last. After their resignation *Smart Set* became a 20-cent all-fiction monthly. William Randolph Hearst's Magus Magazine Corporation purchased it in 1924 and emphasized "true-story" confessional content, with sensation, sentiment, sex, and pictures, as well as a little cheap advertising. Circulation jumped, surpassing 250,000 in 1925. In 1928 James R. Quirk purchased the Magus Magazine Corporation. In 1929 a radical change occurred when the *New McClure's* was merged with *Smart Set* under the latter title with the subtitle *The Young Woman's Magazine*; but the title's reputation handicapped a journal for nice young women. After the magazine's discontinuance the title was taken over as the heading for a society gossip column in the Hearst papers signed by "Cholly Knickerbocker."

1891. *Review of Reviews* (January/April–July 1937) founded in New York as a U.S. edition of a London periodical (f. 1890) by William Thomas Stead (1849–1912). (Other editions were issued in France and Australia.) As editor of the U.S. edition, Albert Shaw (1857–1947) kept the original content types, departmentalization, and numbering system. His monthly was well printed and illustrated; it emphasized information, with some comment, on economics, foreign affairs, and government. Coverage was fair and rational. In 1897 the adoption of a new title, *The American Monthly Review of Reviews*, indicated separation of the American and English editions. Advertising and circulation (200,000) rose. The Spanish-American War was covered in pictures and words; writers included Winston Churchill and James Creelman. By 1900 the magazine was running more original articles: by David Starr Jordan, Jack London, Julian Ralph, Jacob A. Riis, Theodore Roosevelt, Woodrow Wilson, and many others. In June 1907 *Monthly* was dropped from the title. During the muckraking era Shaw preferred constructive planning and suggestions to in-depth exposés. During World War I the *American Review of Reviews's* coverage in words and pictures made a significant war history, and circulation surpassed 240,000 to the magazine's highest. It slipped in the 1920s, and in 1929 the periodical was redesigned and *American* dropped. In September 1932 a merger with another monthly resulted in a combined title, *Review of Reviews and World's Work*, but circulation and advertising declined. In the 1930s the magazine gave more attention to business and finance, becoming more a business journal, although it still published articles by such authors as Raymond Clapper, who wrote about politics. The periodical shrank in pages, and in 1937 it merged into the weekly *Literary Digest* (f. 1890), which for many years had followed a similar editorial pattern and was in similar straits. The combined periodical lasted eight months.

1892. *Newspaperdom* (–1925) founded in New York by Charles S. Patterson as a monthly for publishers of weeklies and small city dailies; weekly at times but mostly semimonthly. In 1901 it was purchased by John Clyde Oswald, in 1912 by H. Craig Dare. After Dare's death in 1923 his widow continued it. In 1925 James Wright Brown (1873–1959) of *Editor & Publisher* purchased it, then issued it a short time as *Advertising*.

1893. *Dun's Review* (5 August–) founded in New York by Robert Graham Dun (1826–1900) as a small and cheaply printed weekly organ of his credit agency. *Dun's Review* soon improved in appearance, size, and prestige, becoming a leading financial journal. In March 1933 it absorbed *Bradstreet's Weekly* (f. 1879) to become *Dun & Bradstreet Monthly Review*, a title that lasted to 1937, when the old title was restored. In August 1953 the magazine absorbed *Modern Industry*.

● *McClure's Magazine* (June–March 1929) founded in New York by Samuel Sidney McClure (1857–1949) and John Sanburn Phillips (1861–1949) as an inexpensive illustrated monthly. McClure, the idea man, and Phillips, the general manager and supervising editor, at first filled their monthly with features and fiction already purchased for the McClure Newspaper Syndicate (f. 1884). In 1894 *McClure's* became a pace setter in the golden age of 10-cent illustrated magazines. The first taste of mass approval came with publication of Ida M. Tarbell's illustrated *Napoleon* biography, which began November 1894; circulation doubled. Illustrated pieces on Lincoln further boosted circulation in the 1890s, helping make *McClure's* a leader in advertising, circulation, and prestige. Contributing to this success was fiction by Stephen Crane, Conan Doyle, Thomas Hardy, Joel Chandler Harris, O. Henry, Anthony Hope, Rudyard Kipling, Robert Louis Stevenson, and William Allen White. Early issues also contained articles on exploration, science, trains, and personalities as well as some poetry. By 1895 the owners abandoned publishing material already in circulation through their syndicate. Coverage of the Spanish-American War included eyewitness reports by James Creelman. By 1900 *McClure's* boasted voluminous advertising and a circulation of 370,000, larger than any other general monthly except *Munsey's*. In 1902 *McClure's* touched off the muckraking movement with the accidental discovery of the power of exposés. It began with Tarbell's exposé of the Standard Oil Company, which ran for two years, and an exposé of St. Louis corruption, which led to Joseph Lincoln Steffens's "The Shame of the Cities" (1903–1905). These series with Ray Stannard Baker's articles on labor union racketeering (1903–1905) and on railroads (1905–1906), made *McClure's* the muckraking leader. Advertising boomed, and by 1907 circulation had climbed to about a half million. A large part of *McClure's* success, however, was based on fiction by Rex Beach, Willa Cather, James Hopper, Myra Kelly, Jack London, Harvey J. O'Higgins, Booth Tarkington, Arthur Train, and Stewart Edward White; poetry by William Butler Yeats; biographical series by Georgine Milmine, Carl Schurz, and George W. Smalley; and illustrations by Charles Dana Gibson and Maxfield Parrish. When in 1906 McClure insisted on a grandiose plan for expansion into a great industrial combination, Phillips and staff members Tarbell, Baker, and Steffens went to the *American Magazine*. McClure recruited others for his staff, including William Henry Irwin (1873–1948), who served a year as managing editor then the editor. Advertising and circulation declined slightly before McClure abandoned his plan. In 1911 *McClure's* was purchased by Cameron Mackenzie and Frederick Lewis Collins under the name McClure Publications. Post-muckraking contributors included Arnold Bennett, Wallace Irwin, Mary Roberts Rinehart, and P. G. Wodehouse. In World War I the magazine was "mobilized" with patriotic articles, and in 1918 circulation hit a peak of 563,000. In 1919 Collins sold the periodical to Herbert Haufman. During the next two years contributors included James Branch Cabell, Edna Ferber, and Zane Grey; but circulation dropped, and McClure Publications went bankrupt in fall 1921. Moody B. Gates came to the rescue and brought McClure back as chairman of the board and as editor to recreate the old magazine. But it published few well-known names, had little sparkle, and lost money. In spring 1924 it was turned over to McClure. Press work was poor, illustrations weak, and advertising sparse, leading to suspension after August 1924. McClure obtained new financing and revived the magazine with a new series beginning May 1925. Although contributors included Herbert Hoover and Tarbell, McClure could not repeat his earlier success, and he gave up with the January 1926 number. *McClure's* was revived for a third time when William Randolph Hearst's International Publications bought the name, added the subtitle *The Magazine of Romance*, and made it a cheap periodical in content and format. Although it published some name writers, including Elmer Davis and Nina Wilcox Putnam, its advertising and circulation lagged. In December 1927 it improved, with contributions by such noted authors as Frazier Hunt and Carl Sandburg. It was becoming an attractive, balanced publication when in 1928 the Magus Magazine Corporation purchased it. Magus made it a man's periodical, the *New McClure's Magazine*, with such contributors as Irvin S. Cobb, James Hopper, Rupert Hughes, Gene Tunny, and Donald Ogden Stewart. After the March 1929 issue it was combined with *Smart Set* (1890–1930).

1898. *Sunset* founded in San Francisco by the passenger department of the Southern Pacific Company to promote train travel to California; named after the railroad's "Sunset Limited." In the first decade of the 1900s, Charles Sedgwick Aiken expanded coverage beyond California to northwest coastal states. He ran departments in books and authors, theater, and amateur photography, as well as published such authors as Mary Austin, Jack London, Stewart Edward White, and Owen Wister. In 1915 Editor Charles K. Field bought *Sunset*, changed its emphasis to literary and political subjects, and promoted western authors, including Earle Stanley Gardner, Zane Grey, Bret Harte, Will Irwin, Jack London, and Kathleen Norris. In 1928 the periodical verged on bankruptcy, and early in 1929 a new owner and publisher, Laurence William Lane (1890–1967), took over. Lane intended to cover the entire range of family and home interests, providing "timely and practical suggestions on gardening, building, home-decorating and furnishings, cooking and home management, traveling, enjoying outdoor life. . . . " Service articles would appeal to women and men. Lane pioneered publication of regional editions, and by 1932 had three; circulation reached 203,000. In 1935 he initiated the "*Sunset* Shopping Center," a collection of small mail-order ads, an innovation copied by other periodicals. In 1936 *Sunset* ran its first photo cover, and two years later redesigned the cover. In 1938 *Sunset* first showed a profit. Bans on beer and tobacco ads had been added to the original liquor-ad ban by

1940. By then *Sunset* was publishing cooking and gardening books, some for bonuses to sell subscriptions; by 1980 it would publish about 100 titles. *Sunset* weathered World War II despite a paper shortage. By 1951 circulation exceeded 733,000. That year the headquarters was moved to a hacienda style building surrounded by gardens in Menlo Park. Within 15 years *Sunset* was the nation's most successful regional magazine. In 1971 circulation first reached 1 million. As circulation continued to rise, hitting 1,350,000 by the next decade, the magazine continued to emphasize service, covering building, food, gardening, and travel only for readers in 13 western sates. Readers could buy newsstand copies only in the West, and subscribers elsewhere had to pay extra. In the middle 1980s "The Magazine of Western Living" still emphasized how-to service features, covering entertaining at home, remodeling, and other subjects that had made it outstanding. There were four editorial zone editions, and circulation was 1,387,855 (1985). L. W. (Bill) Lane, Jr. (1919–), was chairman of the board and publisher.

1899. *The Coming Age: A Magazine of Constructive Thought* (January–August 1900) founded; published in Boston and St. Louis. Co-editors were Mrs. Calvin Kryder Reifsnider and Benjamin Orange Flower (1858–1918). The monthly called itself "a magazine with a mission" but lacked the aggressiveness of Flower's *Arena*. Many former *Arena* contributors wrote for it. The best feature was a series of "Conversations" with notable men.

● *Everybody's Magazine* (September–March 1929) founded in New York by Robert Curtis Ogden (1836–1913) as a general circulation monthly. John O'Hara Cosgrave was editor 1900–1903, 1906. The magazine emphasized nonfiction but did carry some fiction. In May 1903 it was sold to Ridgway-Thayer Company, which increased the number of pages and added illustrations. To build circulation, *Everybody's* ran muckraking articles, including Thomas William Lawson's popular 20-month series, "Frenzied Finance." During World War I content was attractively displayed and well balanced, with war pieces by Vernon Kellogg, Frederick Palmer, Theodore Roosevelt, William G. Shepherd, Lincoln Steffens, and Brank Whitlock. In 1921 *Everybody's* began publishing all fiction; by 1927 it had become a "pulp," printed on cheap paper. After the last issue it became part of *Everybody's Combined with Romance*, a confession magazine. During its 30 years *Everybody's* published some literature and much information and entertainment, including works by Michael Arlen, Dorothy Canfield, O. Henry, Joseph Hergesheimer, James Hopper, Will Irwin, Rudyard Kipling, Kathleen Norris, Frank Norris, Harvey J. O'Higgins, Ernest Poole, James Whitcomb Riley, Mary Roberts Rinehart, Rafael Sabatini, Arthur Train, and Alexander Woollcott.

Motion Pictures

1883. Celluloid film introduced by John Carbutt (1832–1905).

1891. Kinetograph camera and Kinetoscope peephole viewer patents applied for by Thomas Alva Edison (1847–1931). Slow manufacture and distribution delayed their popularity.

• *Fred Ott's Sneeze*, first celluloid close-up and earliest motion picture in Library of Congress. Ott was an Edison mechanic. His sneeze was shot by William Kennedy Laurie Dickson, director of Edison's motion picture project.

1893. Panoptikon (or Eidoloscope) demonstrated by Woodville Latham and his sons, Gray and Otway. One of the first successful projectors, it was a combination of Kinetoscope and magic lantern and produced better results than Edison's. The Latham projector doubled the size of Edison's film to about 70 mm, producing a brighter, clearer, sharper picture. The Lathams gave showings in southern cities and New York, but their invention ended in the obscurity of financial disaster.

1896. Vitascope, prototype of the modern motion picture projector, demonstrated by Charles Francis Jenkins (1867–1934) and Thomas Armat. In 1896 a secret agreement was struck whereby Thomas Alva Edison would sell the projector as his own invention.

• First official public showing of a motion picture to a paying public (using the Vitascope); shown at Koster and Bial's Music Hall, New York City, as one act on a vaudeville bill.

• *The Execution of Mary, Queen of Scots*, an early Edison film; ran for less than 30 seconds. The audience saw Mary decapitated and her head bound away.

• *The Kiss*, Edison's best-known film, a close-up of John Rice and May Irwin (real name Ida Campbell, 1862–1938) reenacting a kiss from their current Broadway stage hit. It was shot originally for Kinetoscope in 1896. When later projected onto a large screen, it elicited the public's first moralistic reaction to movie romance.

1897. *Burglar on the Roof*, first film by Vitagraph Company; filmed on the roof of Vitagraph office building in New York. It was an early attempt at screen narrative.

1898. Two notable films released by Edison. In *Washday Troubles* a boy's prank resulted in a tub of washing dousing people. *Pullman Honeymoon*, an early narrative film, recorded a series of fictional events in one of George Pullman's sleeping cars (actually a stage setup) involving bandits, comics, lovers, passengers, police, and porters. The camera was static, like a spectator at a stage play. The film ran ten minutes.

● *Tearing Down the Spanish Flag*, an attempt to capitalize on the Spanish-American War. It featured a battle scene staged on Vitagraph's roof in New York.

Radio and Television

1885. First radio patent, granted to Thomas Alva Edison (1847–1931). The induction system used antennas to transmit above the curvature of the earth and its conduction.

● American Telephone and Telegraph Company formed from several earlier phone companies. It had a near monopoly on the U.S. telephone system.

1892. Wireless telephone system demonstrated, by Nathan B. Stubblefield (1860–1928). This transmission of voice over the air without wires consisted of sending ground conduction voice signals several hundred yards. Stubblefield had begun experimenting with an electrical radiation system in the late 1880s.

1894. The start of experimentation with television mosaic system, by Charles Francis Jenkins (1867–1934).

1900–1914

The Progressive Era

━━━━━━━━━━━━ ▐●▌ ━━━━━━━━━━━━

Books

1900. Doubleday, Page & Co. (January–), a publishing house, founded in New York by Frank Nelson Doubleday (1862–1934) and Walter Hines Page (1855–1918), who left in 1913. In 1928 Doubleday merged with George H. Doran Co. (f. 1908) to form Doubleday, Doran & Co.

● Two best sellers—*Eben Holden*, by Irving Addison Bacheller (1859–1950), and *To Have and To Hold*, by Mary Johnston (1870–1936). Other books by Johnston, an author of historical romances, included *Ceasing Firing* (1912), *The Great Valley* (1926), and *Miss Delicia Allen* (1932).

● *Sister Carrie*, by Theodore Herman Albert Dreiser (1871–1945), his first novel. This story of a young woman propelled by blind, amoral forces brought threats of censorship and was withdrawn by the publisher; it went largely unread until its renaissance and third edition (1912). Other novels by Dreiser also reflected his naturalistic and realistic view of life; they included *Jennie Gerhardt* (1911), *The Financier* (1912), *The Titan* (1914), *The Genius* (1915), *An American Tragedy* (1925), *The Bulwark* (1946), and *The Stoic* (1947). After World War I Dreiser turned socialist, writing *Dreiser Looks at Russia* (1928), *Tragic America* (1932), and *America Is Worth Saving* (1941).

1901. Two best sellers—*Graustark*, the first novel by George Barr McCutcheon (1866–1928), and *Mrs. Wiggs of the Cabbage Patch*, by Alice Caldwell Hegan Rice (1870–1942). Other works by McCutcheon included *Brewster's Millions* (1902), *Beverly of Graustark* (1904), *Mary Midthorne* (1911), *A Fool and His Money* (1913), *The Prince of Graustark*

(1914), and *The Merivales* (1929). Other works by Rice included *Lovey Mary* (1903), *Mr. Opp* (1909), *A Romance of Billy Goat Hill* (1912), *The Buffer* (1929), *Mr. Pete & Co.* (1933), and *My Pillow Book* (1937).

• *The Great God Success*, the first novel by David Graham Phillips (1867–1911). This novel boldly presented a relationship between man and woman as well as business frauds of modern plutocrats. Phillips published 23 novels, many of them muckraking, including *The Plum Tree* (1905), *Light-Fingered Gentry* and *The Second Generation* (1907), and *Susan Lenox: Her Fall and Rise* (1917). His nonfiction included a collection of muckraking articles, *The Reign of Guilt* (1905).

1902. B. W. Huebsch, a publishing house, founded in New York by Ben Huebsch (1876–1964); absorbed by Viking Press (f. 1925) in 1925.

• *Poems*, by Edward Rowland Sill (1841–1887). The selections reflected the author's stoic idealism.

• *The Virginian*, by Owen Wister (1860–1938), a best seller at this time and later. Wister's other works included *Philosophy 4* (1903), a short story collection, and *Roosevelt* (1930), a biography.

1903. Three best sellers—*The Call of the Wild*, by John Griffith London (1876–1916); *The Little Shepherd of Kingdom Come*, by John William Fox, Jr. (1863–1919); and *Rebecca of Sunnybrook Farm*, by Kate Douglas Smith Wiggin (1856–1923). Jack London's novel, also a later best seller, was an episodic story of a dog in the Far North that escapes from civilization to lead a wolf pack. It was London's first major novel among his 49 volumes of fiction, essays, and drama. London's other works included the short story collections *The Son of the Wolf* (1900) and *The God of His Fathers* (1901) as well as the novels *The Sea Wolf* (1904), *The Iron Heel* (1908), *Martin Eden* (1909), *John Barleycorn* (1913), *The Valley of the Moon* (1913), and *The Star Rover* (1915). Of works by U.S. naturalists, London's were the most widely read at home and abroad. John Fox, Jr., wrote two best sellers, the other being *The Trail of the Lonesome Pine* (1908); his novels and novelettes made the mountaineers of the Cumberlands widely known. Wiggin's *Rebecca* was her most popular book; her first literary success had been *The Birds' Christmas Carol* (1887).

1904. *Freckles*, by Gene Stratton Porter (1868–1924), Porter's first best seller. Others were *A Girl of the Limberlost* (1909), *The Harvester* (1911), and *Laddie* (1913). Her works also included *The Song of the Cardinal* (1902) and *The Fire Bird* (1922), a collection of poems.

1905. *The House of Mirth*, by Edith Newbold Jones Wharton (1863–1937), the author's first major work, a novel of New York's social elite. In 1905 Edith Wharton also published a travel book, *Italian Backgrounds*. Previously, she had published three novels, including *The Touchstone* (1900), and three collections of short stories. Her other novels of New York's social elite included *The Age of Innocence* (1920) and *The Old Maid* (1924). Among her other major works were *Ethan Frome* (1911), a novel, and *Xingu* (1916), a short story collection.

● *Memoirs of an American Citizen*, by Robert Herrick (1868–1938), his first major novel. In that novel, *Clark's Field* (1914), and *Waste* (1924), Herrick made a social protest against acquisitiveness. His other major works included his first novel, *The Man Who Wins* (1897), and the short story collections *Literary Love-Letters* (1897) and *The Master of the Inn* (1908).

1906. *The Jungle*, by Upton Beall Sinclair, Jr. (1878–1968), Sinclair's first major novel. It exposed labor exploitation and corruption among Chicago meat packers. Upton Sinclair's other exposé novels included *Oil!* (1927) and *Boston* (1928). A major novel was *Dragon's Teeth* (1942). A socialist, Sinclair also wrote an expository propaganda series: *The Profits of Religion* (1918), *The Brass Check* (1919), *The Goose Step* (1923), *The Goslings* (1924), *Mammonart* (1925), and *Money Writes* (1927).

● *The Spirit of the Border*, by Zane Grey (1875–1939), a best seller in this period and later. Grey's other long-time best-selling westerns were *The Riders of the Purple Sage* (1912) and *The U.P. Trail* (1918). His other westerns included *The Lone Star Ranger* (1915), *The Mysterious Rider* (1921), *The Wanderer of the Wasteland* (1923), *The Thundering Herd* (1925), *The Vanishing American* (1926), *Code of the West* (1934), and *West of the Pecos* (1937). Grey also wrote books about his hobby, fishing.

1907. *The Shepherd of the Hills*, by Harold Bell Wright (1872–1944), a best seller. Among Wright's other popular novels were *The Calling of Dan Matthews* (1909), *The Winning of Barbara Worth* (1911), *The Eyes of the World* (1914), and *When a Man's a Man* (1916)—all best sellers in their period and later.

1908. *The Circular Staircase*, by Mary Roberts Rinehart (1876–1958), a best seller and the author's first major book. Her other works included *Amazing Adventures of Letitia Carberry* (1911), *The Breaking Point* (1922), *Lost Ecstasy* (1927), *The Romantics* (1929), *The Door* (1930), *Miss Pinkerton* (1932), *Married People* (1937), and *The Wall* (1938).

1909. *The Wine of the Puritans*, by Van Wyck Brooks (1886–1963). In this, his first book, Brooks claimed that the Puritan tradition crushed U.S. culture, a view that he later changed. His other works included *America's Coming of Age* (1915), *The Ordeal of Mark Twain* (1920), *The Pilgrimage of Henry James* (1925), *The Flowering of New England, 1815–1865* (1936), *New England: Indian Summer* (1940), and *On Literature Today* (1941).

1910. *The House of Mystery* by William Henry Irwin (1873–1948),

Irwin's first popular novel, a mystery featuring spiritual medium Rosalie LeGrange. Another LeGrange mystery was Irwin's *The Red Button* (1912). Other novels included *The Readjustment* (1910), *Columbine Time* (1921), and *Youth Rides West* (1925). Irwin's nonfiction books included *The City That Was: A Requiem of Old San Francisco* (1906), *The Confessions of a Con Man* (1909), *Beating Back* (1914), *Highlights of Manhattan* (1927), *How Red Is America?* (1927), *Herbert Hoover: A Reminiscent Biography* (1928), *Propaganda and the News* (1936), and *The Making of a Reporter* (1942). Irwin also wrote two polemics against war, *The Next War* (1921) and *Christ or Mars?* (1923), and three collections of war correspondence, *Men, Women and War* (1915), *The Latin at War* (1917), and *A Reporter at Armageddon* (1918).

1911. *Mother*, by Kathleen Thompson Norris (1880–1966), a best-selling novelette. Other major works included *Saturday's Child* (1914), *Sisters* (1919), *The Sea Gull* (1927), *My California* (1933), and *Heart-broken Melody* (1938).

1912. *The New History*, by James Harvey Robinson (1863–1936). Robinson advocated that historians explain causes and make syntheses.

1913. *An Economic Interpretation of the Constitution*, by Charles Austin Beard (1874–1948), the historian's first major work. A companion monograph was *Economic Origins of Jeffersonian Democracy* (1915). In *The Rise of American Civilization* (four volumes, 1927–1942), written with Mary Ritter Beard (1876–1958), Beard discarded economic determinism for pluralistic historical causation. Beard's other major works included *American Foreign Policy in the Making: 1932–1940* (1946) and *President Roosevelt and the Coming of the War 1941* (1948).

● *O Pioneers!*, by Willa Sibert Cather (1873–1947), her major work. Cather deftly interwove environment and character in this fictional chronicle and others, including *My Antonia* (1918), *A Lost Lady* (1923), *Death Comes for the Archbishop* (1927), and *Shadows on the Rock* (1931). Her novel *One of Ours* (1922) won a Pulitzer Prize.

● *Pollyanna*, by Eleanor Hodgman Porter (1868–1920), a best seller. Porter's first novel was *Cross Currents* (1907).

1914. *Congo and Other Poems*, by Vachel Lindsay (1879–1931). The volume displayed the poet's vigorous rhythms and vivid imagery.

● *Penrod*, by Newton Booth Tarkington (1869–1946), and *Tarzan of the Apes*, by Edgard Rice Burroughs (1875–1950), two best sellers in this period and later. Burroughs also wrote other Tarzan adventures, such as *The Return of Tarzan* (1915). Booth Tarkington's major novels included other Penrod stories and two Pulitzer Prize works, *The Magnificent Ambersons* (1918) and *Alice Adams* (1921). His first novel was *The Gentleman from Indiana* (1899).

Newspapers

1900. Newspapers now a major business: 1,967 dailies published, with total circulation of 15 million and 26 percent of all adults subscribers. Most growth in the previous two decades had been in evening editions. More than 12,000 weeklies were published.

• Associated Press reincorporated, as a cooperative news agency, after an Illinois court found that the incorporation papers of the Associated Press of Illinois (which had taken over the New York Associated Press, f. 1849) were so broadly written that they made the organization a public utility bound to provide its services to all newspapers wanting to buy it. To avoid ending the exclusive membership character, AP's leaders formed a nonprofit membership association under New York State law, with the same general manager, Melville Elijah Stone (1848–1929). AP members now shared costs of exchanging news and of maintaining an association staff to direct news flow and to provide additional coverage. The original members owned bonds with voting rights that kept control of the board of directors in the hands of older, larger newspapers, thus controlling new memberships and competition in members' publication areas. Members were not allowed to subscribe to other news services, a restriction lifted in 1915. In 1913 AP first used teletypes (automatic news printers), which gradually replaced the telegraph. In 1921 Frederick Roy Martin succeeded Stone as general manager. The next year AP won its first Pulitzer Prize, for Kirke L. Simpson's series on the burial of the Unknown Soldier in Arlington. In 1925 Kent Cooper (1880–1965) became general manager. He increased the number of bureaus, expanded the staff and state services, and encouraged human-interest stories. In 1927 AP established a new photograph service. In 1931 the Associated Press Managing Editors Association was formed; in 1948 it began publishing its criticism of AP news coverage and writing style, in *APME Redbook*. In 1933 AP newspapers voted not to furnish news to radio networks and to limit news broadcasts by members (many owned stations) to occasional 35-word bulletins; AP began selling its report to radio outlets in 1940. In 1934 management finally ended old restrictive arrangements (f. 1893) with European news agencies that prevented sale of AP news abroad and began opening foreign bureaus. In 1935 a Wirephoto system was approved to transmit pictures by rented wires, and a year later Byron Price (1891–1981) became AP's first executive news editor. Smaller dailies were given 3 seats on a board of 18 in 1937. In April 1937 the U.S. Supreme Court decided *Associated Press v. NLRB* (301 U.S. 103), ruling that "the publisher of a newspaper has no special immunity from application of general laws." The decision defined the limits of First

Amendment protection the press could expect in government regulation of business. Although the press could not be singled out for discriminatory taxation, the opinion indicated, the press was subject to taxes and other generally applicable regulation. The case had arisen from the 1935 discharge of AP staff member Morris Watson, who asserted that he was dismissed for union (American Newspaper Guild) activities. He appealed to the National Labor Relations Board to order his reinstatement under the Wagner Labor Relations Act (1935). The NLRB ruled for Watson in 1936. AP appealed to the Supreme Court, contending that the Wagner Act was both unconstitutional and not applicable to press associations or newspapers. The court ordered AP to reinstate Watson, saying he had been illegally discharged for union activity. A major Guild victory, the opinion assured the union of a place in the newspaper business. Another major suit, filed in 1942 by Marshall Field, publisher of the Chicago *Sun* (f. 1941), challenged the AP bylaws that permitted a member to blackball an applicant in its own city. To override the veto required a four-fifths vote of the entire membership, rarely obtained; the only way to join AP in larger cities was to buy a newspaper holding a membership. In 1945 the U.S. Supreme Court in *Associated Press et al. v. United States* (326 U.S. 1) held that the bylaws constituted unfair restriction of competition. AP amended its membership rules and elected several newspapers previously denied admission. During World War II AP fielded a distinguished battery of correspondents, including reporters Hal Boyle and Daniel De Luce and photographers Frank Filan, Frank Noel, and Joe Rosenthal—all Pulitzer Prize winners. Rosenthal's picture of six Marines erecting the Stars and Stripes on top of Mount Suribachi memorialized Iwo Jima. Women correspondents included Ruth Cowan and Bonnie Wiley. On the Western front AP chief Edward Kennedy broke U.S. censorship in 1945 to score a beat on Germany's surrender in Europe, although he had pledged with 16 Allied correspondents to withhold the announcement until the officially prescribed time. Kennedy broke his story after German radio had announced the surrender early. Fifty-four colleagues in Paris charged him with an unethical "double cross." In 1946 AP began its World Service. That year radio stations were granted associate membership, without voting rights. In 1948 Cooper was succeeded by Frank J. Starzel. Service by teletypesetter (which produced a perforated tape that automatically ran a typesetting machine) began in 1951; circuits were set up for smaller papers, sports, and financial services. In 1954 AP began supplying photographs by facsimile over its Photofax. In 1962 Wes Gallagher, AP's leading World War II correspondent, succeeded Starzel. Gallagher opened the reporting ranks to younger men and to women and presided over a massive reorganization of transmission wires. Also in the 1960s, AP's Vietnam reporting was distinguished by Pulitzer Prize winners

Malcolm Browne and Peter Arnett, reporters, and Horst Faas and Edward T. Adams, photographers. Adams depicted the moment of execution of a Viet Cong by the Saigon police chief during the Tet offensive. In 1976 AP served 1,181 newspapers. At the close of 1976 Keith Fuller replaced Wes Gallagher as president and general manager. Executive editor was Louis D. Boccardi, managing editor Robert H. Johnson, and star political reporter Walter Mears. In the 1970s AP automated its transmission facilities, using video display terminals and computers for information processing, storage, and retrieval. Domestic news wires could deliver copy at 1,200 words per minute; a news report could be flashed around the world in 1 minute. In the 1980s dish antennas were installed at newspapers to receive satellite transmissions. Using cables, lasers, and satellites, AP transmitted high-quality photos to editors within minutes of events. AP provided reports to radio and television stations and networks as well as to newspapers and a few magazines, and it engaged in teletext, among other technological developments. In 1984 AP served 56 percent of U.S. dailies.

• Chicago *American* (–1974) founded by William Randolph Hearst (1863–1951). In 1956 the Chicago Tribune Company purchased the *American* from Hearst Consolidated; later named the paper Chicago *Today*.

1901. Girard, Kansas, *Appeal to Reason* (–1922) founded as a Socialist paper by J. A. Wayland. Although Wayland devoted only about 20 percent of the space to Socialist theory and party activities, instead concentrating on muckrakinglike protests, his weekly was the largest Socialist newspaper in 1913, with 760,000 copies distributed by rail throughout the nation. On special occasions Wayland distributed millions of copies.

• Boston *Guardian* founded by William Monroe Trotter, with George Forbes, as a provocative, militant black paper.

1902. Chicago *Examiner* founded as a morning edition of the *American* by William Randolph Hearst. In 1918 the *Examiner* and Chicago *Herald* combined to form the *Herald-Examiner*.

1903. Los Angeles *Examiner* (–1962) founded as a morning daily by William Randolph Hearst. The first issue advertised such Hearst writers as Ambrose Bierce, Dorothy Dix, Mrs. John A. Logan, and Ella Wheeler Wilcox. Within a month the *Examiner* claimed 32,500 readers; it remained a strong paper for about 50 years. In 1960 the *Examiner* had a circulation of 369,537 daily and 684,605 Sunday.

1904 First four-year curriculum in journalism organized by the University of Illinois, under direction of Frank W. Scott.

• Boston *American* founded by William Randolph Hearst as an afternoon paper; later issued mornings. In 1938 it became a tabloid. In an early 1960s economy drive the *American* and *Record* (f. 1884, bought by Hearst in 1917) were combined into a profitable morning paper, which reached more than 455,870 readers by 1968.

• New York *Evening Globe* founded by J. J. Wright. In 1905 Wright bought the New York *Commercial Advertiser* (f. 1793 as *American Minerva*) and consolidated the two papers into the *Globe and Commercial Advertiser*, which was purchased by Frank Andrew Munsey (1854–1925) in 1923 and merged into the *Sun*.

1905. Chicago *Defender* founded by Robert S. Abbott (1868–1940). By 1915 the weekly had 230,000 circulation. The early *Defender* crusaded on behalf of black people, challenging the Ku Klux Klan and opposing lynchings, race rioting, and other racial injustices. It sensationalized by emphasizing race in headlines and stories and playing up crime and scandal. By the 1930s Abbott moderated the tone, adding more culture, fashion, personal, and social news. During the depression circulation declined by two-thirds. Upon Abbott's death, John Herman Sengstacke (1912–), a nephew, became editor and publisher. By the close of World War I the *Defender* had become one of the big three black newspapers that could be purchased nationally. Circulation in 1947 was 160,000. The paper went daily in 1956. Circulation dropped to 33,000 by 1970, but the *Daily Defender* and its weekly national edition became the cornerstone of the largest black newspaper group, which had 100,000 circulation in 1983. That year the *Defender* had circulation of 15,000 daily and 21,000 weekly (national edition). In the mid-1980s the daily was published Monday through Friday mornings and had about 27,600 circulation.

1907. United Press Associations founded as a commercial wire service by Edward Wyllis Scripps (1854–1926), who merged two regional news services for his own papers in the Midwest and West. John Vandercook, the first general manager, who helped create the merger, died in 1908. He was succeeded by Roy Wilson Howard (1883–1964), who established bureaus in major European capitals and made arrangements with leading foreign newspapers and with news agencies not connected with the Associated Press. In South America, where AP could not serve because of its contracts with foreign news agencies, he acquired many clients and established bureaus. UP early gave reporters bylines and opportunities to develop writing styles and news specialities (AP reporters covering World War I were mostly anonymous news gatherers). On 7 November 1918 Howard flashed a false armistice report over the UP wire, setting off wild celebrations at home and in France. When he left UP in 1920 to become a partner in the Scripps newspaper chain, the wire service had 780 clients. Helping to sell UP as a second wire for AP member newspapers were young correspondents like Fred S. Ferguson, Webb Miller, Westbrook Pegler, William G. Shepherd, and William Philip Simms. Other notable "Unipressers" included Raymond

Clapper, Paul Mallon, and Thomas L. Stokes. In 1923 William W. Hawkins, who had succeeded Howard, was succeeded by Karl A. Bickel, who expanded international services. In 1925 UP began Acme Newspictures, which in 1952 became United Press Newspictures, transmitting by Telephoto and (from 1954) Unifax (facsimile). In 1928 UP was among the three major press associations supplying election returns to radio stations. In the early 1930s UP bowed to pressures by its newspaper clients to stop sale of news to radio stations, but in 1935 it resumed service (to meet competition from Transradio Press Service), providing a report written for broadcast. Also in 1935 Hugh Baillie (1890–1966) succeeded Bickel as president and Earl J. Johnson became working head of news operations (serving until 1965, when he retired as editor). To meet the pressures of World War II, UP rapidly expanded. Leading war correspondents included Edward W. Beattie, Henry T. Gorrell, Joseph W. Grigg, Dudley Anne Harmon, and Eleanor Packard. UP also distinguished itself in the war in Korea. On 25 June 1950 Jack James first flashed to the world news of the North Korean invasion of the Republic of South Korea. UP rushed in Peter Kalischer and Rutherford Poas, who were backed up by the Tokyo bureau, headed by Earnest Hoberecht. In the early 1950s UP set up teletypesetter circuits for smaller papers and for sports and financial services. In 1955 Frank H. Bartholomew (1898–) succeeded Baillie as president, then in 1958 presided over absorption of International News Service (f. 1909). William Randolph Hearst, Jr. (1908–), and two of his associates took minority seats on the board of directors of the new United Press International. Mims Thomason became UPI president in 1962, and Neil Sheehan went to Vietnam to cover the fighting. White House senior correspondent Merriman Smith (1913–1970) won a Pulitzer Prize for his 1963 coverage of President Kennedy's assassination. A 1966 Pulitzer winner was photographer Kyoichi Sawada, whose prize picture showed a Vietnamese family swimming in a river current. In 1971 Lucinda Franks and Thomas Powers won a Pulitzer for national news. In 1976 UPI served 823 newspapers. Byliners abroad in the 1970s included Arthur Higbee, Wellington Long, Gerard Loughran, and Peter Uebersex in Europe as well as Leon Daniel, Alan Dawson, and Joseph Galloway in Asia. By the late 1970s UPI was using radio teleprinters, satellites, and underwater cables to transmit news reports and photographs over the world. Video display terminals and high-speed computers were used for information processing, storage, and retrieval. Domestic news wires could deliver copy to clients at 1,200 words per minute; a news report could be flashed around the world in 1 minute. UPI used cables, lasers, satellites, and electronic darkrooms to transmit high-quality photographs to editors in minutes. UPI tried to cope with inflation, rising costs, and worldwide recession. After 1980 the parent E. W. Scripps Company reported losses in the millions of dollars; by 1982 UPI's daily newspaper clients had dropped to 639. In June 1982 UPI was sold to William Geissler and Douglas F. Ruhe, who became managing director. A few months later Roderick W. Beaton retired as president, to be succeeded by William J. Small. Maxwell McCrohon became editor in chief. The news headquarters was shifted from New York City to Washington, D.C. UPI increased promotion of services to nonmedia users. In 1983 about half of its income came from its 818 U.S. newspaper clients, most of whom used dish antennas to receive news by satellite. That year H. L. Stevenson became executive vice president/editorial. Women correspondents included Helen Thomas at the White House and Geri Smith and Cindy Karp in El Salvador. In 1984 UPI sold news and photos to 800 newspapers and about 3,800 radio and television stations. Severe financial difficulties continued. Hoping to save $12 million, UPI executed an austerity program, suspending pension contributions and laying off employees; but in spring 1985 the company began operating under protection of a federal bankruptcy court. That November Mexican Mario Vázquez Raña won a bid to buy the press association.

1908. *Christian Science Monitor* (25 November–) founded in Boston by Mary Morse Eddy (1821–1910), née Baker, for the Church of Christ, Scientist, to counter the sensationalism of other daily papers. Mary Baker Eddy, the church founder, did not intend that the afternoon daily be a religious publication but that it play down crime and disaster news and play up positive, good news according to the tenets of her faith. As editor for the first ten years, Frederick Dixon built a staff known for its excellent foreign and cultural news coverage. By 1918 circulation was 120,000. Early in the 1920s, after an internal management fight and a circulation drop, Willis J. Abbot became editor. By 1935 the *Monitor* had built up its staff in leading U.S. and foreign cities and strengthened its circulation. One of the largest staffs of any U.S. newspaper covered World War II. In 1945 Erwin D. Canham (1904–1982) became editor, a position he held until he became editor in chief in 1964. Canham helped make the *Monitor* a nationally and internationally respected newspaper for significant regional stories, arts features, and Washington and foreign correspondence. As a pioneer in interpretive and in-depth reporting and in news analysis, the *Monitor* appealed to educated readers. In a 1961 poll the paper ranked among the top ten dailies. DeWitt John succeeded Canham about the time circulation slumped to 185,000. The *Monitor* modernized with five-column layout, bigger type, better art, and livelier writing. In the 1960s it won Pulitzer Prizes for national and international reporting. Changes in the 1970s began with R. John Hughes's appointment as editor (1970–1979). In 1970 the *Monitor* became the first major newspaper to change from letterpress to offset printing. In 1971 it joined other leading newspapers in printing excerpts from the Pentagon Papers before the U.S. Supreme court officially permitted their publication. That year circulation reached a record high of 239,000. Also in 1971 the *Monitor* began syndicating its news and features; by 1979 it had 200 client newspapers with a combined circulation of almost 16 million. Continuing to lead in new technology, the paper instituted phototypesetting in 1972 and facsimile transmission of pictures to printing plants in 1973, but during the 1970s the *Monitor* faced severe financial problems as circulation and advertising declined. Management, however, continued to refuse alcoholic beverage, tobacco, and drug ads. Circulation fluctuated between 150,000 and 260,000 as quality improved, and advertising revenue halted its downward spiral (1977–1978) then rose slightly (1979). In 1979 circulation was 194,000. Four major moves in the late 1970s were initiation of a news service for radio stations (1977), creation of an endowment fund administered by the treasurer of the mother church (1978), appointment of Earl W. Foell as editor (1979), and installation of an electronic editing and composition system (1979). By the 1980s the *Monitor* had plants for its daily regional editions in Beverly, Massachusetts; Chicago; Glendale, California; and Somerset, New Jersey. A plant near London printed a weekly international edition, distributed in 130 countries. Use of satellites assured fast delivery between Boston headquarters and the plants. In the early 1980s the daily *Monitor*, now long distributed Monday–Friday mornings, had a circulation of about 151,000. In 1983 Katherine W. Fanning succeeded Foell, who became editor in chief. Although circulation fell to about 141,250 in 1985, the *Christian Science Monitor* continued its strong international and cultural news coverage, along with arts and book reviews and advice on finances, food, gardening, and home furnishings.

● School of Journalism, University of Missouri, established as the first separate journalism school. The first dean was Walter Williams.

● New York *Evening Call* (–1923) founded; a major Socialist labor daily.

1909. Sigma Delta Chi founded at DePauw University as a professional fraternity for men in journalism and Theta Sigma Phi founded at the University of Washington as an honorary and professional fraternity for women in journalism. SDX later expanded to include professional chapters and women and changed its name to Society of Professional Journalists, Sigma Delta Chi. Theta Sigma Phi later became Women in Communication, Inc., open to men too.

● International News Service founded by William Randolph Hearst as the third major U.S. press association, an outgrowth of earlier leased wire facilities for Hearst newspapers. The first manager was Richard A. Farrelly. The moving force after 1916 was Barry Faris, editor in chief, who concentrated bureaus in major news centers. By 1918 INS served

400 clients and had a leased wire service about half as extensive as AP or UP. INS offered special coverage of major news events by such talented writers as Bob Considine, Floyd Gibbons, Dorothy Kilgallen, James L. Kilgallen, and H. R. Knickerbocker. In 1928 Faris established 24-hour operations. Early in the 1930s INS, which had supplied 1928 election returns to radio stations, bowed to its newspaper clients' desires (as did UP) and stopped sale of news to the stations. In 1935 INS (and UP) resumed the sale of full news reports to radio to meet competition by Transradio Press Service. Late in the decade business control went to Joseph V. Connolly. During the 1930s INS's foreign service developed a strong reputation, led by foreign editor J. C. Oestreicher. During World War II top correspondents included Lee Carson, Kenneth Downs, Rita Hume, George Lait, Clarke Lee, Merrill Mueller, Inez Robb, Dixie Tighe, and Richard Tregaskis. After 1945 Seymour Berkson ran the business side. In 1951 INS (and UP) began servicing television. In the 1950s Ray Richards was the first correspondent to fly over a battle area after the outbreak of the Korean War, and Howard Handleman headed the Tokyo bureau. Frank Conniff, William Randolph Hearst, Jr., and Kingsbury Smith won a 1956 Pulitzer Prize for their interview with Communist leaders behind the Iron Curtain. In 1958 INS was absorbed by United Press, which then became United Press International.

• New York *Amsterdam News* founded by James H. Anderson; in 1936 purchased by Dr. C. B. Powell and in 1971 by Clarence B. Jones. Concentrating on local news, the paper went from sensational, with emphasis on crime and sex, to moderate, with emphasis on sports and women's news and some crusading. The paper gradually won leadership in competitive Harlem journalism, and became one of the largest standard black community newspapers.

• Norfolk, Virginia, *Journal and Guide* founded; taken over in 1910 by P. Bernard Young, who ran it as a moderate, nonsensational weekly until his death in 1962. The *Journal and Guide* became one of the best black papers and the largest in the South.

1910. Kappa Tau Alpha, journalism scholastic society, founded at the University of Missouri.

• Pittsburgh *Courier* founded as a church-sponsored venture. Later it was taken over by Robert L. Vann, who fought racial discrimination and the Jim Crow tradition. His *Courier* backed black athletes, including Jackie Robinson, whom it helped break the color barrier in baseball. At the close of World War II the *Courier* was one of the big three black newspapers, with virtually national distribution of its editions. Circulation grew from 102,000 to almost 300,000 in the late 1940s; by 1970 it had dwindled to 20,000. In the mid-1980s the weekly was called the *New Pittsburgh Courier* and had about 21,000 circulation. Rod Doss was editor. The paper belonged to the John Sengstacke group.

1911. Chicago *Day Book* (–1917) founded by Edward Wyllis Scripps as an experimental tabloid without advertising. The editor was Negley D. Cochran and the chief reporter Carl Sandburg (1878–1967). The daily was within $500 a month of breaking even on a circulation of 25,000 when rising newsprint costs of the first year of World War I forced discontinuance.

● Milwaukee *Leader* (–1942) founded; a major Socialist labor daily. Editor was Victor L. Berger (1860–1929). During World War I the Post Office withheld the *Leader*'s second-class mailing privileges for violating the Espionage Act of 15 June 1917 by being disloyal to the U.S.-Allied war cause. In 1921 the U.S. Supreme Court upheld the ban, but in June the postmaster general restored the mailing privileges, enabling the *Leader* to once more reach its many out of town subscribers. In the 1930s the daily declined.

1912. American Association of Teachers of Journalism founded; later named Association for Education in Journalism (AEJ), then Association for Education in Journalism and Mass Communication (AEJMC).

● School of Journalism, Columbia University, established by a $2 million endowment from Joseph Pulitzer (1847–1911). The first director, to 1919, was Talcott Williams (1849–1928). In 1912 more than 30 colleges and universities offered courses in journalism.

1913. Circulation of 2 million copies by 323 Socialist newspapers.

● Bell Syndicate founded by John N. Wheeler; featured H. C. (Bud) Fisher, who drew "Mutt and Jeff," the first regular daily cartoon strip, which appeared in the San Francisco *Chronicle* in 1907, and Fountaine Fox, who first portrayed the "Toonerville Folks" in the Chicago *Post* in 1908.

1914. About 1,300 foreign-language newspapers and periodicals published, up about 100 from 1910. Foreign-language dailies peaked at about 160, including 55 German; 12 each French, Italian, Polish; 10 each Japanese, Yiddish; 8 each Bohemian, Spanish; their total circulation was 2.6 million, 823,000 of that German-speaking readers and 762,000 Yiddish-speaking readers. The largest foreign-language daily was *New Yorker Staats-Zeitung* (f. 1845), with 250,000. Much of the foreign-language press served immigrants in large cities; its influence was strong among readers.

● Federal Trade Commission established by Congress to promote fair trade practices; principal federal agency regulating advertising.

● King Features Syndicate founded by William Randolph Hearst. By 1918 the syndicate was a major purveyor of comic strips. A leading color comic for King Features, the "Katzenjammer Kids" (f. 1897), continued into the 1980s. Leading columnists included Bruce Barton, Jim Bishop, and Fulton Lewis, Jr.

Magazines

1900. *World's Work* (November–July 1932) founded in New York by Walter Hines Page (1855–1918) as a quality monthly for discussion of public affairs. Well printed and illustrated, it attained a circulation of 100,000 with 50 to 100 pages of advertising by 1907. Although Page ran some exposure and reform material, including Upton Sinclair's *The Jungle*, he was generally pro-business. Content covered art, business, education, government, literature, technology, nature, politics, etc. Contributors included Ray Stannard Baker, Winston Spencer Churchill, Arno Dosch-Fleurot, Joel Chandler Harris, Rudyard Kipling, and Frank Simonds. In 1913 Page was succeeded by his son, Arthur Wilson Page, the editor to 1926. The magazine ran much material about World War I, when it attained its highest circulation, 140,000. A. W. Page was succeeded as editor by Carl C. Kickey, 1927–1928; Barton Currie, 1928–1929; Russell Doubleday, 1929–1931; and Alan C. Collins, 1931–1932. In the late 1920s leading contributors included Will Irwin, Theodore Joslin, Lowell Thomas, Freeman Tilden, and T. R. Ybarra. During the depression *World's Work*, which had been unstable for several years, lost advertising and circulation. It was absorbed in 1932 by the *Review of Reviews* (f. 1891), its chief competitor.

1901. *Current Encyclopedia* (July–February 1925) founded in Chicago by William E. Ernst as a monthly digest of the *Encyclopedia Britannica* for home study. In 1902 its name was changed to *The World To-Day*, which in 1903 absorbed the new *Christendom*, a weekly publication of the University of Chicago. *The World To-Day* was a copiously illustrated, well-balanced magazine. Upon purchase by William Randolph Hearst (1863–1951) in 1911, the magazine was moved to New York. In March 1912 the name was changed to *Hearst's Magazine*. Content included articles on economic, historical, and political subjects and editorials by Hearst, "Mr. Dooley," and Norman Hapgood. Drawings by such leading illustrators as James Montgomery Flagg and Charles Dana Gibson appeared. Rex Beach, Rupert Hughes, Jack London, and David Graham Phillips contributed outstanding fiction, and Albert J. Beveridge, Louis D. Brandeis, Alfred Henry Lewis, George W. Perkins, and Charles Edward Russell did factual articles. To gain circulation, *Hearst's* in 1914 was made an entertainment magazine. Vincente Blasco-Ibáñez, G. K. Chesterton, Gabrielle D'Annunzio, Elinor Glyn, Rudyard Kipling, Maurice Maeterlinck, H. G. Wells, and other noted writers were featured. In 1925 the magazine was merged into *Cosmopolitan* under the title *Hearst's International Combined with Cosmopolitan* (though only *Cosmopolitan* was displayed on the cover).

● *The Editor & Publisher* (29 June–) founded in New York by James B. Shale, editor 1901–1902 and 1909–1912, as a weekly *Journal for*

Newspaper Makers (subtitle); also ran news about magazine publishing. In 1907 it absorbed *The Journalist* (f. 1884). In 1912 Shale sold to James Wright Brown (1873–1959) and associates, who published their first issue 6 April. Brown, who was president of Editor & Publisher, Inc., 1912–1947 and 1948–1953, crusaded against abuses of press agentry, attempts to undermine freedom of the press, bad advertising, and fraud in the news. Size and advertising increased. In 1915 the weekly adopted the ampersand of the parent company and the founding date of *The Journalist*, jumped its volume numbering from 14 to 47, and called itself "The oldest publishers' and advertisers' newspaper in America." Advertising, circulation, and number of pages increased. In 1918 it dropped *The* from its title. In 1922 Marlen Edwin Pew became editor (to 1936). In the early 1920s *Editor & Publisher* initiated a series of annuals. The first annual directory, which appeared as a supplement to the 28 January 1922 issue, carried a comprehensive list of advertising agencies, advertising rates, circulations, foreign newspapers, syndicates, and other data. The next year the first *International Year Book*, with expanded lists, was issued as a separate section; in 1945 it became a separate publication. In 1924 Brown began publishing an annual syndicate directory. In the 3 December 1924 issue the first market guide for advertisers appeared; it was an annual supplement until 1942, when it became a separate publication. In 1925 Brown bought *Newspaperdom* (f. 1892), which he issued for six months as *Advertising* before merging it with *Editor & Publisher*. In 1927 the *Fourth Estate* was absorbed by "E & P," which reported a circulation of 9,000. In 1933 the magazine initiated its Newspaper Promotion Awards and in 1956 its Color Awards; a "Spring Color issue," which ran data on color linage and related topics, recognized the increasing use of color in newspapers. By the 1950s the magazine had become more of a special pleader for the newspaper industry, antagonistic to radio and television as well as resentful of criticism of newspapers and advertising practices. It frequently attacked Democratic programs, an editorial policy apparently going back to wide newspaper opposition to the National Recovery Administration. The periodical increased its attention to developments in advertising and added a line under its cover nameplate that read: "Spot News and Features About Newspapers, Advertisers and Agencies." In the 1980s Robert U. Brown, the president-editor, published *Editor & Publisher* for newspaper publishers, editors, and other employees as well as for people in advertising, marketing, and related industries. Content stressed news items and articles on the newspaper business, its personalities, and printing technology. Circulation in the mid-1980s was about 29,000.

1905. *Variety* founded in New York by Sime Silverman (1873–1933) as a theatrical trade journal. The weekly became probably the most influential show-business trade journal. In the 1980s Editor

Syd Silverman supervised coverage of the radio, television, theater, motion picture, music, and recording industries. Mid-1980s circulation was about 34,800.

1909. *La Follette's Weekly* founded in Madison, Wisconsin, by Robert Marion La Follette (1855–1925) to espouse the Progressive cause. La Follette edited and wrote for the periodical until his death. In 1928 the title was changed to *The Progressive*. Editors included Morris H. Rubin, 1940–1973. Erwin Knoll was editor in 1979 when the magazine, by then a monthly, became defendant in a prior restraint case after it proposed to publish an article telling how to make a hydrogen bomb. After Knoll voluntarily submitted for federal government review the accurate, definitive article based on unclassified sources and authorized visits to U.S. nuclear installations, he was enjoined from publishing it. In *United States v. The Progressive, Inc. et al.* (467 F. Supp. W.D. Wis.), the government contended the article contained technical data analogous to wartime troop movements and violated the Atomic Energy Act of 1954, which prohibited revealing national secrets. Thus, the government argued, the article fell within the narrow exceptions for prior restraints. The *Progressive* argued that it had not violated the Atomic Energy Act since the information was available to the public and, besides, the act was unconstitutionally broad and vague. Thus, the magazine contended, prior restraint was unjustified. The magazine's appeal on the injunction was never ruled on, however, because the government dropped the case after the *Press Connection*, a Madison paper, published information similar to that in the article; but the government warned that by withdrawing it was not approving violation of the act by anyone. Though the *Progressive* in effect won, litigation costs almost bankrupted the financially marginal nonprofit periodical. Media observers feared anticipation of costly defense against government harassment would have a generally chilling effect on publication. In the mid-1980s Knoll was still editor, running articles interpreting domestic and world affairs from the perspectives of the political Left. The *Progressive* continued its original policy of opposing abuses of power by government and by corporate elites, assaults on the environment, and militarism and war, as well as of championing civil liberties and civil rights. Circulation was about 6,000.

1911. *The Masses* (January–) founded in New York as a monthly edited by Socialists and "devoted to the interests of working people." Editor for the first few issues was Piet Vlag. After three months of no issues in fall 1911, a group of Greenwich Village artists and writers headed by Arthur Henry Young (1866–1943) rescued the magazine and named Max Forrester Eastman (1883–1969) editor effective with the December 1912 issue. Eastman, who was editor to 1917, was soon joined by Floyd Dell (1887–1969), who became managing editor, and John

Reed (1887–1920), who wrote the periodical's statement of purpose: "To everlastingly attack old systems, old morals, old prejudices. . . . " Living up to its purpose, the *Masses* supported birth control, feminism, black rights, pacifism, and sexual freedom, often leavening its criticism with humor. Among the many artists and writers contributing without pay were Sherwood Anderson, Jo Davidson, Walter Lippmann, Amy Lowell, Reed, Carl Sandburg, Wilbur Daniel Steele, Louis Untermeyer, Mary Heaton Vorse, and Art Young. As war fever rose, the *Masses* continued to espouse pacifism and socialism, which led the New York City elevated and subway systems to ban the periodical from their newsstands in 1916. Even after the United States entered the war the *Masses* continued its policy; it not only urged President Wilson to push for repeal of the draft, but also appealed for funds to defend agitators against conscription. In August 1917 the Post Office barred the magazine from the mails for an issue containing four antiwar cartoons and a poem defending radical leaders Emma Goldman and Alexander Berkman. Eastman, Dell, Young, and Merrill Rogers, the business manager, were indicted on charges of "conspiracy against the government" and of "interfering with enlistment," but two hung juries failed to convict them under the Espionage Act of June 1917 and the indictments were dismissed (1919). Soon after the government tried to suppress the *Masses*, it was discontinued, only to be revived in March 1918 as the *Liberator*, which embraced Marxism. In 1924 the *Liberator* was turned over to U.S. Communists, who merged it with other Communist publications. In 1926 Joseph Freeman (1897–1965) and Michael Gold revived the original periodical as the *New Masses*, which increasingly followed the Communist Party line. Editors included Freeman, Gold, Granville Hicks, and James Rorty. Circulation rose from 25,000 in 1929 to 36,500 in 1933. In 1934 the monthly switched to weekly frequency. After World War II, increased production costs and increased hostility to Communism in the United States contributed to the periodical's demise in January 1948. Later that year the *New Masses* name was briefly combined with that of the literary quarterly *Mainstream*.

• *Photoplay* founded as the first motion picture fan magazine. It glamorized screen personalities in articles, interviews, and photographs, with glimpses into their private lives. Publisher James R. Quirk ran honestly critical reviews under stills from films, providing a reliable guide to movies. In the 1970s *Photoplay* was part of the Macfadden group.

• *Twentieth Century Magazine* (–1913) founded in Boston by Benjamin Orange Flower (1858–1918), editor for two years, as a reform monthly.

1912. *Poetry* (October–) founded in Chicago by Harriet Monroe (1860–1936), editor 1912–1936, as a monthly for new trends in poetry. About 66 percent of the content was poetry, both conventional and unconventional, and the rest articles, book reviews, criticism, and news. Early contributors included William Rose Benét, Hart Crane, T. S. Eliot, Robert Frost, Vachel Lindsay, Amy Lowell, Archibald MacLeish, Marianne Moore, Ezra Pound, Carl Sandburg, Wallace Stevens, Rabindranath Tagore, William Carlos Williams, Elinor Wylie, and W. B. Yeats, as well as French, Japanese, and other foreign poets. In August 1913 *Poetry* published two of its most anthologized poems: Helen Hoyt's "Ellis Park" and Joyce Kilmer's "Trees." Prominent contributors in the 1930s included poets Conrad Aiken, Paul Engle, Stephen Spender, and Robert Penn Warren. Prominent in the 1940s were John Ciardi, David Cornel DeJong, Robert Lowell, James Merrill, Muriel Rukeyser, Gertrude Stein, and Dylan Thomas. Circulation increased from 2,000 to 4,000 as the periodical went from temporarily modern, illustrated typography back to its classic look. In 1950 Karl Shapiro became editor, to be succeeded in 1955 by Henry Rago. In the 1950s major contributors included Thom Gunn, Stanley Kunitz, Juan Ramon Jiménez, and Delmore Schwartz. In 1966 circulation exceeded 6,000. In the mid-1980s The Modern Poetry Association published *Poetry*, whose editor was Joseph Parisi. Poetry comprised about 75 percent of each issue. The monthly aimed consistently to publish all forms of the best poetry written in English.

1913. *Dress and Vanity Fair* (September–) founded in New York by Condé Nast (1874–1942) as a sophisticated monthly of art, humor, literature, sports, theater, and the like addressed to a select audience. After four issues, its title was shortened to *Vanity Fair*, making it at least the fourth periodical of that name. In 1914 Francis Welch Crowninshield (1872–1947) became editor. Contributors included Cecil Beaton, Robert Benchley, e. e. cummings, T. S. Eliot, Corey Ford, Paul Gallico, Ferenc Molnar (plays), Grantland Rice, Gilbert Seldes, Robert Sherwood, Edward Steichen, Gertrude Stein, and Alexander Woollcott. The magazine reproduced works of Gauguin, Matisse, Picasso, and Rouault. It opened in the 1920s with about 99,000 circulation and closed the decade with about 86,000. In the early 1920s advertising revenue was about $500,000 annually; by 1935 it had slipped to $292,895, despite Nast's efforts (from 1932) to add substance to the content. In 1936 Nast merged *Vanity Fair* into his *Vogue* (f. 1892), for which Frank Crowninshield became arts editor. In March 1983 *Vanity Fair* was revived in New York; the monthly published nonfiction and fiction.

1914. *The Little Review* (March–May 1929) founded in Chicago by Margaret C. Anderson, editor, publisher, and owner to 1929, as a monthly for artistic and literary experimentation. After April 1920 publication was irregular. It was published in Chicago into 1917, except briefly in San Francisco in 1916; in New York City 1917–1926; in Paris,

France, into 1929. The periodical emphasized music and musicians as well as books and writers; it covered theater and introduced new names and works in painting and sculpture, mostly European, with many reproductions. The *Little Review*'s main contribution was introducing foreign talent and trends to U.S. readers. It was best known for a three-year serialization of James Joyce's *Ulysses*, which led to Anderson's conviction for publishing obscenity. Also, the October 1917 issue was suppressed for Wyndham Lewis's story "Cantelman's Spring-mate." Much space was devoted to works by and about Ezra Pound, the foreign editor 1917–1919, 1921–1924. Sherwood Anderson, William Carlos Williams, and William Butler Yeats were also important contributors. Others included T. S. Eliot, Ford Madox Ford, Ben Hecht, Ernest Hemingway, Aldous Huxley, Llewellyn Jones, Vachel Lindsay, Edgar Lee Masters, Dorothy Richardson, and Carl Sandburg. Circulation probably never much exceeded 1,000.

• *The New Republic* founded in New York by Herbert Croly (1869–1930) and Walter Lippmann (1889–1974), with financial assistance by Willard D. Straight (1880–1918), as a liberal opinion journal of public affairs. Croly was editor 1914–1930. Henry Agard Wallace (1888–1965) was editor briefly in the 1940s. The periodical had several owners, including Gilbert A. Harrison (1953), who sold it to Martin Peretz. In 1969 the *New Republic* joined the conservative *National Review* in selling advertising, but the two remained editorially far apart. In 1974 Harrison and Peretz saw a special role for such a journal as the *New Republic*, "which strives to be scrupulous with fact, independent of fashion, and attentive to the lessons of history." In the mid-1980s the weekly covered the arts as well as public affairs and was published in Washington, D.C. Circulation had increased from its founding 875 to 100,000.

Motion Pictures

1902. Electric Theater, opened in a store by Thomas L. Tally of Los Angeles, the first permanent movie theater.

1903. *The Great Train Robbery*, produced by Edwin S. Porter (1870–1941), the first immensely popular and commercially successful film to tell a unified story. Porter also developed parallel story themes, shifted camera angles, and edited the film to create a flow of narrative sequences. In the last scene he revealed a new editing idea, an elliptical jump in time, by omitting the inessential. The eight-minute film ended with a close-up of a bandit firing at the audience, much as three-dimensional movies would use such devices to thrill audiences some fifty years later. Because of this ending it became almost standard practice for the next five years to end a film with a close-up of its leading figure. Another important story film by Porter was *The Life of an American Fireman* (1903), which sequentially depicted a rescue, cutting between interior and exterior shots. Other films by Porter included *Uncle Tom's Cabin* (1903), which was bound by stage and staging; *The Whole Dam Family and the Dam Dog* (1904), a comedy of cleverly combined live action and animation; *The Kleptomaniac* (1904), one of the earliest film dramas of social commentary; and *The Seven Ages* (1905), which used the metaphoric lighting of a firelight glow for the final old-age scene.

1904. Three notable Biograph films produced—*The Great Jewel Robbery*, in which a thief hid in a coffin on a train; and *The Lost Child* and *Personal*, which each had a seriocomic chase.

1905. Nickelodeon, an early movie house, established in Pittsburgh by Harry Davis and John P. Harris. Although nickelodeons were small and sometimes dirty, they were better than former store theaters. At nickelodeons the practice was to have piano music accompany showings. The usual charge was 5 cents. By 1908 an estimated 8 million Americans (c. 8 percent of the population) patronized the approximately 8,000 nickelodeons weekly. A typical 60-minute program consisted of six one-reel films. To keep customers returning, programs were changed several times weekly, even several times daily, creating a need for more films, which gave rise to middlemen who bought or leased films. Producers knew they could market their films, distributors arranged for their most effective circulation, and exhibitors paid less for a larger supply. This three-part film industry structure (with some modifications) continued into the 1980s.

1906. Three notable Biograph films photographed by Billy Bitzer (1872–1944). For *The Black Hand*, a story of organized crime, Bitzer shot on location—Seventh Avenue, New York. (This was a precursor of *On the Waterfront* (1954), *The Godfathers* (1972, 1975), *Mean Streets* (1973), and other later films that depicted organized crime against a real city background.) In *A Kentucky Feud* Bitzer's cinematography created an appropriate visual context for a tale of the Hatfields and McCoys. *The Paymaster* used available light more creatively than any previous film.

1907. *Ben-Hur*, by Kalem (K.L.M.), first produced.

1908. Motion Pictures Patents Company founded by the nine leading film companies of Biograph, Edison, Essanay, Kalem, Lubin, Méliès, Pathé, Selig, and Vitagraph. They agreed to support each other's business procedures, to share legal rights to machine patents, and to keep all other machines and parties out of the business. Distributors who wanted to handle Patents Company films, then the best, had to accept its terms, which included not handling any other producer's films and paying a fee. These film exchanges, which soon became General Film Company, rented only to exhibitors who paid a weekly licensing fee and agreed to show only Patents Company pictures. This monopoly eliminated bargaining and raised prices. Within months two distributors, Carl Laemmle (1867–1939) of New York and William Swanson of Chicago, went independent and urged other film exchanges to do likewise, igniting a trust war in the courts and streets. Producer and distributor William Fox (1879–1952) sued Patents and its General Film for engaging in illegal trust activities. By 1915 the trust was dead. In 1925 the last of the original trust companies, Vitagraph, disappeared, absorbed by Warner Brothers; most of the original independents survived into the 1980s.

● National Board of Censorship founded by the film trust. Later, the board's power undermined by the film trust's demise, the name was changed to National Board of Review. By establishing acceptable principles and standards, the board reduced state and local censorship.

● *The Adventures of Dollie*, directed by David Lewelyn Wark Griffith (1875–1948), a conventional narrative handled with a fluidity and symmetry unusual in contemporary films. Probably Griffith's most famous film was *The Birth of a Nation*, originally *The Clansman* (1915), the story of a southern family victimized by the Civil War. The production cost $125,000, the most invested in a film to then, and went for years unsurpassed in its magnificent conception, acting, sets, and cinematic devices, including cross-cutting, a typical Griffith technique. *Birth of a Nation* was the first "blockbuster" epic in U.S. film history. Griffith's next major film was *Intolerance* (1916), which grew out of his being publicly condemned for his bigoted treatment of blacks in *Birth of a Nation*. The conception and cost—reputedly $2 million—were even greater than that for *Birth of a Nation*. *Intolerance* consisted of four stories tied together by such themes as the triumph of injustice over justice and the prevasiveness of violence through the centuries. Audiences found the film generally unpleasant and confusingly complex; it was a financial disaster. Other Griffith films included *The Devil* (1908); *A Corner in Wheat*, *The Drunkard's Reformation*, and *The Lonely Villa* (1909); *The Two Paths* and *The Way of the World* (1910); *A Country Cupid*, *The Lonedale Operator*, and *Pippa Passes* (1911); *The New York Hat* (1912); *Judith of Bethulia* and *Home Sweet Home* (1914), *Broken Blossoms* (1919); *Way Down East* (1920); *One Exciting Night* (1922); *The Royle Girl* (1926); and *Abraham Lincoln* (1930). The title of a 1931 sound film about alcoholism was changed from *The Struggle* to *Ten Nights in a Barroom* to make it salable.

1909. Newsreel form probably introduced by Pathé *Gazette*.

1912. Audion tube's amplification potential discovered by its inventor, Lee de Forest (1873–1961). This three-element, or triode, vacuum tube (patented 1906) magnified sounds over speakers so an entire audience could hear them, thus stimulating development of sound film. In the early 1920s de Forest developed a sound-on-film process, Phonofilm. By 1923 he was making and showing short synchronized sound films of comedians, politicans, singers, and variety acts.

• *Traffic in Souls*, produced by Carl Laemmle, the first full-length photoplay.

• Keystone Film Company, an independent producer, founded by Mack Sennett (1884–1960). The first feature film was *Tillie's Punctured Romance* (1914), a typical Sennett formula movie with a string of gags hung on a thin plot. Other Keystone Studios films by Sennett included *Mabel's Dramatic Career* and *Barney Oldfield's Race for a Life* (1913); *Getting Acquainted*, *The Knockout*, *The Masquerader*, and *The Rounders* (1914). In 1916 Sennett discontinued Keystone to direct comedies for larger producers. Among those playing in his films (before or after 1916) were Charlie Chaplin, Buster Keaton, Mabel Normand, and Ben Turpin. In 1930 Sennett left directing to become a producer.

• *Queen Elizabeth*, directed by Louis Mercanton, the first Film d'Art seen in United States. Sarah Bernhardt (1844–1924) and members of the Comédie Française performed in this bombastic tale of Elizabeth's love for Essex, whom she must send to the block. The Film d'Art company of France brought together the leading actors, composers, directors, painters, and playwrights of the time to produce such movies, which were filmed as stage plays. *Queen Elizabeth* demonstrated the static staginess of Film d'Art, proving that film acting and stage acting required different techniques. But the six-reeler's huge success proved that long pictures, as well as quality ones, could make money, contrary to the myth promulgated by the Motion Picture Patents Company, which refused to distribute long films. *Queen Elizabeth*'s U.S. distributor was Adolph Zukor (1873–1976).

• Famous Players Film Co. founded by Adolph Zukor; later reorganized as Paramount Pictures, Inc., dominant in the silent era. In the 1930s B. P. Schulberg ran Paramount Studios, a loose organization of directors and writers such as Cecil B. DeMille, Leo McCarey, Preston Sturges, Josef von Sternberg, and Billy Wilder. Stars included W. C. Fields, Jeanette MacDonald, the Marx Brothers, and Mae West.

1913. *What Happened to Mary*, a serial, evidence of growing interest in this type of film.

• *The Squaw Man*, made for the Jesse L. Lasky Feature Play Company, the first film directed by Cecil Blount DeMille (1881–1959). Other films by C. B. DeMille included *Male and Female* (1919), *The King of Kings* (1927), *Sign of the Cross* (1932), *Cleopatra* (1934), *Union Pacific*

(1939), *The Story of Dr. Wassel* (1944), *The Greatest Show on Earth* (1952), and *The Ten Commandments* (1956).

1914. *A Fool There Was*, Theda Bara's well-publicized debut as a "vamp" (sexual vampire).

Radio

1906. Crystal detector, developed by H. H. C. Dunwoody and Greenleaf W. Pickard, the first easily duplicated and inexpensive sound-detecting device. Pickard discovered that one could detect radio waves on a crystal far less expensively than before by using a small metal point, or "cat's whisker," to find the most effective spot. Dunwoody discovered that electricty flowing in only one direction through carborundum converted into pulses that could be heard over earphones. For decades thousands of individuals received radio signals for a few cents worth of cat's whisker, crystal, and wire and the price of earphones. But the crystal set had major disadvantages. It was difficult to find the exact spot on a crystal with a cat's whisker, and the simple receivers could not amplify incoming signals.

● Audion, or triode, vacuum tube patented by Lee de Forest (1873–1961), leading to amplification; critical to development of broadcasting, as well as to high-fidelity music systems, public address systems, and sound film. De Forest added a third grid to the two in the diode tube, which could function as a detector. In 1912 he discovered the Audion's amplification potential. He sold telephone rights to American Telephone & Telegraph, whose engineers improved it for use on long-distance lines, including the first transcontinental one (1915). Audion's greatest value was amplifying weak incoming radio waves so people could listen over loudspeakers instead of just earphones.

● First publicly announced broadcast and transmission of voice by radiotelephony (24 December), by Reginald Aubrey Fessenden (1866–1932). The program for his Brant Rock, Massachusetts, station consisted of music and voice. Fessenden was the first of many experimental broadcasters.

1909. Broadcasting by the first station with a regular schedule of programs; operated by Charles D. Herrold (1876–1948). Early in 1919 Herrold broadcast news reports and musical programs only on Wednesday nights for about one hour; he soon changed to daily programming. "Doc" Herrold also built and distributed receivers for use in hotel lobbies. After passage of the Radio Act of 1912, his station was licensed. During the San Francisco Exposition (1915), it broadcast six to eight hours daily. During World War I it was closed, as were other amateur stations. Herrold reopened the station in December 1921 or January 1922 under call letters KQW. Later KQW was sold and moved to San Francisco, where in the late 1970s it broadcast as the 50,000-watt KCBS. The delay in returning to the air after World War I destroyed the station's claim as the oldest station still operating in the 1980s.

1910. Wireless Ship Act, which called for a radio and operator on ocean-going passenger vessels. This was the first U.S. radio law.

1912. *Titanic* disaster (April). The catastrophe dramatically demonstrated the value of wireless as 700 were saved in mid-Atlantic by another ship responding to the distress call. Within three hours after ramming an iceberg, the "unsinkable" *Titanic* went to the bottom off the Newfoundland Banks with 1,500 passengers and crew. The responding ship had picked up the wireless call 58 miles away, but a much nearer ship did not assist in the rescue because its only radio operator, after many hours on duty, had been asleep when the distress call was transmitted. The disaster not only emphasized the need for radios on ships, but also for enough radio operators to man each radio.

• Second Wireless Ship Act (July), which amended the 1910 Wireless Ship Act, requiring two radio operators on all ships.

• Radio Act (August), the first regulations for land stations and amateur operators. It stipulated public policy and standards of operations. Provisions included that stations be licensed by the secretary of commerce and labor, that government stations had priority, and that transmitter power and wavelengths be selected for minimal interference. The act governed radio, including the still little-known concept of broadcasting, until replaced in 1927.

• Station 2XN in operation at City College of New York by Alfred Goldsmith (1887–1975).

1914–1919

World War I

━━━━━━━━━━━━━━ ‖●‖ ━━━━━━━━━━━━━━

Books, Leaflets

1915. Alfred A. Knopf, publishing house, founded by Alfred Abraham Knopf (1892–1984) and Blanche Knopf with Knopf's father, Samuel (1862–1932), the treasurer. The company emphasized books by outstanding European authors. In 1954 Knopf launched Vintage Books, paperback reprints of prestigious old titles. In 1960 the firm was acquired by Random House (f. 1927).

● First major works by two noted authors. *The Harbor* was a novel by Ernest Poole (1880–1950), whose other works included the study *Great White Hills of New Hampshire* (1946) and the novel *Nancy Flyer: A Stagecoach Epic* (1949). *Spoon River Anthology* was a poetic commentary on urban standards by Edgar Lee Masters (1869–1950), whose other major works included the biography *Vachel Lindsay* (1935) and the autobiography *Across Spoon River* (1936).

1916. *A Heap o' Livin'*, by Edgar Albert Guest (1881–1959), a best seller in this period and later. Edgar A. Guest, a columnist for the Detroit *Free Press*, wrote many volumes of popular verse.

1917. Books by two noted authors. *Renascence and Other Poems*, the first published volume of poems by Edna St. Vincent Millay (1892–1950), exhibited the poet's technical virtuosity. Millay's other major volumes included *The Harp-Weaver and Other Poems* (1923) and *Fatal Interview* (1931). *Java Head*, by Joseph Hergesheimer (1880–1954), was an escapist novel.

● Boni & Liveright (–1928), publishing house, founded by Albert Boni (1892–1981) and Horace Brisbin Liveright (1886–1933). That spring the company announced the "Modern Library," which became famous under the Random House imprint. In 1926 Boni & Liveright and Thomas Seltzer, Inc., merged.

1918. Two best sellers—*The Education of Henry Adams*, by Henry Brooks Adams (1838–1918) and *Dere Mable*, by Edward Streeter (1891–1976). After having been privately printed in 1907, Adams's autobiography was published posthumously. His other major works included *History of the United States* (nine volumes, 1889–1891) and *Mont-Saint-Michel and Chartres* (privately printed 1904, published 1913). Streeter's other books included *That's Me All Over, Mabel* (1919).

1919. Harcourt, Brace & Howe (June–), publishing house, founded in New York by Alfred Harcourt (1881–1954), Donald Brace (1881–1955), and Will D. Howe (1873–1946). After Howe resigned, about a year later, the name was changed to Harcourt, Brace & Co. This was probably the first publishing house giving equal rights to women, especially through the work of unofficial partner Ellen Knowles Eayres. Soon after absorbing the World Book Co. (f. 1905), largest U.S. publisher of educational testing materials, in 1960, Harcourt, Brace became Harcourt, Brace & World. The company expanded, buying control of Canadian and English publishing houses and diversifying into other media as well as into nonmedia interests. When William Jovanovich (1920–) became chairman in 1970, the company became Harcourt Brace Jovanovich.

• Two landmark cases in the establishment of First Amendment rights of freedom of the press and freedom of speech decided by the U.S. Supreme Court. In *Schenck v. United States* (249 U.S. 47), an Espionage Act (1917) case, the Court upheld the convictions of members of the Socialist Party (Philadelphia) for printing and distributing antiwar leaflets urging draftees to join the party and work for repeal of the conscription law. The leaflets also denounced the war as a ruthless adventure for the benefit of Wall Street. Justice Oliver Wendell Holmes (1841–1935) said that a "clear and present danger" existed that the defendants' actions would cause "the substantive evils that Congress has a right to prevent." The same test was applied in *Abrams v. United States* (250 U.S. 616), a Sedition Act (1918) case, to uphold the convictions of five New York radicals for distributing pamphlets condemning U.S. troop intervention in Russia and urging a general strike to prevent production of munitions. Justice John Hessin Clarke (1857–1945) wrote for the majority that the "clear and present danger" rule mandated the convictions. But Justices Holmes and Louis Dembitz Brandeis (1856–1941), dissenting, argued for "free trade in ideas" and the "power of the thought to get itself accepted in the competition of the market." Wrote Holmes: "Only the emergency that makes it immediately danger-ous to leave the correction of evil counsels to time warrants making any exception to the sweeping command, 'Congress shall make no law . . . abridging freedom of speech.'"

● *The American Language* by Henry Louis Mencken (1880–1956), published. Supplements added in 1945 and 1948. Mencken's other major works included *A Book of Prefaces* (1917), *Prejudices* (six series: 1919, 1920, 1922, 1924, 1926, 1927), *James Branch Cabell* (1927), *Selected Prejudices* (1927), and the autobiography *Days of H. L. Mencken* (1947).

● *Jurgen*, by James Branch Cabell (1879–1958), an escapist novel. Major novels by Cabell included *Figures of Earth* (1921). *These Restless Heads* (1932), *Quiet, Please* (1952), and *As I Remember It* (1955) were autobiographical.

● *Winesburg, Ohio*, by Sherwood Anderson (1876–1941), a series of stories about small-town life. Other works by Anderson, a naturalistic writer, included the novels *Poor White* (1920) and *Dark Laughter* (1925) and the autobiographical *A Story-Teller's Story* (1924) and *Sherwood Anderson's Memoirs* (1942).

Newspapers

1915. About 500 U.S. correspondents covering the war in Europe for newspapers, press associations, magazines, and syndicates; about 50 covering the American Expeditionary Force.

1916. Newspaper prices up in most large cities, ending the penny press, due to cost increases for ink, Linotype metal, machinery, postal delivery, etc. All English-language newspapers in Buffalo adopted (December) the 2-cent price; similar increases occurred in Chicago, Philadelphia, Pittsburgh, and elsewhere. The price of Sunday papers in New York City went (February 1918) from 5 cents to 7 cents, then to 10 cents, usually with temporary declines in circulation followed by recovery to previous levels.

1917. Foreign-language publications at their peak, numbering 1,323.

● Committee on Public Information (April–1919) established by President Thomas Woodrow Wilson (1856–1924) to disseminate facts about the war, to coordinate government propaganda efforts, and to serve as government's liaison with newspapers. George Creel (1876–1953) named chairman. Under the CPI's voluntary censorship code, editors agreed not to print material that might aid the enemy. In May the CPI began publishing an Official Bulletin that contained news releases reprinted in newspaper form; circulation rose to 118,000 before the war ended. During the war the CPI issued more than 6,000 news stories.

• Pulitzer Prizes endowed by Joseph Pulitzer (1847–1911), inaugurated by the trustees of Columbia University, to be granted on recommendation of the Advisory Board of the Columbia School of Journalism. The awards were established for "the encouragement of public service, public morals, American literature, and the advancement of education." Awards were to be made not only for journalism but also for biography, drama, music, novels, poetry, and U.S. history.

• Espionage Act (15 June) provided for prosecution of people considered disloyal to the U.S. war cause. Among crimes punishable by heavy fines and imprisonment were willfully making false reports or false statements with intent to interfere with the operation of the armed forces and willfully trying to promote disloyalty in the armed forces or to obstruct recruitment. The act empowered the postmaster general to declare unmailable books, circulars, pamphlets, newspapers, and other printed materials violating the act. The *American Socialist*, *Solidarity*, and other Socialist, as well as German-language, publications were banned from the mails. In the act's first year about 75 papers lost mailing privileges or retained them by agreeing to print nothing more about the war.

• War Revenue Act (3 October), providing for annual increases in postal rates for four years beginning July 1918 and setting up rates by zones for advertising. Rates remained at the 1921 level until 1928, when the pound rate for the first and second zones was reduced to 1.5 cents. By 1928, however, many newspapers had turned to other distribution methods, mainly trucks and carriers.

• Trading-with-the-Enemy Act (October), authorization of censorship of all communications passing in or out of the country. It also provided that the Post Office could require translations of newspaper stories or magazine articles published in foreign languages—a provision to keep German-language papers in line.

• Censorship Board established (October) by President Wilson to coordinate control of communication facilities. The board censored foreign messages, mostly outgoing, sent by cable, telegraph, and telephone.

1918. *Stars and Stripes* (February–) founded in Paris for the American Expeditionary Force in France. Harold Ross (1892–1951) became chief editor, assisted by Grantland Rice and Alexander Woollcott. Other military units overseas, as well as U.S. camps, also had publications. *Stars and Stripes*, the best known, was discontinued abroad in 1919; later that year it was revived in Washington, D.C., where it was suspended in 1926. In 1942 it was revived as the leading G.I. newspaper; eventually it had Pacific and European editions. During the Vietnam war it fought censorship and was criticized for allegedly undermining morale by reporting the truth about Vietnam.

• Sedition Act (May) amending and broadening the Espionage Act (1917). The new law made it a crime to write or publish "any disloyal, profane, scurrilous or abusive language about the form of government of the United States or the Constitution, military or naval forces, flag, or the uniform"; also to use language intended to bring those institutions and ideas "into contempt, scorn, contumely, or disrepute." The post-master general could ban offending publications from the mails, but he exercised that power sparingly. Unpopular pro-German and radical minorities suffered most under the Sedition Act.

• False armistice celebrations (7 November). They were ignited by the erroneous report from United Press Associations, initiated by UP President Roy Wilson Howard (1883–1964) in France. Next day a second cable from Howard announced that the armistice report was unconfirmed.

1919. The demise of many marginal newspapers—those having difficulty making a profit even in prosperous times—because of the rigors of wartime journalism. In this period the total number of dailies, weeklies, semiweeklies, and triweeklies—including foreign-language and class dailies and all weekly periodicals—decreased by one-eighth, for a total reduction of about 2,430.

• *The Watch on the Rhine* (February) founded for the Army of Occupation in Germany. Next to *Stars and Stripes* (f. 1918), it was the most important military paper published abroad in this period.

• New York *Illustrated Daily News* (26 June–) founded by cousins Joseph Medill Patterson (1879–1946) and Robert Rutherford Mc-Cormick (1880–1955). With emphasis on pictures, the morning tabloid (format one-half broadsheet size) emphasized sensational news of crime and sex. Circulation plummeted from 100,000 in the first month to 26,000 in the second despite heavy promotion, including a full page advertisement in the staid New York *Times* headlined: "See New York's Most Beautiful Girls Every Morning in the Illustrated Daily News." Publisher Patterson discovered a potential audience not among readers of the *Times* but among immigrant and poorly educated U.S.-born New Yorkers. Pictures sold the *Daily News* (*Illustrated* dropped after a few months) on stands where only foreign-language publications had been sold. By 1921 circulation was second only to the *Evening Journal's*; in 1924 the *Daily News* attained the highest daily circulation in the United States (750,000). In 1929 circulation hit 1,320,000 and was still growing while competitors' circulations remained stable. Patterson's news enterprise, including aggressive photographic coverage, went beyond shocking people. After the financial crash (1929) the *Daily News* added to its sensationalism coverage of the depression and its effects on people's lives. The paper supported the New Deal until 1940, when it broke with President Roosevelt over involvement in World War II, becoming isolationist. Despite breaking with the Democrats, the *Daily News* remained a paper for the masses. After Patterson's death, McCormick became publisher. Circulation peaked in 1947 at 2,400,000 daily and 4,500,000 Sunday before the paper felt the effects of television and other factors that contributed to a decline in metropolitan newspaper circulations. An attempt to publish an intellectual evening rival (*Tonight*) to the sensational New York *Post* failed, and the *Daily News* suffered in the recession of the early 1980s. After a futile effort to sell the paper in 1982, management stabilized the paper's financial position through economies. Although the morning tabloid had lost 735,000 daily (and 2,180,000 Sunday) circulation since 1950, in 1983 it had a daily circulation (1,513,941) second to the *Wall Street Journal*'s. In 1985 daily circulation was down to 1,346,840, about 600,000 below the *Journal*.

Magazines

1914. Audit Bureau of Circulations formed by union of two older organizations with similar aims—Advertising Audit Association and Bureau of Verified Circulation—to verify circulations of magazines and newspapers for advertisers. Standardized statements told advertisers how a publication obtained its circulation and how many subscribers paid, under what arrangements. ABC also provided data to help advertisers judge circulation quality. ABC could suspend members who padded figures. Through ABC advertisers helped change the attitude of magazine publishers toward circulation figures, which had been a trade secret or data to be taken merely on faith. In the 1980s ABC was a reasonably convincing guarantee of circulation.

● *Mid-Week Pictorial* (9 September–20 February 1937) and *The New York Times Current History of the European War* (December–) founded by the New York *Times*. George Washington Ochs-Oakes (1861–1931), the publisher's brother, was appointed editor of both magazines (1 July 1915). *Mid-Week Pictorial* was a war extra emphasizing news photographs. After World War I it continued as a rotogravure weekly with 32 pages of news pictures. In 1936 its popularity was waning, and after revamping it for the *Times*, Monte Bourjaily bought the periodical. He increased the number of pages to 60, improved the paper quality, and changed the approach, creating a magazine that told its stories in both pictures and text. Circulation jumped from 30,000 (under *Times* ownership) to 117,750. In November 1936 a similar, competing periodical, *Life*, was launched with heavy promotion, and was soon selling a million copies. Bourjaily suspended publication of *Mid-Week Pictorial* until he could revamp it, which he never did. *Current History: A Monthly Magazine of the New York Times*, as the second magazine was retitled in February 1916 after converting from semimonthly publication, treated news as history, to be contemplated in articles and public documents as well as other matter less timely than newspaper content. The first issue contained contributions by famous authors about the controversial war. Early numbers had special titles, such as "Who Began the War and Why?" (second issue). Illustrations consisted of cartoons, photographs, and maps chronicling the war. The amount of war pictures was eventually reduced, leaving them for *Mid-Week Pictorial*. Stories were reprinted from the *Times* or written for the magazine by *Times* correspondents. Outsiders, such as Norman Angell, Rudyard Kipling, and H. G. Wells, also contributed. In 1918 circulation was 76,000, just 4,000 short of its peak (1923). From 1918 *Current History* carried considerable content about the League of Nations. After the war the periodical groped for a new identity. In October 1923 it dropped the newspaper's name from its subtitle. A month later it began drawing on university professors to review world events and heavily promoted the new editorial policy. In the late 1920s *Current History* contained much material on prohibition. Circulation dropped to 61,000 in 1930 and continued a slow, steady decline; there was little advertising. In 1931 the publisher adopted cheaper paper and abandoned illustrations, except cartoons and maps. By the mid-1930s journalists, such as regular contributors Raymond B. Clapper and Ernest K. Lindley, tended to crowd the professors off the pages. In 1936, with circulation at 42,000, the *Times* sold the magazine to Merle Elliott Tracy. The new editor and publisher's issues began in May with better paper and illustrations; larger pages were added later. About half the content concerned foreign affairs; more was run on books and culture. Tracy wrote anti-New Deal editorials. Contributors included Bernard M. Baruch, Winston Churchill, Rexford Guy Tugwell, and Harry A. Overstreet. But circulation continued to decline. In March 1939 Tracy's firm, Current History, Inc., sold the periodical to interests represented by isolationist Joseph Hilton Smyth, who sold it nine months later. In December 1939 the new management headed by E. Trevor Hill, with John T. Hackett co-editor, opposed U.S. participation in the European war. Frequent contributors included James Truslow Adams and Vincent Sheehan. In July 1940 *Forum and Century* was combined with the magazine under the title *Current History and Forum*, which was livelier. The merger temporarily boosted circulation. By June 1941 Hill was urging the United States to assume world leadership. That summer Hill sold to Spencer Brodney, who had been editor 1931–1936. Resuming that position (to 1943), Brodney began afresh with new staff, numbering, policy, and format, which was between that of pocket and regular magazines (format enlarged in 1947). He eliminated illustration.

Analytical and nonpartisan, the new *Current History* was aimed chiefly at students and librarians; it emphasized foreign and international affairs. Beginning in the mid-1950s many special issues were published, and contributors were drawn from college faculties. In 1959 Daniel G. Redmond, Jr., became publisher. In the late 1960s circulation was slightly more than 26,000. As the 1970s ended, Redmond was publishing the monthly of current world affairs in Philadelphia; Carol L. Thompson had become editor in 1955.

1915. *The Midland* (January–March/April/May/June 1933) founded in Iowa City by Raymond H. Durboraw, John Towner Frederick, Ival McPeak, Roger L. Sergel, others. Frederick was editor throughout its existence, except from May to August 1916, when McPeak took over. Although devoted to the depiction and interpretation of the Midwest, *Midland* was nationally significant. It also ran pieces about the Far West, stories set in the East, articles and verse about foreign countries, and universal poetry. It soon gained a reputation for good short stories by unknown writers; contributors also included such known writers as Ruth Suckow and Raymond Weeks. Poetry included works by Witter Bynner, Carolyn Davies, Hazel Hall, Howard Mumford Jones, and Mark Van Doren. Humor and book reviews were also part of the content mix. Frederick sought literature free from the commercialism of the large circulation magazines. One of his co-editors was Frank Luther Mott (1886–1964), 1925–1930, who also served as co-publisher 1926–1930. *Midland* was moved to Moorhead, Minnesota, in 1917; to Glennie, Michigan, in 1919; to Pittsburgh in 1922; and to Chicago in 1931. It was usually published monthly (1915–1917, 1920–1924, 1926–1927), at other times semimonthly or bimonthly; some issues, including the last, were combined. In summer 1933 *Midland* merged with *Frontier*, forming *Frontier and Midland*.

● *Parisienne* and *Saucy Stories* founded by *Smart Set* (f. 1900) publishers Eugene F. Crowe, Henry Louis Mencken (1880–1956), George Jean Nathan (1882–1958), and Eltinge Fowler Warner. *Parisienne* exploited public interest in French culture, stimulated by the war; it was satirical, "cheap in every sense" (Mencken), and attacked in the courts. Both magazines were risqué and financially successful.

● *Picture Play* founded, early movie fan magazine.

1916. *Theatre Arts Magazine* founded in New York; in 1924 became *Theatre Arts Monthly*; discontinued 1964.

1917. American Association of Advertising Agencies founded.

● *Forbes* (15 September–) founded in New York by Bertie Charles Forbes (1880–1954) as a pioneering general business magazine. In 1954 the founder's older son, Bruce Charles Forbes (1916–1964) took over. In 1957 the second son, Malcolm Stevenson Forbes (1919–), became editor in chief, then in 1964 president, and later chairman. In 1974

Forbes launched an annual issue printed in Arabic to let the Arab world know about U.S. business activities. In the 1970s the family-held biweekly of business, finance, and industry ran inspirational stories, concise articles about company actions and trends, items of interest to investors, etc. In the middle 1980s *Forbes* directed its content to managers in U.S. companies as well as private and professional investors in securities. In case histories and intraindustry comparisons, the magazine evaluated managements' personality, philosophy, and style related to growth, profitability, and stock market performance. In the mid-1980s *Forbes* had a circulation of about 770,000.

1919. *Justice* founded; became largest circulation labor magazine. In the 1960s the International Ladies' Garment Workers Union published it semimonthly in New York; circulation was 400,000 (c. 1968). Going into the 1980s, it was published monthly and edited by Meyer Miller. The claimed circulation was 378,882.

● *True Story* (May–) founded in New York by Bernarr Macfadden (1868–1955) as the first major confession magazine. First editor was John Brennan from Macfadden's *Physical Culture* magazine (f. 1899); Brennan selected editorial content for its emotional appeal to women. *True Story*'s cover motto was "Truth is stranger than fiction." Typical stories were "How I Learned to Hate My Parents" and "My Battle with John Barleycorn." Often by amateur writers, narratives were written in first person and simple, homely language; they were serious, true to life, and carried a moral lesson. Macfadden announced that contributors were required to sign affidavits swearing their stories were authentic, and he threatened to prosecute writers falsifying the statements, but few people in the business took him seriously. An advisory board of clergymen served as "censors." Stories were illustrated with posed photographs to heighten the realism. At first members of the editor's family posed. Then young actors and actresses posed for the publicity value; models who later became movie stars included Jean Arthur, Bebe Daniels, Frederic March, and Norma Shearer. As circulation grew, *True Story* spawned imitators, even by its own publisher, who in the 1920s launched *True Experiences* and *Love and Romance*. William Jordan Rapp became editor in 1926, the year *True Story*'s circulation hit 2 million and its advertising revenue $3 million. During the next 20 years Rapp gradually changed editorial emphasis from "sex to social significance," abandoning outright seduction. While retaining the personal tone, he phased out the gross amateurishness. As his readers grew older, he selected more stories about marriage and family, leaving courtship to *True Story*'s sister periodicals. During the depression and World War II he paid more attention to social problems. By war's end *True Story* had departments and features about child care, homemaking, medicine, and national affairs, as well as confessions. In 1941 Orr J. Elder, who had managed the periodical's business side, became head of Macfadden Publications, Inc. When the new management examined the company records, it discovered that in 1940 the magazine's sales had been falsified by an average of 76,697 copies; management voluntarily made restitution to advertisers. Almost every year in the period 1926–1963 *True Story* had a circulation of at least 2 million. In 1963 it was way ahead of other confession magazines with advertising revenues of $3,214,000. For years it was the most profitable Macfadden magazine. Late in the 1960s circulation was about 2,220,600. The periodical continued to carry shocker titles and posed photos, but first-person fiction was done by professional writers. The wide variety of nonfiction appealing to women that also appeared included beauty secrets, charm, children, courtship, dress design, health, marriage, personality, and popularity. *True Story's* editorial philosophy was typical of confession magazines. In the mid-1980s the magazine belonged to the Macfadden Women's Group. Editor Helen Vincent ran fiction and nonfiction about careers, families, love, marriage, social problems, and other subjects of concern to her readers. Vincent's audience consisted of young married, high school–educated, blue-collar women who were home oriented but sought personal fulfillment outside. Monthly circulation was about 1.7 million.

Motion Pictures

1914. Strand, the first movie palace, constructed on Broadway in New York; managed by Samuel L. Rothafel (née Rothapfel), who went on to develop other huge movie theaters carrying his nickname, "Roxy." The Strand had plush, padded chairs and carpeted floors. It was soon followed by Vitagraph (later Criterion). The new theaters could seat more than 2,000.

• *The Last of the Line*, produced by Thomas Harper Ince (1882–1924), a spectacle. Other Thomas Ince films included *The Coward; Keno Bates, Liar*; and *The Taking of Luke McVane* (1915); also *Civilization* and *The Deserter* (1916). His films usually concentrated on narrative flow. Ince was first to divide artistic responsibility for a film between producer and director.

1915. Exclusion of motion pictures from First Amendment protection by the U.S. Supreme Court in *Mutual Film Corp. v. Industrial Commission of Ohio* (236 U.S. 230). Mutual Film, an Ohio distributor, had tried to have the state's censorship statute enjoined as unconstitutional interference with speech and the press. The complaint was rejected by a federal district court, which held that movies were not so protected. After hearing the plaintiff's appeal the Supreme Court upheld the state law, holding that motion pictures were businesses purely for profit and thus not part of the press. (The decision was overturned in 1952.)

• *The Tramp* made for Essanay by Charles Spencer Chaplin (1889–1977). Like most of Charlie Chaplin's short films, *Tramp* contained pointed social commentary in both action and character. Perhaps Chaplin's most famous short was *One A.M.* (1916), in which he played a drunk. His first two sound films were *City Lights* (1931) and *Modern Times* (1936). His other films included *The Bank, Police,* and *A Woman* (1915); *The Count, The Floorwalker,* and *The Pawnshop* (1916); *The Adventurer, Easy Street,* and *The Immigrant* (1917); *A Dog's Life* and *Shoulder Arms* (1918); *The Kid* (1921); *The Pilgrim* (1922); *The Gold Rush* (1925); *The Great Dictator* (1940); *Monsieur Verdoux* (1947); and *Limelight* (1952).

1917. First National Exhibitors Circuit founded by a group of theater owners to counter block booking by Adolph Zukor (1873–1976). Managed by W. W. Hodkinson and J. D. Williams, First National tried to eliminate film production companies from film making (production companies were trying to eliminate independent exhibitors) by contracting with individual stars to make their own films. Such stars as Charlie Chaplin and Harry Langdon gained financial backing and independence, while theatre owners acquired profitable films by well-known names. First National became the third power, behind Marcus Loew (1870–1927) and Zukor, in the control of production, distribution, and exhibition.

• Technicolor Corporation founded with the support of all major film studios; controlled color experiments and filming. Its first film was *Toll of the Sea* (1922). In the 1920s Technicolor was a two-color process in which two strips of film were exposed by two lenses, then bonded in final processing. Scenery and costumes often looked garish, human flesh sickly. Douglas Fairbanks (1883–1939) used the process in *The Black Pirate* (1926) and *Rio Rita* (1929). By 1933 Technicolor had improved its process, using one strip of film sensitive to blue, one sensitive to red, and one to yellow; but it required a bulky three-lens camera for the three rolls of film. *La Cucaracha* (1935) was the first three-color short, *Becky Sharp* (1935) the first three-color feature. Walter E. Disney (1901–1966) made the first Technicolor cartoon, *Trees and Flowers* (1932). In the 1930s color processing was both a monopoly and a guarded secret. As the corporation's artistic director, Natalie Mabelle Dunfee Kalmus (1883–1965), wife of Technicolor inventor Herbert Thomas Kalmus (1881–1963), composed an official aesthetic code binding on a movie's color values. Companies using the process had to employ Natalie Kalmus as "Technicolor Consultant." During World War II the industry took economy measures that usually precluded the luxury of color. Most color films that were made had propaganda value; for example, *The Story of Dr. Wassel* (1944) was a paean to a U.S. war hero, and *Meet Me in St. Louis* (1944) depicted the homespun life the boys were fighting for. In the 1950s color was used to fight black-and-white television. New, competing processes appeared. Eastmancolor, a copy of German Agfacolor, bonded three strips of color-sensitive film into a single roll; an ordinary one-lens camera could be used. Variations of Eastmancolor were De-Luxe, Metrocolor, and Warnercolor. By the 1960s color movies were common, and color was used more to enhance a story than as a gimmick.

• *Reaching for the Moon*, starring Douglas Fairbanks, a parody of intrigue set in little Vulgaria, a fictional European kingdom. Other early Fairbanks films included *His Picture in the Papers* and *Flirting with Fate* (1916). Fairbanks switched from an energetic go-getter to a swashbuckler and sex symbol in later films, including *The Mark of Zorro* (1920), *Robin Hood* (1922), and *The Thief of Bagdad* (1924). His other films included *The Taming of the Shrew* (1929) and *Mr. Robinson Crusoe* (1932).

1919. "Hollywood," collective name for Los Angeles and suburbs where most feature film companies had settled by 1915, producing three-fourths of the world's movies. Movement west had begun in 1907 when independent film makers fled the eastern film trust's thugs. Los Angeles was not only a long way from New York, the previous film capital, but also near Mexico, to where trust evaders could flee with machines and negatives. By the early 1920s, most major film companies—Columbia, Fox, Metro-Goldwyn-Mayer, Paramount, Universal, Warner Brothers—were regularly taking advantage of the visual appeal of southern California's deserts, mountains, ocean, plains, and dependable sun.

• United Artists Corporation founded by Charles Chaplin, Douglas Fairbanks, David Lewelyn Wark Griffith (1875–1948), and Mary Pickford, née Smith (1893–1979), to control their careers and earnings. Each founder separately produced his or her own films, which were distributed by United Artists. The idea was years ahead of its time; it foreshadowed commercial practices of 1960s–1970s. In the 1980s major studios were chiefly distributors of pictures filmed by independent producers.

Radio and Television

1915. Transmission of radio signals across the Atlantic Ocean from the navy station in Arlington, Virginia, by American Telephone &

Telegraph Company. The signals were picked up as far west as Honolulu. Similar experimentations continued throughout World War I.

• General Electric agreed to sell Alexanderson alternators exclusively to British Marconi. Ernst Frederik Werner Alexanderson (1878–1975), a GE engineer, had built the alternator, a huge high-speed generator of alternating currents for use as a transmitter; it was the first reliable means of long-range wireless communication. Final GE-Marconi agreement was delayed by the war. In March 1919 negotiations resumed, with Marconi still demanding exclusivity, which would give it monopoly on radio communications with Europe. To protect U.S. interests, the navy intervened and GE formed the Radio Corporation of America (1919), Americanizing broadcast development.

• American Radio Relay League founded as an association of amateur operators; established magazine QST. The league became politically influential. During wartime its members served as trained operators. The League as a whole was an important group of listeners, and its members contributed to technological advances.

• Experimental station 9XM, since 1909 an unlicensed experimental transmitter, licensed to University of Wisconsin; operated by Professors Edward Bennett and Earl M. Terry. The station provided telegraphic weather forecasts and market reports for midwestern farmers and Great Lakes mariners. One of the few civilian stations allowed to broadcast during World War I, 9XM assisted in training navy radio personnel and provided weather reports. Resumption of civilian broadcasting apparently began between 29 September 1920–19 January 1921. In 1922 9XM became WHA. In 1985 it was the oldest educational station in the United States.

1916. "Radio Music Box" memorandum prophesied commercial broadcasting into homes. Most industry leaders believed the future lay in narrowcasting (point-to-point communication), but David Sarnoff (1891–1971), commercial manager of American Marconi, disagreed. In a memo to his general manager, Edward J. Nally, Sarnoff proposed wireless transmission of music into homes where people could listen to a table-top set with simple controls for changing to several wavelengths. Wrote Sarnoff: "There should be no difficulty in receiving music perfectly when transmitted within a radius of 25 to 50 miles. . . . The same principle can be extended to several other fields as, for example, receiving of lectures at home . . . events of national importance. . . . " American Marconi officials, interested only in international and ship radio for private messages, filed the memo, forgotten for many years.

• Daily music broadcasts begun by Lee de Forest (1873–1961), from his transmitter in New York. De Forest broadcast presidential election returns 7 November 1916, ending with the estimate that Charles Evans

Hughes had defeated Woodrow Wilson. Despite the error, broadcast of such important news was a landmark in radio's development.

• Experimental station 8XK, founded by Dr. Frank Conrad (1874–1941), on the air in Pittsburgh. It was dismantled for the war (1917–1918) and reopened in 1919. Dr. Conrad, engineer for Westinghouse Manufacturing Company, apparently initiated postwar broadcasting by playing phonograph records, beginning 17 October 1919. After many requests, he began transmitting music two hours on Sunday and Wednesday evenings, sometimes adding live vocals or instrumentals by his young sons or reporting sports scores. Westinghouse saw a new market for its radio sets and applied for the first full commercial license, which the U.S. Department of Commerce granted 27 October 1920. KDKA, 8XK's successor, began broadcasting 2 November 1920 with returns of the Cox-Harding presidential election, using bulletins phoned in from the Pittsburgh *Post*. To stimulate public interest in buying radio receivers, KDKA achieved such radio firsts (1921) as broadcasting market reports, orchestra music, political speeches, public service announcements, and sports events. Westinghouse also opened stations in Boston, Chicago, New York, and Philadelphia. In 1923–1924 the company conducted pioneer network experiments. Shortwave transmissions connected KDKA to satellite stations KDPM, Cleveland, and KFXX, Hastings, Nebraska. With higher power that winter KDKA relayed programs to a station in Manchester, England, for rebroadcast. In the 1980s KDKA was the oldest operating station in the United States.

1917. After the United States entered the war (6 April 1917) most nongovernmental radio operations closed. The navy took over all high-powered stations for national security. It censored wireless communications and suffered shortages of high-quality equipment and trained radio personnel. The personnel shortage was solved through recruiting amateur operators and establishing radio schools; by Armistice (11 November 1918) about 7,000 men had been trained and 3,400 were in training. These people plus thousands of hams influenced postwar developments. So that the best equipment (including triode tube) could be made for wartime use, the government indemnified companies for patent infringement, in effect creating a patent pool. Technological advances during the war included lightweight vacuum tube transmitters and receivers.

1919. Congressional hearings (May–June) about the government's role in the future of wireless. Issues included what to do about employment for mustered-out radio operators, monopoly, patent pool, war factories. A push for government control of wireless was unsuccessful. President Thomas Woodrow Wilson (1856–1924) ordered (11 July) all government-seized stations returned to their owners effective 1 March 1920; amateurs allowed back on the air 1 October 1919.

• Coast-to-coast telephone service established.

● Radio Corporation of America founded (October) by American Telephone & Telegraph, General Electric, and Westinghouse to prevent foreign control of international radio communication. Encouraged by the government, particularly the navy, the three founding companies purchased British-owned Marconi patents for radio equipment, which they pooled with their own patent rights in the new RCA. The 1 July 1920 patent pooling agreement among RCA, GE, and AT&T resulted in legal commercial sale of triode vacuum tubes for the first time. Originally, RCA's primary role was as an instrument of U.S. international communication policy; RCA would operate stations while GE manufactured radio equipment. At first RCA was devoted to wireless message service, operating a worldwide radio-telegraph system. Eventually, RCA acquired Victor phonograph interests and established the RCA-Victor manufacturing unit to make phonographs, radio sets, and tubes. On 30 June 1921 RCA concluded a cross-licensing agreement with Westinghouse, bringing the latter into the patent pooling agreement. Using Westinghouse patents, GE could now manufacture and RCA sell radio receivers to the public, and AT&T could manufacture transmitters and use radio telephony domestically. The navy could deal with one company instead of several. Almost 2,000 patents were pooled. In 1923 RCA assumed control of WJZ, Newark, New Jersey, then opened WJY, New York City. It also owned WRC, Washington, D.C. RCA had no direct income from its three stations, usual for station owners in that period. In 1926 AT&T withdrew from the GE-RCA-Westinghouse consortium (Radio Group) to concentrate on telephone communication with its manufacturing arm, Western Electric (Telephone Group). In September 1926 RCA consolidated its broadcasting interests into what it called the National Broadcasting Company; Merlin Hall Aylesworth (1886–1952) became president (to 1936). NBC inaugurated regular network (or "chain") broadcasts 15 November 1926. In December NBC formed a second network, based at WJZ. On 1 January 1927 the two networks joined to produce the first coast-to-coast broadcast, a Rose Bowl football game announced by Graham McNamee. The two NBC networks were the superior Red (flagship WEAF) with 22 affiliates and the inferior Blue (flagship WJZ) with 6 affiliates—a total of almost 7 percent of all stations. In April 1927 NBC began a third chain, Pacific Coast Network, based on San Francisco stations KGO and KPO, ranging from Los Angeles to Seattle. It was organized chiefly for sales rather than programming and closed in late 1928, when NBC established full-time coast-to-coast programming on both its Red and Blue networks, linking 58 stations. Early in 1930 GE, RCA, and Westinghouse joined their manufacturing of radio receivers, leading the U.S. Department of Justice to file an antitrust suit (May). At the time RCA was the most important force in radio manufacturing and broadcasting. Under a consent decree GE and Westinghouse disposed of their RCA holding (1932), leaving RCA an independent manufacturing, selling, broadcasting, and international communication company. RCA gained complete ownership of NBC. As a convenience, RCA continued to administer the no-longer exclusive patent pool. In 1931, meanwhile, RCA had transmitted a 120-line (low-resolution) television picture; quality increased steadily. In 1932 RCA built a TV studio in New York to house experimental station 2XBS, while it continued to expand its radio networks. In 1933 Red had 28 stations, Blue 24; 36 were supplemental. The 88 stations comprised almost 15 percent of all stations in the nation. The more important Red, called "NBC" over the air, had the choice stations and programming as well as more advertising than Blue, called "the Blue Network," which carried mostly sustaining (unsponsored) programs. NBC owned 10 stations: WEAF (later WRCA, then WNBC) and WJZ (later WABC) in New York; WMAQ and WENR in Chicago; KPO and KGO in San Francisco; WRC and WMAL in Washington, D.C.; KOA (later sold) in Denver; and WTAM (later WKYC) in Cleveland. In 1934 the two networks had 127 affiliates. In a city with two owned and operated (O&O) stations, one was Red, one Blue. NBC programmed both its O&Os and its affiliates against each other and engaged in price cutting that few other stations could match, giving NBC a strong advantage in the industry (until 1943). In 1935 RCA announced a multimillion dollar TV research program. That year NBC turned a studio into a large TV production area, and the next year RCA formed experimental station W2XF. In 1937 W2XF sent a mobile unit into New York's streets and in 1938 made its first live telecast, of a fire. Putting millions of dollars into research and patent acquisition, RCA worked toward standardization of TV for commercial purposes, with the goal of selling receivers. At the New York World's Fair (1939) RCA made the first large public demonstration of electronic TV, and Franklin Delano Roosevelt became the first U.S. president to appear on TV. David Sarnoff, RCA operating head, demonstrated a 441-line (high-resolution) system. On 23 March 1940 the Federal Communications Commission granted RCA limited commercial TV, and the corporation raced ahead manufacturing and selling sets, hoping their widespread sale would make FCC consideration of any other standard than RCA's futile. Opponents launched a legal and political offensive, and on 3 May 1941 the FCC ordered a superior standard, opening industry development of TV. In 1943 RCA suffered another setback when the U.S. Supreme Court upheld (May) chain broadcasting rules that limited ownership, and the FCC forced NBC to sell either network. In July 1943 Edward J. Noble (1882–1958) purchased the Blue, which he named (1945) the American Broadcasting Company. After World War II RCA worked within the industry for acceptance of its TV standards, then reaped the benefits from TV's rapid expansion to sell sets and collect huge royalties on patents. FCC approved RCA's all electronic compatible color system in December 1953, but too few color programs existed for RCA to sell many of its expensive, complicated receivers. While developing TV, RCA had diversified, and in the 1960s and 1970s economic reverses led management to drop out of computer and space activities to concentrate on electronics. In the early 1970s RCA briefly tried to sell NBC's radio stations and network but could not find an acceptable buyer of the package. In 1975 NBC started a radio News and Information Service— a 24-hour all-news network for affiliates and any stations that would buy it, but an insufficient number of takers ended the venture in 1977. In the early 1980s NBC still was only one of RCA's subsidiaries, which included book publishers, recording agencies, and nonmedia firms. RCA was also involved with pay cable, satellites, and other video enterprises. In December 1985 plans were announced for GE to buy RCA.

1920–1929

The Jazz Age

=ıı●ıı=

Books, Pamphlets

1920. Two best sellers—*The Americanization of Edward Bok*, by Edward William Bok (1863–1930), and *Main Street*, by Harry Sinclair Lewis (1855–1951). Other books by Edward W. Bok (editor of the *Ladies' Home Journal* 1889–1919) included *Why I Believe in Poverty* (1915), *A Man from Maine* (1923), *Twice Thirty* (1924), *Dollars Only* (1926), and *Perhaps I Am* (1928). Sinclair Lewis's *Main Street*, also a later best seller, was a novel depicting small-town petty meanness. Other best sellers by Lewis, the first U.S. author to receive the Nobel Prize for literature (1930), included *Elmer Gantry* (1927) and *Kingsblood Royal* (1947). Among his other works were *Babbitt* (1922), *Arrowsmith* (1924), *Dodsworth* (1929), *It Can't Happen Here* (1935), and *Gideon Planish* (1943).

● *This Side of Paradise*, Francis Scott Key Fitzgerald's first novel, an expression of jazz-age cynicism. Other novels by F. Scott Fitzgerald (1896–1940) included *The Beautiful and the Damned* (1922), *The Great Gatsby* (1925), *Tender Is the Night* (1934), and *The Last Tycoon* (1941). He also published five volumes of short stories.

1921. *The Brimming Cup*, by Dorothea Frances Canfield Fisher (1879–1958), a best seller. Dorothy Canfield's many other books included the novel *The Bent Twig* (1915), three volumes of short stories, a children's book, a translation, and essays and studies in education and literature.

1922. *Etiquette*, by Emily Price Post (1873–1960), a best seller in this period and after. More editions followed.

● *The Waste Land*, by Thomas Stearns Eliot (1888–1965), Eliot's major poetic work. Two other books published before T. S. Eliot became a British subject in 1927 were *Poems* (1919) and *The Sacred Wood* (1920), one of his major works of criticism. His other major volumes included *Ash-Wednesday* (1930), poetry, and *Murder in the Cathedral* (1935), a play; both showed concern for the Church of England.

1923. *Cane* by Jean Toomer (1894–1969), a collection of rural sketches and the author's best known volume. Toomer was part of the 1920s Harlem Renaissance.

1924. Simon & Schuster (January–), founded in New York by Richard Leo Simon (1899–1960) and Max Lincoln Schuster (1897–1970), a leading publishing house. In 1966 Simon & Schuster bought Pocket Books, a pioneer paperback book publisher.

• *So Big* by Edna Ferber (1887–1968), a best seller and Pulitzer Prize winner. Ferber's *Cimarron* (1930) was a best seller too. Her other major works included *Show Boat* (1926), *Saratoga Trunk* (1941), and *Giant* (1952), novels, as well as *One Basket* (1947), one of three volumes of short stories.

• *How to Write Short Stories* and *The Love Nest* by Ringgold Wilmer Lardner (1885–1933), collections of short stories. Ring Lardner's other books included *What of It* (1925), *Round Up* (1929), and *First and Last* (1934).

• Two notable volumes of poetry published—*Chills and Fevers*, by John Crowe Ransom (1888–1974), and *Tamar*, by John Robinson Jeffers (1887–1962). Ransom's other books included *Selected Poems* (1935); Jeffers's, *The Selected Poetry of Robinson Jeffers* (1938).

1925. Three best sellers published: *Gentlemen Prefer Blondes*, by Anita Loos (1893–1981); *The Man Nobody Knows*, by Bruce Barton (1886–1967); and *The Private Life of Helen of Troy*, by John Erskine (1879–1951). Other works by Barton included *Better Days* (1924), *The Book Nobody Knows* (1926), *What Can a Man Believe?* (1927), and *On the Up and Up* (1929). Other volumes by Erskine included *Galahad* (1926), *Adam and Eve* (1927), and *Penelope's Man* (1928).

• *Barren Ground* by Ellen Anderson Gholson Glasgow (1874–1945), the author's first major novel, although she had 12 novels previously published. In many works Ellen Glasgow analyzed ironies of decaying Virginia society. Her later works included *The Romantic Comedians* (1926) and *In This Our Life* (1941), novels; *A Certain Measure* (1943), essays; and *The Woman Within* (1954), autobiography.

• First *Cantos* by Ezra Loomis Pound (1885–1972) published. Ezra Pound, a leader of the Imagists, worked on the *Cantos*, poetic syntheses of the world's cultural history, into the 1960s.

• *Manhattan Transfer* by John Roderigo Dos Passos (1896–1970), a notable example of the author's maturing work. John Dos Passos's other major novels included *Three Soldiers* (1921) and the *U.S.A.* trilogy

(1930, 1932, 1936); another important volume, *The Ground We Stand On* (1941), concerned social theory.

• *Gitlow v. People of the State of New York* (268 U.S. 652). In this decision the U.S. Supreme Court upheld the conviction of Benjamin Gitlow, who violated a New York State criminal anarchy law by issuing Socialist manifestos, including the *Left Wing Manifesto*. More significantly, the conservative majority stated that it was proper for the Supreme Court to extend First Amendment protections to the states under the Fourteenth Amendment; this landmark theory was applied to later cases concerning freedom of the press.

1926. Two major book clubs founded: the Book-of-the-Month Club, by Harry Scherman (1887–1969), and the Literary Guild of America, by Harold Guinzburg (1889–1961). The clubs were examples of a major post-World War I distributing trend. Their quick success inspired imitators: by 1947 there were more than 50 clubs; by the 1970s there were more than 100 book club companies, some operating several clubs.

• Two best sellers in this period and later—*The Story of Philosophy*, by William James Durant (1885–1981), and *Topper*, by Thorne Smith (1892–1934).

• *Abraham Lincoln: The Prairie Years*, by Carl August Sandburg (1878–1967), published in two volumes, beginning the author's monumental Lincoln biography. Carl Sandburg won a Pulitzer Prize for history for *Abraham Lincoln: The War Years* (1939), in four volumes. Sandburg's other major works included *Complete Poems* (1950), another Pulitzer winner; *Remembrance Rock* (1948), a historical novel; and *Always the Young Strangers* (1952), an autobiography.

• *The Sun Also Rises*, by Ernest Miller Hemingway (1899–1961), the author's first novel. It depicted U.S. expatriots in Europe. Ernest Hemingway's *For Whom the Bell Tolls* (1940) was a best seller when published and after. Other major volumes included the short story collection *Men Without Women* (1927) and the novels *A Farewell to Arms* (1929) and *The Old Man and the Sea* (1952). Hemingway won the Nobel Prize for literature in 1954.

• *Weary Blues* by James Langston Hughes (1902–1967) published. Langston Hughes was probably the most popular poet of the 1920s Harlem Renaissance. His volumes included *Not Without Laughter* (1930), *The Dream Keeper* (1932), *The Ways of White Folks* (1934), and *Shakespeare in Harlem* (1942). *The Big Sea* (1940) was autobiographical.

1927. Random House (January–) founded in New York by Bennett Alfred Cerf (1898–1971) and Donald Klopfer to create and distribute "books of typographical excellence." Their first book, published in January 1928, was Voltaire's *Candide*. Random House published the Modern Library series. To survive the depression the firm became a trade publisher. In 1960 Alfred A. Knopf, Inc. (f. 1915), merged with Random House, becoming an autonomous division. Soon afterward, the firm further expanded, acquiring Pantheon Books and L. W. Singer Co., a major publisher of elementary and high school textbooks. Also Random House organized Blaisdell Publishing Co., Inc., to specialize in engineering, mathematics, and scientific books (division later sold to Ginn & Co.). In 1965 the Radio Corporation of America acquired Random House, which was reorganized, Robert Bernstein replacing Cerf as president. In 1973 the acquisition of Ballantine Books gave Random House a mass paperback division. In 1980 RCA sold Random House to the S. I. Newhouse newspaper group.

• *The Bridge of San Luis Rey*, by Thornton Niven Wilder (1897–1975), a best-selling novel that won a Pulitzer Prize. Another major novel by Thornton Wilder was the *Ides of March* (1948). Two of his major plays were *Our Town* (1938) and *The Skin of Our Teeth* (1942), a Pulitzer winner.

• *Home to Harlem*, by Claude McKay (1890–1948). This won the poet recognition as a novelist. Other major works by McKay, a member of the 1920s Harlem Renaissance, included *Harlem Shadows* (1922) and *Banjo* (1929).

1928. *The Art of Thinking*, by Ernest Dimnet (1866–1954), a best seller. Dimnet was a French abbé who wrote many books in English.

• *John Brown's Body*, by Stephen Vincent Benét (1898–1943), a Pulitzer Prize-winning narrative poem of the Civil War. Benét's other major works included *The Devil and Daniel Webster* (1937), a play; *America* (1944), history; the two-volume *Selected Works* (1942) and *The Last Circle* (1946), collections.

1929. Four best sellers—*Bambi*, by Felix Salten, pseudonym of Felix Salzmann (1869–1945), Hungarian writer; *Believe It or Not*, by Robert Leroy Ripley (1893–1949), also a later best seller; *The Cradle of the Deep*, by Joan Lowell (1902–1969); and *The Magnificent Obsession*, by Lloyd Cassel Douglas (1877–1951). Other best sellers by Lloyd C. Douglas were *Green Light* (1935), *The Robe* (1942), and *The Big Fisherman* (1949). The last was reissued in 1953, when it again was a best seller.

• *Look Homeward, Angel*, by Thomas Clayton Wolfe (1900–1938), an autobiographical novel of Thomas Wolfe's youth. His other major works included *Of Time and the River* (1935), *The Story of a Novel* (1936), *The Web and the Rock* (1939), *You Can't Go Home Again* (1940), and *The Hills Beyond* (1941). Wolfe's fiction was known for its brooding depths, lyrical passages, and satirical portraits.

• *The Sound and the Fury* by William Faulkner (1897–1962), a major novel. Faulkner's others included *As I Lay Dying* (1930), *Sanctuary* (1931), *Light in August* (1932), and *Intruder in the Dust* (1948). Faulkner's published works included eighteen novels, four volumes of short stories, and three volumes of poems and essays. He won the Nobel Prize for literature in 1949.

Newspapers

1920. German-language press reduced to 258 publications by impact of World War I—from 627 in 1910. They had peaked at 750 in 1890.

● Newspaper Classified Advertising Managers Association founded, reflecting growth in newspaper advertising.

1921. Washington *Daily News* founded by Scripps-McRae League as a nonsalacious evening tabloid; edited for many years by Lowell Mellett.

1922. American Society of Newspaper Editors founded under the leadership of Casper S. Yost, editor of the St. Louis *Globe-Democrat*, to consider common problems of large newspapers and to promote professional ideals. The original 107 members were editors in chief, editorial page editors, and managing editors of newspapers in cities of at least 100,000 population. At their first annual meeting (1923), they adopted a code of ethics, the "Canons of Journalism," which called for accuracy, decency, fairness, impartiality, independence, sincerity, and truthfulness. In 1923 ASNE began publishing its proceedings in a series of books, *Problems of Journalism*. The association also published the *ASNE Bulletin*. In 1924 membership was opened to editors of newspapers in cities of at least 50,000, increasing the size to 174. Later editors of smaller dailies were admitted. After World War II ASNE campaigned for freedom of access to government information and for photographers' access to courtrooms.

● North American Newspaper Alliance (–1980) founded by 50 major U.S. and Canadian newspapers. It became a leading specialized news agency. NANA was originally managed by Loring Pickering, Jr.; later by John N. Wheeler, who also headed the Bell Syndicate (f. 1913). Associated Newspapers, Inc. (f. 1912), Consolidated News Features, Inc. (f. 1920), and McClure Syndicate (f. 1884) eventually linked with NANA and Bell, which retained their separate identities under unified administration. In 1976 NANA had 41 clients.

● Baltimore *Post* founded by Scripps-Howard.

1923. Tabloid boom. Tempted by the success of the New York *Daily News* (f. 1919), publishers in other cities tried the tabloid format in new or revamped eight-column papers; between 1919 and 1924 11 tabloids appeared in nine other cities. In 1923 the Los Angeles *Illustrated News* and San Francisco *Illustrated Herald* were founded by Cornelius Vanderbilt, Jr., as nonsalacious, nonsensational picture tabloids. The

Illustrated News was soon sold to Manchester Boddy; the *Illustrated Herald* was discontinued in 1926.

1924. Two major sensational picture tabloids founded in New York: *Daily Mirror* (June–1963) by William Randolph Hearst (1863–1951) and *Evening Graphic* (15 September–1932) by Bernarr Macfadden (1868–1955). The *Daily Mirror* imitated the New York *Daily News* (f. 1919). The *Mirror* resuscitated a four-year-old murder case in New Jersey involving a New Brunswick minister, Edward Hall, and his choir-member sweetheart, Eleanor Mills, both of whom had been found dead, ostensibly suicides, in 1922. The *Mirror* scored a beat with pictures of the arrest of Hall's widow, who was tried for the murders. New Brunswick became an important news center, with about 200 reporters covering the trial. (Mrs. Hall was acquitted.) In 1928 Hearst sold the paper to Alexander P. Moore (1867–1930), then in 1930, after Moore's death, took it back. To strengthen coverage, Hearst installed Arthur Brisbane (1864–1936) as editor, 1934–1935, and hired gossip columnist Walter Winchell from the *Evening Graphic*. The *Mirror* never was profitable. Under Editor Emile Gauvreau, the *Daily Graphic* was the most lurid and notorious tabloid. It eschewed a press association and fed readers a "hot-news" diet of murders and scandals. Applying confession-story techniques successful in Macfadden's *True Confessions* magazine, *Graphic* reporters wrote first-person stories signed by newsmakers, and editors wrote such headlines as "For 36 Hours I Lived Another Woman's Love Life," "I Know Who Killed My Brother," and "He Beat Me—I Love Him." The paper became known as the "Porno-Graphic." One of its innovations was the "composograph," a faked photograph (by combining pictures) of what might have happened. Although from the beginning the *Graphic* had sold well on newsstands, it lost millions of dollars.

● New York *Daily Worker* founded as a Communist Party paper. Circulation was about 100,000 in the late 1930s, down to 5,600 in 1958, when the paper became a weekly and the name changed to *The Worker*. It then became the *Daily World*, a daily, in 1968 and issued a weekly supplement.

1925. Miami, Florida, *Illustrated Daily Tab* (–1926) founded by Cornelius Vanderbilt, Jr.; third in his projected but unsuccessful chain of nonsalacious, nonsensational tabloids.

● Two tabloids founded in Philadelphia: *Daily News*, taken over late 1925 by Bernarr Macfadden, and *Sun* (–1928), by Cyrus Hermann Kotzschmar Curtis (1850–1933).

1926. New York *National Enquirer* founded by William Randolph Hearst as the only Sunday afternoon newspaper in the city; sensational. After several owners, Generoso (Gene) Pope, Jr., acquired the paper in 1952, when circulation was 17,000. With sensational content similar to Hearst's paper—playing up gore, mutilation, perversion, and the like—

Pope built circulation to 1 million by 1962. To make the tabloid salable in convenience stores and especially supermarkets, Pope toned down the sensationalism, shifting emphasis to features on celebrities, health, psychiatric advice, psychic predictions, and romance. Stories about UFOs and medical treatments were staples. Circulation soared. In 1971 Pope moved the *National Enquirer*'s headquarters to Lantana, Florida. With circulation exceeding 5 million, the paper switched to color in 1979, printing in rotogravure in Buffalo and Dallas plants. By 1980 the *National Enquirer* ranked fourth among weekly magazines in circulation and sixteenth among consumer magazines in total gross revenues. Pope paid the highest editorial salaries of any U.S. publication. In the 1970s and early 1980s the paper was a defendant in several libel or privacy suits by celebrities, including Carol Burnett, who won a large judgment for libel. To counter criticism of inaccuracy, the *National Enquirer* in 1977 set up a research department of almost 30 persons who checked stories for accuracy. In the early 1980s the weekly tabloid was edited by Iain Calder, who ran pieces appealing to a mass audience. Content included stories about health and scientific breakthroughs, personalities, the occult, and how government wasted taxpayers' money. Human drama was emphasized. Publisher was James B. Martise, advertising director Ralph S. Gallagher. In the 1985 "Folio: 400" the *National Enquirer* ranked thirteenth among all consumer magazines and fifth among general-interest magazines in total revenue ($178,881,000); rankings by circulation (4,612,927, down 5.7 percent from 1983) were fourteenth and fourth, respectively.

1929. Chicago *Daily Illustrated Times* (September–), founded by Samuel Emory Thomason, the most important tabloid daily founded after the New York tabloid war among the *News*, *Graphic*, and *Mirror*. First editor was Richard L. Finnegan. The Windy City's first tabloid, the afternoon *Times* avoided crass sensationalism in favor of fair, lively reporting. Democratic, it supported President Roosevelt's New Deal during the depression and gained steadily in circulation. After Thomason died, Marshall Field III (1893–1956) bought (1948) the *Times* and merged it with his *Sun* (f. 1941) to form the morning tabloid *Sun-Times*.

● Detroit *Daily* (–1932) founded by Bernarr Macfadden as a tabloid; later sold to Joseph Medill Patterson (1879–1946) and Robert Rutherford McCormick (1880–1955) and named the *Mirror*.

Magazines

1920. *The Freeman* (17 March–5 March 1924) founded in New York by Francis Neilson and Albert Jay Nock, editors throughout its life, with financial backing of Mrs. Helen Swift Neilson, the co-founder's wife. (Nock did most of the work.) The weekly advocated intelligent, peaceful anarchy and opposed direct political action. It was open-minded to labor unions and forms of industrial organization that might circumvent government controls. Its radicalism dwindled as it aged. The *Freeman*'s wide variety of thought-provoking, witty content included articles, commentary, and editorials on economic, political, and social affairs; translations from German and Russian; light essays, short fiction; verse; and book reviews. Literary editor for 1921–1924 (except for six months in 1923) was Van Wyck Brooks. Contributors included the publisher, B. W. Huebsch (1876–1964), Lewis Mumford, Harold Stearns, John Dos Passos, Arthur Gleason, and Constance Rourke. In 1930 a *New Freeman* was founded in New York by Peter Fireman, with Nock as "contributing editor" and Clara Suzanne La Follette, associate editor (1921–1924) of the original *Freeman*, as editor. The new periodical attracted some contributors from the original, which it resembled. Too pro-Soviet for 1930, however, the *New Freeman* was discontinued after 14 months. Circulation had reached about 10,000. In the early 1980s another *Freeman* was edited in Irvington-on-Hudson, New York, by Paul L. Poirot for readers interested in limited government and in private enterprise. This monthly's aim was to present in scholarly analyses the case for individual responsibility and choice in a free market economy.

• *Screenland* founded for movie fans.

1921. *Love Story* (May–) founded by Amita Fairgrieve for Street & Smith as a quarterly; semimonthly then weekly. In 1928 Daisy Bacon began more than 20 years as editor. The romance magazine emphasized love without illicit sex. Its formula was widely imitated.

1922. *The Reader's Digest* (February–) founded in New York by DeWitt Wallace (1889–1981), editor, and Lila Acheson Wallace (1889–1984) as a pocket-size monthly of condensed articles from intellectual, general, and women's magazines. According to the cover of the first issue, DeWitt Wallace aimed to provide "thirty-one articles each month from leading magazines—each article of enduring value and interest, in condensed and compact form." He ran no fiction. As circulation grew from the initial press run's 5,000, headquarters was moved to Pleasantville, New York. At first Wallace reprinted articles with the permission of publications merely for the publicity provided by an appearance in *Reader's Digest*. Then he began paying an annual fee for digest and reprint rights. Eventually, Wallace paid both the publication and the author for articles reprinted. In 1933 *Reader's Digest* began producing a limited number of original articles because some magazines Wallace had drawn on had been discontinued, a few others (e.g., *New Yorker*) had refused reprint rights, and a limited supply existed of the folksy, humorous, inspirational, optimistic, sentimental, and journalistically provocative material that Wallace wanted. Staff and free-lance writers' articles were placed in other publications, then condensed and reprinted in *Reader's Digest*. In the early 1930s Wallace also began such departments as "Drama in Everyday Life," "Life in These United States," and "My Most Unforgettable Character." Staple content appealing to the average person included anecdotes of good triumphing over evil, biographical sketches of interesting characters, homey success stories, and popularized medical pieces. Articles showed how ambition, kindness, and thrift paid high rewards, sometimes material, always spiritual. Bureaucratic financial bungling in government was a favorite target. Sex was handled subtly. In 1935 *Reader's Digest* ran one of the most widely circulated magazine articles ever published: "—And Sudden Death." In it author J. C. Furnas realistically described highway killings and maimings at a time when accidents were killing 13 people for every 100,000 autos in use. His shocking account was widely reprinted and some 5 million copies distributed. Despite the depression, circulation soared from 500,000 in 1933 to 3 million in 1938. In 1939 offices were moved to a Georgian-style building on spacious, landscaped grounds in Chappaqua, near Pleasantville. Now more than half of the articles were original, some appearing for the first time in *Reader's Digest*. Criticism of Wallace's conservative, pro-government bias notwithstanding, circulation increased, reaching 9 million in the United States and 4 million abroad by the end of World War II. A popular feature was condensed books (some financed by the periodical), which Wallace also sold through a book club; from the early 1950s Reader's Digest Condensed Books sold in the millions. As rising postal rates and costs of paper and production ate into the *Reader's Digest's* normally high profits, the magazine continued to sell at its original rate of 25 cents per copy and $3 per year. In 1954 magazine operations suffered a $500,000 deficit, with larger losses anticipated unless something was done. Polled, readers said they would prefer advertising to a price increase, so management decided to accept advertisements in the U.S. edition for the first time (ads had already appeared in foreign editions). Ad orders poured in; management selected them carefully, rejecting all for alcoholic beverages, medical remedies, and tobacco. Ads first appeared in the April 1955 issue; during the first decade they brought in more than $351 million. No liquor ad was accepted until 1979. From the beginning Wallace had heavily promoted his magazine by mail, and in 1961 he launched his first of many successful sweepstakes. In 1964 the Wallaces created their first office of the president, choosing Hobart D. Lewis as president and executive editor; in 1969 he became the periodical's first editor in chief. By 1970 circulation had risen to more than 17 million in the United States, 29 million worldwide. The periodical was published in Arabic, Chinese, Danish, Dutch, Finnish, French, German, Italian, Japanese,

Norwegian, Portuguese, and Spanish. It was said to be read by 100 million and called the world's largest, most international magazine. In 1980 it ranked among the top three U.S. magazines, with an estimated average circulation of 18,045,968 (behind *Parade* and *TV Guide*) and total revenue of $261,205,000 (behind *TV Guide* and *Time*); it ranked ninth in total advertising revenue with $94,056,000 (ahead of *Better Homes and Gardens*). By the end of 1981 *Reader's Digest* had regained the circulation lead it had once held, with 17,927,542. After Wallace's death in 1981, Editor Edward T. Thompson (1928–) instituted no major changes. The periodical continued its emphasis on free enterprise but was less consistently Republican. Still appealing to the average person, articles and features entertained, informed, and explained how to solve personal and social problems. Now about 75 percent of the content was staff inspired or written. To boost sales on newsstands and at supermarket checkout lanes, larger type and colors were used in the old familiar table of contents on the cover. Circulation reached about 18.5 million U.S. and 12.5 million foreign in 40 editions in 16 languages in 163 countries. No other magazines challenged the *Reader's Digest* in worldwide coverage. Plans were made for African, Chinese, Greek, and Hindi editions. Renewal rate in the early 1980s was more than 70 percent (exceeded only by *National Geographic* among major magazines). *Reader's Digest* did not sell its subscription list but used it extensively for company book sales (including a condensed Bible), record sales, sweepstakes, and other projects. In the mid-1980s, with the cover price at $1.50, the editors still aimed for the broadest spectrum of readers with general-interest content. A staff shakeup, including dismissal of Thompson, in 1984, however, left future editorial policy open to speculation.

• *The Fugitive* (April–December 1925) founded in Nashville, Tennessee, by publishers and editors Walter Clyde Curry, Donald Grady Davidson (1893–1968), James Marshall Frank, Sidney D. Mttron Hirsch, Stanley Phillips Johnson, John Crowe Ransom (1888–1974), Alec Brock Stevenson, and John Orley Allen Tate (1899–1979) as a dignified magazine of poetry. The periodical was published quarterly in 1922 and 1925, bimonthly 1923–1924. In the beginning it was written, edited, and published by the eight founders, friends of some years. They represented a wide variety of poetical philosophies, mostly modern. Ransom's poetry stood out. *The Fugitive*, whose circulation probably never exceeded 500, was one of many little magazines that flowered in the 1920s.

• *Fruit, Garden and Home* (July–) founded in Des Moines, Iowa, by Edwin Thomas Meredith (1876–1928) as a monthly emphasizing service to middle-income town and city homeowners for 35 cents per year. Meredith intended to provide a forum for readers to exchange experiences, ideas, and practical information. First editor was Chesla C.

Sherlock, to 1927. Early issues contained many practical short articles on subjects reflecting the title. The magazine was planned, written, and edited locally; staff members owned homes and enjoyed spending time with their family and working around the house. With the August 1924 issue the periodical became *Better Homes and Gardens*. By then it ran at least 50 pages per issue, larger illustrations, and substantial advertising; monthly circulation was about 500,000. Also in 1924 the periodical initiated a landscape planning service. In 1925 it stated that it would provide a money-back guarantee for products advertised. In 1927 the ampersand replaced the *and* in the title (until 1945). Shortly after the founder's death, Fred Bohen (Meredith's son-in-law) became publisher; the next year (1929) he was named president of Meredith Publishing Company. Meanwhile, E. T. Meredith, Jr., had joined the company; he served in high positions until his death in 1966. In 1928 *Better Homes & Gardens* became probably the first magazine to achieve 1 million circulation without running fashions or fiction; it looked prosperous, with some issues exceeding 150 pages. Also in 1928 the magazine set up a test kitchen for recipes. Two years later Meredith offered the *My Better Homes & Garden Cook Book* as a premium for subscriptions; in 1941 it became available in bookstores; in 1978 the 20-millionth copy sold. In 1930 *Better Homes & Gardens* advocated a comprehensive national home-building plan, a campaign that helped bring about the National Housing Act. The periodical weathered the early years of the depression with difficulty, but business improved in the latter 1930s: the April 1937 issue consisted of 186 pages. In 1937 *Better Homes & Gardens* founded its idea annuals with *Home Building Ideas*; annuals on gardens, home furnishings, etc. followed during the next decades; circulation of each usually exceeded 1.5 million. By 1940 the magazine's circulation passed 2 million. With the World War II paper shortage, advertising dropped from 1941 levels by about $1 million in 1942; to offset losses, the publisher tried to build linage by such techniques as expanding the editorial department on meal preparation to attract more food ads. The periodical was a leader in the Victory Garden campaign. In 1943 Meredith issued its *Baby Book*, which sold 1.5 million copies within ten years. Immediately after the war the magazine's advertising gross leaped ahead. In the title *and Gardens* appeared in smaller type (beginning 1945), reflecting less advertising support for gardening articles; but flower cultivation remained important. By 1950 *Better Homes and Gardens* was a leader among shelter magazines in total advertising revenue. As staff members left for other jobs, they carried to other magazines Meredith's editorial philosophy and techniques of practical service, extending the magazine's influence. In 1950 circulation was almost 3.5 million. As articles on building, remodeling, and home furnishings increased, the pages per issue occasionally exceeded 400. In the 1960s home management increased in importance, and food preparation pieces for men and women remained prominent; typical titles: "How To Be a Great Hostess!" and "How To Get Dinner in 30 Minutes." In 1963 *Better Homes and Gardens* printed ten editions and offered advertisers custom-made editions. It was one of the largest selling magazines, with a circulation of 6,228,000; but advertising revenue, which had not kept pace with circulation, was down from 1953 to $21,260,000. In the 1970s spinoffs, including special-interest books and a real estate business, helped financially. Of continued significance was the periodical's assistance with readers' daily activities and problems as well as reader involvement. Like many magazines, *Better Homes and Gardens* experimented with delivery alternatives to the increasingly expensive U.S. Postal Service; some delivery cost was offset by selling advertising space in circulars accompanying the magazine. According to *Folio's* 1980 survey of the top 400 magazines, *Better Homes and Gardens* ranked sixth in average circulation with 8,055,040 (third among monthlies), tenth in advertising revenue with $94,004,000, and ninth in total revenue with $162,909,000. In the mid-1980s the monthly was still published in Des Moines. Editor David Jordan aimed for "middle-and-up" income families and home owners who were active in their communities. Content excluded politics and included automobiles, health, home entertainment, and money management. Circulation hovered around 8 million.

● *True Confessions* (August–) founded by Fawcett Publications as a monthly emphasizing actual confessions of criminals in such articles as "Memoirs of a Con Man." The magazine soon became an imitation of *True Story*, running first-person pieces about women's romances. After 1937 *True Confessions's* circulation sometimes exceeded 1 million; for years it was second only to *True Story* among confession magazines. Eventually, Fawcett toned down the sexual aspects and added respectability by publishing such contributors as Eleanor Roosevelt. In mid-1963 Fawcett sold *True Confessions* to Macfadden Publications. In the mid-1980s the publisher was Macfadden Women's Group, New York; editor was Barbara J. Brett. Circulation was about 250,000. The monthly's target audience was blue-collar women with a high school education, from teens through maturity. Content emphasized emotional first-person stories with high moral tone, romantic interest, and an exciting climax.

1923. *The New Leader* founded as an organ of the U.S. Socialist Party. In 1930 S. M. Levitas became general manager, and a few years later took over editorial direction. In the mid-1930s the periodical broke with the party because the editors thought a faction was undemocratic. For more than 30 years Levitas made the *New Leader* a forum for a wide variety of democratic opinions. The weekly was staunchly anti-

Communist but concerned with Russia and international communism. Besides political articles, Levitas ran arts criticism. Although the periodical could not afford to pay contributors, regulars included name writers Daniel Bell, Max Eastman, James T. Farrell, and Sidney Hook. In 1950 the *New Leader* changed from tabloid to magazine format. Graphic artist Herbert Frederick Lubalin (1918–1981) restyled it in 1961 free. In the 1960s management appealed to subscribers and friends for financial contributions. Circulation was about 18,500.

● *Time* (3 March–) founded in New York by Henry Robinson Luce (1898–1967) and Briton Hadden (1898–1929) as *The Weekly News-Magazine* (subtitle). Hadden was editor 1923–1927, Luce 1928–1949 (with Manfred Gottfried (1943–1946); Luce was editor in chief 1945–1964, then editorial chairman. The founders concisely departmentalized the week's news "for busy men," mainly college graduates. The first issue had 7 pages of advertisements and 24 of departments, beginning with "National Affairs" (later "The Nation"); it had 9,000 subscription sales and a few thousand newsstand sales. For inverted syntax, puns (e.g., sexational), and blended words (e.g., cinemactor) *Time* became known. To deemphasize lateness of week-old news, *Time* played up colorful side events and interpretation. Soon it became known for its descriptive settings, dramatic narratives, and editorial commentary. To economize, in 1925–1927 the periodical was headquartered in Cleveland. By 1927 circulation had risen to 136,000 and advertising revenue to $501,000. Prospering, the owners moved *Time* back to New York. After Hadden's death, Luce took over entirely, becoming the principal stockholder in Time Inc. In 1929 circulation reached 200,000; in 1930 advertising grossed more than $3 million. Beginning in 1931 *Time* sponsored a radio "March of Time," a dramatization of news based on the magazine. *Time*'s competitive position was strengthened in 1938 with absorption of the *Literary Digest* (f. 1890). In 1941 *Time* launched a Latin American edition (in English); in 1943, a Canadian edition; in 1944, an Atlantic Overseas edition; and in 1946, a Pacific edition, later split in two. In 1960 five international editions circulated 621,000 copies, many to influential readers. That year advertising revenue, growing faster than circulation, totaled more than $50 million. Among editorial contents, particularly notable were such arts departments as "Cinema" under James Agee, 1941–1955, and "Theatre" covered by Louis Kronenberger, 1938–1961. To broaden and deepen comprehensive coverage of news, *Time* editors went from merely rewriting newspapers (chiefly New York *Times*) and the Associated Press wire (acquired 1936) to building a news-gathering network. Thus *Time* kept its lead over rivals through the depression and World War II. By the 1960s the network had 12 U.S. bureaus, including Washington, and 113 U.S. stringers, plus 18 foreign bureaus and 179 foreign stringers; about 70 fact checkers worked in the large New York headquarters staff. Regularly using color (begun editorially 1945), *Time* continued to appeal to a wide audience of college-educated readers. Luce was staunchly anti-Communist, Protestant, and Republican—an influential conservative (critics said a propagandist). From *Time*'s founding Luce had acknowledged some prejudices, including his free enterprise philosophy; he had expressly not aimed for impartiality (objectivity) but for "fairness." But *Time* was criticized for being unfair as well as biased because it mingled facts and opinion in new items. After World War II *Time* supported Dwight D. Eisenhower, among other Republicans, and attacked President Truman, Secretary of State Dean Acheson, and Adlai Stevenson, among other Democrats. In 1962 *Time* claimed 3 million circulation for domestic, Canadian, and three overseas editions. In 1963 it attacked the U.S. press corps in Saigon, saying its members were propagandists plotting to overthrow the Diem government and reporting distortions compounding the confusion they should be untangling for U.S. readers. In protest, correspondents Charles Mohr and Matt Perry resigned. When Luce in 1964 retired as editor in chief, Hedley W. Donovan (1914–) succeeded him; in 1979 Donovan was succeeded by Henry Anatole Grunwald (1922–). In 1965, with circulation near 3 million, *Time* began its "Essay" feature (first topic: United Nations). In 1976 *Time* published its first special edition, a bicentennial issue (4 July) with the periodical's largest press run (5.5 million). In 1979 *Time* led magazines in worldwide ad revenues with $296 million. Many readers especially liked the specialized back-of-the-book departments, which included art, business, education, medicine, press, religion, and science. In 1980 the editors upset some readers by putting the Ayatollah Ruhollah Khomeini of Iran on the cover as "Man of the Year" (a feature begun in 1927 with Charles A. Lindbergh), without endorsing his activities, much as it had so honored Adolf Hitler (1938) and Joseph Stalin (1939, 1942). *Time* continued among the top magazines (1980) with circulation of 4,407,928, ranking it fifth among weeklies (between *National Enquirer* and *The Star*); with ad revenue of $214,139,000, ranking it second (between *TV Guide* and *Newsweek*); and with total revenue of $346,623,000, ranking it second (between *TV Guide* and *Reader's Digest*). In 1981 ad revenue jumped to $253,440,762, returning *Time* to the top (just above *TV Guide*). In 1982 worldwide circulation was 5.8 million, ad revenue $350 million. Satellites transmitted page images to printing plants in the United States, Hong Kong, and Netherlands. There were 23 foreign bureaus, 10 domestic; 450 people staffed the New York headquarters. In 1984 *Time* ranked thirteenth in circulation with 4.6 million, but second (behind *TV Guide*) in total revenue with $540,742,000 and first in advertising revenue with $335,589,000. In 1985 *Time* won a libel suit brought by Ariel Sharon, who contended the magazine had accused him of condoning a massacre of Palestinians in Lebanon (1982) when he was defense minister of Israel. Despite the legal victory, *Time* was criticized by the jury and other observers for not reporting more carefully. Still, it remained the most successful and perhaps the most influential news magazine.

1924. Three "true" periodicals founded, including confession magazines *True Marriage Stories* and *True Love Stories* (the latter edited for some years by Daisy Bacon) and *True Detective Mysteries*, one of the first major factual detective magazines. *True Detective Mysteries* was one of the best written and edited magazines of its genre and a circulation leader. In it founder Bernarr Macfadden (1868–1955) tried to prove that factual crime mysteries could be as interesting as fictional mysteries in the pulps. *True Detective Mysteries* was successful, durable, and widely imitated.

● *The American Mercury* (January–) founded in New York by Henry Louis Mencken (1880–1956), George Jean Nathan (1882–1958), and others as a critical and literary monthly review. H. L. Mencken was editor 1924–1933; Nathan co-editor 1924–1925 and contributing editor 1925–1930. Their iconoclastic magazine challenged complacency, shocked conventional people, and delighted young rebels. Mencken reveled in debunking middle-class values. By 1927 circulation exceeded 77,000. As the public's mood changed with the depression, subscribers dropped away—to about 62,000 by 1931, 40,000 by 1932, 33,000 in 1933—although Mencken published top new writers, including Charles Beard, Elmer Davis, Theodore Dreiser, William Faulkner, F. Scott Fitzgerald, Sinclair Lewis, and Vachel Lindsay. Henry Hazlitt became editor for 1934. In the mid-1930s Paul Palmer bought the *American Mercury*, which had 30,000 circulation, and as editor 1935–1939 reduced its size to digest format, shortened articles, halved the price, created a politically conservative tone, and continued to aim for "the intelligent minority." Circulation more than doubled. In 1939 Palmer sold to Lawrence Edmund Spivak (1906–), business manager since 1933. Eugene Lyons was editor 1939–1944, then Spivak 1944–1950. Authors included Major Alexander de Seversky, crusader for air power, and Thomas Wolfe, novelist. Circulation peaked at 84,000 in 1945, but the periodical never made a profit. Spivak published paperback books and mystery and science fiction magazines to help underwrite *American Mercury*. In 1950 Clendenin J. Ryan bought it; editor was William Bradford Huie, who soon took over. Content under Huie's direction included conservative political commentary, sensationalized inside stories, and *Reader's Digest*-like articles of lasting interest. In 1952 J. Russell Maquire bought the money-losing periodical. Huie stayed as editor until 1953, when content became too reactionary for him. Maquire was editor 1955–1957. In the 1980s La Vonne Doden Furr edited the quarterly in

Houston, Texas, where it was published by American Mercury Patrons, Inc.

• *The Saturday Review of Literature* (August–) founded in New York by Henry Seidel Canby (1878–1961), editor, and others, with the help of Time Inc., as a literary weekly. It grew out of a New York *Evening Post* supplement, *The Literary Review* (f. 1920), which Canby (and others) had edited. The early *Saturday Review of Literature* was noted for its book reviews and erudite discussion of the literary scene. Bernard DeVoto (1897–1955) was editor 1936–1938. In 1940 circulation was 20,000. Contributors included Goodman Ace, William Rose Benét, John Ciardi, H. L. Mencken, Fulton Sheen, and Leon Trotsky. In 1938 Harrison Smith bought the periodical; in 1942 he sold it to the Saturday Review Association. After becoming editor in 1942, Norman Cousins (1915–) added articles on business, mass communication, music, and travel as well as issuing special supplements; he occasionally crusaded. By 1944 the magazine had lost $1 million, which was made up by Thomas Lamont and other wealthy benefactors. In 1952 *of Literature* was dropped from the title; it had been included at the beginning to differentiate the magazine from a widely known English periodical. In 1961 McCall Corporation bought the *Saturday Review*, whose circulation was then about 265,000; later Norton Simon, Inc., bought it. Advertising revenues rose to $2,741,000 (1963). In 1970 circulation was 615,000. In 1971 the *Saturday Review* was purchased by Nicholas H. Charney, editor, and John James Veronis. They moved the offices to San Francisco. They also changed the single weekly edition to four rotating weeklies, in effect creating four new monthlies—on the arts, education, science, society— that one could subscribe to singly or together. This innovation confused readers and potential advertisers; by 1973 the experiment had failed. Cousins acquired ownership, combining the *Saturday Review* with a recently founded periodical of his own, the *World*. In 1977 *Saturday Review/World*, which had 520,000 circulation, was sold to a group headed by Carll Tucker, who edited the periodical in New York. In 1980 Robert I. Weingarten became the new owner, Tucker editor, and Al Kingon editor in chief. They broadened coverage and improved graphics. In late 1980 Weingarten reported that *Saturday Review* had become profitable with a circulation of more than 500,000, but in 1982 the magazine was discontinued. In March 1983 it was revived by Jeffrey and Debra Gluck in Columbia, Missouri; Cousins contributed. In the mid-1980s the periodical was published by the Saturday Review Publishing Co. as a bimonthly for highly literate people. Content included nonfiction book excerpts, interviews with and profiles of artists and authors, and coverage of artistic and cultural events. Managing editor was Frank Gannon, circulation 250,000.

• *National Motorist* founded. In the mid-1980s it was published in San

Francisco by the National Automobile Club. Editor Jane M. Offers emphasized motor travel in the 11 western states, nonfiction on auto care, and profiles and interviews with personalities in the transportation and energy fields. The bimonthly had a circulation of about 233,000.

1925. *The Golden Book Magazine* (January–) founded by Henry Wysham Lanier, editor, with financial assistance from Charles Day Lanier (brother). H. W. Lanier persuaded the Review of Reviews Corporation to publish the periodical. Circulation rose to 165,000 (1927), its highest. The new monthly was well printed, with attractive typography, but without illustration, on wood pulp paper. Content emphasized reprinted material, especially short stories, and included humor poetry and excerpts from novels and plays. The *Golden Book* drew on the works of such leading American and English authors as Sherwood Anderson, Willa S. Cather, Irvin S. Cobb, Joseph Conrad, Stephen Crane, Richard Harding Davis, Charles Dickens, Theodore Dreiser, Robert Frost, Bret Harte, O. Henry, Jack London, Katherine Mansfield, Eugene O'Neill, "Saki," Robert Louis Stevenson, Mark Twain, Stewart Edward White, and Owen Wister. It also ran translations of works of leading European authors, especially French and Russian writers. In 1927 the *Golden Book* absorbed one of its many imitators, *Famous Stories Magazine* (f. 1925). In early 1928 circulation and advertising—mostly for books, household luxuries, and travel—declined. At the end of 1928 the Laniers withdrew; Edith O'Dell became editor, 1929–1930. She maintained the Laniers' editorial policy but increased illustration. As the depression ravaged the periodical, editorial policy became inconsistent; desperately, editors ran a few original stories and in the last few months tried emphasizing sex. In October 1935 the periodical was merged into *Fiction Parade* (f. 1935) to form Fiction Parade and Golden Book, which lasted until February 1938.

• *The New Yorker* (19 February–) founded in New York by Harold Wallace Ross (1892–1951), editor, and Raoul Fleischmann (1885–1969) as a sophisticated, humorous weekly for a select metropolitan audience. Ross wanted the *New Yorker* to reflect city life urbanely and satirically; he would not edit "for the old lady in Dubuque." The first issue sold 15,000 copies. Circulation dropped before picking up; after 1928 the magazine made a profit. Advertising grew with its reputation. Art Editor Rea Irvin drew Eustace Tilley, the dandy who became the magazine's symbol. Such artists as Charles Addams, Peter Arno, Helen Hokinson, and Otto Soglow contributed cartoons. E. B. White conducted the "Talk of the Town," a department of anecdotes and comment. Other noted contributors included Wolcott Gibbs, A. J. Liebling, Ogden Nash, John O'Hara, S. J. Perelman, and James Thurber. More than 700 "Letter from Paris" pieces, signed by "Gênet," were written by Janet Flanner 1925–1975. Regular features were "Profiles" and "Reporter at Large." The periodical also became known for its arts reviews and plotless fiction. In 1946 the *New Yorker* devoted an issue to John Hersey's "Hiroshima," an account of the devastation from the atom bomb dropped on Japan near the end of World War II. When Ross died, the editorship went to William Shawn (1907–), who edited in the Ross tradition and continued the editorial department's complete independence from the advertising department. In 1952 he published Lillian Ross's "The Picture," a factual report in novel form of a film production. Other writers who helped sustain the periodical's success included Michael Arlen, Elizabeth Drew, Richard Rovere, Jonathan Schell, Calvin Trillin, and John Updike. In the 1960s correspondent Robert Shaplen realistically appraised the quagmire in Vietnam. In 1968 Peter F. Fleischmann (1922–) became president of the firm, in 1969 board chairman. The periodical, fat with advertising, had one of the best profit records in the industry. In 1980 the *New Yorker* joined the leaders in advertising among consumer magazines, ranking thirteenth with 4,223 pages. In the mid-1980s circulation was about 500,000. In 1985 the magazine was purchased by the Newhouse family's Advance Publications Inc.

• *Screen Play* founded for movie fans.

1926. *Children* (October–) founded by George Joseph Hecht (1895–1980) and family as "The Magazine for Parents." It covered raising children from crib to college and offered practical suggestions for parents. Clara Savage Littledale, editor 1926–1956, ran articles on child care by leading authorities and by parents. She extended the scope to include housing and marriage problems because she thought they affected children, and the magazine's subtitle became *Family Home Guide*. With the August 1929 issue *Children* became *Parents' Magazine*. By 1932 it had about 100,000 readers, 30 years later almost 2 million. As the monthly grew, it reflected changing attitudes toward child rearing. In the 1960s *Parents'* initiated a seal for products it approved. In the late 1970s it was mainly a magazine for women 18 to 30 years of age. Five thousand copies went to offices of obstetricians each month; 99 percent of the circulation went to subscribers. By 1978 circulation had declined from 2 million to 1.5 million. That year Gruner + Jahr, a West German publisher, bought *Parents'* and began concentrating on single-copy sales and made other changes. In 1980 the periodical was edited for women when they graduated from school, set up their households, got married, and had children. Thus *Parents'* uniquely covered both parents and children. In 1985 *Parents Magazine* (without the apostrophe) was published in New York and edited by Elizabeth Crow, who ran well-documented articles on development and behavior of preschool, school-age, and adolescent children; baby care; family and marriage relationships; new trends and research findings in education and mental and physical health; women's issues, etc. Articles encouraged informed action on social issues. Monthly circulation was 1,670,000.

1927. *Tide* (April–1959) founded by Henry R. Luce and Briton Hadden as a news magazine for the advertising industry. *Tide* resembled *Time* in format and news summaries. In 1930 Time Inc. sold *Tide* to Raymond Rubicam. Four more ownership changes occurred before the periodical was discontinued.

1928. *Screenbook* founded for movie fans.

1929. Two movie fan magazines founded—*Screen Romances* and *Screen Stories*.

● *Master Detective* founded by Bernarr Macfadden. In the mid-1980s it was part of the Official Detective Group, R. G. H. Publishing Corporation, New York. Editor in chief was Art Crockett, who ran factual stories about outstanding detective work. Monthly circulation was 350,000.

● *Business Week* founded by McGraw-Hill Publishing Company to report news of business and industry. By 1962 it had 400,000 circulation; by 1981, almost 762,000, with several U.S. and foreign editions. In the early 1980s the publisher was R. B. Alexander; editor, Lewis H. Young. The weekly, still published in New York in the mid-1980s, not only reported but also interpreted business news; worldwide circulation was about 857,000.

Motion Pictures

1920. Loew's, Inc., theater chain, founded by Marcus Loew (1870–1927). In 1924 Loew formed Metro-Goldwyn-Mayer by combining the three corporations of Metro Pictures, Goldwyn Pictures, and Louis B. Mayer Pictures. Addition of the production and distribution facilities gave Loew control of the three facets of the film business (including exhibition). As M-G-M's vice president in charge of production, Louis Burt Mayer (1885–1957) headed the studio for almost 30 years. By the 1930s M-G-M was one of the largest studios. In that decade it produced black-and-white three-dimensional shorts that were forerunners of the color 3-D feature films of the 1950s. In the 1950s M-G-M's influence waned, and in the 1970s M-G-M virtually withdrew from the motion picture business to concentrate on hotels and other ventures. In 1981 M-G-M bought United Artists from Transamerica, Inc.

1921. *The Cabinet of Doctor Caligari*, an expressionistic German film, exhibited in United States; significant foreign influence. Made in 1919, the film was directed by Robert Wiene.

• *The Four Horsemen of the Apocalypse*, Rex Ingram's best-known film, a notable early spectacle.

• *The Playhouse*, one of the best films starring comedian Buster Keaton (1895–1966). Another noted Keaton silent was *The General* (1927). Keaton's popular style was deadpan, unsentimental.

• *The Sheik* released, one of the most popular films starring Rudolph Valentino (1895–1926), the most popular matinee idol of silent films. Another major Valentino film was *Blood and Sand* (1922). Almost as famous as a "Latin lover" was Ramon Novarro (1899–1968). Both actors' films had exotic settings.

1922. Motion Picture Producers and Distributors of America founded for self-regulation by the industry, which was reacting to threats of increased government censorship provoked by the new frankness of postwar pictures and Hollywood's reputation for debauchery. Censors were already active in 36 states, including New York, which licensed films for exhibition; and the possibility of federal regulation loomed. Under President Will H. Hayes (1879–1954) the MPPDA policed film morals, especially nudity, profanity, and sex. Films with the MPPDA's seal of approval usually would not arouse state censors, parent groups, or religious organizations. Few distributors would handle films that did not, and fewer exhibitors would dare show them. In the 1930s MPPDA's Office of Production Code Administration extended regulations, such as prescribing that film makers must punish criminals and could not ridicule ministers. Some film makers tried to circumvent the code. (The powerful trade association also carried out other industry activities, including bargaining with foreign governments for U.S. exports.) Through the MPPDA the eight major film companies, which in 1939 produced 76 percent of feature films released and collected 86 percent of total rental revenue, dominated the industry. In 1945 Eric Johnston succeeded Hayes as president. When in the 1950s the U.S. Supreme Court dissolved industry control by the five largest studios and television challenged motion pictures, the MPPDA liberalized its code. Until then no important movie had been distributed without the Production Code Administration seal since 1934. In the 1950s two major films were denied the seal: *The Moon Is Blue* (1953), which included talk about sex, and *The Man With the Golden Arm* (1956), which dealt with narcotic addiction, expressly prohibited by the code. These were released anyway. In 1956 the code was revised mainly to permit the subject of narcotics. About 1966, when Jack Valenti succeeded Johnston, the MPPDA further liberalized its code, permitting use of common profanity and treatment of abortion and justifiable suicide. As explicitness in films grew, most protests were raised against movies' effects on children. In 1968 the MPPDA switched from trying to control screen content to regulating audience attendance by an age classification system that put the burden of enforcement on theaters. The system: G = general, suitable for all people; M = mature, soon changed to PG = parental guidance suggested; R = restricted, moviegoers under 17 must be accompanied by parent or adult guardian; X = moviegoers must be at least 18 years old. (In 1984 PG-13 was added to indicate parents should exercise additional discretion for children below teen age.) The Production Code Administration became the Classification and Rating Administration. In the 1970s the MPPDA changed its name to the Motion Picture Association of America.

● *Nanook of the North*, a pioneer documentary produced by Robert Flaherty (1884–1951).

1923. Warner Brothers Pictures incorporated by the Warner (née Eichelbaum) brothers: Albert (1884–1967), Harry Morris (1881–1958), Jack Leonard (1892–1978), and Samuel Louis (1887–1927). Harry was president, the others vice presidents. The four had been exhibitors since 1903, producers since 1912. In the mid-1920s the corporation began expanding to achieve full vertical integration of production, distribution, and exhibition so it could compete against the big three of First National, Loew, and Zukor, whose control of distribution severely limited the market for Warner Brothers films. Warner Brothers bought the Vitagraph Company, last of the original motion picture trust companies, and pioneered sound film, using the Vitagraph system, which mechanically synchronized phonograph discs to projector motors and electrically amplified sound. On 5 August 1926 Warner Brothers presented a program of short sound films and a feature, *Don Juan*, the first feature with sound accompaniment, a symphonic score, and some sound effects (e.g., swords clashing). For more than a year Warner Brothers presented similar programs. Vitaphone's success was limited because few theaters were equipped for it and audiences were used to live music (e.g., local organist or pianist). On 6 October 1927 Warner Brothers exhibited *The Jazz Singer*, a feature film with synchronized speech as well as music and other sound; still, titles carried most the conversation. *The Jazz Singer* not only gave birth to the "talkie" but also foreshadowed the backstage musical film (though *Jazz Singer* contained no dancing), a significant early subgenre. In July 1928 Warner Brothers released the first all-talking picture, *The Lights of New York*—also the first gangster talkie. By 1929 Warner Brothers had absorbed most of First National and its theaters. In the 1930s Warner Brothers was one of the five largest film companies, producing more than 50 pictures annually. The studio specialized in biographies, gangster films, and musicals as well as in fast, sharp dialogue. Directors included Busby Berkeley, Michael Curtiz, Howard Hawks, Mervyn LeRoy, and William Wellman. Stars included Joan Blondell, Humphrey Bogart, James Cagney, Bette Davis, Ruby Keeler, Ida Lupino, Paul Muni, Dick Powell, and Edward G.

Robinson. After World War II the corporation developed Warnercolor, a new color process. Warner Brothers was among the first film companies to make television commercials and weekly shows. After changing ownership twice in the 1960s, the company became Warner Communications. Its studio became the Burbank Studio and in the 1980s was shared with Columbia and other production companies.

● *The Covered Wagon*, directed by James Cruze, released; first epic western.

1924. Columbia Pictures, Inc., founded by the Cohn brothers: Jack (1889–1956) and Harry (1891–1958). In the 1930s it was one of the three smaller studios but among the eight largest. In 1951 it was probably the first film studio to establish a television production division, Screen Gems. In the latter 1950s Columbia sold feature films to TV. Coca-Cola Company bought the studio in 1981. In the 1980s it shared the Burbank Studio with Warner Brothers (f. 1923) and other production companies.

1925. *The Big Parade*, directed by King Vidor (1895–1982), a prototype war film that effectively mixed World War I humor, antiwar message, and syrupy love story.

● *Greed*, made in 1923, released. This ambitious, detailed, experimental, and literal translation of *McTeague* (1899), a novel by Frank Norris (1870–1902), was director Erich von Stroheim's masterpiece. Shot mostly in San Francisco, the original film ran 45 reels, about 10 hours, before it was cut to 20 reels. Metro-Goldwyn-Mayer further cut it to the conventional 10 reels, the final rendition, which Stroheim disavowed. Stroheim (1885–1957) also directed probably the first million-dollar motion picture, *Foolish Wives* (1922), produced by Carl Laemmle (1867–1939). Other Stroheim films included *Blind Husbands* (1919), *The Devil's Passkey* (1920), *Merry Widow* (1925), and *The Wedding March* (1928). His last film was *Queen Kelly* (1928), from which he was fired during production. Stroheim was a producer and actor as well as director.

1926. Motion picture business the fifth largest U.S. industry, accounting for 90 percent of the world's motion pictures.

● *Don Juan* (5 August), starring John Barrymore (1882–1942), probably the first film with sound. It used the Vitaphone sound system.

1927. *The Jazz Singer* (October), starring Al Jolson (1880–1950), opened in New York. Probably the first feature with which an audience could hear spoken dialogue and (mostly) singing; but printed titles carried most of the conversation, making the film look like a silent. It used the Vitaphone sound system. *The Jazz Singer* both foreshadowed the important backstage musical subgenre of the 1930s and modern "talkies." Early in the 1930s sound film quickly replaced silent, halting careers of some silent screen idols. For example, Douglas Fairbanks and John Gilbert could not make the transition, but Ronald Colman and Greta Garbo did.

• *Shaw Talks for Movietone*, a visually static interview with George Bernard Shaw (1856–1950), the first newsreel with sound, by Fox-Movietone News, introduced by William Fox (1879–1952). Fox's sound system was a slight modification of Lee de Forest's Phonofilm. Fox-Movietone News produced shorts, mainly actualities and documentaries, with music and narration, little dialogue.

• *Sunrise*, directed by F. W. Murnau, basically a silent film, though titles minimized; released with a musical score.

• *Underworld*, one of many silent gangster movies of the 1920s.

1928. RKO Radio Pictures, Inc., formed by combining Radio Corporation of America (R), interested in sound aspects, and Keith-Orpheum (K-O) theater circuit, survivor of the era when vaudeville competed with film for audiences. With the theater chain, Radio-Keith-Orpheum became one of the big five studios. In 1948 Howard Hughes (1905–1976) bought control. In 1953 the studio was sold to Desilu. After Hughes's withdrawal in 1955, RKO, facing financial collapse, became the first major film company to release old feature films to television, selling 740 to General Teleradio (December 1955). Other film companies soon followed. In the 1950s RKO was purchased by a General Tire subsidiary, then became RKO General, a broadcasting and cable TV company (no film).

• *The Lights of New York* (July), directed by Bryan Foy, probably the first complete talking motion picture and first talking gangster movie. This Warner Brothers Pictures release contained more talk than action, at least partly due to limitations of stationary hidden microphones. The film was noted for its authentic "Roaring Twenties" atmosphere.

• *The Crowd*, directed by King Vidor, and *The Wind*, directed by Victor Seastrom, notable realistic silents.

• Two landmark shorts released by Walter E. Disney (1901–1966)— *Plane Crazy*, Walt Disney's first cartoon, and *Steamboat Willie*, the first animated film with synchronized sound and his first hit. Disney's studio (f. 1928) was a pioneer creator of animated movies and such famous characters as Donald Duck, Goofy, and Mickey Mouse. In 1929 it began the innovative Silly Symphonies with *Skeleton Dance*, drawn to Saint-Säen's *Danse Macabre*. The series, which ended in 1939, included *Flowers and Trees* (1932), the first movie to utilize three-color Technicolor successfully; *Three Little Pigs* (1933), and *The Old Mill* (1937). Multiplane cel animation gave depth and dimension to the Silly Symphonies. In the 1930s Disney's studio developed techniques that became animation standards. In 1937 Disney introduced feature-length animation in *Snow White and the Seven Dwarfs*, a Technicolor "musical." Other features included *Fantasia* (1940), which set seven animated ballets to classical music and introduced stereophonic sound, and *Dumbo* (1941). In 1953 *Toot, Whistle, Plunk, and Boom* effectively explored the recently introduced CinemaScope (wide) screen. The Disney studio also extended into film and television with live actors.

• First Oscars awarded by American Academy of Motion Picture Arts and Sciences. Best motion picture: *Wings* (Paramount). Best actor: Emil Jannings (1886–1950), *The Last Command, The Way of All Flesh*. Best actress: Janet Gaynor, originally Laura Gainer (1906–1984), *Seventh Heaven, Street Angel, Sunrise*. Best director: Frank Borzage (1893–1962), *Seventh Heaven,* and Lewis Milestone (1895–1980), *Two Arabian Knights*.

1929. *In Old Arizona,* directed by Raoul Walsh. This release added sound to the western genre motion picture; it was probably the first sound feature recorded largely outdoors (instead of sound stage). *In Old Arizona* and *The Virginian* (1929), directed by Victor Fleming (1883–1949), expanded and continued the genre's traditions, including wide vistas and the show-down shootout.

• *The Broadway Melody*, probably the first all dancing, singing, and talking musical, beginning the only new genre in sound film.

Radio and Television

1920. Radio stations seized by the navy for World War I returned to civilian control (March).

• Experimental station 8MK (20 August–), licensed to Radio News and Music Company, a Lee de Forest radio equipment sales organization. It began daily operations, sponsored by the Detroit *News*. On 31 August 8MK began carrying music, news, and talk programming part of each day. On 2 November the station broadcast election returns (as did KDKA, Pittsburgh). On 15 October 1921, 8MK was licensed to the *News* as WBL; on 3 March 1922 call letters changed to WWJ.

1921. Broadcasting by 30 stations on the only two frequencies available. Six stations were owned by Westinghouse, the others by Radio Corporation of America and General Electric.

• WJZ, Newark, New Jersey, and WBZ, Springfield (later Boston), Massachusetts, founded by Westinghouse. On 5 October 1921, WJZ began the first World Series broadcast. The sports editor of the New York *Sunday Call*, Sandy Hunt, telephoned the play-by-play of the Giants-Yankees game to announcer Tommy Cowan in Newark. In October 1922 WJZ, WBZ, and WGY (f. 1922), Schenectady, New York, jointly broadcast the World Series (Giants v. Yankees again)—precursing chain (network) broadcasting. The broadcasts included descriptions by sports-writer Grantland Rice of the New York *Herald Tribune*. In December

1926, WJZ became the flagship station for the National Broadcasting Company's Blue network, which in 1945 became the American Broadcasting Company.

● KYW (1921–), founded by Westinghouse in Chicago, began broadcasting the Chicago Civic Opera on 11 November. After several moves, KYW landed in Philadelphia.

● About 50,000 broadcast receivers in use.

1922. Broadcasting begun by more than 600 stations; many short-lived. Stations were often founded to promote churches, colleges, newspapers, radio manufacturers, and department stores selling crystal sets. Newspapers founding stations included the Atlanta *Journal*, Chicago *Daily News* and *Tribune*, Dallas *News*, Detroit *News*, Kansas City *Star*, Los Angeles *Times*, Louisville *Courier-Journal*, and Milwaukee *Journal*.

● WGY (22 February) founded in Schenectady, New York, by General Electric to encourage sale of receivers. In fall 1922 the station began offering weekly programs by the "WGY Players," radio's first dramatic series. In October WGY joined with WJZ of Newark, New Jersey, and WBZ of Springfield, Massachusetts, to broadcast the World Series, precursing network broadcasting.

● Radio conference convened (27 February) in Washington, D.C., by U.S. Secretary of Commerce Herbert Clark Hoover (1874–1964), who requested advice about his regulatory powers. The conferees, representatives of industrial and regional radio interests, asked for federal regulation to eliminate the chaos of interfering stations on the limited frequencies (channels), commonly considered in the public domain. Broadcasters, radio manufacturers, listeners, and the American Newspaper Publishers Association (many members owned stations) wanted regulation. Conferees also wanted limited advertising and classes of stations based on kinds of service. (Three more radio conferences would follow: 1923, 1924, 1925.) In August 1922 Herbert Hoover added a new frequency for stations of high power and high-quality programming; and stations first used four-letter call signs.

● WEAF (16 August–), built in New York by American Telephone & Telegraph, began broadcasting, beginning commercial radio. AT&T announced that WEAF would be (the first station) supported by advertising time sales. On the evening of 28 August, WEAF broadcast the first paid-for "commercial" (a term borrowed from AT&T accounting practice), a pitch by the Queensboro Corporation for cooperative apartment houses in Jackson Heights, New York City. The commercial lasted 10–15 minutes and cost $100; it was repeated for five days. The advertiser reported several thousand dollars in sales. By March 1923 WEAF had about two dozen sponsors paying for air time.

● Experiments by AT&T using telephone lines for intercity broadcasts. On 4 January 1923 chain broadcasting began experimentally when telephone lines connected WEAF and WNAC of Boston for a five-minute saxophone solo originating at WEAF. In June 1923 WEAF, KDKA of Pittsburgh, KYW of Chicago, and WGY of Schenectady joined for a special program on the anniversary of the electric light. In July 1923 the first continuing chain was founded when WEAF piped programs to WMAF of South Dartmouth, Massachusetts. WMAF was owned and supported as a public service by E. H. R. Green, who paid for three to four hours of daily programming from New York. In 1924 the WEAF-led chain consisted of 26 outlets and stretched west as far as Kansas City. In 1926 the Radio Corporation of America purchased WEAF from AT&T for $1 million and made the station the flagship of the National Broadcasting Company's Red network. On the night of 15 November 1926, WEAF originated the program that launched regular network broadcasting. Connected by 3,600 miles of special telephone cables, 21 NBC affiliates and 4 other stations carried the program, a live variety show before 1,000 guests in the Grand Ballroom of New York's Waldorf-Astoria Hotel with remote pickups from Chicago and Kansas City.

• More than 60,000 broadcast receivers in use.

1923. 576 radio stations as of 1 February. Owners included 222 electrical or radio dealers and manufacturers, 72 educational institutions, 69 publications, 29 department stores, 18 jewelry, music, and musical instrument stores. Other owners included churches, cities, fire and police departments, hardware stores, power companies, railroads, telephone companies, and YMCAs. Stations were still often promotional, noncommercial.

• Second radio conference convened (20 March) in Washington; iterated suggestions of first conference (1922) and called for temporary licensing until Congress would act. Conferees asked Secretary of Commerce Herbert Hoover to regulate hours and wavelengths to prevent interference detrimental to the public interest. (Two more conferences would follow: 1924, 1925).

• First public demonstration of mechanical picture transmission over wireless in United States. Charles Francis Jenkins (1867–1934) transmitted a photograph of President Harding from Washington to Philadelphia. In 1925 Jenkins transmitted via mechanical television moving silhouettes, then motion pictures (not live figures). In 1929 he organized the Jenkins Television Company to manufacture receiving and transmitting equipment. The company licensed other manufacturers to use its patents and announced commercial programs for 1930. In the depression it went into receivership. De Forest Company purchased its assets, then sold them to the Radio Corporation of America.

• National Association of Broadcasters (April–) founded as a trade group to seek government technical regulation, protect members from unwanted regulation, and fight the American Society of Composers, Authors, and Publishers, which demanded that broadcasters pay fees for airing music by ASCAP members. The first NAB president was Eugene F. McDonald, Jr., president of Zenith Radio Corporation; the first managing director, Paul Klugh. After 1923 NAB's role expanded to include relations with advertisers and the Federal Communications Commission (f. 1934). In 1929 the NAB adopted its Code of Ethics and Standards of Commercial Practice, the first self-imposed regulations on broadcasters. Later the more detailed radio and television codes were added. Shortly after the Japanese attack on Pearl Harbor (7 December 1941) the NAB issued a list of 16 guidelines to help broadcast reporters avoid disseminating news of benefit to U.S. enemies; the government soon made most of the guidelines official. After scandals of rigged quiz shows on TV in the 1950s, NAB founded the Television Information Office (October 1959–), New York, to provide the public favorable information about the medium. In the 1950s the NAB (and other media organizations) fought for photographers' access to courtrooms. Head-quartered in Washington, D.C., the NAB had a large staff to handle legal problems, public relations, research, stations services, and other matters. In the 1980s the Code Authority staff heard complaints about subscribers' code violations. NAB continued as the collective voice of U.S. broadcasters.

● Three classes of stations announced (May 15) by Secretary of Commerce Herbert Hoover, who assigned a greatly lengthened frequency spectrum to two. The spectrum increase outdated many receivers but firmly established AM radio and made possible adequate regulation.

● *Hoover v. Intercity Radio Co., Inc.* (286 F. 1003). This decision limited regulatory powers of the secretary of commerce. U.S. Court of Appeals for the District of Columbia ruled (25 February) that the secretary could only assign wavelengths and not otherwise regulate radio.

● Iconoscope, the first electronic camera tube, patented by Westinghouse and Vladimir Kosma Zworykin (1889–1982). The iconoscope was a key to an electronic TV system. In 1928 Zworykin patented a greatly improved iconoscope. He was one of the two major U.S. inventors (the other Philo T. Farnsworth) of electronic TV.

● Federal Trade Commission report criticizing monopoly—particularly of the Radio Corporation of America—in radio patents and manufacture. The report led to federal antitrust prosecution of RCA and others.

1924. Third radio conference (October) in Washington, D.C. Conferees called for broadcast use of entire 550–1,500 kHz band and urged research into monopoly. (Other conferences in 1922, 1923, 1925.)

• WNYC, New York, founded; early municipally owned radio station.

• "Barn Dance" on WLS, Chicago. The country-western music program was the precursor of "National Barn Dance," on national radio from 1933. This was one of the most famous programs of a popular type.

1925. Fourth radio conference (19 November) in Washington, D.C. Conferees agreed that limited advertising was acceptable, that radio was not a public utility, and that restrictions on the number of stations might be required. Afterward Secretary of Commerce Herbert Hoover refused to issue more licenses. (Other conferences in 1922, 1923, and 1924.)

1926. *United States v. Zenith Radio Corporation et al.* (12 F.2d 614). The limits of the Federal Radio Act of 1912 were clarified. The U.S. Department of Commerce had sued after Zenith, a receiver manufacturer and a broadcaster, had jumped frequencies from 930 kHz to 910 kHz (other stations intended to follow) against the department's will. The U.S. District Court of Northern Illinois held (16 April) that the secretary of commerce could not prevent the company from changing frequencies. The U.S. attorney general subsequently opined that under the 1912 act the secretary could only process license applications, not regulate them. Controls ended, 200 newly licensed stations began operations, and the interference chaos on airwaves in major urban areas grew. In December almost 700 stations existed, many interfering with each other.

• Three-part agreement (July) by telephone and radio groups ending their commercial war. Competition between the Telephone Group (American Telephone & Telegraph, its manufacturing subsidiary Western Electric, WEAF, and allied stations and companies) and the Radio Group (Radio Corporation of America, General Electric, Westinghouse, and their stations) had affected decisions on patents, equipment manufacture, programming, and station interconnections. Under 1919–1921 patent agreements, the Radio Group contended, only companies in the patent pool had the right to make receivers and sell them to the public, any station could at least recover program costs from sponsors, and stations could be interconnected by any available means. The Telephone Group contended that it had exclusive right to make and sell transmitters for broadcasting, to sell advertising time ("toll" broadcasting, as in long-distance calls), and to interconnect stations by wire for chain (network) broadcasting. In 1922–1924 attempts made to reconcile the two groups' differences failed. In 1925 the groups agreed to binding arbitration but stalemated over the outcome. In early 1926 the complex three-part agreement broke the stalemate and clearly defined the functions of the radio and telephone interests. Essentially, the agreement (1) redefined the patents arrangement in the context of the 1926 broadcasting industry, (2) gave AT&T a monopoly to provide wire interconnections between stations, and (3) provided for AT&T's withdrawal from station ownership. AT&T agreed to sell WEAF to RCA, and to refund part of the $1 million purchase price if it became a station owner in eight years. Weary of the broadcasting battle, AT&T management preferred to operate in a monopoly situation and to concentrate on the point-to-point communication at which it excelled.

1927. United Independent Broadcasters, Inc. (January–), founded by Arthur Judson, George A. Coats, and others to purchase time on radio, sell time to advertisers, and provide programming. WOR of Newark, New Jersey, which covered New York City, soon became UIB's main affiliate. On 5 April 1927 UIB and Columbia Phonograph Corporation, sales arm of Columbia Phonograph Record Company, merged, but maintained separate corporate identities, and created Columbia Phonograph Broadcasting System, Inc. On 25 September 1927 CPBS went on the air with a broadcast from the New York Metropolitan Opera to its 16-station network. After losing $100,000 in the first month, the record company withdrew from the operation. With added monies from Jerome H. Louchheim, who bought control of UIB, on 19 November 1927 CPBS became the Columbia Broadcasting System. CBS and UIB briefly co-existed to operate the network. After further losses, CBS-UIB's controlling interest was offered for sale. On 28 September 1928 William S. Paley (1901–), vice president of his family's Congress Cigar Company, bought controlling interest; in early 1929 he became network president. In 1930 he hired Edward Klauber (1887–1954) to set up a network news service. With assistant Paul White, Klauber staffed offices in Chicago, Los Angeles, London, New York, and Washington with newspapermen and established an extensive system of correspondents. Rising to second in command at CBS, Klauber became instrumental in its growth, serving Paley to 1943. In 1932 Raymond Gram Swing (1887–1968) and Cesar Saerchinger conducted the first transatlantic radio interview. By 1933 CBS owned seven stations: WABC (later WCBS), New York; WJSV, Washington, D.C.; WKRC, Cincinnati; WBBM, Chicago; WBT, Charlotte, North Carolina; WCCO, Minneapolis; and KMOX, St. Louis. These owned and operated (O&O) stations were its main sources of income. Its affiliates had increased from 17 (c. 4 percent of all stations) in 1928 to 91 (c. 16 percent of all stations) in 1933. On 12 March 1938 Edward R. Murrow (1908–1965) in Vienna and William Lawrence Shirer (1904–) in London made the first multiple news pickup in history, with newspaper correspondents reporting from Berlin, Paris, and Rome. Robert Trout (1908–) anchored the program, which set a pattern for modern newscasts. On 1 July 1941 CBS's WCBW became one of the first television stations to begin commercial operations. On 7 December 1941 it offered bulletins on the Pearl Harbor attack and showed its small audience maps of the war zones. In 1944 CBS unsuccessfully sought Federal Communications Commission approval of its mechanical color system as the industry standard. The system, which was incompatible with black-and-white TV, used a wheel to filter, transmit, and reconstitute the primary colors in sequence. The wheel was noisy, large, and difficult to synchronize and maintain. However, CBS's system provided a slightly better color quality than the Radio Corporation of America's competing system. In October 1950 the FCC approved the CBS color system; but the approval was later rescinded. In December 1953 the FCC approved RCA's compatible, electronic system. In 1970 CBS modified its spinning disc system to send the first color transmissions from moon to earth. In 1946 Frank Stanton (1908–) had become CBS president; he became vice chairman of the CBS board in 1971 and retired in 1973. In 1948 the network hired Douglas Edwards (1917–) to begin a TV news program and began (September) talent raids on other radio networks, luring "Amos 'n' Andy," Jack Benny, and Edgar Bergen and Charlie McCarthy from the National Broadcasting Company; Bing Crosby from the American Broadcasting Company; etc. On 18 November 1951 CBS brought Murrow's radio show "Hear It Now" to television live as "See It Now" (–9 July 1958). In 1953 Murrow began the TV interview show *Person to Person* (–June 1959). Murrow was also associated with "CBS Reports," for which he narrated *Harvest of Shame* (1960), a documentary exposé of the plight of migrant workers. In the 1960s Walter Cronkite (1916–) became the leading CBS-TV news personality, anchoring such programs as "CBS Reports," "Eyewitness to History," and "Twentieth Century" as well as specials on assassinations, presidential elections, racial conflicts, space flights, Vietnam, and Watergate. In 1962 he began anchoring the "CBS Evening News." In September 1963 Managing Editor Cronkite in New York, with Eric Sevareid (1912–) in Washington, broadcast the first half-hour network news program. An outstanding CBS reporter was Morley Safer, who broadcast controversial reports of the Vietnam war. In the late 1960s CBS began to diversify its holdings; it purchased Creative Playthings; Fender Guitars; Holt, Rinehart and Winston, and other publishing properties. In 1971 CBS management stood up to the government criticism of its critical documentary "The Selling of the Pentagon." In 1972 Arthur Taylor succeeded Stanton at CBS; in 1977 John D. Backe was named Chief Executive Officer and Paley withdrew from daily control but remained active. In September 1982 Paley announced he would step down as board chairman of the company in which he owned $90 million stock; CBS was then making $4 billion annually. On 28 February 1983 CBS had the highest rated single program in TV history to then: a 2½-hour final episode of its 11-year comedy series "M*A*S*H," the tale of a

Mobile Army Surgical Hospital team during the Korean War (Alan Alda starred). The finale pulled 77 percent of all homes watching TV that evening; more than 125 million people saw some part of the show. It also set advertising records, including the time charge for a 30-second commercial, $450,000. Another outstanding ratings success was the weekly "Sixty Minutes," a magazine format news show of interviews and short documentaries. Also in the early 1980s Dan Rather (1931–) succeeded Cronkite as anchor of the evening news; Diane Sawyer (1945–) became co-anchor of the morning news. CBS earned substantial profits through its news and sports divisions in the 1980s. Its TV enterprises included pay cable and satellites. It ran one of eight major radio groups. Subsidiaries included book publishers, magazines, recording agencies, and nonmedia organizations. In early 1985 a libel suit by retired army General William Westmoreland was abruptly resolved in the network's favor. In 1982 Westmoreland had accused CBS of defaming him in "The Uncounted Enemy: A Vietnam Deception," a documentary accusing him of conspiring to alter estimates of enemy troop strength during the Vietnam war. CBS had claimed that estimates were lowered below those of intelligence reports for political purposes. CBS stood by the essence of its report. After weeks of trial, during presentation of the defense's case, which seemed to run against Westmoreland, he withdrew his suit.

• Radio Act (bill enacted 18 February) law (president signed 23 February). It provided that the government owned the airwaves (in behalf of the public) and stipulated that all licenses would expire in two months. Censorship, except for obscenity, was prohibited. The act established a five-member Federal Radio Commission for one year to regulate all forms of radio communications; after several short-term extensions, the FRC became continuous (December 1929). Because the number of license applicants was larger than the limited number of frequencies that could be used without interference, Congress established the criterion of the "public interest, convenience, and/or necessity" for choosing licensees. Practically, the phrase (not defined by statute) meant that broadcasters were responsible for their operations and that the government would intervene only if they failed to provide an adequate service to listeners. The FRC, which began functioning in March 1927, maintained control of all frequencies to provide "fair, efficient, and equitable service" throughout the country. Licenses were granted for use of specific frequencies for three-year periods. In April the FRC ordered stations back to frequencies assigned by the secretary of commerce and put the broadcast band at 550–1,500 kHz. In March 1928 Congress passed the Davis Amendment (repealed 5 June 1936), which was intended to promote equality of radio service in five regions. In May 1928 the FRC aimed General Order No. 32 at the 164 stations believed to be causing the most interference. After hearings the FRC removed 109 stations from the air, reducing the total to about 590. Three months later General Order No. 40 outlined the FRC's station classification plan for local, regional, and clear AM channels to improve radio reception. In November 1928 the FRC reassigned existing stations. By the early 1930s, despite challenges in court, the FRC had solved the interference problem, but equalization was still an issue.

• First electronic television pictures transmitted, by Philo Taylor Farnsworth (1906–1971). The first picture was a 60-line (low-definition) image of a dollar sign. By 1930 Farnsworth had developed a new scanning and synchronizing system. He was one of the two major U.S. inventors (the other, Vladimir K. Zworykin) of electronic TV.

• First transmission, by wire, of still and moving pictures with synchronized sound, by Herbert Eugene Ives (1882–1953). In one demonstration (7 April) Secretary of Commerce Hoover spoke from Washington to a New York audience watching on a neon-tube screen that was 2 feet by 2½ feet; definition was a low 50 lines. In 1919 Ives had joined AT&T's Bell Telephone Laboratories, where he worked on mechanical TV and researched wire-photo transmission. These experiments generated the Picturephone, first shown to the public in 1927. By 1928 Bell had a three-channel color system that could pick up outdoor scenes. Rather than promote the system commercially, Bell opted just to keep up with development, aiming eventually to interconnect TV stations.

• Radio coverage (May) of Charles A. Lindbergh's solo transatlantic flight (the first). Millions of people tuned in.

• First automobile radios produced, by Philadelphia Storage Battery Company (Philco).

1928. Advertising clearly the main source of revenue for broadcasters, although radio carried only 2 percent of total ad expenditures. At first only a few advertisers—among them a department store, political organization, motion picture producer—had recognized radio's sales potential. Many people objected to mixing advertising and programming.

• "Empire Builders" first thriller drama. In its first season (1928–1929) it was heard only in the Midwest.

• "National Farm and Home Hour" for housewives. It was produced with assistance from the U.S. Department of Agriculture.

1929. Sales of radio receivers and components more than $840 million, an increase of about $200 million in less than two years and of about $780 million in eight years.

• First broadcast rating service, Crossley's Cooperative Analysis of Broadcasting, offered by Crossley Radio Company, founded by Archibald Maddock Crossley (1886–). The service was established for the Association of National Advertisers and funded largely by networks and stations to learn how many people listened to sponsored shows of the Columbia Broadcasting System and National Broadcasting Company. Ratings, used to sell advertising, measured a percentage of set-owning families listening to a network or program. CAB used a modified recall telephone interview method. CAB divided each day into four parts and asked if the program was turned on. Most people listened at night: half the sets were used between 9 and 10 P.M., about one-third 7 to 11 P.M. Thus originated the "prime-time" concept. CAB was the standard for five years, though many local stations began to conduct informal, unscientific audience research for potential advertisers who wanted data before buying time. CAB opened offices in 33 cities, 14 on the East Coast.

• "Amos 'n' Andy" from local radio broadcast on WMAQ, Chicago, to National Broadcasting Company's Blue network (August). The program was the first and, for many years, most popular continuing comedy drama. Each self-contained episode starred Freeman F. Gosden (1899–1982) and Charles J. Correll (1890–1972) in all the roles. The two white actors had brought their blackface vaudeville act to radio. It ran for two years on WGN, Chicago, as "Sam 'n' Henry." The title was changed when Gosden (Amos) and Correll (Andy) moved to WMAQ. In 1948 the Columbia Broadcasting System lured "Amos 'n' Andy" to television with black actors playing the leads. The TV show was discontinued in 1966 because blacks resented the stereotypes and whites never liked it as much as the radio version.

1930–1941

The Great Depression

Books

1931. *Axel's Castle*, by Edmund Wilson (1895–1972), a major work of criticism of literature for the period 1870–1930. Wilson, a critic who became prominent in the 1930s, had wide-ranging interests. His other works included the novel *I Thought of Daisy* (1929), *Memoirs of Hecate County* (1946), poems, and travel books, but mostly criticism. He edited *The Shock of Recognition* (1943), a collection of works by U.S. authors.

● *The Dutch Shoe Mystery*, by Ellery Queen, a best seller in this period and later. Ellery Queen was the pseudonym of cousins Frederick Dannay (1905–1982) and Manfred Bennington Lee (1905–1971) as well as the name of the fictional writer-detective hero. Other Queen best sellers included *The Egyptian Cross Mystery* (1932), *The Chinese Orange Mystery* (1934), and the *New Adventures of Ellery Queen* (1940). Dannay–Lee wrote at least 40 Queen mystery novels, which sold about 150 million copies. Stories also appeared in magazines and were adapted for movies, radio, and television. As Barnaby Ross, Dannay–Lee wrote other mysteries, including *The Tragedy of X* (1932).

1932. *The Good Earth*, by Pearl Sydenstricker Buck (1892–1973), a best-selling novel in this period and later. It won a Pulitzer Prize and established Pearl Buck as the most popular woman author of her time. In the 1930s she also published *Sons* (1932), *The Mother* (1934), *A House Divided* and *House of Earth* (1935), *The Exile* and *Fighting Angel* (1936), and *The Patriot* (1939). In 1938 Buck won the Nobel Prize for literature. Her other major works included the novels *Dragon Seed* (1942), *The Promise* (1943), and *Kinfolk* (1949). Buck also wrote, among other books, *Of Men and Women* (1941); *American Unity and Asia* (1942);

Water-Buffalo Children and *What America Means to Me* (1943); *Yu Lan, Flying Boy of China* and *Talk About Russia* (1945); *The Big Wave* (1948); and *American Argument* (1949).

• *Tobacco Road*, by Erskine Preston Caldwell (1903–), the author's most popular novel. It exemplified the social problem novel, revitalized in the depression. Other works by Erskine Caldwell, a southern writer, included *Poor Fool* (1930), *American Earth* (1931), *God's Little Acre* and *We Are the Living* (1933), *Journeyman* and *Some American People* (1935), *Tragic Ground* (1944), and *Call It Experience* (1951). Major short story collections were *Kneel to the Rising Sun and Other Stories* (1935), *Georgia Boy* (1943), and *Complete Stories* (1953).

1933. Three best sellers—*Anthony Adverse*, by William Hervey Allen (1889–1949); *The Case of the Sulky Girl*, by Erle Stanley Gardner (1889–1970); and *Lost Horizon*, by English author James Hilton (1900–1954). Hervey Allen's other novels included *Action at Aquila* (1937) and *It Was Like This* (1940). He also wrote *Israfel* (1926), a biography of Edgar Allan Poe. The mystery by Gardner, one of the all-time best-selling authors, was also a later best seller. His other best sellers during and after their initial publication included *The Case of the Curious Bride* (1934), *The Case of the Counterfeit Eye* (1935), *The Case of the Stuttering Bishop* (1936), *The Case of the Dangerous Dowager* and *The Case of the Lame Canary* (1937), and *The Case of the Substitute Face* (1938). Gardner also wrote under the pseudonyms of Kyle Corning, Charles M. Green, Carleton Kendrake, Charles J. Kenny, Robert Parr, etc. His works included nonfiction and westerns.

• *The Autobiography of Alice B. Toklas*, by Gertrude Stein (1874–1946), published. Stein's other books included the short story collection *Three Lives* (1909), *Wars I Have Seen* (1945), *Brewsie and Willie* (1946), and *First Reader and Three Plays* (1948). Stein was a long-time resident of France.

• *United States v. One Book Called "Ulysses"* (5 F. Supp. 182). The decision provided a new definition of obscenity for other courts to consider. In this prosecution under the Tariff Act of 1930 customs officers prevented a woman from bringing James Joyce's stream-of-consciousness novel into the United States. Intervening in the case, Random House, Inc., book publisher, asked Judge John Woolsey of the federal District Court for the Southern District of New York to read the entire book to see if it was truly obscene. Woolsey did, and ruled *Ulysses* was art, not obscenity. Woolsey defined a book as obscene if it "tends to stir the sex impulses or to lead to sexually impure and lustful thoughts. Whether a particular book would tend to excite such impulses must be the test of the court's opinion as to its effect (when judged as a whole) on a person with average sex instincts." The decision enunciated four principles that had not been accepted by most other courts. Whether a book is obscene, according to Woolsey, could be based on (1) the purity of the author's purpose, rather than "impure" words; (2) the dominant effect of the book as a whole, rather than on isolated passages; (3) the effect of the book on normal adults, rather than on children or abnormal adults; and (4) artistic or literary merit of the book balanced against incidental obscenity.

1935. *Studs Lonigan* trilogy (1932–1935), by James Thomas Farrell (1904–1979), which exemplified the social problem novel, revitalized in the depression. *Studs Lonigan* naturalistically portrayed squalor among the Chicago Irish. Among Farrell's other works were novels and short stories, including *The Short Stories of James T. Farrell* (1937).

1936. *Gone With the Wind*, by Margaret Mitchell (1909–1949), and *How to Win Friends and Influence People*, by Dale Carnegie (1888–1955), best sellers in this period and later. Mitchell's novel won a Pulitzer Prize in 1937. (A film version, released in 1939, was still being shown in the 1980s.) Carnegie's work was based on his course.

1938. Four best sellers—*The Best of Damon Runyon*, by Alfred Damon Runyon (1880–1946); *Fast Company*, by Marco Page (1909–1968); *Singing Guns*, by Max Brand (1892–1944); and *The Yearling*, by Marjorie Kinan Rawlings (1896–1953). The books by Damon Runyon and Brand, pseudonym for Frederick Schiller Faust, were also best sellers later. Other works by Runyon included *Tents of Trouble* (1911), verse, and *Rhymes of the Firing Line* (1912), short stories. *Fast Company* was the first mystery by Page, pseudonym of Harry Kurnitz, who under his real name wrote movie scripts and Broadway plays. Other Page mysteries included *The Shadowy Third* (1946) and *Reclining Figure* (1952). *The Yearling* won a Pulitzer Prize. Rawlings's other works included *South Moon Under* (1933), *Golden Apples* (1935), and *Cross Creek Cookery* (1942).

1939. Pocket Books (May–) founded by Robert Fair de Graff (1895–1981) to publish inexpensive unabridged paperback reprints of best sellers. Pocket Books's huge success spurred a new paperback revolution; other publishers had tried to sell paperback reprints of popular books for 25 cents to 35 cents with little success. De Graff's pocket-size books sold at the uniform low price of 25 cents. Printing costs were lowered by using cheap paper on rotary presses, but the books had attractive covers in colors. A key to his formula was distribution through newsstands and other dealers serviced by newspaper and magazine wholesalers. Paperback publishing flourished in World War II (especially for armed services personnel); by 1950 about 90,000 dealers sold paperbacks. Pocket Books became one of the three major paper publishers, and in July 1966 it merged with Simon & Schuster, becoming a division of that company and retaining its own reprint. By the 1970s more than 100,000 paperbound titles by many publishers were in print, and in the 1980s paperbacks continued to flourish.

● *The Grapes of Wrath*, by John Ernst Steinbeck (1902–1968), a best seller in this period and later. John Steinbeck humanistically portrayed the Dust Bowl disaster of the 1930s and the dislocation of the Okies. His other major novels included *Tortilla Flat* (1935), *Of Mice and Men* (1937), *Cannery Row* (1945) and *East of Eden* (1952); short stories volumes included *Nothing So Monstrous* (1936) and *The Long Valley* (1938). Steinbeck received the Nobel Prize for literature in 1962.

1940. *The Ox-Bow Incident* by Walter van Tilburg Clark (1909–1971), published. Clark's other major novels included *The Track of the Cat* (1949).

Newspapers

1930. English-language dailies of general circulation down 258 from 1910 to 1,942. In the two decades 1,391 dailies had been discontinued or changed to weeklies, 362 merged with rivals, and 1,495 founded. One-fourth of the new papers had been discontinued within the first year. Some newcomers had thrived in expanding small towns and cities as the nation became increasingly urban. The number of towns and cities of at least 8,000 population had increased from 768 to 1,208 as the national population increased from 92 million to 122 million (1930). Daily newspaper circulation increased at a faster rate than the population, rising from 22.5 million per day in 1910 to 39.6 million per day by 1930. During that time Sunday circulation rose from 13 million to 27 million. The number of cities with dailies increased from 1,207 to 1,402. The number of one-daily cities increased from 509 to 1,002, and the number of one-combination (morning and afternoon) newspaper cities from 9 to 112, while the number of cities with competing dailies declined from 689 to 288. Reasons for declines, mostly economic, included business depressions, competition for advertising and circulation, declining economic or social need, ineffective management, planned consolidation, standardization of content (resulting in loss of individuality, reader appeal), technological changes, wartime inflation.

1931. *Near v. Minnesota ex rel. Olson* (283 U.S. 697). In this landmark case the U.S. Supreme Court prohibited prior restraint of publication. A Minnesota statute (1925) permitted suppression of a "malicious, scandalous and defamatory newspaper, magazine, or other periodical." This law had been designed to halt publication of the *Saturday Press*, a Minneapolis "scandal sheet" highly critical of government officials. H. M. Near was enjoined from publishing his paper until he could convince the lower court that he would operate without the objectionable aspects indicated in the "gag law." Chief Justice Charles Evans Hughes (1862–1948) wrote the 5–4 majority decision, holding the Minnesota statute unconstitutional because it permitted prior restraint on publication. Hughes said that suppression presented a greater danger than an irresponsible attack on public officials, who could have properly sued for libel. Following the 1925 doctrine of *Gitlow v. New York* (168 U.S. 652), the Supreme Court applied the First Amendment to the state through the due process clause of the Fourteenth Amendment.

1933. Largest declines of daily newspaper advertising and circulation in the depression. Advertising dropped from $860 million (1929) to $473 million. Circulation dropped from 39,600,000 (1930) to 34,850,000.

• American Newspaper Guild (15 December–) founded in Washington, D.C., by delegates from 30 cites "to preserve the vocational interests of the members," to improve their working conditions by collective bargaining, and "to raise the standards of journalism." First national president was Matthew Heywood Campbell Broun (1888–1939), columnist for the New York *World-Telegram*, who served to his death; first executive secretary was Jonathan Eddy. By the first annual convention (June 1934), in St. Paul, Minnesota, the Guild had 8,000 members, mostly editorial employees of newspapers. The convention called for contracts providing minimum wages, maximum hours, overtime pay, paid holidays and vacations, sick leave, severance pay, etc. The first contract was negotiated with the Philadelphia *Record*. In 1936 the Guild affiliated with the American Federation of Labor, in 1937 with the Committee on Industrial Organization. In 1937 it won a case against the Associated Press, which was accused of discharging Morris Watson for union activities. The National Labor Relations Board had ruled against AP, which carried the case to the U.S. Supreme Court, claiming the National Labor Relations Act contravened the guarantee of press freedom in the First Amendment. In *Associated Press v. National Labor Relations Board* (301 U.S. 103) the high court upheld the NLRA's constitutionality and the NLRB decision. The press was held not immune from general laws. In 1938 the Guild signed a contract with United Press, its first with a press association. In the 1930s the Guild negotiated contracts with 91 dailies and conducted 31 strikes, which were more successful in winning recognition and salary scale adjustments than closed shops. In the 1940s the union was anti-Communist but liberal. It increased its power and membership, in 1946 admitting business and clerical employees of newspapers. By 1949 it had more than 23,000 members; 173 contracts with dailies and several independent Sunday papers; and 59 contracts with news magazines, news services, radio stations, weeklies, and other communication companies. By 1954 the Guild had reached its 1946 goal of a $100 per week minimum wage for the most experienced employees; by 1983 average top minimum for reporters nationally was more than $450. In the 1960s the Guild revived efforts to raise journalistic standards, a goal that had been largely dormant since the 1930s, with a notable exception of an annual reward established (1941) for newspaper work "in the spirit of Heywood Broun." The Guild established the Mellett Fund for a Free and Responsible Press to finance community press councils and encouraged publication of critical media reviews. On some papers Guild members sought a voice in management. Other issues included racial discrimination, reporters' privilege, and restrictions on the press. U.S. and Canadian membership in the Newspaper Guild, as it became known, passed 33,000, concentrated in larger dailies and in press associations.

1934. National Association of Science Writers founded. By the mid-1980s there were approximately 1,100 members.

1935. Syndicated column by Mrs. Anna Eleanor Roosevelt (1884–1962) for United Features Syndicate, unprecedented for a First Lady.

1936. *Grosjean v. American Press Co.* (297 U.S. 233). In this case the U.S. Supreme Court prohibited discriminatory taxation. In 1934 the machine of Louisiana political boss Huey Long pushed through the state legislature a bill that levied a special 2 percent tax on the gross advertising income of Louisiana newspapers with at least 20,000 circulation weekly. Of the 13 papers affected, 12 opposed Long. In 1936 the Supreme Court found the tax punitive and unconstitutional. In the unanimous decision written by Justice George Sutherland (1862–1942), the Court held that Long's law was a "deliberate and calculated device in the guise of a tax to limit the circulation of information to which the public is entitled in virtue of the constitutional guarantees. A free press stands as one of the great interpreters between the government and the people. To allow it to be fettered is to fetter ourselves."

• Detroit *Michigan Chronicle* founded for blacks. In 1983 it was the largest paper in the John H. Sengstacke group, with a weekly circulation of about 31,000. L. M. Quinn was publisher and editor in the mid-1980s.

1937. Daily newspaper advertising and circulation at new highs. Advertising climbed from $473 million (1933) to $630 million. Circulation climbed from 34,850,000 (1933) to 41,500,000.

1938. Wheeler-Lea Act (April) authorizing the Federal Trade Commission (f. 1914) to stop false and misleading advertising, particularly for cosmetics, drugs, and food. It applied to all media.

1940. Hempstead, New York, *Newsday* (9 September–) founded by Alicia Patterson Guggenheim (1906–1963) and Harry F. Guggenheim

(1890–1971) as a community newspaper for Long Islanders. By mid-century it had grown with Long Island to become the outstanding suburban daily in the nation. It was lively, loaded with advertising, and one of the most attractive tabloids. Mr. Guggenheim, who had been president, succeeded Mrs. Guggenheim as publisher and editor after her death. By 1970 circulation had grown from the first year's 11,000 to 450,000. That year the Times Mirror Company bought *Newsday* and William Attwood (1919–) became president and publisher (to 1978). In April 1972 *Newsday* began a Sunday edition, which attained 350,000 circulation by late 1973. Highly ranked in polls, sometimes among the ten best dailies, *Newsday* was by 1974 the fifth largest evening newspaper and read by more than half the families in Suffolk and Nassau counties, Long Island, the ninth largest metropolitan market. Considered liberal, the paper was known for local, national, and international coverage, investigative reporting, features, and interpretation. By the late 1970s *Newsday* ranked as the fourth largest evening newspaper and the eleventh daily. In the early 1980s David Laventhol was publisher, Anthony Insolia, editor. Published at Melville, New York, *Newsday* had circulations of more than 500,000 daily and more than 570,000 Sunday. In 1983 it began a New York City edition.

● PM (–1949) founded in New York by Marshall Field III (1893–1956) as a liberal, adless tabloid. Under founding editor Ralph Ingersoll (1900–1985) the daily was noted for the "left-wing" point of view expressed in the news columns, excellent pictures, and skilled staff. During World War II correspondent Leah Burdette was killed in Iran. In 1946 Field began accepting advertising in an attempt to bolster sagging finances. In 1948 he sold *PM*, which became the New York *Star*, with Joseph Barnes editor, then the *Compass*.

1941. *Bridges v. California* and *Times Mirror Co. v. Superior Court* (314 U.S. 252). In this decision the U.S. Supreme Court widened the scope of press comment on pending litigation. Harry Bridges, longshoreman union leader, had been fined for contempt for sending to the secretary of labor a telegram—published in newspapers—that criticized a court decision in a labor case and threatened a retaliatory strike. The Times Mirror Company and the managing editor of its Los Angeles *Times* were fined for publishing three editorials while a trial court was considering sentences in a labor case. One editorial urged the court to make "examples" of the defendants, who had been convicted of intimidating nonunion workers. In a single 5–4 decision the Supreme Court reversed the lower courts, saying the appellants were protected by the First Amendment through the due process clause of the Fourteenth Amendment. Applying the "clear and present danger" test, the majority found that the publications were not likely to disrupt the functions of the courts—to interfere with justice. Newspapers could now supposedly comment on unclosed court actions without fear of punishment, unless a judge could hold that the comment created so immediate and great a danger that the court could no longer function. But state courts resisted this idea, and such newspapers as the Miami *Herald*, in *Pennekamp v. Florida* (328 U.S. 331 [1946]), and the Corpus Christi *Caller-Times*, in *Craig v. Harney* (331 U.S. 364 [1947]), had to fight to avoid penalties for contempt.

• Chicago *Sun* (4 December–) founded by Marshall Field III as a liberal tabloid competitor to the conservative broadsheet *Tribune* (f. 1847); both morning dailies. Barred by the *Tribune* from obtaining Associated Press service, Field challenged the press association under the Sherman Antitrust Act (1890). In the early 1940s, an AP member could bar an applicant in its own city, unless overridden by a four-fifths vote of the membership, a rare occurrence. Field sued in 1942, and three years later in *Associated Press et al. v. United States* (326 U.S. 1) the U.S. Supreme Court held that the AP bylaws unfairly restricted competition. By court order AP rescinded its rule, and several previously barred newspapers, including the *Sun*, were elected to membership. The *Sun*, meanwhile, had one of the largest newspaper staffs covering World War II. In 1948 Field bought the Chicago *Times* (f. 1929), a terse, liberal daily, and combined it with the reliable, somewhat sensational *Sun*, maintaining tabloid format. In 1959 Marshall Field IV, then owner of the morning *Sun-Times*, bought the afternoon *Daily News* (f. 1876) from John S. Knight (1895–1981) for a record $24 million. In 1962 the *Sun-Times* began syndicating cartoonist Bill Mauldin (1921–). In 1968 Ralph Maurice Otwell (1926–) became *Sun-Times* managing editor, in 1976 editor. A 1982 survey ranked the paper high regionally but below the top 15 dailies nationally. In 1983 it had the eighth largest circulation among dailies: 654,957. Marshall Field V, who had taken over in 1969, sold the paper in 1983 for $90 million to Rupert Murdoch (1931–), who sensationalized it. In the mid-1980s circulation was about 649,900, tenth among dailies.

Magazines

1930. *Fortune* (February–) founded in New York by Henry Robinson Luce (1898–1967) to cover business and industry for upper management. Originally, Henry R. Luce had conceived a magazine that would print material crowded out of *Time*'s business pages. By late 1928 a prospectus announced the purpose as "to reflect industrial life in ink and paper and word and picture as the finest skyscraper reflects it in stone and steel and architecture." *Fortune* would be sumptuously printed on quality paper and sell for $1 a copy. After the financial crash, Time Inc. executives reconsidered the launch, then proceeded with more hope than optimism. The first issue began with 30,000 subscribers and finished the year with 34,000. From the beginning the monthly was luxuriously printed in a large format of 11¼ by 14 inches. Articles were thoroughly researched and carefully written, with close attention to accuracy. *Fortune* pioneered the detailed analysis of the finances, policies, problems, and structure of one company—an article type that eventually became a staple in general business periodicals. The magazine also was well illustrated, with photographs by Margaret Bourke-White, Peter Stackpole, and Erich Salomon, a pioneer in candid camera photography who excelled at making executives look interesting. Soon after the founding, *Fortune*, under Luce's continuing influence, broadened coverage to deal not only with business but also government, politics, and social questions. By the late 1930s, an issue might cover an entire industry, a single corporation, an influential or wealthy community, and a foreign nation. Despite the high cover price, *Fortune* thrived. By 1936 advertising gross revenues had increased from $247,000 (1930) to $1,963,000 and circulation had risen to 139,000. In October 1948 an improved *Fortune* appeared, with new departments, layout, and typography as well as more, shorter articles. Writers analyzed industrial communications, experimented with group biography, and studied the rise of suburbia. In the 1950s gains continued in advertising and circulation. In 1955 *Fortune* first printed its list of 500 largest corporations. In January 1956 the periodical appeared with redesigned cover, table of contents, and inside layout. In the early 1960s circulation reached about 383,000, ad revenues a record $11,996,000. In 1972 another facelift accompanied a reduced format to save paper, postage, and printing costs, all of which were rising rapidly. With the January 1978 issue came more changes, including fortnightly frequency, new body type, and fewer and larger photos. In the early 1980s *Fortune*'s demographic and regional editions were printed twenty-six times a year, published by Edward Lenahan and edited by William S. Rukeyser (1939–). In the mid-1980s circulation was about 710,000.

1931. Controlled Circulation Audit founded to review nonpaid circulation publications, which Audit Bureau of Circulations refused to consider; verified circulation figures for potential advertisers. In 1953 CCA became Business Publications Audit of Circulation, Inc.

• *Apparel Arts* (15 October–) founded in New York by David Archibald Smart (1892–1952), William H. Weintraub, et al., with Arnold Gingrich (1903–1976) first editor, as a quarterly for the men's clothing trade. In 1957 *Apparel Arts* spawned *Gentlemen's Quarterly*, a men's fashion consumer magazine.

1933. *News-Week* (17 February–) founded in New York by Thomas John Cardell Martyn as a news digest. Martyn (former foreign news editor of *Time*) became business manager, Samuel T. Williamson editor. Advertisers were guaranteed 50,000 circulation. Departmentalized, the 32-page magazine reported and explained the news in newspaperlike writing style, accompanied by many photographs. Covers consisted of seven photos representing an important event for each day of the week; they confused newsstand customers and were discontinued in June 1934. By 1937 *News-Week* had 250,000 circulation and financial problems, solved that February by merging with *Today* (f. 1933). New president was Vincent Astor, new editor Raymond Moley (1886–1975), both from *Today*. In October 1937, after Malcolm Muir became publisher and president, the magazine's title was revised to *Newsweek: The Magazine of News Significance*, and the news digest formula was replaced with reporting, backgrounding, and interpreting the news. Signed columns supplemented the anonymous news reports. To supplement press associations, management established a staff of researchers and a news-gathering system of bureaus and correspondents. *Newsweek* had one of the largest staffs covering World War II and produced "pony" editions for military personnel. In 1949 Theodore F. Mueller became publisher. Profits and circulation rose through the 1950s. Gibson McCabe succeeded Mueller in 1958, became president in 1959. In 1961 Phillip L. Graham (1915–1963) bought *Newsweek* for $8,985,000. In 1962 his periodical had 1,531,000 circulation and $27,504,000 advertising revenue. Upon Graham's death his widow, Katharine Meyer Graham (1917–) took over. In the 1960s *Newsweek* had about 230 editorial employees and about 200 correspondents. Its Vietnam staff included Beverly Deepe, Everette Martin, Mert Perry, and François Sully. The magazine stuck to the 1937 formula with such improvements as new departments, greater flexibility, and faster production. In the 1970s editors tended to give more emphasis to the arts and popular culture, until the decade's end, when they renewed emphasis on news coverage. Modern electronic equipment was installed. The magazine was put together in New York, then material sent on a private wire to a pre-press center in Carlstadt, New Jersey, where film was made for weekend printing in plants in Chicago; Hong Kong; Jonesboro, Arkansas; Lancaster, Pennsylvania; London; Los Angeles; and Pewaukee, Wisconsin. In 1980 *Newsweek* ranked among the top ten consumer magazines in advertising income (third with $175,049,000, between *Time* and *Parade*) and in total revenue (fourth with $256,805,000, between *Reader's Digest* and *Playboy*); among consumer weeklies it ranked seventh in circulation with 2,958,397 (between *The Star* and *People*). In the early 1980s *Newsweek* published 18 foreign editions; in 1984 it discontinued the Australian edition to publish an insert (*Newsweek*'s first) in the *Bulletin*, an Australian news weekly. In 1982 William Broyles, Jr. (1944–), became *Newsweek* editor. The periodical had 11 U.S. and 16 foreign bureaus. In the mid-1980s circulation exceeded 3 million.

• *Esquire* (October–) founded in New York by David A. Smart, Alfred Smart, William H. Weintraub, and Editor Arnold Gingrich as a new kind of men's periodical, with emphasis on fashions, humorous illustrations, and short stories. The first issue was an oversized quarterly on glossy paper, with about 40 of its 116 pages in color. Over articles or stories were such bylines as Erskine Caldwell, Morley Callaghan, Dashiell Hammett, Ernest Hemingway, Bobby Jones, John Dos Passos, and Gene Tunney. Demand was so great for the first issue's 105,000 copies at 50 cents each that *Esquire* became a monthly with its second issue, dated January 1934. By 1937 circulation was about 625,000. For most of the first ten years the periodical was known for distinctive articles, essays, and stories by such authors as F. Scott Fitzgerald, Ernest Hemingway, D. H. Lawrence, Thomas Mann, André Maurois, George Jean Nathan, Ezra Pound, and Thomas Wolfe. It was also known for its art work, including the (George) Petty girls, idealized women with graceful curves, long limbs, and gossamer garb; and later the (Joaquin Alberto) Vargas girls, similar idealizations. E. Simms Campbell created "Esky," the little man with ogling eyes and jaunty upturned moustache who became the periodical's symbol. After Gingrich left in 1942, content, makeup, and typography changed. The magazine became preoccupied with sex. In 1943 Postmaster General Frank Comerford Walker (1886–1959) revoked second-class mailing privileges on grounds that *Esquire* was ineligible for that preferential rate. The periodical was not, Frank C. Walker contended, "published for the dissemination of information of a public character, or devoted to literature, the sciences, arts, or some special industry," as the law required, nor did it make a "special contribution to the public welfare." Walker's move meant that the magazine would have to pay the fourth-class rate, which would cost about $500,000 a year more. To restrain the postmaster general *Esquire* filed suit, which terminated in the U.S. Supreme Court in 1946. Robert Emmett Hannegan was then postmaster general. In *Hannegan v. Esquire* (327 U.S. 146) the high court restored the second-class privilege, saying that the postmaster general had "no power to prescribe standards for the literature or the art which a mailable periodical disseminates." The unanimous decision in effect limited the Post Office to continue excluding publications only for obscenity. In 1952 Gingrich returned and tried to recapture *Esquire*'s distinction; he deemphasized sex and emphasized a serious purpose. Content followed no standard forumla but provided variety and surprise; subject areas included history, politics, and racism. Fiction and nonfiction came from new and previous contributors, including Vance Bourjaily, William Inge, Norman Mailer, Arthur

Miller, Howard Nemerov, Philip Roth, Arthur Schlesinger, Jr., Anthony West, and Tennessee Williams. In the 1960s *Esquire* led the *New Journalism* movement with such authors as Gay Talese and Tom Wolfe; top editors included Harold T. P. Hayes and Con Erickson. By 1962 circulation had risen to about 884,000, advertising gross revenues to about $7,470,000. *Esquire* was praised for editorial diversity and creativity, for reporting social trends, and for original typography and design. An innovation was the use of seven regional covers (June 1968). The 564-page fortieth anniversary edition included contributions from 41 Pulitzer Prize winners and 15 Nobel Prize winners. After Gingrich's death, former staff member Clay Felker (1925–) took over and, with art direction by Milton Glaser (1929–), mixed fresh ideas with successful aspects of past issues and published fortnightly. After losing money, *Esquire* in 1979 was sold to Phillip Moffitt and Christopher Whittle, who infused new monies and ideas. In March 1980 the magazine began coming out monthly again, with a new logo and inside appearance. Early in the 1980s circulation stood at almost 651,000. In mid-decade Senior Executive Editor Betsy Carter and Editor Moffitt provided a wide range of subject matter for intelligent, sophisticated readers. Circulation was about 700,000.

• *Today* (November–) founded by Raymond Moley, editor to 1937, with financial support from Vincent Astor and W. Averell Harriman, to popularize the New Deal; widely quoted. Its largest circulation was 75,000 before it merged with *News-Week* in February 1937.

• *United States News* founded in Washington, D.C., by David Lawrence (1888–1973) as the weekly successor to the *United States Daily* (f. 1926), a national newspaper; reported, analyzed, and forecast national events. In 1940 the format was changed from newspaper to magazine. The new look included a red, white, and blue cover; more inside color; more charts, illustrations, and photographs. In January 1948 *United States News* and its sister publication, *World Report* (f. 1946), which consisted only of international affairs, were combined as *U.S. News* and *World Report*. With the 19 March 1948 issue the periodical became *U.S. News and World Report*. The first issue using the ampersand was 2 April 1948. The combined periodical covered national and international affairs, with emphasis on economic and political subjects. Content, usually fair but politically conservative, included analyses, interviews, and on-the-scene reports as well as many full texts of documents and statements. It was not departmentalized. Circulation increased to 1,256,000 in 1962, the year Lawrence sold the magazine to his employees. In the mid-1970s the owners added advanced electronic publishing methods; 1977 brought new typography, 1980 more color. *U.S. News & World Report* entered the 1980s with a reputation for accurate, balanced, reliable coverage and with a circulation of about 2.1

million, where it remained in the mid-1980s. Editor was Marvin L. Stone. In 1983 the magazine ranked about tenth in circulation. In 1984 the employee-owners sold to Mortimer Zuckerman for a record $168.5 million; the deal included a typesetting company (Publishers Services International) and a Washington real estate development. *U.S. News & World Report* ended 1985 with a new editorial policy that included strengthened visual appeal and business, lifestyle, and personal finance coverage.

1936. *Coronet* founded in New York by Esquire, Inc., with Arnold Gingrich as the first editor. Publisher David A. Smart wanted to make *Coronet* a beautiful, pocket-size magazine without advertising. The first issue had a five-color cover and ran drawings, etchings, color reproductions of paintings by Raphael and Rembrandt, photographs, articles, and fiction; its 250,000 copies quickly sold. Subsequent 1930s issues were also profusely illustrated, including color reproductions of classical and modern paintings and cartoons. Artistic, clever writing included satire. After initial success circulation declined from about 200,000 in 1936 to about 100,000 in early 1940. That year Oscar Dystel took over editorial operations and replaced classical reproductions with photographs of models and starlets. Imitating *Reader's Digest*, Dystel made *Coronet* inspirational. During World War II circulation increased to an estimated 2 to 5 million. When *Coronet* accepted ads in 1947 (for the first time, except for briefly in 1937) to meet rising costs, the circulation guarantee was 2 million. With ads came new emphasis on reader participation content, including games and puzzles. Competing against the newly popular television medium in the 1950s, *Coronet* joined the numbers chase for circulation. Despite sales in the millions by the early 1960s, the magazine was losing hundreds of thousands of dollars annually due to insufficient ad revenue. After Esquire, Inc., discontinued *Coronet*, Hy Steirman's H.S. Publications inaugurated a similar-looking *Coronet* emphasizing general-interest material, including topical articles on family problems, relationships between the sexes, and self-help guidance. This formula continued to 1972, when a Warner Communications division purchased the periodical and made it a women's psychological service magazine. Yvonne Dunleavy directed the editorial changes. In 1972 the monthly had about 350,000 circulation. Before expiring, it became a general-interest magazine for men and women published by Challenge Publications, Inc., of Canoga Park, California, with about 200,000 circulation.

● *Life* (19 November–) founded in New York by Henry R. Luce as a large-format photojournalism weekly; became the most successful of its kind. Experimentation had begun in 1933, with Luce and his staff drawing on *Time*, *Fortune*, and "March of Time" for ideas. In October 1936 Luce bought the title of the defunct *Life* humor magazine. The new

Life's goals were, according to its prospectus, "to see life; to see the world; to eyewitness great events; to watch the faces of the poor and the gestures of the proud; to see strange things—machines, armies, multitudes, shadows in the jungle and on the moon; to see man's work—his paintings, towns and discoveries; to see thousands of miles away, things hidden behind walls and within rooms, things dangerous to come to; the women that men love and many children; to see and to take pleasure in seeing; to see and be amazed; to see and be instructed. . . . " Luce appointed John Shaw Billings managing editor and remained active in operations. The first issue of 96 large slick pages quickly sold out its 466,000 press run at 10 cents a copy. Heavily promoted, *Life* was soon selling a million copies a week. Advertising failed to keep up with costs of heavy coated stock, etc., and *Life* lost $6 million before it began paying back many times over. Wilson Hicks (1897?–1970) was picture editor then executive editor (to 1950); publisher was Roy Larsen (1899–1979), who replaced Luce as Time Inc. president in 1939 (to 1960). Photographers included Margaret Bourke-White, Robert Capa, David Douglas Duncan, Alfred Eisenstaedt, Carl Mydans, Gordon Parks, W. Eugene Smith, and Peter Stackpole. *Life* covered World War II thoroughly with artistry, timeliness, and historical consciousness. In 1943 it ran its first occasional fiction, which in 1952 included Ernest Hemingway's *The Old Man and the Sea*. In the 1940s and 1950s the periodical also ran memoirs of famous persons, including Winston Churchill, General Douglas MacArthur, and Harry S Truman. It occasionally ran such cultural content as the award-winning series "The World We Live In" (1953). In 1959 *Life* signed (for $500,000) the first seven astronauts to tell their eyewitness stories. Going into the 1960s with several million circulation, *Life* battled other magazines and especially television. In January 1961 the magazine published a special souvenir supplement covering President Kennedy's inauguration. That year management regrouped editorial and advertising content, revised layouts, and altered the cover. The periodical, which was read by an estimated 25 percent of all U.S. adults, proclaimed its intention to be a great magazine of adventure, better living, fine and lively arts, history, nature, politics, science, and sport. Multiple U.S. and Canadian editions for advertisers grew. In 1962 *Life* ran articles by 12 prominent people on "The National Purpose." After Kennedy's assassination in 1963 *Life* published a special memorial edition. In 1963 *Life* led all magazines in advertising gross revenue with $143,875,000; in 1966 figures peaked at almost $170 million. Circulation peaked in 1969 at 8,548,500; in 1971 it was down to 7,110,000. Advertising gross revenue dipped $32 million in a year to slightly below $110 million, and *TV Guide* took over the lead in ad revenues. In 1968–1972 *Life* lost about $30 million. Ad revenue had increased insufficiently to cover rising costs of production and distribution, despite forced circulation reductions; many advertisers could not pay the necessarily high rates even for demographic editions. With a circulation of 5.5 million *Life* was suspended in 1972—another mass magazine death in the changing marketplace. After the suspension *Life's* name occasionally appeared on special reports and books. In October 1978 the magazine was resurrected as a general-interest picture monthly with goals similar to its original purpose but with less emphasis on news and more emphasis on pictorial quality. The 10⅛ by 13⅛ inch format, high-quality coated paper, and rotogravure printing contributed to excellent photo display. Rather than hire the best photographers again, management drew on other Time Inc. staff and free-lancers. Content included many four-color and black-and-white photos, artists' illustrations, and a few articles and columns. Publisher Charles A. Whittingham directed the periodical toward a smaller, more affluent audience that would appeal to advertisers. Cover price was $1.50, subscription $18 per year, without the discounts of the previous *Life*. The new *Life's* first issue set a record, with ads on 56 of its 149 pages reaping $848,568; within eight months ad revenues passed $1 million. The rate base in April 1979 was 1 million. The magazine apparently was profiting by its new staffing and marketing approaches as well as the public's interest in pictures, perhaps stimulated by TV. In the 1980s *Life* added a newsprint section of news photos. Mid-decade circulation exceeded 1.4 million, and Managing Editor Richard B. Stolley (1928–) edited the monthly for people of all ages, backgrounds, and interests. A few articles supplemented pictures.

1937. *Commentator* (January–1942) founded by Charles Shipman Payson; pocket-size monthly. In 1939 the *Commentator* bought *Scribner's* (f. 1887), a failing quality magazine, and became *Scribner's Commentator*. Under new management, the periodical became strongly isolationist in the early 1940s. In 1942 Publisher Joseph Hilton Smyth pleaded guilty to an indictment under the Foreign Agents Registration Act for accepting funds from Japanese officials to publish propaganda for their government.

● *Look* (January–) founded in Des Moines by Gardner Cowles, Jr. (1903–), as an offshoot of the rotogravure section of the Cowles family's Des Moines *Register and Tribune* newspaper. *Look* was intended to be a monthly mass magazine covering beauty, current events, education, science, and sports. Through pictures and words it would inform people of what was happening in the world. The first issue sold more than 700,000 copies. At first *Look* was printed by rotogravure on cheap pulp paper and emphasized animals, fashions, foods, personalities, photo quizzes, photo mysteries, and the spectacular and thrilling. About mid-1937 frequency was changed to biweekly. No advertising was accepted until after ten months, when 1.7 million circulation provided a substantial rate base. In 1939 ad revenue totaled $2,250,000. In 1940 "Mike" Cowles moved the advertising and editorial offices to New York. In 1945 circulation reached 2 million; in 1946 ad revenue hit $6,429,000. Growth continued, ad revenue increasing to $17,765,000 in 1950. In the early 1950s sensationalism gave way to an editorial formula that included beauty, entertainment, fashion, foods, health, home living, national and international affairs, science, and sports. *Look* began annually selecting All-American Cities, communities improved by citizen action. By late 1950s the periodical had become more serious. Photo mysteries had been dropped, but there were cartoons and other humor. Photos still were prominent, but more full-length textual articles were run. Topics included civil liberties, highway safety, and problems of minorities. Contributors included Adlai Stevenson, Bertrand Russell, the Duchess of Windsor, Ernest Hemingway, and Walter Lippmann. Ad revenue and circulation increased rapidly as *Look* raced with other mass magazines for high numbers by aggressive promotion, bargain rates, and use of lists from discontinued periodicals. In 1959 *Look* became one of the first large-circulation magazines to publish regional editions, offering advertisers a choice from seven. By 1960 *Look* was one of the four circulation leaders with *Life, Reader's Digest,* and *Saturday Evening Post.* In 1961 *Look* reached an estimated 21 percent of all U.S. adults. In 1963 management was embarrassed by an article that suggested President Kennedy could be defeated in the next election—the piece appeared just after Kennedy's assassination. But that year circulation exceeded 7 million and ad revenue hit $74,198,000, one of the highest ad figures among magazines. In 1966 ad revenue peaked at $80 million, and in 1967 circulation peaked at almost 8 million. Then both figures declined as management fought television and higher costs, including rising postal rates. Cutting off 1 million subscribers to reach 6.5 million who would attract advertisers, *Look* shifted circulation to the best metropolitan markets. In 1969 it offered advertisers "Top/Spot," the first "geodemic" edition for zip code zones with high median incomes; eventually it offered about 160 separate editions of some issues. Among other *Look* innovations were improved high-speed reproduction processes. Due to rising costs and dropping ad revenue, the periodical was discontinued in 1971. Over the years *Look* had been produced by many skilled people, including art directors William Hopkins and Allen Hurlburt, photography director Arthur Rothstein, editors Daniel D. Mich and William B. Arthur, and photographers Paul Fusco, Phillip Harrington, and John Vachon. They had favored people over things, fact over fiction, features over spot news, and photos over text. In September 1978 a pilot issue came out for a new *Look*, founded by Daniel Filipacchi, who intended to combine with new ideas aspects of *Paris Match* (which he had restored) and of the old *Look* and *Life*. The first public issue, 19 February 1979, was published under the supervision of Robert Gutwillig. It had for the East a cover with a photo of Nelson A. Rockefeller, recently deceased, and for the West a cover with a picture of Patty Hearst, recently freed from prison. Format was an unusual 9 by 12 inches. The biweekly emphasized celebrities, photographs, and crisp layouts. Circulation guarantee was 600,000. Sales and financial losses both rose. Frequency was changed to monthly, the editor-publisher to Jann S. Wenner (1946–), who sought a new mass audience unconcerned with the *Look* tradition. In his first issue, July 1979, readers noticed a shift in emphasis from gossip and spot news to in-depth profiles of people who reflected trends. Losses rose to an estimated $8 to $10 million, and in August 1979 *Look* was discontinued again.

1938. *Ken* (March–3 August 1939) founded in New York by David A. Smart and Arnold Gingrich (both of Esquire, Inc.) as a liberal magazine backgrounding events as insiders viewed them. Smart and Gingrich had idealistically begun laying plans a year before for a radically liberal periodical, but before the first issue business pressures forced them to moderate editorial policy. Some staff thought the magazine played too safe, opposing both communism and fascism to appease commercial interests. For a while *Ken* sold about 500,000 copies per issues, with such contributors as Ernest Hemingway and with many large photographs, but it gradually lost advertising. To boost the total monthly guarantee to advertisers, management in April 1939 changed frequency from semi-monthly to weekly. In June the price was cut from 25 cents to 10 cents. The changes were ineffective.

1941. *Parade* (13 July–) founded by Marshall Field III (1893–1956) as *The Weekly Picture Newspaper* (subtitle). The magazine carried no advertisements and sold on newsstands for 5 cents; later, newspapers began carrying it as a Sunday supplement. In 1947 Jess C. Gorkin (1913–) became editor, serving to 1978. With the addition of ads and other changes, *Parade* became financially successful in the early 1950s. In 1958 Marshall Field IV sold the magazine to John Hay Whitney (1904–1982). Circulation climbed to 9.5 million in 1960, making *Parade* one of eleven magazines with more than 5 million. By 1974 circulation exceeded 17 million in about 100 newspapers. Editorial policy included keeping on top of the news and providing stories newspapers could not get for themselves. In 1975 James M. McAllister became president and chief executive officer, in 1978 board chairman. In 1976 Newhouse Newspapers bought *The Sunday Newspaper Magazine*, as it was now subtitled. In the late 1970s ad revenues reached $100 million and circulation exceeded 20 million in more than 100 newspaper. By 1980 circulation was 21,644,000, the highest for consumer magazines. *Parade* was fourth in advertising income with $135,899,000. By the mid-1980s circulation had climbed to 23,681,200 and total revenue to $157,346,000, ranking *Parade* first and eighteenth respectively in those categories. Advertising director was Anne Holton, editor Walter Anderson, and publisher Carlo Vittorini. Headquartered in New York, the weekly was published for a general audience and emphasized special articles of national interest on such topics as business, celebrities, health, and newsmakers. Themed editorial sections were edited by Julia Child, on food; Carl Sagan, science; and Earl Ubell, health. Departments included Intelligence Report, Laugh Parade, and Personality Parade (questions and answers about famous people).

Motion Pictures

1930. *All Quiet on the Western Front*, directed by Lewis Milestone (1895–1980), the first major sound film of war. It indicted World War I militarism.

• *Little Caesar*, the beginning of the gangster genre in the sound era. It depicted a mobster's rise and fall. The film was directed by Mervyn LeRoy (1900–) and starred Edward G. Robinson (1893–1973), originally Emanuel Goldenberg. Two other significant early gangster sound films were *Public Enemy* (1931), starring James Cagney (1900–1986), and *Scarface* (1932), starring Paul Muni (1895–1967), original surname Weisenfreund. These three genre classics glamorized amoral underworld brutality. Imitations, most of which were inferior, included *Manhattan Melodrama* (1934), *The Roaring Twenties* (1939), and *Johnny Eager* and *High Sierra* (1941). Gangster movies typically were fast paced, laconic, and tough—and reminded moviegoers that crime does not pay.

• *Morocco*, Director Josef von Sternberg's first U.S. film, starring Marlene Dietrich (1902–), originally Maria von Losch. The hero was Gary Cooper (1901–1961). Von Sternberg (1894–1969) had made *The Blue Angel*, starring Dietrich, in 1929. Other von Sternberg movies of the 1930s included *An American Tragedy* (1931), *Shanghai Express* (1932), *The Scarlet Empress* (1934), and *The Devil Is a Woman* (1935). His films were visually beautiful and full of psychological details.

1932. *I Am a Fugitive From a Chain Gang*, a social protest film, critically depicting prison brutality in the South; directed by Mervyn LeRoy, starred Paul Muni.

• *Million Dollar Legs*, one of the first sound comedies starring W. C. Fields (1880–1946), originally William Claude Dukenfield, who had successfully transferred his talents from silent pictures. Fields's cynical and misanthropic humor attacked cherished bourgeoise values, especially sentimentality. His verbal wit, delivered in a gravelly voice tinctured with whiskey, complemented his somewhat bloated physical appearance, which was adorned with the apparel of conventional society. Fields's other films of the period included *Tillie and Gus* (1933), *It's a Gift* and *Six of a Kind* (1934), *The Old Fashioned Way* (1935), *Poppy* (1936), *The Bank Dick* and *My Little Chickadee* (1940), and *Never Give a Sucker an Even Break* (1941).

● *Trouble in Paradise*, a sophisticated and polished urbane comedy of manners. It starred Kay Francis (1903–1968), Miriam Hopkins (1902–1972), and Herbert Marshall (1890–1966). It was the masterpiece of Ernst Lubitsch (1892–1947), a silent comedy director who made comedies of manners with clever dialogue, and they often focused on upper-class foibles. Other Lubitsch films included *Design for Living* (1933), *Ninotchka* (1939), and *To Be or Not To Be* (1942).

1933. For first time severe effects of the depression felt by the motion picture industry. Admissions and production dropped, theaters closed. The Catholic Legion of Decency threatened an economic boycott because of perceived immoral content of films.

● *Duck Soup*, a hilarious farce, one of the Marx Brothers' funniest films. It was directed by Leo McCarey (1898–1969), who specialized in comedies. The brothers Chico (originally Leonard, 1891–1961), Groucho (Julius, 1890–1977), Harpo (Arthur, 1893–1964), and Zeppo (Herbert, 1901–1979) combined zany visual and verbal humor; Gummo (Milton, 1894–1977) early left the act to become business manager. Their films in this fertile period included *Horsefeathers* (1932), *A Night at the Opera* (1935), *A Day at the Races* (1937), *At the Circus* (1939), and *Go West* (1940). Their first was *The Cocoanuts* (1929).

● *Flying Down to Rio*, directed by Thornton Freeland, the first movie pairing Ginger Rogers (1911–), originally Virginia Katherine McNath, and Fred Astaire (1899–), original surname Austerlitz. The film featured their dancing. Other films in which Astaire and Rogers established a musical tradition included *Top Hat* (1935), directed by Mark Sandrich, and *Swing Time* (1936), directed by George Stevens (1904–1975).

● *42nd Street*. This film established the backstage film as the major new genre of the sound era. In the backstage formula characters usually were performers preparing a show. *42nd Street*, directed by Lloyd Bacon and Busby Berkeley (1895–1976) before the Hollywood Production Code (1934), had tough, sexually candid dialogue.

● *She Done Him Wrong*, the most sexually suggestive of Mae West's films, which also included the sanitized *I'm No Angel* (1933), *Belle of the Nineties* (1934), and *Goin' To Town* (1935). The buxom, hefty blonde parodied amoral women who enjoyed nice clothes, good food, and sex. West (1892–1980) briefly was film's leading comedienne, until her risqué jokes and gyrations were squelched by the Hollywood Production Code (1934), which suppressed sexuality and a glamorous portrayal of vice.

1934. Hollywood Production Code (–1968) drafted (1930) by Daniel Lord, S. J., and Martin Quigley, Roman Catholic layman, adopted by motion picture industry to avert economic boycotts and government censorship. The moral code prohibited brutality, sexual promiscuity, glorification of illegal or immoral activities, and words such as "damn," "God," "guts," "hell," "nerts," and "sex." The new Production Code Administration, run by Joseph I. Breen, a Roman Catholic layman, would refuse the industry's seal of approval to any picture violating the code and impose a $25,000 fine for releasing a film without the seal.

● *Gold Diggers of 1933*, directed by Mervyn LeRoy and Busby Berkeley, a backstage musical with saccharine, sterilized dialogue that contrasted to *42nd Street*'s (1933) vulgarity.

● *It Happened One Night*, directed by Frank Capra (1897–), a popular escapist film starring Claudette Colbert (1905–), originally Lily Claudette Chauchoin, and Clark Gable (1901–1960), who won an Oscar for it. Capra, an important figure in the new sound era, emphasized the down-home, ingenuous manners of Americans. Capra and Robert Riskin, who wrote the pair's major scripts, pitted the honest little fellow against powerful, inimical social forces. *Mr. Deeds Goes to Town* (1936) and *Mr. Smith Goes to Washington* (1939) particularly depicted the period's conventional, folksy optimism. Capra won Oscars for *One Night* and *Deeds*. Other Capra films included *Lost Horizon* (1937), *You Can't Take It With You* (1938), *Arsenic and Old Lace* (1944), *It's a Wonderful Life* (1946), and *State of the Union* (1948).

● *The March of the Wooden Soldiers*, a comedy starring Stan Laurel (1890–1965), originally Arthur Jefferson, and Oliver Hardy (1892–1957), silent screen comedians who succeeded in talking pictures.

● *The Thin Man*, directed by Woodbridge Strong Van Dyke (1887–1943), the first movie in an outstanding detective series and a prime example of the genre that flourished in this period. It starred William Powell (1892–1984) and Myrna Loy (1905–), originally Myrna Williams, as Dashiell Hammett's husband-wife detective team of Nick and Nora Charles. In addition to light comedy-mystery films, W. S. Van Dyke directed operettas, historical romances with music, costume pageants, and adventures, including *Tarzan, the Ape Man* (1932).

● *Twentieth Century*, one of the best backstage comedies and one of Director Howard Winchester Hawks' best films. It starred Carole Lombard (1908–1942), originally Jane Peters, and John Barrymore (1882–1942), originally John Blythe. Howard Hawks (1896–1977), who wrote or co-wrote his scripts, created at least one movie representative of the finest in most genres. By genres they included gangster, *Scarface* (1932); mystery, *The Big Sleep* (1936); newspaper, *His*

Girl Friday (1940); prison, *The Criminal Code* (1930); screwball comedy, *Bringing Up Baby* (1938); western, *Red River* (1948) and *Rio Bravo* (1957).

1935. Twentieth Century-Fox, the last of the major film combines, founded by William Fox (1879–1952), who had been a distributor and theater owner before becoming an independent producer. His company excelled in adventure and historical films starring Henry Fonda and Tyrone Power, in folksy comedies starring Will Rogers and Shirley Temple, and in show business musicals starring Don Ameche and Alice Faye and, later, Dan Dailey and Betty Grable. To compete against television, Twentieth Century-Fox introduced wide-screen Cinema-Scope, pictures shot and projected using anamorphic lenses, with *The Robe* (1953). The studio joined the competition eventually by making commercials and weekly shows for TV.

● *Naughty Marietta*, the first operetta pairing Jeanette MacDonald (1901–1965) and Nelson Eddy (1901–1967).

1936. *Fury*, a social protest film indicting mob violence; directed by Fritz Lang (1890–1976), whose other films included *You Only Live Once* (1937) and *The Big Heat* (1953).

● *My Man Godfrey*, a screwball comedy directed by Gregory LaCava, who specialized in comedies.

1937. *Nothing Sacred*, one of many films written by Ben Hecht (1894–1964). Others in this period included *Gunga Din* (1939) and *Wuthering Heights* (1939). Many of Hecht's films were in the gangster, newspaper, and prison genres. His crisp style was marked by colorful, tough, fast-paced dialogue, and widely imitated.

1939. Two classics released—*Gone With the Wind* and *The Wizard of Oz*. Both were directed by Victor Fleming (1893–1949) and continued to be shown in theaters or on television in the 1980s. Both used the developing color technology effectively. *Gone With the Wind*, which starred Clark Gable and Vivien Leigh (1913–1967), originally Vivien Hartley, set box office records; it long held a record for revenue returned in relation to cost of production. This Civil War picture, set in the South, was begun by George Dewey Cukor (1899–1983), whose films in this period included *Dinner at Eight* (1933), *David Copperfield* (1934), *Camille* (1936), and *The Philadelphia Story* (1940). Judy Garland (1922–1969) originally Frances Gumm, played the heroine in *The Wizard of Oz*.

● *Stagecoach* directed by John Ford (1895–1973), originally Sean O'Feeney. It set a much imitated pattern for westerns. The film dramatically contrasted the humanism of the stagecoach people against the savagery of the Apaches. Other westerns by Ford included *My Darling Clementine* (1946), *Fort Apache* (1948), *She Wore a Yellow Ribbon* (1949), *Wagonmaster* (1950), and *The Man Who Shot Liberty Valance*

(1962). Ford drew on his Irish background to direct *The Quiet Man* (1952), *The Last Hurrah* (1959), etc. His other films included *The Grapes of Wrath* (1940) and *How Green Was My Valley* (1941).

1940. *Rebecca*, which won an Oscar for Alfred Joseph Hitchcock (1899–1980), a filmmaker of British origin who became known as a Hollywood master of suspense. Alfred Hitchcock's movies combined psychology and mystery. Later Hitchcock films included *Suspicion* (1941), *Saboteur* (1942), *Lifeboat* (1944), *Spellbound* (1945), *Notorious* (1946), *The Rope* (1948), *Strangers on a Train* (1951), *Rear Window* (1954), *To Catch a Thief* (1955), *Vertigo* (1958), *North by Northwest* (1959) *Psycho* (1960), *The Birds* (1963), *Frenzy* (1972), and *Family Plot* (1976).

• *The Great McGinty*, the first film directed by Preston Sturges (1898–1959), previously a screenwriter. Sturges charmingly and wittily ridiculed the naive notion that voters controlled government. He wrote and directed spirited comedies challenging many optimistic clichés about 1940s America. His other social satires included *The Lady Eve* and *Sullivan's Travels* (1941), *The Miracle of Morgan's Creek* (1943), and *Hail, the Conquering Hero* (1944).

1941. *Citizen Kane*, a daring, bitter, innovative, unconventional motion picture that became one of the most influential in U.S. history; regarded by some critics as the finest U.S. sound film. It was the first film by Orson Welles (1915–1985), who produced it, starred in it, and supervised most production aspects; Herman J. Mankiewicz (1897–1953) wrote and directed. They and cameraman Gregg Toland (1904–1948) made effective use of such new technology as bright lights and fast film. The complexly structured narrative unflatteringly drew on the life of newspaper publisher William Randolph Hearst, who saw infuriating parallels between himself and Welles's egomaniacal Charles Foster Kane, between his own actress protégée Marion Davies and Kane's singer protégée Susan Alexander, and between his own San Simeon castle in California and Kane's Xanadu castle in Florida. Negative press reaction, particularly by Hearst papers, contributed to limited profits. Audience reaction was restrained. Many moviegoers missed the Hollywood gloss and a happy ending. They found *Citizen Kane* sprawling (it covered some 60 years), gloomy, unpleasant. Welles's next film, *The Magnificent Ambersons* (1942), contained fine acting and, tacked on, a happy ending, but it fared no better at the box office. Other Welles films included *The Lady from Shanghai* and *Macbeth* (1948), *Touch of Evil* (1958), *Mr. Arkadin* (1962), and *The Trial* (1963).

• *The Maltese Falcon*, a classic example in the hardboiled detective genre that became popular in the 1940s; first film directed by John Huston (1906–), previously a screenwriter. Humphrey Bogart (1899–1957) starred as the tough detective, Sam Spade.

Radio and Television

1930. National Advisory Council on Radio in Education and National Committee on Education by Radio founded. The council advocated nonprofit educational programming on commercial radio stations. The committee advocated 15 percent nonprofit educational programming on commercial stations and attacked "commercial monopolies." Both organizations reflected educational radio's struggle in the marketplace.

● "Death Valley Days," one of the first westerns on radio. In 1955 the anthology began on television. One of the hosts was Ronald Reagan (1911–).

1931. Three cases represent the trend toward definition of the Federal Radio Commission's right to evaluate programming for the public interest. In February the denial of license renewal to Dr. John R. Brinkley's KFKB of Milford, Kansas, was upheld in court. Renewal had been denied because programming included personal attacks and prescriptions of Brinkley's own patent medicines. Brinkley was a precedent for the two subsequent cases. In June FRC revoked the license of Norman Baker's KTNT of Muscatine, Iowa, because programming included personal attacks and promotion of his medical ideas and cancer hospital. In November FRC revoked the license of Reverend Robert P. Schuler's KGEF (licensed to a church), Los Angeles, for personal attacks, violent language, obstruction of justice, and the like.

● Metropolitan Opera broadcasts began in the fall over the National Broadcasting Company's Blue network. The Saturday afternoon programs from New York City were announced by Milton Cross until his death in 1974.

● "March of Time," weekly news magazine on NBC-Blue. Created by *Time* magazine, the show dramatized news events. The signature, "Time marches on," delivered by announcer Westbrook Van Voorhis, became a popular phrase.

● "Sherlock Holmes," one of first crime programs on network radio; long running.

● Bing Crosby variety show, on network radio. In 1946 Harry Lillis Crosby (1904–1977) crossed from NBC to the American Broadcasting Company, where he could tape his programs instead of doing them live, and in 1948 he switched to the Columbia Broadcasting System. His nighttime radio show was discontinued in 1957, his daytime show in 1962.

● "Little Orphan Annie," first of many children's adventure serials. It was based on the comic strip.

1932. Edward Petry & Co. founded to help local radio stations sell time in major cities; first modern station representative firm. Most reps had been brokers for sponsors. The new type represented one station in a market and sold its time to sponsors through their advertising agencies. This way important stations received more regional and national advertising. Station reps became increasingly important in this period.

• Kidnapping of 19-month-old son of aviation hero Charles A. Lindbergh, one of first calamities covered on the air (March).

• "Vic and Sade," popular series with same cast and different situations each week. It originated in Chicago, as many early radio programs did.

• "One Man's Family," first national program from West Coast (San Francisco); long running.

1933. First "fireside chat" (12 March) delivered by President Franklin Delano Roosevelt (1882–1945); indicated rising influence of radio as a political tool. In the early broadcasts Roosevelt talked conversationally about depression problems. In his three presidential terms, he delivered 18 chats, mostly highly rated half-hour programs in prime time.

• "Biltmore Agreement" signed (December) in New York City by major networks and press associations to eliminate independent radio reporting by the networks. In the depression competition for advertisers' dollars had intensified between radio and newspapers. In 1933 Associated Press, a cooperative controlled by newspapers, had limited sale of news to local stations. International News Service and United Press Associations had bowed to pressures from their newspaper clients to stop sale of news to stations. At the Biltmore Hotel representatives of the newspaper industry and networks agreed to restrict network news reporting to two brief newscasts daily, to broadcast only commentary and interpretation (no hard news), to halt network news operations, to use only a new Press-Radio Bureau (f. 1934), and to broadcast only sustaining news programs.

• Four key patents to new frequency modulation (FM) radio system received (December) by Edwin Howard Armstrong (1890–1954). Edwin H. Armstrong had discovered (1930) that the key to successful FM was a channel much wider than the standard AM channel of 10 kHz. His system contained almost no static, even in electrical storms, which could ruin AM reception. In November 1935 Armstrong first publicly demonstrated FM, transmitting from his amateur station W2AG (the world's first FM radio station) in Yonkers, New York, to a meeting of engineers in Manhattan (New York City). In April 1938 the first lasting FM station, Armstrong's W2XMN in Alpine, New Jersey, went on the air.

• "Ma Perkins," radio serial. On 25 November 1960 the National Broadcasting Company soap opera was discontinued after its 7,065th broadcast.

1934. Press-Radio Bureau (1 March–1938) established; received press association copy for rewriting in radio style.

• WLW of Cincinnati began experimenting around the clock (May–March 1939) with 500,000 watts to test superpower effects. Main effect: better signal in WLW's already wide coverage area. The experiment was discontinued by Federal Communications Commission order. WLW was an advocate of greater power for wider service to increase station prestige and advertising. Opponents of this clear channel broadcasting argued super power would give some stations too much economic advantage. The experimentation and debate were suspended during World War II.

• Communications Act (19 June), effective 1 July. The new law incorporated most provisions of the Radio Act of 1927, including the three-year broadcast license term, but also set up a seven-person Federal Communications Commission (replaced Federal Radio Commission) and added jurisdiction over telephone communication (to broadcast and telegraph communication). FCC was prohibited from censoring broadcast content but could decide if a station's policies and programs served the public interest. The premise of the Communications Act was that individual licensees were responsible for their stations' operations.

• Quality Network (September–), under cooperative ownership and operation by WGN of Chicago, WLW of Cincinnati, WOR of Newark, New Jersey, and WXYZ of Detroit. Its purpose was to improve the stations' economic status outside established networks. WXYZ brought "The Lone Ranger" (f. 1933), a popular western for children, to the network; the other three stations were high-powered clear-channel operations. On 29 September 1934 the network changed its name to the Mutual Broadcasting System, reflecting its unique organization. Most programs emanated from the founding or affiliate stations, and a small central news service operated in New York. In 1934–1935 less than ½ percent of all stations belonged to Mutual, which, nonetheless, was heard in much of the Midwest and East. After WXYZ switched to the National Broadcasting Company in 1935, the place was filled by CKLW of Windsor, Ontario, Canada, which served the same area. In 1936 13 affiliates of the Colonial Network in New England and 10 affiliates of the Don Lee Network on the West Coast joined Mutual, making it national. Acquiring other small networks as well as independent stations brought Mutual strengths to more than 19 percent of all stations, although many new members, primarily affiliated with NBC and the Columbia Broadcasting System, used MBS programs only as fillers. Most MBS affiliates were low-power local and regional stations with comparatively small audiences; NBC and CBS had much larger audiences and advertising revenues. As the largest networks concentrated on television in the mid-1950s, MBS became the largest radio network in the number of affiliates. In 1956–1959 ownership changed six times; scandals rocked MBS, causing many stations to quit. But in the 1980s Mutual ranked among the eight top station groups in the three largest markets (Chicago, Los Angeles, New York).

● National Association of Educational Broadcasters founded. Its progenitor was the Association of College and University Broadcasting Stations (f. 1925). NAEB was instrumental in establishing national radio.

● "Major Bowes and His Original Amateur Hour," on WHN, New York. In 1935 the show moved to the National Broadcasting Company's Red network and quickly became the most popular program on radio. Host Major Edward Bowes (1874–1946) presented amateur performers, some of whom went on to fame; they included Frank Sinatra (1915–), who debuted on radio in the program's first year. Ted Mack (1904–1976) took over after Bowes's death. The show ran on radio until 1952. In 1949 Mack took it to television, where it ran for almost 20 years.

1935. International News Service and United Press Associations began selling full news reports to stations and networks, effectively ending the Biltmore Agreement (1933). INS and UP were released (May) from the Press-Radio Bureau arrangement to meet the competition of Transradio Press Service, not a signer of the agreement.

● "Backstage Wife," radio serial about "what it means to be the wife of a famous Broadway star—dream sweetheart of a million other women." It ran for about 25 years.

● "Gangbusters," recreated "true" crime stories. A popular phrase, "coming on like gangbusters," was based on the loud opening of sirens, machine-gun fire, and marching feet.

● "Mr. District Attorney," opening with the D.A. reciting the oath of office; depicted the law as both protector and prosecutor.

● "Your Hit Parade," with popular songs performed by major orchestras and singers. The selection of tunes was purportedly based on a national survey identifying the top-selling sheet music and records. "Your Hit Parade" began on television in 1950, and shows ran on both media for some years. The format declined in popularity with the rise of rock music.

1937. Radio coverage of disastrous Mississippi and Ohio valleys floods; one of the medium's greatest performances in a domestic crisis. The stations' cooperation demonstrated radio's portability and immediacy. Stations flooded out loaned their employees to stations still on the air, which replaced regular programming with information directing flood victims to food and shelter. Some stations provided message services for official agencies. Many stations helped raise funds for victims.

● *Hindenburg* disaster at Lakehurst, New Jersey, recorded (May) by

Herb Morrison of WLS, Chicago; one of the most dramatic radio reports in history. Morrison was recording on disc the landing of Germany's huge hydrogen-buoyed dirigible when it burst into flames and in less than a minute crashed, a charred mass of twisted girders; 30 crew and passengers died. Although overwhelmed by the unexpected catastrophe, Morrison continued to record for about 30 minutes, except for intervals helping rescuers. The next morning WLS broadcast his report, and the three major networks suspended their no-recordings rule to play segments.

● American Federation of Radio Artistes (July–) founded as a union for announcers and performers; later known as American Federation of Radio Artists, then American Federation of Television and Radio Artists (AFTRA).

● National Broadcasting Company Symphony Orchestra began broadcasts of classical music; a major radio program of the period. Arturo Toscanini (1867–1957) organized and conducted the orchestra.

● Canon 35 (September–) adopted by American Bar Association; banned radio and photography in courtrooms. Grew out of massive and chaotic coverage of the trial (1935) of Bruno Richard Hauptmann for the kidnapping-murder (1932) of the 19-month-old son of aviation pioneer Charles A. Lindbergh. (Hauptmann was executed in the electric chair.) ABA's new rule of judicial procedure limited radio's access to courtrooms to avoid similar pandemonium during trials. After 1952 Canon 35 included television. Media opposed the rule (later Canon 3A [7]) as violation of the First Amendment's free press and speech provisions; proponents cited the Sixth Amendment's fair trial provision. In isolated cases some judges permitted TV in their courtrooms. Debate continued into the 1980s.

● "The Fall of the City" (4 March), a major radio program of the 1930s. It was a blank verse drama by poet Archibald MacLeish (1892–1982).

1938. Munich crisis (12–29 September) coverage by Columbia Broadcasting System and National Broadcasting Company. It was the first major shortwave live coverage of international events. Bulletins interrupted entertainment programs to bring listeners news of Hitler's threat to Czechoslovakia.

● "The War of the Worlds" broadcast (30 October); one of the most famous single radio programs. H. G. Wells's novel was adapted for the "Mercury Theater on the Air" (f. fall 1938) by Orson Welles (1915–1985) and Howard Koch, who changed the time to the present, the location to New Jersey, and the narrative to radio format, including a simulated remote band pickup interrupted by simulated news bulletins. Although this Columbia Broadcasting System program of an invasion from Mars, broadcast at Halloween, contained announcements that it was fiction, many listeners, reports of impending war in Europe in mind, thought it was true and panicked. Overnight Welles, who produced and narrated the show, won national fame.

• Twenty-five channels in the 40 MHz band authorized by the Federal Communications Commission; first educational allocation.

1939. Associated Press supplying news (February–) without charge for sustaining programs on National Broadcasting Company; press-radio war soon ended when AP began to sell news (June) to broadcasters.

• Memorandum on 14 types of programming not in public interest issued (March) by Federal Communications Commission. The types: (1) defamation; (2) religious or racial intolerance; (3) fortune telling and the like; (4) favorable reference to hard liquor; (5) obscenity; (6) depiction of torture; (7) excessive suspense on children's programs; (8) excessive playing of recorded music to take up air time; (9) blatant solicitation of money; (10) frequent and long commercials (11) interruption of "artistic" programs with commercials; (12) fraudulent, false, and other misleading advertising; (13) presentation of just one side of a controversy; and (14) refusal to give equal treatment to both sides in a controversy. In the late 1970s the FCC still considered objectionable the first 9 types at all times and the last 5 in some situations.

• Broadcast Music, Incorporated (September–) founded by National Association of Broadcasters as a music licensing organization to compete against the American Society of Composers, Authors and Publishers, which demanded higher license rates (royalties) to play copyrighted music.

• "This is London" (–1941), by Edward (Egbert) Roscow Murrow (1908–1965), for the Columbia Broadcasting System. Night after night, Edward R. Murrow reported from London how the war affected average residents.

• Two situation comedies over the National Broadcasting Company's Blue network—"Li'l Abner" and "Henry Aldrich." The latter, misadventures of an adolescent whose voice was changing, had been a segment on other programs for years. "Li'l Abner" was based on the comic strip.

• Initiation of regular television broadcasting (30 April–) by NBC. President Franklin D. Roosevelt was featured on this first telecast, from the World's Fair in New York.

• First televised sports event (17 May), a baseball game between Princeton and Columbia universities; on NBC.

1940. Commercial FM radio authorized (20 May) by Federal Communications Commission to commence 1 January 1941 on 40 frequencies, the lowest 5 reserved for educational stations. A new, wider broadcast band was provided. Development was delayed by single ownership of both FM and AM stations in a community, which provided little incentive to expand FM commercially; by a freeze on construction permits during an FCC investigation (1941–1944) of newspaper control of radio stations; and by national defense preparations, which increasingly required construction materials.

● Combined broadcast (June) by William Kerker of National Broadcasting Company and William Lawrence Shirer (1904–) of Columbia Broadcasting System in Compiégne forest when France surrendered to Germany (while most correspondents waited in Berlin for the news).

● "Truth or Consequences," comedy-quiz radio program. As a consequence of failing to answer silly questions, contestants from the audience had to do silly stunts. The program was later on television.

1941. "Mayflower decision" issued (16 January) by the Federal Communications Commission (8 FCC 333) prohibiting station licensees from using their properties to disseminate their own opinions; interpreted to prohibit editorializing. While passing on the Mayflower Broadcasting Corporation's challenge to WAAB's request for license renewal (in Boston), the FCC ruled that "the broadcaster cannot be an advocate." Most broadcasters did not editorialize anyway, lest they antagonize advertisers or listeners. In 1949, after hearings, the FCC issued a report, *In the Matter of Editorializing of Broadcast Licensees,* to "clarify" the 1941 decision. The precedent-setting clarification permitted broadcasters to editorialize if they allowed "all responsible viewpoints" on issues and operated in the public interest. Editorializing expanded slowly in the 1950s, but was still limited (then often innocuous) in the 1980s.

● Investigation of newspaper ownership of radio stations called for in Order No. 79 issued (March) by the FCC. Newspapers, one of the largest ownership classes, controlled about one-third of the radio stations, many in the same markets as the papers; newspaper applicants had received almost one-fourth of FM construction permits. FCC intended to determine if it should issue any policy or rules governing applications for high-frequency stations associated with newspapers. Publishers cried violation of First Amendment. FCC froze construction permits to newspaper-controlled FM stations during the hearings and investigated newspaper ownership of AM stations. Hearings ran July–October 1941, then intermittently until January 1944, when the FCC decided to forego any rule on the topic.

● North American Regional Broadcasting Agreement in effect (March), fairly dividing the broadcast spectrum among Canada, Cuba, Mexico, and United States; reduced interference. Most Canadian, Mexican, and U.S. stations changed frequencies at least slightly.

● *Report on Chain Broadcasting* issued (2 May) by FCC to eliminate abuses of monopoly; limited network control of affiliates. With Order No. 37, FCC study had begun in 1938 to learn if rules were necessary to curtail network monopolistic tendencies. FCC (1) limited network affiliation contracts to one year, replacing the practice of binding stations for five years, networks for one; (2) prohibited exclusive affiliations, enabling affiliates to air other networks' programs; (3) prohibited networks from demanding options on large amounts of station time, enabling stations to control their programming; (4) allowed affiliates to reject any network program that they thought failed to meet the public interest, convenience, or necessity; and (5) blocked network control over affiliates' rates for non-network programs. FCC also (6) decided not to issue a license to a standard broadcast station affiliated with an organization that maintained more than one network, except when such networks operated at different times or covered different areas. Not in the chain broadcasting regulations was a seventh rule, which also prohibited duopoly—specifically, one licensee owning two stations in the same service area. The sixth rule in the report most upset the industry, except the Mutual Broadcasting System, which expected to become more competitive with the largest networks. National Broadcasting Company would lose most under rule 6, being forced to give up either its Red or Blue network. NBC and Columbia Broadcasting System filed suit to set aside the new regulations, and the federal government prepared antitrust suits against the two major networks and NBC's parent Radio Corporation of America. In *National Broadcasting Co., Inc., et al. v. United States et al.* (319 U.S. 190), the U.S. Supreme Court on 10 May 1943 upheld, 5–2, the FCC's authority to enforce chain broadcasting regulations. The decision reinforced the FCC's power under the Communications Act (1934) to exercise its best judgment in behalf of the "public interest, convenience, or necessity." Selection and regulation of licensees was, the court ruled, within the FCC's jurisdiction as assigned by Congress. Contrary to the networks' claim, the court said, no conflict existed with the First Amendment. The decision was the most important holding on the FCC's authority to that time. Reluctantly, NBC sold its Blue network (which in 1945 became American Broadcasting Company). The government withdrew its antitrust suits. And the new FCC regulations became effective in mid-1943, leading to sale of some stations in cities where a licensee owned more than one station.

• Arthur Godfrey (1903–1983) took his radio show from Washington, D.C., to New York City and CBS. The singer and master of ceremonies had begun his broadcast career in Baltimore as the "warbling banjoist." In 1949 his network show, "Arthur Godfrey's Talent Scouts," went to TV (continuing on radio), where it lasted about ten years. The show helped spur copies on some local stations.

• Full commercial television operations approved (3 May) by FCC; effective 1 July 1941. FCC authorized FM audio and 525-line video, basic standards still used more than 40 years later. By 1 July, CBS and NBC were operating stations. World War II would drastically curtail programming and equipment manufacturing. In 1941 the 853 stations broadcasting included the 2 commercial TV, 2 educational FM, 18 commercial FM, and 831 AM stations.

1941–1945

World War II

━━━━━━━━━━━ ‖●‖ ━━━━━━━━━━━

Books

1942. American Textbook Publishers Institute founded; in 1970 joined with American Book Publishers Council (f. 1946) to become Association of American Publishers.

• *See Here, Private Hargrove*, by Marion Hargrove, a young draftee's humorous story of his army experiences and one of the war's biggest best sellers.

• *They Were Expendable*, by William Lindsay White, and *Torpedo Junction*, by Robert Casey, two popular war accounts by eyewitnesses.

1943. Three best sellers—*Here Is Your War*, by Ernest Taylor Pyle (1900–1945); *One World*, by Wendell Lewis Willkie (1892–1944); *A Tree Grows in Brooklyn*, by Betty Smith. Ernie Pyle's book was a compilation of his columns for Scripps-Howard Newspaper Alliance. The Pulitzer Prize-winning reporter's compilation *Brave Men* led all nonfiction titles in 1944. Other compilations by Pyle included *Ernie Pyle in England* (1941) and *Last Chapter* (1945). Wendell Willkie's argument for world peace through world unity became the season's fastest seller soon after its publication in April.

1944. Two censored best sellers—*Forever Amber*, by Kathleen Winsor, and *Strange Fruit*, by Lillian Smith; both banned in Massachusetts particularly.

1945. Three best sellers—*The Black Rose*, by Thomas Bertram Costain; *Captain from Castile*, by Samuel Shellabarger; and *The Egg and I*, by Betty MacDonald.

Newspapers

1941. At least 200 U.S. correspondents gathering news abroad when the U.S. declared war against Japan (8 December) and Germany and Italy (11 December). Many were trapped in enemy territory and interned with diplomats, some for months. Several hundred more correspondents for U.S. media were citizens of the countries where they worked.

● Office of Censorship (19 December–15 August 1945) established by presidential order to censor U.S. communication; directed by Byron Price (1891–1981). Office of Censorship scrutinized all communication entering and leaving the country by cable, mail, and radio and passed it in full or part, delayed it, or suppressed it. Another important function of the Office of Censorship was directing voluntary press censorship. On 15 January 1942 the office issued its *Code of Wartime Practices for the American Press* to publishers and radio station managers. The code explained improper handling of news and urged suppression of information about aircraft, armaments, fortifications, shipping, troops, war production, weather, etc. Most media voluntarily followed the code, which included no legal penalty for violations, erring toward overly suppressing news possibly harmful to the war effort. The Office of Censorship was headquartered in Washington, D.C., and had offices along U.S. borders.

● Most of the year's total advertising expenditures of almost $2 billion to newspapers (32 percent); direct mail 16 percent, radio 12 percent, and magazines 9 percent.

1942. War Advertising Council established by advertisers, agencies, practitioners, media representatives to offer the government assistance.

● *Yank* (April–1945) founded in New York by and for military personnel. Printed by rotogravure, the large-format weekly was well illustrated, including cartoons and pin-up girls. Some content was of literary distinction. *Yank* had its own correspondents in combat areas and editions scattered around the world. Highest circulation was about 2.5 million. Long-time Managing Editor Joe McCarthy received credit for much of *Yank*'s success.

● Office of War Information (13 June–) set up by presidential order to originate and coordinate government war propaganda; directed by Elmer Holmes Davis (1890–1958). OWI provided cartoons, features, fillers, news releases, pictures, and weekly digests as well as background information on government objectives. The agency worked closely with the War Advertising Council (f. 1942) to place patriotic advertising in newspapers and magazines and on billboards and radio. Palmer Hoyt (1897–1979) directed the domestic operations, Robert Emmet Sherwood (1896–1955) the overseas operation, which conducted the widest propaganda effort in U.S. history to then. Robert E. Sherwood's division disseminated all official information abroad, except to Latin America, served by Office of Coordinator of Inter-American Affairs. After OWI was discontinued following the war, the Department of State took over the overseas services, continuing "Voice of America" radio broadcasts and running the United States Information Agency (f. 1953).

● Camp Newspaper Service founded to assist military camp editors, provide syndicated materials, and supervise use of printing supplies. The approximately 1,200 U.S. camp newspapers, mostly weeklies, reported camp news, ran pin-ups, and included diverse features. To advise editors, CNS published a manual and a monthly journal, *G.I. Galley*.

● First-time recognition on a wide scale of Marine Corps Combat Correspondents for their reports of the assault on the Solomon Islands in the Pacific. The unique correspondents were Marines trained both as fighters and reporters.

1943. Army News Service (January–) founded in New York to furnish bylined columns, features, military analyses, and a news report to domestic and overseas publications; also to provide scripts and news for army stations and networks.

● More than 430 full-time U.S. newspaper correspondents covering the war at the fronts or in foreign news centers.

● More than 60 photojournalists for newspapers, newsreel companies, and magazines accredited. Newspapers also received pictures from Signal Corps and public relations photographers. Photos were shot by Speed Graphic (most used combat camera) and transmitted by cable, wireless, and other methods. Common in combat areas was picture pooling, whereby photos were made available to all newspapers and press associations. Photographers played a larger part than ever before in reporting a war.

1945. A record 135 women reporting (January) from the House of Representatives and Senate press galleries. The situation reflected the wartime manpower shortage that gave women opportunities to hold many journalistic positions from which they had been excluded, including copy desk and foreign assignments. Some women became outstanding war correspondents. After the war many women journalists kept their jobs, despite domination of males on newspapers.

● Harry S Truman's first presidential press conference (17 April), a record number of reporters (348) attending.

● Rise of newspaper prices by mid-1945 to 5 cents per copy for about half the dailies; circulation usually not adversely affected in the long run.

● War advertising totaling more than $98.8 million from August 1943 to July 1945. All of it (except recruiting) was paid by private advertisers (no cost to government). Although forced to turn down profitable advertising because of a newsprint shortage, newspapers donated much space for salvage drives, food rationing and saving, war loans, and other war-related causes.

Magazines

1942. *American Family* founded for distribution through stores by Independent Grocers Alliance; suspended soon after first issue, revived in 1948, discontinued in 1954.

• *Baseball Digest* founded for fans. Circulation reached about 240,000 in late 1970s and declined to about 225,650 in early 1980s, when it was published monthly in Evanston, Illinois, by Norman Jacobs, edited by John Kuenster.

• *Movieland* founded; fan magazine.

• *Negro Digest* founded in Chicago by John H. Johnson (1918–), edited by Ben Burns; serious content. Within three years circulation was 110,000, but profits lagged after World War II. In 1970 *Negro Digest* became *Black World*. Editor Hoyt W. Fuller ran nonfiction, fiction, and poetry concerning blacks, with emphasis on cultural and political subjects. The monthly had about 100,000 circulation in the mid-1970s, shortly before its demise.

• *Organic Gardening and Farming* founded by Jerome Irving Rodale (1898–1971). His son, Robert David Rodale, became editor in 1954. In the late 1970s the periodical had a circulation of about 1,250,000, which dropped to about 1,200,000 by the mid-1980s, when the monthly was published at the Emmaus, Pennsylvania, offices of Rodale Press Publications for readers interested in conservation, health, growing fruits and vegetables without chemicals, and preserving the environment. *Organic Gardening* emphasized practical, how-to advice, especially on growing food.

1944. American Society of Magazine Photographers founded. By 1980 ASMP had more than 2,200 members. They were engaged in advertising, documentary, industrial, and journalism photography for film, print, and tape. ASMP published *Professional Business Practices in Photography*.

• *Fishing and Hunting News* founded. In the early 1980s it was published by Bill Farden and edited by Vance Malernee in Seattle, Washington. It covered fishing, hunting, other outdoor sports. Circulation was 119,406 in eight western editions. It soon moved to New York and then became a general outdoor service periodical covering backpacking, conservation, camping, fishing, hunting, and related activities. Editor was Jack Samson.

● *Human Events* founded in Washington, D.C.; reported governmental activities, especially in Congress and major executive departments. By the late 1970s the conservative weekly had a circulation of 78,000. It was about 60,000 in the early 1980s, when Jerry M. Roberts was publisher, Thomas S. Winter editor.

● *Pageant* founded by Alex L. Hillman as a slick pocket monthly without advertising. First editor Eugene Lyons was succeeded in a few months by Vernon L. Pope. With a limited wartime paper supply and increasing production costs, *Pageant* lost money; circulation dropped from its initial 500,000 to 170,000 by August 1947. Frequency was changed to bimonthly. Harris Shevelson, who replaced Pope in late 1947, brightened content and used more photographs. By 1949 circulation had climbed to about 400,000 and the periodical was at least breaking even. In 1961 Hillman Periodicals, Inc., sold *Pageant*, whose circulation was then about 500,000, to Macfadden (which in 1962 became Macfadden-Bartell Corporation). In the mid-1970s it was published in Rouses Point, New York, and edited by Nat K. Perlow for a general audience. Content included articles about history, medical advances, newsmakers, and personal experiences, as well as how-tos, humor, and off-beat briefs. A monthly again, *Pageant* had 150,000 circulation.

● *Reader's Scope* founded as a digest running half reprinted, half original material. Articles, including biographical pieces and humor, were liberal and timely. Periodicals agreeing to let Editor Leverett Gleason use their material included *Mademoiselle*, *New Yorker*, *Saturday Review of Literature*, and *Woman's Day*. Rising postwar costs forced *Reader's Scope* to begin soliciting advertising in 1947. Publication discontinued about 1950.

● *Seventeen* founded for girls under 20 years of age; monthly circulation 400,000. It went from a large format to a reduced format and over the years adjusted to serve the changing interests and everyday problems of readers 13 to 19. Content included beauty, careers, fashions, hobbies, and sports; some fiction. By the mid-1980s circulation had risen to 1.5 million. *Seventeen* was owned by Walter Annenberg's Triangle Publications Inc. and published in New York. Publisher was Frank Wolf, editorial director Merrill Panitt. Executive Editor Ray Robinson (1920–) ran topical, helpful articles and features of general interest to young women; quality fiction emphasizing the concerns and problems of adolescent girls, and poetry by teenagers. Robinson encouraged reader participation by teen contributions of book reviews, essays, exposés, profiles, puzzles, and reportage to a "Free-for-All" department.

1945. *Ebony* founded in Chicago by John H. Johnson as a picture magazine emphasizing the "positive, everyday achievements" of U.S. blacks; edited by Ben Burns. The first issue, printed on slick paper, contained many pictures, similar to *Life*; the press run was 50,000. When *Ebony* began accepting advertising (1946), it had some difficulty attracting major companies, but it soon demonstrated to advertisers that blacks were important consumers. During 1952–1962 ad revenues tripled, to $3,631,000. By the mid-1960s *Ebony* had become known for advocating full, equal treatment of blacks. Content included features on the heritage and future of blacks, riots, and the war on poverty. By the late 1970s *Ebony* had a circulation of 1.3 million and a total audience of about 7 million, mostly upscale urban black men and women. The most successful black magazine, it was edited for readers in Africa and the Caribbean as well as the United States. Its content (nonfiction) included humor, interviews, and profiles emphasizing achievement and human interest. Johnson was editor, Charles L. Sanders managing editor.

• *Cats* founded; ran articles on cat care and health, including breeding, exhibiting, and selling. Circulation was 64,000 in the late 1970s, 75,000 by the mid-1980s, when the magazine was published monthly in Pittsburgh, Pennsylvania. Executive Editor Jean Amelia Laux ran nonfiction (mainly), fiction, and poetry about cats.

• *Commentary* founded by The American Jewish Committee as a journal of opinion on contemporary Jewish issues. The monthly, published in New York, covered a wide range of cultural, political, and social topics, including economics, international affairs, literature, and popular culture. *Commentary* entered the 1980s with 50,000 circulation, which remained stable into the mid-decade, as Norman Podhoretz (1930–), editor since 1960, continued the editorial policy.

• *Lakeland Boating* founded, a monthly for fresh-water boaters in mid-United States. For years it was edited in Michigan, but when former editor David G. Brown took over (mid-1980s), he moved the offices to Port Clinton, Ohio, and emphasized power boating. In the mid-1980s circulation was about 41,000.

• *The Retired Officer* founded by Retired Officers Association for military personnel. In the mid-1980s it was published in Alexandria, Virginia, and edited by Colonel Minter L. Wilson, Jr., USA-Ret., for military officers and their families. Monthly circulation was 325,000.

Motion Pictures

1941. *Swamp Water*, a U.S. film made by French director Jean Renoir, who lived in the United States during the war. Others included *The Southerner* (1945). Renoir returned to France after the war.

• *They Died with Their Boots On*, directed by Raoul Walsh

(1887–1980). Walsh was known for his consistency and individuality. His other films included *They Drive by Night* (1940) and *White Heat* (1949).

1942. Two of the period's best comedies released—*The Man Who Came to Dinner*, starring Monty Woolley (1888–1963), and *Woman of the Year*, starring Katharine Hepburn (1909–) and Spencer Tracy (1900–1967). *Woman* was directed by George Stevens (1904–1975), whose subsequent films included *I Remember Mama* (1948), *A Place in the Sun* (1951), *Shane* (1953), and *Giant* (1956).

● *Yankee Doodle Dandy*, starring James Cagney (1900–) as show-business figure George M. Cohan, one of the top box office hits during the war. The musical was directed by Michael Curtiz (1898–1962), née Mihály Kertész. Two other outstanding wartime films by the versatile Curtiz were *Casablanca* (1942), starring Humphrey Bogart (1899–1957) and Ingrid Bergman (1915–1982), and *Mildred Pierce* (1945), starring Joan Crawford (1908–1977), originally Lucille le Sueur. Curtiz's previous films included *The Charge of the Light Brigade* (1936), starring Errol Flynn (1909–1959).

1944. *Double Indemnity*, starring Barbara Stanwyck (1907–), originally Ruby Stevens, and Fred MacMurray (1908–) as murderous adulterers. It was directed by Billy Wilder (1906–), who co-scripted it with Raymond Chandler (1888–1959). Another film directed by Wilder, master of *film noir* (dark, psychological movies), in this period was *The Lost Weekend* (1945), an alcoholic's story. Wilder also directed comedies, co-authored with I. A. L. Diamond, often mixing a sinister setting with verbal wit; for example, *A Foreign Affair* (1948), *Sunset Boulevard* (1950), *Stalag 17* (1953), *Sabrina* (1954), *Love in the Afternoon* (1957), *Some Like It Hot* (1959), *The Apartment* (1960), and *One, Two, Three* (1962).

● *Going My Way*, a comedy directed by Leo McCarey (1898–1969), a top box office hit of the war years. Other McCarey films included *Ruggles of Red Gap* (1935) and *The Awful Truth* and *Make Way for Tomorrow* (1937).

● *I Married a Witch*, a film made by French director René Clair in the United States. Another was *And Then There Were None* (1945). Clair returned to France after the war.

● *Murder, My Sweet*, starring Dick Powell (1904–1963) as Raymond Chandler's private detective Philip Marlowe, directed by Edward Dmytryk. It won the first Edgar award given by the Mystery Writers of America for the best mystery film of the year.

● Other 1944 movies of note—*The Purple Heart*, a morale-boosting war film; *Since You Went Away*, directed by John Cromwell; and *Up in Arms*, starring comedian Danny Kaye (1913–), originally David Kaminsky.

1945. *The Story of G.I. Joe,* starring Burgess Meredith (1909–), originally George Burgess, as columnist Ernie Pyle, one of the most popular realistic war movies. It was directed by William Wellman (1896–1975), whose other works included *Wings* (1929), *Public Enemy* (1931), *Wild Boys of the Road* (1933), *The President Vanishes* (1934), *Nothing Sacred* and *A Star Is Born* (1937), and *Battleground* (1949).

● Other 1945 films of note—*Back to Bataan,* a morale-boosting war story; *State Fair,* directed by Walter Lang (1898–1972); and *To Have and Have Not,* directed by Howard Hawks (1896–1977).

Radio and Television

1941. "We Hold These Truths," by Norman Corwin (1910–), one of the first patriotic war programs. The theme was the Bill of Rights.

● Amateur stations closed (–November 1945).

● Between 10,000 and 20,000 television sets in use (December): half in New York, the rest in Chicago, Los Angeles, Philadelphia.

1942. New station construction limited (January) by Federal Communications Commission. In February the FCC announced that to conserve materials and equipment for war use it would issue no new station construction permits. More than 900 AM stations existed; FM was just beginning. In April the War Production Board backed up the FCC, limiting construction only to those licensees already having all the required materials or to builders of educational (noncommercial) stations. FCC also froze major alterations to existing stations and reduced power limits and broadcast hours. Wartime restrictions were lifted in August 1945.

● "Code of Wartime Practices for American Broadcasters"—voluntary restrictions—issued (15 January) by the government Office of Censorship (code revised May 1942 and December 1943). The code, based on National Association of Broadcasters guidelines, prohibited broadcasts about specific military installations or units and disposition of enemy prisoners in the United States; it also banned man-on-the-street interviews, most quiz shows, other ad-lib programs, and all weather reports. The government investigated stations broadcasting German or Italian programs; the Office of Censorship required stations broadcasting in foreign languages to file English translations and to hire a linguist to preview program content. These requirements led to discontinuance of many foreign-language programs and of some of the 127 foreign-language stations.

● "Voice of America" (January–) founded to broadcast propaganda abroad. Using privately owned shortwave stations (taken over for the duration) and new government-owned transmitters, VOA broadcast in foreign languages. Office of War Information (f. June 1942) rapidly expanded VOA's international operations. Music programming was supplemented with news, commentary, and entertainment, including shows from domestic radio, as well as special VOA productions with well-known radio personalities. By war's end VOA operated production centers in New York and San Francisco.

● "This Is War!" radio series (14 February–), an example of a new program series focusing on the war or reflecting home-front impact. It was the first all-networks production. Funding was by the government. The 13-week series of one-hour Saturday evening programs, each focusing on an aspect of the war, aired on all four national networks and 700 stations, live or by transcription. Norman Corwin directed the series and wrote half the programs; other contributors included Maxwell Anderson, Stephen Vincent Benét, and Philip Wylie as well as radio and movie stars. An estimated 20 million people tuned in.

● "Army Hour" (April) on National Broadcasting Company, one of the new programs focusing on the military. Army-produced, it gave civilians an image of army life through a format combination of drama, features, music, and news.

● AM radio receiver production halted (April) by War Production Board. Radios were in 31 million homes and more than 9 million autos. The ban soon applied to the new FM and television receiver industry. Production of receivers for civilian use resumed after the war (1945).

● Radio Bureau founded as part of the domestic division of the Office of War Information (f. 1942) to guide voluntary flow of war information through privately owned radio stations. Station managers had been buried under an avalanche of war information early in 1942, and the Radio Bureau's first job was to coordinate, clear, and prioritize all government messages. The bureau inserted war messages into regular entertainment shows and emphasized quality rather than quantity so as not to blunt the messages' impact. To a lesser extent, the bureau produced programs, such as "Command Performance," and backed series, such as "This Is Our Enemy" and "You Can't Do Business with Hitler."

● American Federation of Musicians struck (August–), refusing to play for recording sessions. The strike had been called (June) by AFM President James Caesar Petrillo (1892–1984), who demanded that existing fees for playing recorded music on the air be paid directly to the union. Petrillo ignored requests (summer 1943) to lift the recording ban for national morale or at least for the combat forces. He also refused to honor a National War Board order to lift the ban (mid-1944). Neither would he heed President Roosevelt's request (October 1944) to end the strike. The beginning of the strike's end came in November 1944 when Columbia Broadcasting System and Radio Corporation of America agreed to Petrillo's demands.

1943. Armed Forces Network began operating in England. Soon it had more than 50 low-power stations on United Kingdom bases broadcasting to U.S. troops.

● Federal Communications Commission investigation by House of Representatives (June). Hearings chaired by Representative Eugene E. Cox, leader of an anti-FCC group of congressmen, broadcasters, and newspaper publishers; many thought the FCC had gone too far in promoting the public interest. (Other people thought the FCC had not gone far enough.) Tangible results of the hostile hearings were few, mainly some FCC personnel changes, but the long investigation made the FCC cautiously responsive to Congress.

● National Broadcasting Company's Blue network to be sold by Radio Corporation of America (f. 1919) to Edward J. Noble (1882–1958), owner of New York's WMCA. The announcement was made in July, and the FCC approved in October. Blue had been less lucrative than NBC's Red, having fewer affiliates and carrying more sustaining programs. The $8 million sale laid the foundation for the American Broadcasting Company (f. 1945).

● Stations to be licensed for the full three years permitted by the Communications Act of 1934. Prior to the announcement by the FCC, licenses had been issued for two-year periods. The longer period meant less paperwork for the FCC and the stations, both short of manpower.

● Own radio programs by two future television stars—Perry Como (1912–) and Ed Sullivan (1902–1974). Como, a singer known for his informal, relaxed style, began his own network television TV show in 1950. Sullivan, a newspaper gossip columnist known for his stiff, hesitant style, began his TV program in 1948.

1944. By this year newscasts and news specials comprised 16 to 20 percent of network programming, although the amount of radio news had begun to decline to 1943, after reaching more than 1,000 hours per year. Network reporters continued to cover the war in both the European and Pacific theaters.

● Networks permitted (January–) FM stations to carry AM programs. Duplication had been extremely limited. The new policy reduced the amount of independent FM programming. Only by carrying popular AM programs could fledgling FM substantially expand its audience—so argued many AM owners, FM advocates, and network officials.

● Singer Kate (Kathryn Elizabeth) Smith (1909–) in 57 appearances in one day (1 February) to sell War Bonds; probably the most famous of the special broadcasts to sell War Bonds, appeal for scrap materials, and get support for the war effort. Smith helped sell $112 million in bonds.

• Television Broadcasters Association founded; their first trade association.

• George Hicks (1905–1965) of the National Broadcasting Company recorded troops heading ashore from a navy ship during Allied D-day invasion of Normandy (6 June), with antiaircraft guns and aircraft heard in the background. One of the most notable radio reports of the war, it was transmitted to the United States by shortwave for later broadcast.

• Television station WABD founded in New York; named after owner Allen B. Dumont (1901–1965), who announced plans for a postwar TV network. After the war Dumont founded WTTG (after his chief engineer, Thomas T. Goldsmith) in Washington, D.C., and, with money from his successful TV manufacturing company, developed the only early network not built on radio. The network became national as the number of affiliates grew, but few carried many Dumont programs. Dumont was usually the fourth network in a market when most markets had fewer than four TV stations. At best Dumont's revenue was one-third that of the other national networks. In January 1955 Dumont fed 21 hours per week, the three prime-time hours a day, and in August fed only five hours a week to about 160 affiliates. The Dumont company eventually sold its owned and operated stations to concentrate on research and manufacture.

• "The Paul Harvey News," on radio from Chicago. In the mid-1980s Paul Harvey Aurandt (1918–) continued to give the news his personal touch from Chicago. He broadcast twice daily for the American Broadcasting Company and for syndication. Another radio show was "The Rest of the Story." His "Paul Harvey Comments" was on television.

1945. American Broadcasting Company (April–) founded in New York; based on former Blue network of National Broadcasting Company. Blue-purchaser Edward J. Noble held controlling interest. To catch up with Columbia Broadcasting System and NBC, ABC quickly expanded into television and sought additional financing. In May 1951 ABC and United Paramount Theaters (former exhibition arm of Paramount motion picture company) announced a merger, with Noble as board chairman and UPT head Leonard Harry Goldenson (1905–) as president. The merger (after FCC approval in February 1953) gave ABC cash to continue TV expansion. Two Walt Disney Productions programs— "Disneyland" (1954) and "Mickey Mouse Club" (1955)—and an increase in three-station markets improved ABC's competitive position in the late 1950s. But it was still far third. On a new tack, ABC divided (1 January 1968) its regular radio network into four networks: American FM, Contemporary, Information (largest), and Personality (later Entertainment). Thus for the first time networks customized for specialized station formats, which had become predominant after TV diminished network radio. Each specialized network had a 15-minute segment of each broadcast hour. The new setup allowed ABC to have four radio affiliates in each market—one station per network. Soon more than 1,200 stations (about 30 percent of all stations) affiliated with the four ABC networks, making ABC the largest radio operation. ABC also innovated in TV. In 1968 it veered from standard gavel-to-gavel reporting of the political conventions to concentrate coverage in late evening, giving the network the ratings advantage of its entertainment programs. In the 1960s and 1970s ABC became known for innovations in TV sports coverage. Its "Wide World of Sports" weekend anthology (1961–) added viewers who rarely watched sports. Its reporting of the Olympics (1964–) was detailed, technically innovative, and expertly narrated, often by former athletes. "Monday Night Football" (1969–) captured audiences unreached by standard entertainment programs on CBS and NBC. Given much credit for these achievements was ABC sports chief Roone Arledge (1931–), who in 1977 was promoted to ABC News president. Another innovation was hiring a woman (1976), Barbara Walters from NBC's "Today Show," at a million-dollar salary to co-anchor the evening news and to do some specials. In 1972 Goldenson became chairman of American Broadcasting Companies, Inc., the network's parent company, and Elton Rule president. In 1975 the network hired Fred Silverman of CBS, and in 1975–1976 ABC for the first time moved into first place among the three full-service networks. In 1976–1979 35 more stations affiliated with ABC, giving it 203 (CBS 198, NBC 212). The parent company depended on about two-thirds of its income from broadcasting but also held interests in such varied ventures as cable, magazines, recordings, and theme parks. In 1985 ABC was purchased by Capitol Cities Communications.

● President Roosevelt's death reported (12 April–) by all networks; first intensive radio coverage of the death of a U.S. president in office. After the flash announcing his death in Georgia, radio reported his background, public reaction in the United States and abroad, the funeral, etc.

● Final Reports on FM radio and television spectrum allocations issues (May and June) by Federal Communications Commission, following weeks of hearings (September–November 1944). FM moved up to 88–106 (later 108) MHz and was given 100 channels (60 more than before), 20 reserved for educational use. Allocated 13 very high frequency (VHF) channels, TV won primary attention over radio for FM.

● In 1942–1945 start up of 28 FM stations and 34 AM stations. Previously between 30 and 50 AM stations had started annually. The reduced growth rate was due to government policy. At war's end the

FCC began to process a backlog of station applications. During the war network programming had dominated radio, with affiliation rising from 60 percent of all stations (1940–1941) to 95 percent (1945), the all-time peak. Most of the about 950 stations operating were affiliated with at least one network—the largest proportion, 40 percent (1945), with Mutual.

• Radio advertising flourishing. During the war it increased its share of ad dollars from 12 percent (1941) to 18 percent on an expanded base (1945). In 1943 radio passed newspapers as a national advertising medium, and by 1945 radio garnered more than 37 percent of national advertising, ahead of magazines and newspapers. Gross revenues for networks and their owned and operated stations almost doubled, from $56.4 million (1940) to $100.9 million (1945). Gross revenues of stations not owned by networks more than doubled, rising from $90.6 million (734 stations, 1940) to $198.3 million (873 stations, 1945); before-tax profits grew from 21 percent to 30.5 percent of revenues. Returns on station investments ranged up to 800 percent (1939–1945). Many national and regional manufacturers that had switched to producing war materiel (e.g., auto companies) used institutional advertising to keep their good name before the public. Most product advertising was for such attainable but frequently rationed items as drugs, foods, tobacco, and toiletries.

• "Ozzie and Harriet," situation comedy starring Ozzie Nelson (1906–1975) and Harriet Hilliard Nelson (1914–), originally Peggy Lou Snyder. The long-running network radio show later became a television program starring the real Nelson family, including sons Rick and David.

• "Queen for a Day," audience-participation show with strong human interest. Host Jack Bailey showered prizes on selected women from the audience with sad personal stories to tell. The national radio show later went to television.

1946–1953

Cold War Period

Books

1946. Two best sellers—*Peace of Mind*, by Joshua Loth Liebman, and *The Foxes of Harrow* by Frank Garvin Yerby (1916–), also author of the best-selling *The Golden Hawk* (1948) and *Pride's Castle* (1949). *Foxes of Harrow* was set in the pre–Civil War South. Frank Yerby specialized in historical romances. His other books included *A Woman Called Fancy* (1951), *The Garfield Honor* (1961), and *Western: A Saga of the Great Plains* (1982).

- *All the King's Men*, by Robert Penn Warren (1905–), a Pulitzer Prize winner. Inspired by Louisiana's Huey Long, the novel was about a corrupt southern governor. Other books by Warren, a leading southern writer, included *Night Rider* (1939), *At Heaven's Gate* (1943), *Band of Angels* (1955), *The Cave* (1959), *Flood* (1964), *Meet Me in the Green Glen* (1971), and *A Place To Come To* (1977). Warren was known as a poet, too, having published such works as *Promises* (1957), a Pulitzer Prize winner; *Being Here* (1980); and *Chief Joseph of the Nez Perce* (1983).

- *Lord Weary's Castle*, by Robert Lowell (1917–1977), a leading postwar poet. This volume exemplified Lowell's work, as did his *Life Studies* (1959).

- *Member of the Wedding*, by Carson McCullers (1917–1967), née Smith, a major novel. Her other books included *The Heart Is a Lonely Hunter* (1940), *Reflections in a Golden Eye* (1941), and *Clock Without Hands* (1961).

1947. Two best sellers—*Gentleman's Agreement*, by Laura Z. Hobson (1900–), and *Inside U.S.A.*, by John Gunther (1901–1970), whose other behind-the-scenes analyses included *Inside Europe* (1936),

Inside Asia (1939), *Inside Latin America* (1941), *Inside Russia Today* (1958), and *Inside Europe Today* (1961). Gunther's novels included *The Troubled Midnight* (1962) and *The Lost City* (1964). Hobson's other books included *Over and Above* (1979) and *Untold Millions* (1982).

• *The Age of Anxiety,* by Wystan Hugh Auden (1907–1973), a major poet, awarded a Pulitzer Prize. Other volumes of poems by W. H. Auden in this period included *Collected Shorter Poems 1930–1944* (1950) and *Nones* (1951); his *Collected Poems* was published in 1976.

• *A Free and Responsible Press,* by The Commission on Freedom of the Press, published. It suggested government intervention in the mass media system if the media did not exercise social responsibility. The commission, chaired by University of Chicago Chancellor Robert M. Hutchins (1899–1977) and including no media people, had studied books, magazines, motion pictures, newspapers, and radio. Noting a consolidation trend, commissioners saw increasingly limited public access to the free marketplace of ideas and decreasing opportunity for truth to defeat error (two premises for interpretations of the First Amendment). Society could no longer afford to allow the First Amendment to sanction irresponsibility as the price of press freedom. The "Hutchins commission" recommended self-regulation by the media, with public participation. If that did not work, the commission said government should step in.

1948. Three best sellers—*Sexual Behavior in the Human Male,* by Alfred Charles Kinsey (1894–1956); *Dinner at Antoine's,* by Frances Parkinson Keyes (1885–1970), née Wheeler; and *The Naked and the Dead,* by Norman Mailer (1923–). Previous Keyes novels included *The Old Gray Homestead* (1919), *The Career of David Noble* (1921), *Queen Anne's Lace* (1930), *Written in Heaven* (1937), *Fielding's Folly* (1940), and *Crescent Carnival* (1942). *The Naked and the Dead,* a novel about World War II, established Mailer as an author. In the 1960s he was included among practitioners of the "new journalism," freely using fiction techniques to report, as in *Miami and the Siege of Chicago* (1968), his view of the 1968 Republican and Democratic conventions. Mailer's *The Armies of the Night* (1968) and *The Executioner's Song* (1979) won Pulitzer Prizes. His other books included *Barbary Shore* (1951), *The Deer Park* (1955), *Advertisements for Myself* (1959), *An American Dream* (1965), *Of a Fire on the Moon* (1970), *The Prisoner of Sex* (1971), and *Tough Guys Don't Dance* (1984).

• New American Library founded by Kurt Enoch (1895–1982) and Victor Weybright. NAL introduced the well-printed king-size paperback, including *An American Tragedy* by Theodore Dreiser and *God's Little Acre* by Erskine Caldwell, thus setting the standard for distribution of literary paperbacks. In 1966 NAL was purchased by Times Mirror Company.

• *Crusade in Europe*, by Dwight David Eisenhower (1890–1969), a wartime memoir.

• *Terror and Decorum*, by Peter Robert Edwin Viereck (1916–), recipient of a Pulitzer Prize (1949). Other books of poems by Peter Viereck in this period included *Strike Through the Mask* (1950) and *New Poems* (1952).

• *The Young Lions*, by Irwin Shaw (1913–1984), a novel about World War II. This established the playwright and short story writer as a novelist. Other Shaw books included *Two Weeks in Another Town* (1960), *Rich Man, Poor Man* (1970), *Evening in Byzantium* (1973), and *Beggarman, Thief* (1977).

1949. *The Man With the Golden Arm*, by Nelson Algren (1909–1981), the story of a Chicago narcotics addict. Another major Algren novel was *A Walk on the Wild Side* (1956).

• *Annie Allen* by Gwendolyn Brooks (1917–) published; a Pulitzer Prize winner (1950). Brooks was the first black woman to win a Pulitzer for poetry. Her works were racially oriented, as in *In the Mecca* (1968) and *Primer for Blacks* (1980).

1950. Two best sellers—*The Cardinal* by Henry Morton Robinson and *Betty Crocker's Picture Cook Book*.

1951. Four best sellers—*The Caine Mutiny*, by Herman Wouk (1915–); *From Here to Eternity*, by James Jones (1921–1977); *Look Younger, Live Longer*, by Gayelord Hauser; and *The Sea Around Us*, by Rachel Carson (1907–1964). Another popular work by Carson, a zoologist, was *Silent Spring* (1963). *From Here to Eternity* was a naturalistic novel of army life on Hawaii on the eve of the Japanese attack on Pearl Harbor. Jones's *Some Came Running* was a best seller in 1958. His other books included *The Pistol* (1958), *The Thin Red Line* (1962), *Go to the Widow-Maker* (1967), and *Whistle* (1978). *The Caine Mutiny*, a World War II navy story, won a Pulitzer Prize (1952). Wouk's *The Winds of War* (1971) and *War and Remembrance* (1978), a best seller, comprised a World War II saga. Another Wouk best seller was *Marjorie Morningstar* (1955).

• *The Catcher in the Rye*, by Jerome David Salinger (1919–), a picaresque novel that became a youth cult classic. J. D. Salinger's other works included the best sellers *Franny and Zooey* (1961) and *Seymour: An Introduction* and *Raise High the Roof Beam, Carpenters* (1963).

• Books by two major poets—*Collected Poems*, by Marianne Craig Moore (1887–1972), and *Collected Poems* and *Autobiography*, by William Carlos Williams (1883–1963). Marianne Moore's collection won a Pulitzer Prize. Her books included *Poems* (1921), *The Pangolin and Other Verse* (1936), *What Are Years?* (1941), and *Complete Poems* (1967). Williams's other works of poetry included *The Complete Collected Poems of William Carlos Williams 1906–1938* (1939) and *Paterson* (1946). He also wrote novels, short stories, and essays.

1952. *The Holy Bible: Revised Standard Version*, a best seller in this period and later.

• *The Invisible Man*, by Ralph Waldo Ellison (1914–), a leading black writer. It was a naturalistic novel of a black man trying to discover himself as an individual among his race and society. Ralph Ellison's other works included *Shadow and Act* (1964), essays.

1953. Two best sellers—*A Man Called Peter*, by Catherine Marshall, and *The Power of Positive Thinking*, by Norman Vincent Peale.

• *The Adventures of Augie March*, by Saul Bellow (1915–). *Augie March* established Bellow among the top living writers. His *Herzog* (1965) was a best seller, and his *Humboldt's Gift* (1975) won a Pulitzer Prize. His other books included *Dangling Man* (1944), *Henderson the Rain King* (1958), and *Mr. Sammler's Planet* (1969). In 1976 Bellow received the Nobel Prize in literature.

• *The Shocking History of Advertising*, by E. S. Turner, a critical study of the ad business.

• Books by two major poets—*Collected Poems, 1917–1952*, by Archibald MacLeish (1892–1982), and *Selected Poems*, by Conrad Potter Aiken (1889–1973). Other volumes of verse by Conrad Aiken included *Earth Triumphant* (1914), *Priapus and the Pool* (1922), and *In the Human Heart* (1940). He also wrote short stories and novels, including *Blue Voyage* (1927). MacLeish, librarian of Congress 1939–1944, won a Pulitzer Prize for his collection, as he had for *Conquistador* (1932). His other major works included *Actfive and Other Poems* (1948) and *New and Collected Poems* (1976). MacLeish also wrote plays and essays.

Newspapers

1946. Administrative Procedures Act, 5 U.S.C. 1002, passed by Congress to prevent imposing bureaucratic secrecy on the rapidly expanding administrative actions of the federal government. Not intended as a public information law, it required disclosure of information in official records only to persons directly concerned with the subject of inquiry—sometimes interpreted to exclude reporters. The law broadly provided that information could be kept secret for "good cause found," for "internal management of an agency," and for "the public interest." Editors and reporters thought those vague phrases were used by federal agencies as excuses to withhold information that should be released. In the 1950s and 1960s newspaper editors pressed for an improved law, which was finally passed in 1966. Strongly endorsing disclosure of information, President Lyndon Baines Johnson (1908–1973) signed

Public Law 89-487 on 4 July 1966 to become effective 4 July 1967. The new "freedom-of-information act," which applied only to the federal executive branch, clearly indicated that most records unessential to national security were public information, provided access to anyone who could reasonably identify the requested records, and eliminated previous loopholes. The media considered the new law better than the old but still too restrictive. In the 1980s President Ronald Wilson Reagan (1911–) weakened the FOIA by increasing federal agencies' authority to exclude materials from FOIA provisions and by encouraging agencies to charge fees for filling information requests.

• American Press Institute and Inter-American Press Association founded to increase communications among journalists.

1948. New York *Guardian*, a pioneer "alternative" or "underground" paper, founded; radical.

• Los Angeles *Mirror* (11 October–January 1962) founded as an evening tabloid by Norman Chandler (1899–1975), president of the morning Los Angeles *Times*. The publisher was Virgil Pinkley. The *Mirror* emphasized features and offered advertisers run-of-the-paper color.

• Public Relations Society of America founded.

1949. As of 1 October, 1,780 daily newspapers with 52,845,550 circulation and 546 Sunday papers with 46,498,970 circulation.

• Electronic photocomposition demonstration. It replaced lead (hot type) with photographed characters on film (cold type). An early phototype machine was Intertype's Fotosetter.

• New York *Daily Compass* (May–November 1952) founded as a liberal tabloid with financial backing of Mrs. Anita McCormick Blaine; publisher and editor was Ted O. Thackery.

1950. An estimated 19,000 men and women practicing public relations professionally. Growth of the vocation was stimulated by postwar business expansion.

• Korean War covered (fall), with little censorship, by about 300 correspondents from 19 countries as United Nations troops under the command of General Douglas MacArthur (1880–1964) advanced toward the Yalu River. On 18 December leading newspaper, radio, and wire service representatives, meeting with Defense Secretary George Catlett Marshall (1880–1959), adopted a resolution explicitly giving the military responsibility for security of information from combat areas. Regarding this as media approval for strict, formal censorship, MacArthur tightened restrictions. On 23 December Eighth Army headquarters began requiring that all magazine articles, newspaper reports, photographs of military operations, and radio broadcasts be cleared by censors. Early in January 1951 Tokyo headquarters allowed the release of stories that were accurate and did not contain military information, and prohibited any story that would injure U.S. or Allied forces' morale or embarrass the United States, Allies, or neutrals. Also prohibited were reports of any result of enemy action that might tend to make Americans or Allies despondent. Censors were to examine messages at the Korean point of dispatch, Tokyo point of receipt, and the point of transmission abroad. After President Truman removed MacArthur as commander (11 April 1951) for insubordination, censorship declined. By June there was censorship at only one point: Korean headquarters. When truce negotiations began in Korea (July), the U.N. Command insisted that reporters be permitted at the truce site. In December 1952 the U.S. Defense Department instituted a uniform field-censorship plan for the air force, army, and navy. Censorship duties were transferred from intelligence officers to public relations officers, who were to censor only for security reasons; censors and journalists disagreed about the definition of "security."

1951. Expansion of teletypesetter circuits, which transmitted tape ready for composing machines, by Associated Press, International News Service, and United Press Associations. In 1952 the circuits were used by about 600 dailies.

• Executive Order 10290 issued by President Harry S Truman (1884–1972) to Defense and State departments; extended restrictions on military information. After persistent media pressure, President Dwight David Eisenhower (1890–1969) in 1953 issued Executive Order 10501 easing Truman's order; but the media considered the new policy still too restrictive. In a March 1960 memorandum Eisenhower clarified authority to classify defense information by agencies established since his 1953 order. Before leaving office he eliminated blanket classification in 30 agencies and bureaus.

• *Lorain Journal Company v. United States* (342 U.S. 143). In this decision the U.S. Supreme Court enjoined the Lorain, Ohio, *Journal* (f. 1879) from a boycott to destroy a competitor. The daily had rejected advertising of merchants advertising with a competing radio station in nearby Elyria. Under the Sherman Antitrust Act (1890), the station had obtained a lower court injunction barring the boycott. The Supreme Court found that the injunction was not unconstitutional, holding that the First Amendment was not intended to protect monopolistic practices that would force a competitor out of business.

1952. Newsprint prices, rising with inflation and greater advertising and circulation, at $126 a ton, up from about $100 a ton in the recent past. Paper prices continued upward.

• International Press Institute founded.

1953. Two important decisions by the U.S. Supreme Court affecting the press. One upheld a union rule; the other overturned an injunction against a combination advertising plan. In *American News-*

paper Publishers Association v. National Labor Relations Board (345 U.S. 100) the Supreme Court upheld the International Typographical Union's "bogus-matter" rule. To protect against job loss by automation, the rule stipulated that advertising provided a newspaper in ready-to-print form must be reset by compositors. In *Times-Picayune Publishing Company v. United States* (345 U.S. 594), a Sherman Antitrust Act case, the Supreme court reversed a lower court decision barring the New Orleans company, which also published the *States*, from selling advertising in its morning and evening papers under a unit-rate plan. The Supreme Court held that the plan did not violate antitrust laws, but the 5–4 decision was confined to the New Orleans case. The complaint had been initiated by the competing *Item*, sold to Times-Picayune Publishing in 1958.

● *I. F. Stone's Weekly* (–1971) founded by Isidor Feinstein Stone (1907–) as a liberal, "alternative" paper. His *Weekly* became nationally known for its well-researched exposés, often documented with information from government records. The paper attacked McCarthyism and covered Korean War controversies, problems of blacks, U.S. involvement in Vietnam, and government encroachments on private rights in reaction to demonstrations against that involvement.

● United States Information Agency founded, stabilizing a program established in 1945 when the government had decided to continue in peacetime the wartime international propaganda of the Office of War Information. Abroad the USIA became known as the United States Information Service. It provided magazines, motion pictures, news services, and pamphlets and operated libraries and reading rooms in 70 nations. In 1977 President Jimmy (James Earl) Carter (1924–) initiated merger of the USIA with the State Department's cultural and educational functions in a new International Communication Agency.

Magazines

1946. *Freedom and Union* founded and edited by Clarence Kirshman Streit (1896–); dedicated to promoting peace. The monthly had about 10,000 subscribers in 1963.

● *Our World* founded as a picture magazine for blacks.

● *Salute* (–August 1948) founded to capture readership of World War II veterans. It had some of the flavor and tone of *Yank*. Publisher Leverett Gleason staffed the magazine with former *Stars and Stripes* and *Yank* editors and writers. Three months after its founding, ownership changed; the new publishers broadened the appeal to include nonveterans. In early 1948 the appeal to ex-servicemen was dropped. *Salute*'s peak circulation was 300,000.

1947. *Changing Times* founded for businessmen, with articles covering a wide variety of business topics. By the 1970s the monthly had broadened subject areas to include automobiles, career planning, education, health, home, insurance, investments, recreation, taxes, and social security. As *Changing Times* continued to help businessmen and other adults manage their affairs better, Publisher and Editor-in-Chief Austin H. Kiplinger (1918–) began accepting advertisements (1980) to meet rising costs. In the mid-1980s "The Kiplinger Magazine" was edited in Washington, D.C., for readers wanting consumer information. Circulation was 1,350,000.

• *Country Music* and *Country Song Roundup* founded to cover similar areas.

• *Lapidary Journal* founded for hobbyists making jewelry with rocks. Articles covered gem collecting, cutting, etc. In the mid-1980s the monthly was edited in San Diego by Pansy D. Kraus.

1948. Association of Comics Magazine Publishers founded by 14 major comic books publishers to curtail criticism and restrictive legislation. ACMP adopted an ethics code urging members, who published about 30 percent of comic magazines, not to publish periodicals that glorified crime, detailed methods of crimes committed by youths, depicted "sadistic torture," contained obscene or vulgar language, or were "sexy, wanton."

• *American Square Dance Magazine* founded as a monthly for callers, dancers, and teachers of square dancing; some round dancing coverage.

• *Presbyterian Life* founded, a leading Protestant denominational magazine. It carried features with broad appeal and covered church news.

1949. Protestant Church-owned Publishers' Association established by 24 publishing houses. In the mid-1980s it included the major church publishers and was headquartered in Nashville, Tennessee.

• *American Heritage* founded by Earle W. Newton as a quarterly to dramatize U.S. history; backed by the American Association of State and Local History. Circulation in 1951 was 50,000. In 1954 new management, seeking a larger readership, dressed up the periodical with hard covers and four-color illustrations. Frequency was increased to six issues annually. Bruce Catton (1899–1978) became editor. Circulation rose to 300,000 in 1958. In the mid-1980s *American Heritage* was published bimonthly and edited in New York by Byron Dobell, who ran historical articles for lay readers. Circulation was 125,000.

• *Quick* founded by Gardner Cowles, Jr. (1903–); the first miniature (4 by 6 inches) magazine with popular appeal. Its 68-page first issue covered news items in one to six sentences; other content included features and photographs. Because the small page size required advertisers to prepare special printing plates, Cowles had not planned to accept advertising; but he finally did when production costs exceeded circulation revenues. During the early 1950s *Quick* continued to lose money. In 1953, with 1.3 million circulation, the title was sold to Walter Annenberg (1908–) of Triangle Publications, Inc. Annenberg made *Quick* a larger, adless biweekly, then discontinued it in 1954. The magazine was widely imitated. The title floated around the industry, other publishers using it singly and in title combinations.

• *The Reporter* (April–) founded by Max Ascoli (1898–1978) for an educated, liberal audience. The fortnightly became known not only for its opinion pieces, but also for its depth reporting about domestic and foreign affairs. Topics included the China lobby, the press as a fourth branch of government, the trucking lobby, use of lie detectors by government agencies, and wire tapping by government and industry. Douglas Cater was the star Washington correspondent. With a circulation of 174,000 the *Reporter* in 1963 carried $689,000 worth of advertising. Circulation peaked at about 200,000, but then waned as Ascoli supported the escalating Vietnam war. In 1968 *Harper's* purchased the *Reporter* and discontinued it.

1950. *Prevention* founded by Jerome Irving Rodale (1898–1971) to show people how to avoid becoming sick. The monthly campaigned against food additives, refined white flour, sugar, etc. J. I. Rodale refused advertisements for alcoholic beverages, cigarettes, commercially prepared foods, and household appliances and toiletries it deemed harmful. The number of subscribers went from the original 50,000 to more than 1 million by 1971. In the next ten years circulation rose to almost 2,400,000 and in 1985, neared 2,821,000. *Prevention* was published by the Rodale Press, Inc., in Emmaus, Pennsylvania; publisher was Marshall Ackerman. The editor since 1964 was Robert Rodale (1930–). Under the supervision of an advisory board of nutritionists and physicians, Rodale edited for women interested in appearance, exercise, and nutrition. Content included new information about fitness techniques, medical technologies, and pharmaceutical products.

• *Tan* (–1981) founded in Chicago by John H. Johnson (1918–); later named *Black Stars*. It covered black stars in music, theater, sports, and the media.

• *Flair* founded by Gardner Cowles, Jr., and edited by Fleur Fenton Cowles (1910–) for a select audience. Editor Cowles aimed to produce an unconventional monthly that combined the best in the arts, decoration, entertainment, fashion, and humor. Impressively designed, *Flair* had different papers, gatefolds, inserts, peepholes, and pullouts. Circulation reached 200,000, but costs outran revenues. The "class" periodical lasted about a year.

• *People Today* founded by the publishers of *Newsweek* as a *Quick* imitator. *People Today* aimed to depict people's lives through words and pictures. After eight months Hillman Periodicals, Inc., purchased the magazine. Circulation peaked at about 500,000 before diminishing to the 1957 level of 219,000.

1951. Comic magazines a big business, as circulation figures (June) for three of the largest publishers indicated: Marvel Comic Group, 11,057,830; National Comics Group, 7,906,690; and Harvey Comics Group, 5,458,860.

● *Army Times* and *Navy Times* founded for military personnel and their families. Published by Army Times Military Group, which included *Air Force Times* (f. 1947). Content included information about legislation, pay, and promotions. The group's parent Army Times Publishing Company also published nonmilitary periodicals.

● *Jet* (November–) founded in Chicago by John H. Johnson as "The Weekly Negro News Magazine." The pocket-size periodical covered events involving U.S. blacks. With more than 750,000 circulation by 1980, *Jet* was the second most successful magazine in the Johnson Publishing Company (first: *Ebony*). By the mid-1980s circulation had reached 800,000. Executive Editor and Associate Publisher Robert E. Johnson supervised coverage of current events and trends and ran features on African affairs, civil rights, education, entertainment, religion, and other black concerns.

1952. *Confidential* founded by Robert Harrison; specialized in intimate gossip about the private lives of celebrities. It also exposed corruption and harmful medicines. The bimonthly's specialty was the lurid article built less on facts than innuendo. Illustrations were at times edited to appear sensational. Printed on cheap paper and selling for 25 cents, *Confidential* achieved 3,442,536 circulation in 1956. In 1957 the publisher was indicted for criminal libel and obscenity. Some charges were dismissed; but in Los Angeles Harrison, who also published *Whisper*, was fined $5,000 for conspiring to publish obscene material. In March 1958 *Confidential* appeared in a new format with a new policy of not exposing private lives. In May 1958 Hy Steirman purchased *Confidential* and *Whisper*, and made more changes. *Confidential* was widely imitated in the 1950s.

● *Mad* founded as a comic book by William Maxwell Gaines (1922–). In 1955 Gaines raised the price from 10 cents to 25 cents and changed format. As the first satirical magazine for children, *Mad* dealt primarily with the adult environment, drug use, school, and sexuality. It stressed visual presentation. Its symbol was the smiling, gap-toothed, jug-eared Alfred E. Neuman, whose slogan was "What, me worry?" Appealing more to boys than girls, mostly teens, *Mad* achieved 2.3 million circulation in the mid-1970s before declining to 1,850,000 about 1980, when it was published eight times a year. Circulation was boosted by parodies of widely known newspapers, such as the *National Enquirer* and the *Wall Street Journal*. The magazine was owned by Warner Communications. In the mid-1980s Al Feldstein edited *Mad* in New York.

● *Numismatic News* founded; covered coin collecting. In the mid-1980s Krause Publications of Iola, Wisconsin, published the weekly for beginning and advanced collectors of U.S. coins, medals, and tokens. Circulation was 55,000.

● *Tropical Fish Hobbyist* founded for people interested in commercial, educational, and recreational uses of tropical fish. Circulation reached 52,000 in the mid-1980s. The monthly was published in Neptune City, New Jersey. Edward C. Taylor edited *Tropical Fish Hobbyist*, running personality profiles about notable aquarium hobbyists and providing advice about breeding and caring for amphibians, reptiles, and tropicals.

1953. *Family Weekly* (13 September–) founded by Downe Publications as a Sunday supplement for newspapers. In 1976 it was sold to a company representing the four newspaper groups of Donrey Media Group, Holies Newspapers, Howard Publications, and Small Newspapers. In 1979, when it was sold to CBS Inc., it ranked fourth among consumer magazines and third among weeklies. More than 350 newspapers distributed it, giving it 13.3 million circulation. Emphasizing service, *Family Weekly* carried articles on such topics as food, health, money management, and sports. In the mid-1980s the Gannett media conglomerate purchased the magazine, whose circulation was then about 12.5 million. In 1985 Gannett radically changed its appearance, added more features, and called it *USA Weekend*.

● *Playboy* (December–) founded in Chicago by Hugh Hefner (1926–) as an entertainment monthly for indoor urban males between the ages of 18 and 80. Fifty-one copies of the first issue, which contained a nude photograph of actress Marilyn Monroe, were sold at 50 cents each. By the end of 1954 circulation was 175,000. Early content included fiction and nonfiction by such authors as Nelson Algren, Wolcott Gibbs, Herbert Gold, Jack Kerouac, Alberto Moravio, Carl Sandburg, and Evelyn Waugh. Hefner went from publishing material in the public domain and buying inexpensive reprint rights to paying well for original material. He ran articles on fashions, food, jazz, sex, sports cars, travel, etc. The "playmate of the month," a nude or nearly nude young woman photographed in color and displayed in a gatefold insert, became one of *Playboy*'s most talked about features. Editors selected models with a fresh, girl-next-door look. With toned-up quality and toned-down sexual content, *Playboy* began soliciting advertising in 1956. The "pleasure-primer for the sophisticated, city-bred male" (as the periodical called itself) grew rapidly, hitting a million circulation in 1958. In 1961 operating profit from circulation and sales passed

$1,757,000. Two years later circulation passed 1.3 million. The *Playboy* symbol, a rabbit (in a tuxedo for a sophisticated touch), became famous. In the 1970s editors continued running articles and stories by top authors and experimented with one-shot specials (the first: *Playboy's Guide to Electronic Entertainment*). *Playboy* ranked among the top ten magazines in circulation by the late 1970s. Foreign editions for Australia, Brazil, France, Germany, Italy, Japan, Mexico, etc. added more than 2 million circulation to the domestic figure of about 5.5 million. In 1980 *Playboy's* total revenue of $199,279,000 ranked it fifth among magazines. The periodical's success spawned not only widespread criticism of its sexual content but also many imitators—at one time more than 160 "girlie" or "skin" magazines. In the mid-1980s *Playboy's* editorial offices were divided between Chicago, where Don Gold was managing editor, and New York, where G. Barry Golson was executive editor. Articles accented topical, timely topics, including notable contemporary men in business, finance, politics, music, science, and technology. Fiction was both serious and light but above all clever and smoothly written or fraught with contemporary ideas and style. Story types included adventure, fantasy, horror, humor, mystery, psychology, and science. Color photographs of nude young women added visual appeal. Other content included reviews of books, movies, and records. Editors aimed for educated, well-informed urban males (whose median age was about 30). In 1984, according to *Folio:*, *Playboy* ranked fifteenth among consumer magazines in both total revenue, with $171,354,000, and circulation, with 4,209,824; the figures were down slightly from 1983. In late 1985 the magazine based its advertising rates on 4.1 million circulation.

• *True West* founded. Circulation rose to almost 150,000 by 1980. In the mid-1980s the national magazine was published by Western Publications of Perkins, Oklahoma, and edited by Jim Dullenty, who ran fast-paced pieces about gunfights, Indian raids, and other adventures in the frontier West of 1830–1910 as well as articles about lawmen, outlaws, and other personalities of the Old West.

• *TV Guide* (April–) founded in Philadelphia by Walter H. Annenberg, who purchased and combined *TeleVision Guide* of New York, *TV Digest* of Philadelphia, and *TV Forecast* of Chicago. In 1954 Annenberg's Triangle Publications, Inc., published *TV Guide* in 27 editions for a total 2,222,000 circulation. In 1962 *TV Guide*, headquartered since 1957 at Radnor, Pennsylvania, went to 70 editions and became the first weekly to attain 8 million circulation. In 1963 circulation was second only to *Reader's Digest's* 14.5 million. As *TV Guide* rose to first in magazine circulation for 1976–1980, the staff grew to about 1,400, about half in Radnor and the others in 34 U.S. offices. By 1980 *TV Guide* topped all magazines in total revenue. Advertising passed $200 million annually, a giant leap from its first year's $750,000, and annual profits were estimated between $35 million and $50 million. Probably no other magazine in the world sold a billion copies a year. Content included behind-the-scenes and critical articles, but the backbone consisted of computer-compiled (since the 1960s) local program listings with brief explanations. In 1980 Triangle tested its first Cable-Pay Edition in the Southwest, and the next year shifted *TV Guide* to perfect binding, which permitted more inserts for cable and other special listings. In 1981 *TV Guide*'s 17,670,543 circulation slipped under first-place *Reader's Digest*'s; its $253,440,762 ad revenue was second to *Time*'s. In the mid-1980s David Sendler, national section editor, stressed trends; local sections editor was Roger Youman. Merrill Panitt continued as editorial director, a post he had held since the founding. In 1984, according to *Folio:*, *TV Guide* had the highest total revenue of any consumer magazine, with $743,750,000. It ranked third (behind *Parade* and *Reader's Digest*) in circulation, with 17,230,353. In latter 1985 the advertising rates were based on 17 million circulation.

Motion Pictures

1946. *The Best Years of Our Lives,* directed by William Wyler (1902–1981), probably the most popular film about returning servicemen adjusting to civilian life. This was partly because of its absorbing story, its study of human relationships, and the subtle camera work by Gregg Toland (1904–1948). The House Un-American Activities Committee, however, condemned the Academy Award-winning *The Best Years of Our Lives* as unpatriotic. Wyler's *Mrs. Miniver* (1942) and *Ben-Hur* (1959) also won Oscars. Other films by Wyler, one of many Hollywood directors who made documentaries for the government during World War II, included *Wuthering Heights* (1939), *The Little Foxes* (1941), *Roman Holiday* (1953), *Friendly Persuasion* (1956), and *Funny Girl* (1968).

● Movie industry box office receipts at their peak: $1.7 billion gross, the highest in the half-century history of the film business.

1947. House Un-American Activities Committee hearings into Communist infiltration of the motion picture industry. The congressional committee cross-examined directors, producers, and screenwriters. Ten witnesses were labeled Communist sympathizers. This "Hollywood Ten" accused HUAC of violating their constitutional right to freedom of speech and were sentenced to a year in prison for contempt of Congress. Frightened, industry leaders instituted blacklisting, which barred any suspected or known Communist or sympathizer from working on a Hollywood movie. In a second set of hearings witnesses had two choices: (1) they could plead the Fifth Amendment guarantee against self-incrimination and refuse to answer any questions, which would keep them both out of jail and out of work (blacklisted); or (2) they could admit previous membership in the Communist Party, which meant they must name everyone they had known in the party or face prison for contempt. Along with blacklisting, the HUAC hearings generated damaging publicity in the media, American Legion threats to boycott Hollywood films, and a spate of movies glorifying the Federal Bureau of Investigation and the crusade against communism, as if flattery would exonerate movie makers. In all, the accusations came at probably the worst time for the movie industry—just as it was suffering from the effects of the Paramount decision (1948) and rising competition by television.

• *Body and Soul*, directed by Robert Rossen (1908–1966), a *film noir* gangster story. In *film noir* gangsters were not tough but sick and gangsterism was rooted in society. Later Rossen films included *All the King's Men* (1949), *The Hustler* (1961), and *Lilith* (1964).

• *Brute Force*, directed by Jules Dassin (1911–), depicting prison brutality. Later Dassin films included *Naked City* (1948), *Thieves' Highway* (1949), *Night and the City* (1951), *Rififi* (1954), *Never on Sunday* (1960), and *Topkapi* (1964).

• *The Ghost and Mrs. Muir*, directed by Joseph L. Mankiewicz (1909–). His later films included *All About Eve* (1950), *Julius Caesar* (1953), *The Barefoot Contessa* (1954), and *Suddenly Last Summer* (1959).

1948. *United States v. Paramount Pictures, Inc.* (334 U.S. 131). In this case the U.S. Supreme Court ended vertical control and block booking by Hollywood movie companies. Defendants included not only Paramount but also the four other major studios: Loew's, Incorporated, Radio-Keith-Orpheum, Twentieth Century-Fox Film Corporation, and Warner Bros. Pictures, Inc. Each had full vertical integration—control of production, distribution, and exhibition. The Supreme Court upheld a lower court decision enjoining the defendants from block booking, a practice in which a studio insisted that exhibitors take its mediocre films in order to obtain its quality films. Features were licensed in blocks before production. Ruling that vertical control was in restraint of trade, violating the Sherman Antitrust Act, the Supreme Court ordered the majors to sell their theaters and thus give up a guaranteed market for hundreds of features produced each year. The majors could continue to produce and distribute films, just not exhibit. A film would have to be good enough to sell itself. This breakup of the movie monopolies sent panic waves through the industry.

• *Call Northside 777*, directed by Henry Hathaway (1898–),

stretched conventions of the newspaper genre, a close relation of the gangster film, by using real locations that made it seem realistic, immediate.

• *Easter Parade*, directed by Charles Walters (1903?–1982), a show business musical. In this period Walters also directed another film in that genre, *Summer Stock* (1950), as well as *Lili* (1953).

• *The Treasure of the Sierra Madre*, an Academy Award winner directed by John Huston (1906–). The picture was successful despite lack of a Hollywood formula happy ending. Huston's background as a screenwriter was apparent in his subtle and taut scripts that revealed human frailties, not only in *The Treasure of the Sierra Madre* but also in *The Asphalt Jungle* (1950), which epitomized a postwar genre of urban crime films, *The African Queen* (1951), and *Beat the Devil* (1954). Among his other films were *Key Largo* (1948), *The Red Badge of Courage* (1951), *Moulin Rouge* (1953), *Moby Dick* (1956), *The Misfits* (1961), *Freud* (1963), and *Night of the Iguana* (1964).

1949. Motion picture attendance off by one-fifth, employment down by one-fourth. Blaming these statistics on television, studios tried to boycott TV.

• *Force of Evil*, directed by Abraham Polonsky, a *film noir* gangster picture.

• *I Shot Jesse James*, directed by Samuel Fuller (1911–). It stretched conventions of the western genre, foreshadowing psychological westerns for the next two decades. With this film and *Run of the Arrow* (1957) Fuller shattered old ideals by portraying violence as corrupting and brutalizing the good guys who gunned down the bad guys. To Fuller, violence profaned rather than purified.

• *On the Town*, directed by Stanley Donen (1924–) with Gene Kelly (1912–), a Metro-Goldwyn-Mayer musical, as were *Singin' in the Rain* (1952), co-directed by and starring Kelly; *Seven Brides for Seven Brothers* (1954); and *Funny Face* (1957). These films combined appealing scores, imaginative numbers, scintillating color, and humorous, spoofing stories. Donen's other films included *Two for the Road* (1967), *Bedazzled* (1968), and *Movie Movie* (1978), which parodied old Hollywood.

1950. *Winchester 73*, directed by Anthony Mann (1906–1967), a conventional, classic-style western, portraying violence as a legitimate way for good men to eliminate evil enemies and to establish law and order. Another Mann film in this period was *Bend of the River* (1952).

1951. *An American in Paris*, directed by Vincente Minnelli (1913–1986), a musical starring Gene Kelly, who choreographed exuberant dance sequences to George Gershwin's music. The movie featured a long, sensuous, impressionistic ballet acclaimed for its integration of abstract sets, cinematography, color, costumes, dance, and music into formal, virtually "pure" cinema. Later Minnelli films included *The Bad* and the Beautiful (1953), *Lust for Life* (1956), *Designing Woman* (1957), *Gigi* (1958), *The Reluctant Debutante* (1958), *Some Came Running* (1959), and *Bells Are Ringing* (1960).

• *A Streetcar Named Desire*, directed by Elia Kazan (1909–). It featured the new "method-acting" style that spread from Actors Studio in New York to Hollywood. Such actors as "Streetcar" star Marlon Brando (1924–) approached acting more naturalistically. Kazan, a liberal in the ultraconservative Hollywood blacklisting period, avoided losing his job and offending audiences by translating social problems into human problems in such movies as *A Streetcar Named Desire*, *Viva Zapata!* (1952), *On the Waterfront* (1954), *East of Eden* (1955), and *A Face in the Crowd* (1957). In these films dynamic method-acting performances were delivered by Brando, James Dean, Andy Griffith, Vivien Leigh, Rod Steiger, and Jo van Fleet. Other postwar Kazan films included *Gentleman's Agreement* (1947), *Pinky* (1949), *Wild River* (1960), *Splendor in the Grass* (1961), and *The Last Tycoon* (1976).

1952. By this year more than one-fifth of theaters closed; only drive-ins continuing to increase. Hollywood employment was down. Blacklisting and television competition created fear and economic uncertainty.

• *This Is Cinerama*, introducing the first wide-screen process, invented by Fred Waller, as Hollywood desperately sought to compete against TV's small screen. The movie was shot with three cameras and the films simultaneously projected onto a 165-degree curved triple screen that provided peripheral movement, drawing the audience into the picture; stereo sound enhanced the effect.

• *House of Wax*, which horrified and delighted audiences with spectacular three-dimensional effects, another Hollywood gimmick to draw people into theaters. Such 3-D films required audiences to wear cardboard and plastic glasses to fuse two images that sometimes seemed to leap out of the screen. Three-D's novelty eventually wore off, and many exhibitors disliked handling the glasses or could not afford to renovate for the new technology.

• *Joseph Burstyn, Inc. v. Wilson* (343 U.S. 495). In this decision the U.S. Supreme Court first recognized motion pictures as an important medium for the expression of ideas. Burstyn's film distributing company claimed unconstitutional a New York statute that prohibited exhibiting a motion picture unless it was licensed. After bomb threats, picketing, and other protests, the New York State Board of Regents had revoked a film's license on the grounds of sacrilege. In the film, *The Miracle*, an Italian production by Roberto Rossellini, Anna Magnani played a simple-minded peasant "Mary" and Frederico Fellini a bearded, itinerant "Joseph." Mary was raped by Joseph, who she thought was St. Joseph, and consequently ostracized from her village. New York courts supported the regents. The Supreme Court held that the statute and "sacrilege" were vague, therefore insufficient grounds for revoking the license; Burstyn's First Amendment rights had been abridged. This was the first case since 1915 (*Mutual Film Corporation v. Ohio*) to raise the issue of whether motion pictures were protected by the First Amendment. The landmark *Miracle* decision foreshadowed a weakening of social controls on motion picture content.

• *High Noon*, directed by Fred Zinnemann (1907–), one of the best westerns in this period; stretched the genre. Reflecting the contemporary social climate, *High Noon*, which starred Gary Cooper (1901–1961), attacked the think-alike timidity of the conventional, respectable majority. Zinnemann's later films included *From Here to Eternity* (1953), *The Nun's Story* (1959), *A Man for All Seasons* (1966), and *Julia* (1977).

1953. *The Moon Is Blue*, directed by Otto Preminger (1906–1986), the first major film to lack the Hollywood Production Code's seal of approval and the first significant break in movie self-censorship in more than 20 years. The film broke new ground in subject matter—depicting the prohibited topic of adultery—and in candor—including a few prohibited "naughty" words like "mistress" and "virgin." Otherwise it was an inoffensive comedy of manners. With *The Moon Is Blue* Preminger launched a war on the code (replaced about 15 years later with a flexible system of rating film content maturity). His *The Man with the Golden Arm* (1955), story of a drug addict, also was a successful code violator. Later Preminger films included *Anatomy of a Murder* (1959), *Exodus* (1960), and *Advise and Consent* (1962).

• *The Robe* introduced CinemaScope, the most successful wide-screen process. CinemaScope used new wide film and special anamorphic lenses to make the image about half again as wide as normally viewed; instead of almost square, new screens were almost twice as wide as high.

Radio and Television

1946. *Public Service Responsibility of Broadcast Licensees* (7 March), the Federal Communications Commission's first major report on programming policy. In it the FCC emphasized licensees' responsibility for public service programming. The FCC's "Blue Book" (for its blue paper cover) contained five major parts. The first compared examples of programming promises, such as limited advertising and local live public service shows, with actual performance, such as many commercials and low-cost recorded music. The second part provided the legal rationale for FCC's involvement in programming, mainly as it affected the choice of competing applicants for a license. The third part outlined public service factors, including the need for sustaining programs to balance advertiser-supported programs, to experiment with new kinds of programs, to serve minorities and nonprofit organizations, and to provide for unsponsorable types of programs. According to charts and tables, networks broadcast advertiser-supported programs in prime time, relegating sustaining programs to times when few people could listen. When networks did offer a public service program, most affiliates rejected it for a local sponsored program. Local station advertising and programming practices, the Blue Book indicated, made discussion of public issues difficult. The fourth part presented statistics showing the increase in broadcast profits during 1937–1944, implying that broadcasters could afford some of the recommended improvements. The summary fifth part emphasized that a licensee must police its own programming. The FCC indicated that when considering renewal applications it would give preference to stations that had fulfilled their public service responsibilities by airing discussion of public issues, local live shows, and sustaining programs as well as by avoiding excessive advertising. The FCC intended that the Blue Book not promulgate new rules or regulations but, rather, codify the commission's philosophy to help both licensees and regulators. Broadcasters protested that Blue Book policies violated the freedom of speech clause of the First Amendment; broadcasters pointed out that the Communications Act (1934) prohibited the FCC from censoring.

• First television receivers, manufactured by Dumont, on sale (May). Several weeks later sets made by Radio Corporation of America went on sale. In 1947 Philco sets were available. Within two years many other brands were on the market. Early marketing was disorganized, manufacturing slow. Contributing to the confusion and delay were a shortage of manufacturing facilities, which were concentrated on filling the demand for AM radio sets; the color controversy, which could make black and white TV sets obsolete; uncertainty over spectrum allocations; unsophisticated manufacturing techniques; and high prices. In 1948 5-inch to 7-inch receivers cost $375 to $500 plus $45 to $300 for installation. By the early 1950s competition and an increase in set sales lowered the price of a typical small screen set to about $200.

1947. "Howdy Doody," one of the first popular children's television programs; others followed, including "Super Circus" (1949) and "Ding Dong School" (1952).

• Coaxial cable extension from New York to Boston (November) completing interconnection of population centers on the Northeast coast.

1948. "Texaco Star Theater" (–1956) and "Toast of the Town"

264

(–1971), outstanding successes in early television programming. "Texaco Star Theater" was popular for five years. It starred Milton Berle, originally Berlinger (1908–), who presented top guest stars, one-liners, and lots of visual humor, including strange costumes. The "Toast of the Town" variety show, later called the "Ed Sullivan Show," after columnist-host Edward Vincent Sullivan (1902–1974), ran 23 years. Weekly live anthology dramas such as "Kraft Theater," "Studio One," and "U.S. Steel Hour" were also early TV successes.

• Transistor demonstrated (June) at Bell Telephone Laboratories. Inventors John Bardeen (1908–), Walter Houser Brattain (1902–), and William Bradford Shockley (1910–) received the Nobel Prize for it. Advantages of transistors over tubes included compact construction of products, use of less electricity, and cooler operation for longer life. Until costs dropped around 1960, transistors had little impact on broadcasting. By the 1970s the public could buy tiny transistor radios for as low as $5.

• TV stations in Midwest connected by coaxial cable (September).

• Freeze on TV station license applications (September–1952) ordered by Federal Communications Commission while it tried to solve expansion and interference problems. FCC permitted stations with construction permits to begin operations but would not consider new applicants while it studied standards for color TV, spectrum locations for more channels, assignments of channels by city, channel reservations for educational TV, and reduction of tropospheric interference. FCC and industry girded for what would be four years of hearings that would shape TV's future.

• Liberty Broadcasting System founded in Texas by Gordon McLendon (1921–). McLendon skillfully simulated play-by-play broadcasts of baseball games by combining wire service reports of games in progress with records of sound effects. The legality was questionable, but the popularity was not. In 1949 he fed game reports to more than 80 stations in the Southwest. By 1950 Liberty had expanded to 200 stations and six hours of daily programming, including direct play-by-play broadcasts as well as re-creations of both baseball and football games. Just as American Broadcasting Company, Columbia Broadcasting System, and National Broadcasting Company were emphasizing television and deemphasizing radio, Liberty announced plans for a national radio network with 16 hours daily programming. By June 1951 Liberty network consisted of 400 affiliated stations and an effective news operation. Then lawsuits by ball clubs and financial problems jolted the network; advertisers and stations left. In mid-1952 operations were discontinued.

1949. Completion of eastern and midwestern coaxial cable networks connections, enabling major stations in those two areas to receive network programs at the same time.

● Emmy Awards, named after the image orthicon television camera tube, first made, honoring outstanding TV programs of the previous season. These covered Los Angeles stations initially, but became national in 1952.

● "The Goldbergs" (–1953), based on a popular radio show, "Rise of the Goldbergs" (f. 1929), about a poor Jewish family in New York's Bronx. The story revolved around "Molly," portrayed by series creator and writer Gertrude Berg (1899–1966).

● "Father Knows Best" on radio. The show, which starred Robert Young (1907–) and Jane Wyatt (1912–), went on television in 1957.

● Federal Communications Commission (September) hearings, at first focusing on selection of color technology. The choice was essentially between Columbia Broadcasting System's mechanical-electronic, noncompatible (with black and white) system and Radio Corporation of America's electronic, compatible system.

1950. WOI-TV of Iowa State University, Ames, the first (February) nonexperimental educational television station; broadcast on a nonreserved channel.

● *Red Channels: The Report of Communist Influence in Radio and Television* issued (22 June) by American Business Consultants of New York, publishers of *Counterattack* anti-Communist newsletter (f. 1947) and a leading blacklisting group. *Red Channels*, the most widely circulated blacklisting publication, gave detailed background on 151 broadcast personalities whom ABC considered at least sympathetic to communism. It cited reports of government and private groups, mixed in innuendo, and implied guilt by association. Blacklisting ran from the late 1940s into the 1950s. It was perpetuated by anti-Communists who threatened to create controversy, which would turn away advertisers, if certain broadcasters even sympathetic to the "Far Left" were hired. Secret reports circulating among advertisers, agencies, stations, and networks specified persons who should not be hired. No one while in broadcasting admitted blacklisting existed. The practice finally faded with the end of the postwar Red scare and lawsuits by radio personality John Henry Faulk (1913–). In 1957 Faulk lost his sponsor and his Columbia Broadcasting System job in New York and found himself unemployable. He blamed his blacklisting on Aware, Inc., an organization that attacked alleged Communist influence in broadcasting. Faulk finally won his court battles in 1962.

● Korean War restrictions on civilian construction. These led to reduced production of radio and television sets.

● Joint Committee on Educational Television founded to push for educational TV channel reservations. The committee, later called Joint Council on Educational Television, lobbied the Federal Communications Commission and conducted a public information campaign to generate public support; latter subsequently taken over by the cooperating national Citizens Committee for Educational Television.

• CBS's mechanical-electronic, noncompatible color television system approved (October) by FCC (approval later rescinded).

• "Voice of Firestone," a live semiclassical music show, carried over from radio, one of the few serious programs regularly on TV.

• "Superman," first television version. It was based on the hero of comics, radio, and motion pictures.

• "Broadway Open House," perhaps the first late-night television show. Host of the National Broadcasting Company program was comedian Jerry Lester (1911–).

1951. Senate hearings into organized crime, chaired by Senator Estes Kefauver (1903–1963) of Tennessee. These hearings had the most audience impact of any television news programming in this period. The high point was the testimony of Frank Costello, reputed gangster leader; because he demanded that cameras not show his face, they focused on his nervous hands. The hearings put Kefauver in the public eye and made him a Democratic contender for high elective office.

• Three-month test of Phonevision, a wire system of pay-TV, conducted by Zenith. After the successful test Zenith petitioned (1952) the Federal Communications Commission to permit regular pay-TV programming in major markets. After hearings on the request (1955) the FCC authorized testing of pay-TV to determine its commercial viability. After inconclusive tests and FCC delays, proponents set aside pay-TV (revived in 1960s).

• Intercoastal microwave relay system opened by President Truman's address to the Japanese peace treaty conference in San Francisco (4 September). American Telephone & Telegraph had constructed 107 concrete and steel towers 30 miles apart between San Francisco and New York at a cost of $40 million. Ninety-four stations carried the speech live to about 95 percent of U.S. TV sets; other equipment manufacture halted (October) for Korean War duration.

• One of first demonstrations of magnetic videotape recording given by Bing Crosby Enterprises. Videotape would enable Harry Lillis (Bing) Crosby (1904–1977) to do his TV musical variety program when he wished rather than at broadcast times. Kinescopes (film), widely used for video recording, required time for processing, were grainy, and could not be re-recorded; tape could be played back immediately, had live-TV quality, and could be re-recorded. Several companies were developing electronic videotape systems to replace kinescope recordings, but tape would not become commercially practical until 1956.

• "See It Now," based on radio's "Hear It Now," the first continuing documentary public affairs series on a network (Columbia Broadcasting System). The weekly half-hour program was produced by Fred W.

Friendly (1915–) and hosted by Egbert (Edward) Roscoe Murrow (1908–1965). It usually focused on a newsworthy, often controversial event or person. In 1954 Edward R. Murrow exposed the tactics of Senator Joseph McCarthy, Wisconsin Republican, who was investigating communism in the federal government, distorting facts, and indiscriminately ruining reputations.

• Two popular television series—"Dragnet" and "I Love Lucy." "Dragnet" (–1959, 1967–1970), which starred its creator, Jack Webb (1920–1982), was a realistic, matter-of-fact account of a Los Angeles police detective team's work. It helped establish a new TV genre, the police-based series. "I Love Lucy" (–1960), which starred Lucille Ball (1911–), established a standard for TV situation comedies; rerun into the 1980s.

• *Amahl and the Night Visitors* (24 December), an opera by Gian Carlo Menotti (1911–), a cultural highlight of early television; the first of many Christmas showings. An estimated 5 million persons, a large audience at the time, viewed the National Broadcasting Company show.

1952. "The Today Show" debuted (14 January), hosted by Dave Garroway (1913–1982). The one-hour television show consisted of short segments of features, interviews, news, weather, and some performances. The format was innovated by Sylvester Laflin "Pat" Weaver, Jr. (1908–), president of the National Broadcasting Company network.

• "Omnibus," another notable show debuting, one of the most critically acclaimed programs of its time (–1957). It was a 90-minute series of diverse parts.

• "The Bob Hope Show," a radio crossover to television. Bob Hope (1903–), originally Leslie Townes Hope, had been on radio since 1933. During World War II he began entertaining the armed forces abroad, and he continued to do so on television.

• *Sixth Report and Order* (14 April) by the Federal Communications Commission, ending the television freeze. Intending to create more competition (which did not occur), the FCC opened the 70 channels of the ultra-high-frequency (UHF) band (470–890 MHz) for telecasting. To provide TV service to all sections of the country, the FCC established priorities for geographic distribution of VHF and UHF channels, which would intermix in communities; no existing stations would be shifted. FCC considered VHF and UHF channels equal, an error that later became obvious. According to the *Sixth Report and Order*, the FCC would issue two kinds of licenses: for (1) commercial stations (1,809) and (2) noncommercial educational stations (242). Educational channels were reserved in the assignment table. Tropospheric interference was eliminated by increasing the distance between stations using the same channel, thus creating a safety margin. The color controversy was not yet resolved (until 1953).

• "Checkers" speech by Richard Milhous Nixon (1913–), television coverage of a major political event (23 September). Republican presidential nominee Dwight D. Eisenhower was about to dump Nixon as his vice presidential running partner, after the California senator had been accused of accepting large sums of money from wealthy contributors. In an emotional appeal on national TV, Nixon turned the issue to his advantage. The speech tag came from his reference to his daughters' pet dog, Checkers, a gift that the family was going to keep "no matter what."

• Presidential campaign first televised nationally; political spots televised. Coverage included preconvention activities, both conventions, and election night.

1953. KUHT of the University of Houston, Texas, the first educational television channel on a reserved frequency (25 May).

• TV coverage of Queen Elizabeth II's coronation in London, an outstanding technical feat that overcame distance and time problems. Still photographs were in New York ten minutes after being shot, transmitted by Wirephoto. Newsreel film was flown to North America then fed on network lines, enabling Americans to view the events within 12 hours of their occurrence.

• Ownership of stations limited by Federal Communications Commission to five VHF television (extended to seven with addition of two UHF in 1954), seven AM radio, and seven FM radio, unless such ownership was excessive concentration. FCC allowed appeal for exceptions and grandfathered current owners of too many stations, except as it affected future station purchases.

• Approval (December) by FCC of Radio Corporation of America's electronic, compatible color television system as the industry standard, settling the color controversy for consumer purposes.

• United States Information Agency (USIA) founded to coordinate U.S. government propaganda abroad, including Voice of America. VOA broadcast in many languages, transmitting news, music, and other kinds of programs to many parts of the world. Other Cold War broadcast weapons included Radio Free Europe and Radio Liberty. USIA distributed limited material for showing on foreign TV; commercial networks and program packagers did most of the exporting.

1954–1963

Era of Fear and Hope

Books

1954. *Not as a Stranger,* by Morton Thompson, a best seller.

1955. *Gift from the Sea,* by Anne Spencer Morrow Lindbergh (1906–), a best seller. Other books by Anne Morrow Lindbergh included *Dearly Beloved* (1962) and *Earth Shine* (1969).

● "Howl," by Allen Ginsberg (1926–), the most publicized poem of the Beat Generation.

1956. Five best sellers—*Arthritis and Common Sense,* by Dan Dale Alexander; *Don't Go Near the Water,* by William Brinkley; *The Last Hurrah,* by Edwin Greene O'Connor (1918–1968); *Peyton Place,* by Grace de Repentigny Metalious (1924–1964); and *The Search for Bridey Murphy,* by Morey Bernstein. *Peyton Place* was also a best seller later; other books by Grace Metalious included *Return to Peyton Place* (1959). Other books by Edwin O'Connor included *The Oracle* (1951); *The Edge of Sadness* (1961), which won a Pulitzer Prize; and *I Was Dancing* (1964).

1957. *Butler v. Michigan* (352 U.S. 380). In this case, the U.S. Supreme Court declared unconstitutional a Michigan obscenity statute. In Detroit Alfred E. Butler had been convicted of selling an allegedly obscene book, *The Devil Rides Outside,* by John Howard Griffin, about a young man's life in a monastery. The state law outlawed circulation of passages tending to corrupt the morals of young people; it provided that books be judged for their effect on children rather than adults. The Supreme Court unanimously agreed with appellant that the statute could be applied to ban from sale adult books that were unsuitable only for children, thus arbitrarily curtailing adults' constitutional rights.

• The landmark obscenity case of *Roth v. United States* (354 U.S. 476), which laid the foundation for modern obscenity law by enunciating a more liberal, rational standard for testing obscenity. This was of far greater effect than *Butler v. Michigan*. Although known as the *Roth* case, this was a joint U.S. Supreme Court decision also involving *Alberts v. State of California* (352 U.S. 962). In Los Angeles police had seized books from Davis S. Alberts, a mail-order book dealer. Under California statute, a municipal court judge found obscene *The Pleasures of the Torture Chamber, She Made It Pay, Sword of Desire, To Beg I Am Ashamed,* and *Witch on Wheels*. In New York a district court jury convicted Samuel Roth, a book dealer, of violating a federal obscenity law by mailing circulars and a book, *American Aphrodite*. In upholding the convictions, the Supreme Court for the first time upheld the constitutionality of obscenity laws; obscenity was not protected by the freedom of speech and press clauses of the First Amendment. The Supreme Court did not rule whether the publications were obscene. Writing the majority opinion, Justice William Joseph Brennan, Jr. (1906–), defined the test for obscenity as "whether to the average person, applying contemporary community standards, the dominant theme of the material taken as a whole appeals to prurient interest." These criteria provided the key for judicial attempts to determine obscenity. The new "Roth test" tended to have a freeing effect on publications by more clearly defining obscenity.

• Five best sellers—*Anatomy of a Murder*, by Robert Traver; *By Love Possessed*, by James Gould Cozzens (1903–1978); *Compulsion*, by Meyer Levin (1905–1981); *The Hidden Persuaders*, by Vance Oakley Packard (1914–); and *Kids Say the Darndest Things*, by Art Linkletter (1912–), also a nonfiction best seller in 1958. Robert Traver was the pen name for John Donaldson Voelker (1903–), whose other books included *Trouble-shooter* (1943), *Danny and the Boys* (1951), *Small Town D.A.* (1954), *Trout Madness* (1960), and *Laughing Whitefish* (1965). Another major novel by James G. Cozzens was *Guard of Honor* (1948), a Pulitzer Prize winner. His works also included *Confusion* (1924), *Cockpit* (1928), *S. S. San Pedro* (1931), *Men and Brethren* (1936), *Ask Me Tomorrow* (1940), *The Just and the Unjust* (1942), and *Morning, Noon, and Night* (1968). Vance Packard's other books included *The Status Seekers* (1959), *The Waste Makers* (1960), and *The Pyramid Climbers* (1962).

• *Collected Poems*, by Wallace Stevens (1879–1955), published. Stevens's poems were known for their imagery, precision, and intensity.

• *On the Road*, by Jack Kerouac (1922–1969). It epitomized the antiestablishment Beat Generation novel.

1958. Two best-selling novels—*Dr. Zhivago*, by Boris Pasternak (1890–1960), and *Exodus*, by Leon Marcus Uris (1924–). Other best sellers by Leon Uris included *Topaz* (1967), *Trinity* (1976), and *The Haj* (1984).

● *Lolita* by Vladimir Nabokov (1899–1977), a satirical novel. Other books by Nabokov, a Russian émigré, in this period included *Invitation to a Beheading* (U.S. 1959, Soviet Union 1938) and *Pale Fire* (1962).

● *Madison Avenue, U.S.A.*, by Martin Mayer. Mayer gave readers a "peek" at advertising agency operations.

1959. Four best sellers—*Act One*, by Moss Hart (1904–1961); *Advise and Consent*, by Allen Stuart Drury (1918–); *Only in America* by Harry Lewis Golden (1903–1981); and *Twixt 12 and 20*, by Pat Boone (1934–). Allen Drury's political novel won a Pulitzer Prize. His other books included the best seller *A Shade of Difference* (1962), *Throne of Saturn* (1971), *Come Nineveh, Come Tyre* (1973), and *The Hill of Summer* (1981).

1960. Three best sellers—*Folk Medicine*, by D. C. Jarvis; *Hawaii*, by James Albert Michener (1907–); and *The Rise and Fall of the Third Reich*, by William Lawrence Shirer (1904–). William L. Shirer's other books included *Berlin Diary* (1941), *The Rise and Fall of Adolf Hitler* (1961), and *20th Century Journey* (1976). James A. Michener's other best sellers included *The Source* (1965), *Centennial* (1974), *Chesapeake* (1978), *The Covenant* (1980), *Space* (1982), *Poland* (1983), and *Texas* (1985).

1961. Two best sellers—*The Agony and the Ecstasy*, by Irving Stone (1903–), and *The New English Bible: The New Testament*, also a later best seller. Stone's book was a fictional biography of Michelangelo. His other fictional biographies included *Sailor on Horseback* (1938), about Jack London, and *The Origin* (1980), about Charles Darwin.

● *Catch-22*, by Joseph Heller (1923–), a darkly satirical novel of the air corps in World War II; perhaps the best satire by a U.S. author. Heller's other books included *Something Happened* (1974), *Good as Gold* (1979), and *God Knows* (1984).

1962. Two best sellers—*Calories Don't Count*, by Dr. Herman Taller, and *Ship of Fools*, by Katherine Anne Porter (1894–1980). Other books by Porter included *Flowering Judas and Other Stories* (1930), *Pale Horse, Pale Rider* (1939), and *The Leaning Tower* (1944).

1963. *Bantam Books v. Sullivan* (372 U.S. 58). In this case the U.S. Supreme Court held unconstitutional a Rhode Island law that restrained the sale of allegedly obscene publications without a hearing. The state legislature had established a Commission to Encourage Morality in Youth, whose duties included advising book and magazine distributors when a publication was "objectionable" (obscene) and should be removed from sale. The commission threatened that if the listed publication was not removed, the case would be turned over to law enforcement authorities. The appellants were four New York publishers of paperback books whose wholesale distributor for most of Rhode Island was Max Silverstein & Sons, which had received at least 35 notices from the commission. Among the books the commission listed as objectionable were *Peyton Place*, written by Grace Metalious and published by appellant Dell Publishing Co., Inc., and *The Bramble Bush*, written by Charles Mergendahl and published by appellant Bantam Books, Inc. (*Frolic, Playboy, Rogue*, and similar magazines were also listed as objectionable.) The Supreme Court considered the commission's actions prior restraint, since they aimed to suppress certain publications without providing constitutionally required safeguards, and in violation of the First and Fourteenth amendments. Also, censoring publications because they might adversely influence someone under 18 years of age unconstitutionally curtailed adult access to them. The Supreme Court reversed the lower court decision that had enjoined distributors from displaying certain publications the commission believed objectionable.

• Two best sellers—*Happiness Is a Warm Puppy*, by Charles Monroe Schultz (1922–), and *The Shoes of the Fisherman*, by Morris Langlo West (1916–). Morris L. West's later books included *The Salamander* (1973), *The Navigator* (1976), *Clowns of God* (1981), and *The World Is Made of Glass* (1983).

• *The Fire Next Time*, by James Baldwin (1924–), consisting of two "letters" describing the state of U.S. blacks. Earlier books by Baldwin, a leading black author, included the novels *Go Tell It on the Mountain* (1953), *Giovanni's Room* (1956), and *Another Country* (1962).

• *In the Clearing*, by Robert Lee Frost (1874–1963), a collection of the poet's verse. Robert Frost in his lifetime won four Pulitzer Prizes: for *New Hampshire* (1923), *Collected Poems* (1930), *A Further Range* (1936), and *A Witness Tree* (1942).

• *V.*, Thomas Pynchon's first novel. Other books by Pynchon (1937–) included *The Crying of Lot 49* (1966) and *Gravity's Rainbow* (1973).

Newspapers

1954. PR News Association, Inc., founded in New York by Herbert Muschel to transmit business publicity releases to newspapers and broadcasting stations. Teletype receivers were installed without cost to media using the service. Public relations news wires were later founded in Chicago and Los Angeles.

1955. Newsprint consumption a record 6.6 million tons; price to $136 per ton.

• *Village Voice* founded in New York's Greenwich Village by Edward Fancher (publisher), Norman Mailer (1923–), Daniel Wolf (editor), and others; one of the first major alternative papers; antiestablishment Democratic. Content included liberally slanted cultural and political news. Contributors included cartoonist Jules Feiffer and writers Mailer and Jack Newfield. *Village Voice* was the first major paper to report without language taboos, including free use of four-letter obscenities and profanity. In the mid-1970s the tabloid weekly led alternative papers with a circulation of about 150,000. In June 1974 Clay S. Felker (1928–) purchased control, relinquished in 1977 to Rupert Murdoch (1931–). In 1985 John B. Evans was publisher; circulation exceeded 151,800.

1958. Semiconductor chip invention (1958–1959) by Jack St. Clair Kilby (1923–) and Robert Norton Noyce (1927–); a revolutionary commercial and technological breakthrough affecting all media. Chip integrated into one tiny piece all parts of an electronic circuit (capacitors, diodes, resistors, transistors).

● International Public Relations Association founded; members in 50 nations.

● *The Realist* founded in New York by Paul Krassner; an alternative paper.

● International News Service (f. 1909) and United Press Association (f. 1907), wire services, merged to form United Press International.

1959. Postal rate hike for newspapers began (1 January); postage to rise gradually over three years. The rise spurred newspaper efforts to seek greater distribution efficiency by nonpostal means.

● "Housekeeping Act," 5 U.S.C. 22, amended by Congress to reduce its use as an excuse to withhold information from the press and public. The act had been passed in 1789 to make heads of executive departments responsible for the care and custody of records. Its vague wording made it susceptible to broader interpretation, and department heads used it as justification for denying access to information in official records. The one-sentence amendment stated: "This section does not authorize withholding information from the public or limiting the availability of records to the public."

● Advertising volume for all media doubled during the decade, rising from $5.5 billion (1950) to $11 billion (1959). Newspapers ran about one-third of the volume. Newspaper advertising/editorial ratio gradually reversed from 40 percent/60 percent to 60 percent/40 percent. National milline rate (price of agate line per million circulation) rose about 25 percent.

● Harris-Intertype's slugcasting "Monarch" attained a record speed of 750 operations per minute by using a Fairchild-designed tape, as mechanical developments in the decade accelerated composing room production.

1960. In the 50 U.S. states—1,763 English-language general-circulation dailies, a 9-paper decline in the decade; and 9,325 weeklies, semiweeklies, and triweeklies, a 778-paper decline. Suburban and neighborhood newspapers had increased phenomenally with population shifts after World War II, until there were about 2,000 suburban and 2,000 neighborhood papers. There were more than 100 newspaper chains, or groups, most organized within single states; the largest nationals were Hearst, Newhouse, and Scripps-Howard.

• Run-of-paper (originally "run-of-press") color (by 1960) used by about half of the dailies, which controlled about 83 percent of daily circulation. (R.o.p. color was applied in regular press runs rather than preprinted.) The amount of advertising using at least two colors (including black) more than tripled in the 1950s.

• In public relations more than 30,000 men and women professionally employed (1960), most in business services, communications, finance, insurance, manufacturing, public administration, and religious and other nonprofit areas.

1961. *Muhammad Speaks* founded as the Black Muslim organ by Malcolm Little (1925–1965), known as Malcolm X. It proclaimed the programs of Elijah Muhammad and condemned the Vietnam war. Nationally sold on street corners and in shopping centers, *Muhammad Speaks* led the black press around 1970 with an estimated 700,000 circulation. Later the paper became the Islamic *Bilalian News*, distributed nationally in the 1980s.

1962. *Arizona Journal* founded in Phoenix; probably the first attempt to produce by offset a metropolitan daily in a competitive situation. Suspended in 1964, it was briefly revived in 1965.

• *National Observer* (February–July 1977) founded in New York by Dow Jones & Company as a national weekly to provide information about cultural, governmental, and other developments in an attractive newspaper format for a general audience. At first the *National Observer* analyzed and summarized news and ran topical features for a family audience. It the middle 1960s it interpreted new political and social trends. In the 1970s it emphasized consumer service and human interest features. In 1973 circulation peaked at 560,000, small for a national paper; in 1977 it was about 400,000. Editors were William Giles, Don Carter, and Henry Gemmill. Writers included Dickey Chapelle, who covered the Vietnam war, and Jim Perry, who covered national politics. Although widely regarded as a quality newspaper, the *National Observer* never had a profitable year and losses totaled more than $16 million. The paper had no clearly defined audience to attract adequate advertising.

Magazines

1954. Comic Magazines Association of America (September–) established for self-regulation of its member publishers; headed by Charles F. Murphy of New York. The association adopted (27 October) a voluntary code that banned horror, obscene, terror, and vulgar comic books by its member firms. Comic magazines represented an estimated $150 million industry with aggregate monthly circulation as high as 90 million copies. Most readers were children.

• *Popular Electronics* founded as a monthly for citizen-band radio users, computer hobbyists, electronics experimenters, ham radio operators, and high-fidelity enthusiasts. In the early 1980s the New York-based periodical was published by Ziff-Davis Publishing Company and edited by Arthur Salsberg; circulation exceeded 400,000. The title was soon changed to *Computers and Electronics, for Computer Enthusiasts*. Circulation rose to 600,000. Editor in chief was Seth R. Alpert. Authoritatively written for readers with some knowledge of computers and electronics, the periodical emphasized how-to and other technical articles.

• *Sports Illustrated* (16 August–) founded in New York by Henry Robinson Luce (1898–1967) as a national sports news weekly for well educated, upper income readers. A magazine with the title had been published for two years in the 1930s and briefly after World War II, and Henry R. Luce had purchased the title from Stuart Scheftel for $5,000. As major league sports expanded in the late 1950s and early 1960s, circulation rose from 575,000 (1954) to 1 million (1962). Time Inc. published five custom editions for advertisers. Emphasizing features, *Sports Illustrated* covered baseball, basketball, boating, boxing, bridge, dog and horse shows, field trials, football, fox hunts, golf, mountain climbing, snorkeling, swimming, etc. It crusaded for conservation, exposed connections between boxing and racketeering, and examined drug use by athletes. Although the magazine was mostly staff written, also included were such bylines as Catherine Drinker Bowen, William Faulkner, Robert Frost, President-elect John F. Kennedy, John P. Marquand, William Saroyan, and John Steinbeck. *Sports Illustrated* was lavishly illustrated with drawings and color paintings and photographs. By 1980 circulation exceeded 2,250,000; about half the readers were college educated and around 31 years old. In 1984, according to *Folio:*, *Sports Illustrated* had total revenue of $343,619,000, fifth among consumer magazines; advertising revenue of $230,766,000, fifth among consumer magazines; and circulation of 2,668,678, fifth among news magazines. In the mid-1980s *Sports Illustrated* ran national and regional nonfiction about sports and extensive regional advertising.

1955. Industrial Communication Council founded by communication managers, consultants, and editors from government, industry, and not-for-profit organizations to improve communication with customers, educators, employees, governments, and the public. The New York-based association entered the 1980s with 250 members. Its publications included the *ICC Newsletter*.

• *Fishing World* founded for fishermen. Published in Floral Park, New York, the bimonthly had a circulation of 285,000 in the mid-1980s. Editor Keith Gardner ran nonfiction on fishing sites, tackle, techniques, and similar topics.

• *Guns* founded for firearms enthusiasts. Published in San Diego, the monthly had 135,000 circulation in the mid-1980s. Content included firearms roundup articles, gunsmithing and reloading how-to pieces, and new firearms test reports.

• *National Review* (November–) founded by William F. Buckley, Jr. (1925–), publisher and editor, and Priscilla Buckley, managing editor. Politically conservative, the brother-sister team early ran opinion pieces by L. Brent Bozell, James Burnham, Whittaker Chambers, Max Eastman, Russell Kirk, and others of similar philosophy. Contributing editors included Jackson Kilpatrick and Ralph de Toledano. By 1960 *National Review* had 32,000 readers and an $860,000 deficit. The next year Buckley reported a loss of about $100,000. Donations and Buckley family subsidies kept the New York-based magazine going. By 1965 circulation had risen to 100,000, by 1977 to 110,000. In 1969 *National Review* joined with its liberal counterpart, the *New Republic*, to sell advertising. Entering the 1980s *National Review* remained the leading voice of the Far Right, with about 90,000 circulation. In the mid-1980s circulation exceeded 121,900. William A. Rusher was publisher; Robert F. Sennott, Jr., advertising director; and W. F. Buckley, editor in chief.

1956. *Africa Report* founded to provide U.S. readers information about Africa, particularly its lesser-known nations. It entered the 1980s with 10,500 circulation. In the mid-1980s the New York-based bimonthly was edited by Margaret A. Novicki, who emphasized African cultural, economic, and political affairs in relation to U.S. business objectives and foreign policy.

• *Bon Appetit* founded as a free promotional periodical; later became a fine-food monthly. It entered the 1980s with 1,145,000 circulation among people who enjoyed cooking and entertaining; content included features about elaborate meal preparations and many recipes. Published by a subsidiary of Knapp Communications Corporation of Los Angeles in the mid-1980s, *Bon Appetit* appealed to young, affluent women and men. Publisher was Robert S. Phelps; advertising director, George B. Dippy; editor in chief, Paige Rense; editor, Marilou Vaughan; and writers, authorities on food and wine. With circulation exceeding 1,300,000, *Bon Appetit* was one of the most successful fine-food magazines.

• *Christianity Today* founded. Widely read by clergy, it entered the 1980s with about 188,000 subscribers. In the mid-1980s the semimonthly was published in Carol Stream, Illinois, and edited by V.

Gilbert Beers, who ran ethical, historical, informational, and theological material.

● *Horseman* founded; published in Houston, Texas. In the mid-1980s the monthly had about 192,900 circulation among people who owned and rode mostly western stock horses for business and pleasure. Editor Linda Black aimed to inform readers how better to enjoy, keep, ride, and train their horses.

● *Signature* founded; Diner's Club organ. The monthly entered the 1980s with about 600,000 subscribers, mostly men. In the mid-1980s *Signature—The Citicorp Diners Club Magazine* was published in New York. The 750,000 circulation was mostly among club members: affluent, urban, traveled business people. Under familiar bylines, Editor Horace Sutton ran nonfiction on the arts, finance, fitness, photography, sports, and travel.

● *Together* founded as a slick monthly for Methodist lay families. Content ranged broadly among such areas as education, evangelism, family life, history, international affairs, successful Methodists, urban problems, and world missions. In geographical inserts *Together* covered denominational news. In 1963, before its demise, circulation was about 757,000.

● *Trump* (–1957) founded by Hugh Hefner (1926–) as a satirical magazine similar to *Mad.*

1957. *Pacific Travel News* founded. It entered the 1980s with 25,000 circulation among travel agents serving Pacific and Asian destinations.

● *The Real West* founded for readers interested in factual accounts of the Old West. In the latter 1970s circulation exceeded 130,000; in the mid-1980s, 122,000. It was published by Charlton Publications, Inc., Derby, Connecticut.

1958. *AutoWeek* founded for motoring enthusiasts. Published by Crain Automotive Group of Detroit, the weekly tabloid reported about 143,000 circulation in the mid-1980s. Publisher was Keith Crain. Editor-in-Chief Leon Mandel emphasized motor sports as well as the domestic and foreign automobile industries. Content included news reports, nostalgia, personality profiles, sneak previews of products, and technical analyses.

● *Guns and Ammo* founded for firearms enthusiasts. Published by Petersen Publishing Co. of Los Angeles, the monthly entered the 1980s with circulation approaching 500,000; by 1985 it exceeded 512,800. Content included technical material on guns, reloading, and shooting. Publisher was Jay Hard; editor in chief, Howard E. French.

● *Horizon* founded by publishers of *American Heritage* as an arts bimonthly; later (1964) quarterly. In 1978 Gray D. Boone of Tuscaloosa, Alabama, acquired the periodical. As publisher and editor in chief, Boone ran articles on cultural and visual arts. Entering the 1980s

Horizon, by then a monthly (1985: ten times a year), had about 105,000 circulation. Contributors to this expensive ($4 a copy), hardbound, lavishly illustrated periodical included distinguished critics and scholars.

• *Modern Maturity* founded by American Association of Retired Persons for its members. Published in Long Beach, California, *Modern Maturity* was a leader among periodicals for older citizens, with circulation of about 7 million in the late 1970s. In the mid-1980s the bimonthly reported more than 9 million circulation among readers over 50 years of age. Editor-in-Chief Ian Ledgerwood ran nonfiction of many types and photo features.

• *Stereo Review* founded for stereo music enthusiasts. It entered the 1980s with more than 540,000 readers; in the mid-1980s circulation exceeded 581,000. In 1985 Ziff-Davis Publishing Company sold *Stereo Review* and its annual specialized buying guides to CBS, Inc.

1959. *Golf* founded for beginning and expert golfers. Published by Times Mirror Magazines, Inc., of New York the monthly entered the 1980s with circulation exceeding 900,000; in the mid-1980s it was about 800,000.

• *Western Flyer* founded as a regional publication for aircraft owners and pilots. Content included features on antique airplanes, home builts, and business use of planes as well as news of government actions. Published by N. W. Flyer, Inc., of Tacoma, Washington, the biweekly tabloid in the mid-1980s reported 25,000 circulation.

1960. *Bicycling* founded. Circulation passed 173,000 in the early 1980s. Published nine times a year by Rodale Press, Inc., of Emmaus, Pennsylvania, *Bicycling* carried how-to, technical, travel, and other articles as well as photo features. Publisher and editor was James C. McCullagh.

• *Surfer* founded for avid water surfers; published monthly in Dana Point, California. In the mid-1980s, *Surfer* reported 91,000 circulation among teens and young adults. Content included authoritatively written articles on surfing spots abroad. Editor was Paul Holmes.

• *Western Outdoors* founded as a regional sports periodical. Published in Costa Mesa, California, in the mid-1980s, the 150,000-circulation monthly emphasized boating, camping, fishing, and hunting in the 11 western states; Baja, California; Alaska; Hawaii; and Canada.

1961. *Atlas* founded by Eleanor Davidson Worley and Quincy Howe (1900–1977), editor, to provide readers a sampling of the world's press; later became *World Press Review*. Howe aimed to provide U.S. readers with a wide range of unabridged, translated selections, including economic and political articles, criticism and reviews, poetry, short stories, and travel pieces—all originally published outside the United States. Monthly the staff screened more than 600 publications in 25 languages. Content covered all shades of opinion. Under Stanley

Foundation ownership in the late 1970s and the 1980s, the monthly gained circulation, reaching about 150,000. Under Publisher and Editor Alfred Balk the staff regularly reviewed more than 1,000 foreign publications.

• *Columbia Journalism Review* founded at Columbia University (New York), with support from educational foundations, to monitor the media. Content included articles on media issues and performance, critical analyses, and National News Council reports. In 1985 CJR was one of the few surviving media reviews founded in the 1960s. Bimonthly circulation exceeded 35,000.

• *Cycle World* founded for motorcyclists. Published in Newport Beach, California, for affluent, educated, young motorcyclists, the monthly reported 375,000 circulation in the mid-1980s. Editor Allan Gridler ran a wide variety of features; topics included custom bikes, racers, mechanical modifications, and road tests.

• *Harvest Years* founded as an outgrowth of the first White House Conference on Aging (1960). Peter A. Dickinson, the first editor, emphasized retirement planning and living. In 1972 *Harvest Years* became *Retirement Living*, which in 1978 became *50 Plus*. Content included articles on money management, nutrition, and travel; celebrity profiles; crossword puzzles; and motion picture and television reviews. Monthly circulation entering the 1980s was almost 200,000. It was more than twice that in the mid-1980s.

• *Show* (October–May 1965) founded by Huntington Hartford (1911–) as a handsomely designed, lavishly illustrated performing arts monthly. After a few issues Hartford broadened content to cover all the arts, including books, painting, and sculpture, as well as dance, motion pictures, music, television, and theater. In 1961 *Show* absorbed *Bravo*, a concertgoers' quarterly. In 1962 Hartford bought *Show Business Illustrated* (f. 1961) and *USA-1* (f. 1962). Despite additional readers from these purchases, *Show* lost money, and Hartford offered it for sale in 1964.

• *Show Business Illustrated* (August–February 1962) founded by Hugh Hefner to cover the entertainment arts; went from biweekly to monthly.

1962. *Manual Enterprises, Inc. v. J. Edward Day* (370 U.S. 478). In this decision the U.S. Supreme Court added the new element of "patent offensiveness" to the definition of obscenity. Appellant published *Grecian Pictorial*, *Trim*, and *MANual* magazines, which had been banned from the mail as obscene. (Day was postmaster general.) The magazines, published mainly for homosexuals, carried pictures of nude males. The Supreme Court reversed the lower court judgment upholding the ban. Justice John Marshall Harlan (1899–1971), writing the majority opinion, held that the magazines were not obscene and therefore were mailable because they were not "patently offensive," meaning "so offensive on their face as to affront current community standards of decency." Nudity was not in itself enough to support conviction for obscenity.

• *Civil War Times Illustrated* founded for U.S. Civil War buffs. Published monthly, except July and August, in Harrisburg, Pennsylvania, the periodical reported 120,000 circulation in the mid-1980s. Editor John E. Stanchak ran profiles, photo features, and other historical material.

• *Four Wheeler* founded for four-wheel-drive vehicle enthusiasts. Published in Canoga Park, California, the monthly reported 170,000 circulation in the mid-1980s. Content emphasized competition and off-road adventure.

• *Sergeants* founded for career enlisted women and men in the active and reserve air force. Published by the Air Force Sergeants Association of Temple Hill, Maryland, the monthly had 125,000 circulation in the mid-1980s. Editor Belinda Reilly ran articles on all aspects of the air force and related legislation.

• *USA-1* (April–July 1962) founded by Rodney C. Campbell to put current events into historical perspective. The handsome monthly gained 70,000 subscribers before *Show* (f. 1961) absorbed it.

1963. *Bow & Arrow* founded for archers. Circulation exceeded 100,000 in the early 1980s. Published in Capistrano Beach, California, for bow hunters and competitors, the bimonthly in the mid-1980s carried nonfiction on equipment, hunting, techniques, tournaments, and other archery topics.

• *Christian Reader* founded for evangelical Christians. The bimonthly published in Wheaton, Illinois, reported 225,000 circulation in the 1980s. Kenneth N. Taylor was publisher; Ted Miller, editor.

Motion Pictures

1954. *Bad Day at Black Rock*, directed by John Eliot Sturges (1910–). The film mingled action and setting of the western genre with contemporary moralizing. Other John Sturges westerns included *Gunfight at the OK Corral* (1957) and *The Magnificent Seven* (1960).

• *La Strada*, an example of foreign films that enabled many neighborhood theaters, unable to continue as fourth-run houses for Hollywood movies, to remain in business. Two other examples were *Les Diabolique* (1955) and *Nights of Cabiria* (1957). Such foreign movies differed from any show a television network could present. They were introspective, mature sexually, and sensitive to social problems; also they presented fresh insights into other cultures. English subtitles provided translation of dialogue. Producers or distributors were not required to submit imports for Hollywood Production Code approval. Thus while TV became a mass medium, at least some film became an elitist medium.

1955. *Oklahoma!*, directed by Fred Zinnemann (1907–), an example of the adaptations of Broadway hit musicals that were virtually replacing original film musicals.

• *Marty*, directed by Delbert Mann (1920–), with New York locations and actors to break Hollywood studio clichés.

• *Rebel Without a Cause*, directed by Nicholas Ray (1911–1979). The picture epitomized the new "rebellious youth" genre of the 1950s. As the youth, James Byron Dean (1931–1955) rebelled against adult standards and societal values; James Dean became a heroic symbol for his generation. Other films by Ray included *They Live by Night* (1949), *Johnny Guitar* (1954), and *Bitter Victory* (1958). Ray's *Lightning Over Water* (1979) was an autobiographical mixture of fiction and fact completed after his death by German director Wim Wenders.

1956. Hollywood studios selling pre-1948 films to television. Unable to defeat the new medium, the studios decided to join it—but tentatively at first. Along with this gradual change came a shakeup among production chiefs at major studios as more movies were independently produced.

• *All That Heaven Allows*, directed by Douglas Sirk (1900–), veiled criticism of the characters' bourgeois values with a conventionally melodramatic plot. Other films by Sirk, originally Dietlef Sierck, in this period included *Magnificent Obsession* (1954), *Written on the Wind* (1957), *The Tarnished Angels* (1958), and *Imitation of Life* (1959).

• *Around the World in 80 Days*, produced by Michael Todd (1909–1958), filmed in Todd A-O, the first wide-screen system to use 70 mm film.

1957. *Decision at Sundown*, a western directed by Oscar Boetticher (1916–). Budd Boetticher's other westerns included *The Tall T* (1957) and *Buchanan Rides Alone* (1958). Boetticher continued the genre's conventional attitudes about killing. Violence was a legitimate way for men to establish civilization and uphold the law or to maintain their self-respect against enemies.

• *Paths of Glory*, directed by Stanley Kubrick (1928–). The film condemned war and the French army of World War I. Another Kubrick antiwar film of this period was the dark satire *Dr. Strangelove: Or How I Learned To Stop Worrying and Love the Bomb* (1963). Kubrick established his reputation as one of the most important filmmakers of his time with the above two films plus *Lolita* (1962), *2001: A Space Odyssey* (1968), *A Clockwork Orange* (1972), *Barry Lyndon* (1975), and *The Shining* (1980). Kubrick filmed *2001* in Cinerama but made the curved screen's spectacular effects enhance the story rather than smother it. In his films he achieved irony by mixing horror and humor, and with penetrating cynicism he exposed polite societies' hypocrisies (e.g., French military society in *Paths of Glory*).

● *Twelve Angry Men*, directed by Sidney Lumet (1924–), based on a live television drama. It avoided Hollywood clichés. Lumet became especially known for filming on location in New York with experienced local actors. He made such realistic New Yorker films as *The Pawnbroker* (1965), *Serpico* (1973), *Dog Day Afternoon* (1975), and *Network* (1976). Much credit for the success of such location films, which depended partly on realistic lighting and illusive spontaneity, went to cinematographer Boris Kaufman (1906–1980). Lumet displayed different styles in such movies as *A Long Day's Journey into Night* (1962), *Murder on the Orient Express* (1974), *Equus* (1977), and *The Wiz* (1978).

1958. By now independent producers making half the new films, usually released through major studios.

● Drop of box office revenue to under $1 billion and continuing downward.

● *The Defiant Ones*, directed by Stanley E. Kramer (1913–), a study of race relations. Chained together, two escapees from a southern prison, one white man and one black, were forced to cooperate. Liberal films by Kramer also included *On the Beach* (1959), which sentimentally depicted humanity on the verge of extinction from fallout of atomic war, and *Judgment at Nuremberg* (1961), which melodramatically depicted post-World War II war crime trials. Other Kramer movies included *Inherit the Wind* (1960) and *Guess Who's Coming to Dinner* (1967).

1959. *Kingsley International Pictures Corp. v. Regents of University of State of New York* (360 U.S. 684). In this decision the U.S. Supreme Court held that motion pictures are protected by the First Amendment. The Motion Picture Division of the New York Education Department had refused a license to show a French film version of D. H. Lawrence's *Lady Chatterley's Lover*, distributed by Kingsley. The ban was under a New York statute requiring license denials to films portraying "acts of sexual immorality as desirable, acceptable or proper patterns of behavior" or presenting "adultery as being right and desirable for certain people under certain circumstances." The state justified its action because the film favorably portrayed a relationship contrary to the legal code, moral standards, and religious precepts of its citizens. Appellant contended that the statute violated its constitutional right to advocate ideas. Reversing a lower court decision, the Supreme Court said that even such ideas as adultery, which conflicted with social norms, were protected. With other cases, including *Joseph Burstyn, Inc. v. Wilson* (1952), *Kingsley* reflected a trend toward giving films broader freedom of expression. (The Supreme Court did, however, refuse to decide if the controls a state could impose upon motion pictures were precisely the same as those allowable for the print media.)

1960. Movie attendance down to 40 million weekly (all-time high, in 1946: 90 million). Drive-in theaters had sprouted on urban fringes, and small movie houses were being built in shopping centers.

● Columbia Pictures selling post-1948 films to television, blazing a trail other studios soon followed. As TV showed a greater number of more recent movies, people stayed home, and many late-run neighborhood theaters closed.

1961. *Times Film Corp. v. Chicago* (365 U.S. 43). In this decision the U.S. Supreme court upheld a Chicago censorship ordinance, taking a constitutional step backward. Attempting to have the ordinance declared unconstitutional, Times Film, a small distributor of foreign movies, refused to submit *Don Juan*, an Italian version of Mozart's opera *Don Giovanni*, to Chicago's Board of Censors for a license to exhibit. Times Film paid the license fee but contended that requiring screening and licensing of films before public exhibition was prior restraint and therefore in violation of the First and Fourteenth amendments. Upholding lower court decisions against the appellant, the Supreme Court majority, in a 5–4 decision, said that the law was unconstitutional because motion pictures were not subject to rules governing other modes of expression.

1962. In four years box office receipts down by about $100 million to about $900 million. As ticket sales continued falling, costs of equipment, labor, and materials continued rising in the inflated economy.

● *The Longest Day*, an expensive and spectacular re-creation of famous World War II battles for the wide screen—example of a popular genre in the 1960s. Another example was *Battle of the Bulge* (1965).

● *The Wonderful World of the Brothers Grimm*, the first Cinerama movie using one 70 mm film instead of three 35 mm films. In *Brothers Grimm, How the West Was Won*, and *It's a Mad, Mad, Mad, Mad World* (1963), filmmakers blended narrative with Cinerama's unique effects, smothering character, ideas, and plot under spectacle.

Radio and Television

1954. Army–McCarthy hearings televised (April–June), most important live TV reporting since Kefauver organized-crime hearings (1951). The Senate subcommittee hearings were chaired by Senator Joseph Raymond McCarthy (1908–1957), Wisconsin Republican, who was investigating Communist influence in the U.S. Army. Networks carried live all or part of the hearings, boosting daytime ratings about 50 percent.

• National Educational Television and Radio Center (May–) founded in Ann Arbor, Michigan; later moved to New York. In 1963 name changed to National Educational Television, which provided ETV programming.

• The most UHF television stations yet on the air. Soon after the Federal Communications Commission lifted its TV freeze (1952), 120 began broadcasting.

• "The Tonight Show," late-night television program on the National Broadcasting Company network (27 September–). First host of the 11:30 P.M. (EST) show was Steve Allen (1921–). Jack Parr (1918–) became host in 1957, Johnny Carson (1925–) in 1962. The unique format of guests, jokes, music, sketches, and talk was devised by Sylvester Laflin "Pat" Weaver, Jr. (1908–), network president.

1955. Subsidiary Communications Authorizations for FM stations to transmit music into stores and other businesses authorized by Federal Communications Commission. SCAs provided critical source of station income.

• "The $64,000 Question" (June–) on Columbia Broadcasting System television. Within a month it became the most popular program on TV. It was derived from an old radio program that doubled the potential winnings—to a maximum $64—as contestants answered succeeding questions. TV version was followed by "The $64,000 Challenge," on which winners from "Question" were challenged by new contestants. At one time the two programs were first and second in ratings. In 1957 "The $64,000 Question" shared top rating with another quiz show, "Twenty-One." On that show answers to more difficult questions received more points as contestants tried to garner a match-winning twenty-one. Ratings of "The $64,000 Question," "The $64,000 Challenge," and "Twenty-One" dropped in 1957–1958. But quiz shows were the most popular type of TV programs for years. Other popular types in this period were drama, episodic series, movies, and spectaculars.

• Conclusion of first major congressional investigation of television's relation to juvenile delinquency (August) with a call for FCC program censorship and tougher National Association of Broadcasters Code. A Senate subcommittee chaired by Senator Estes Kefauver (1903–1963), Tennessee Democrat, in 1954–1955 had studied how frequent TV violence affected children. Parents feared that daily violence on TV would accustom and desensitize children to that behavior and even cause them to adopt it. According to some experts' testimony, adult action-adventure programs were viewed by children, who often emulated adults. Other experts suggested that watching mayhem could be cathartic, removing children's need for committing violence.

● "Monitor" weekend radio network program (–1975) announced by National Broadcasting Company; foremost radio program innovation in the 1950s. The 40-hour magazine format show of comedy, interviews, music, news, sports, and talk was a hit with advertisers and listeners. Major credit for "Monitor" went to Sylvester Weaver, Jr.

● "Gunsmoke," crossover from radio to television. This archetype adult western emphasized incident and character rather than action and good versus bad. It became one of the most popular series in TV history, running 20 seasons. The star was James Arness, originally Aurness (1923–).

● "Peter Pan" (7 March), early television spectacle. The two-hour show, which starred Mary Martin (1913–), was broadcast live, in color on the National Broadcasting Company network to what was then the largest audience for one event—70 million viewers, half of the U.S. population. Thus "Peter Pan" heralded the arrival of the "age of television."

1956. Practical videotape recording system unveiled (April) by Ampex. Videotape led to greater flexibility in production and programming. Columbia Broadcasting System was one of the first broadcast organizations to use VTR (November), which soon replaced kinescopes. Tape cost less than film, required no processing time, was editable electronically and thus faster, allowed easy removal of mistakes in performances, made special effects easy, and provided live-quality pictures. With VTRs program production was no longer tied to dates and hours of airing. Network orders and high unit costs delayed VTR equipment sales to all but large stations in major markets until the 1960s. In the latter 1960s new electronic devices made editing easier and cheaper. In 1965 the first home videotape recorders appeared.

● Radio-Keith-Orpheum first to sell pre-1948 motion pictures for television showing. Other studios soon followed. Televised Hollywood movies as well as the growing popularity of quiz shows, situation comedies, and westerns, along with spreading use of videotape recording, contributed to the demise of live TV.

● Debut of two notable television programs on CBS—"Captain Kangaroo" and "Playhouse 90." "Captain Kangaroo," a morning show for preschool children, was a combination of education, games, and songs. Bob Keeshan (1927–) played the casual, elderly sea captain. "Playhouse 90" was one of the best anthology dramas. The 90-minute live, original dramas emphasized characterization and plot.

1957. Major pay television test (September–April 1958) on a cable system in Bartlesville, Oklahoma. Two channels offered programs, mostly first-run movies repeated over a short period, from noon to midnight at $9.50 a month. Some of the original 800 subscribers dropped out after the novelty wore off, and payment was changed to per program. The test was halted because of financial losses of $10,000 a month. Contributing to the test's failure, operators said, was the release of new movies to commercial TV. Pay-TV opponents saw the failure as proof that viewers preferred regular TV.

• "American Bandstand," a teenage dance program on the American Broadcasting Company network. The show, hosted by Dick Clark (1929–), introduced a rock music format to television.

1958. Regulation of cable television ruled beyond authority of Federal Communications Commission. FCC decided (April) that it could not regulate community antenna television under the Communications Act (1934) because CATV was not broadcasting and was not interstate. As CATV grew slowly in the 1950s and early 1960s, the FCC tried to ignore or discourage developments. In the late 1950s broadcasters began seriously objecting to CATV picking up their programs (off the air) without paying for them and selling them to advertisers.

• Rumors of TV quiz show rigging turned out true, as it was revealed (August–December) that contestants on "The $64,000 Question," "The $64,000 Challenge," and "Twenty-One" had been given answers. About 20 quiz shows were discontinued. The program scandals, TV's first major ones, led to investigations by a New York grand jury, which did not make its report public, and by the U.S. House Commerce Committee's Special Subcommittee on Legislative Oversight, which heard former contestants admit complicity in riggings. FCC also heard testimony. Rigging was generally considered defrauding the public, who expected honest contests. The networks, meanwhile, effected procedures for close supervision of the few remaining quiz shows. About the time the shock of the quiz show scandals had subsided another scandal jolted the broadcast industry: allegations of "payola." To induce the playing of certain records, some manufacturers bribed disc jockeys with gifts of liquor, money, women, and occasionally drugs. Payola defrauded the public because listeners depended on the disc jockeys' professional judgment rather than their self-interest in selecting records. Many older people thought the practice was as reprehensible as the new rock and roll flooding the airwaves. The FCC and a congressional subcommittee investigating payola also discovered "plugola," which consisted of radio or TV performers intentionally mentioning the name of a service or product for some reward: e.g., some of the product, a case of liquor, or money. The practice was not sponsorship because networks or stations received nothing; in fact, plugola undercut advertising rate cards. In December 1959 Attorney General William Pierce Rogers (1913–) reported to President Eisenhower that legislation was needed to eradicate deceptive and false advertising and programming. In January 1960

Rogers issued the opinion that the Federal Trade Commission and FCC had the authority to deal with quiz show rigging, payola, and plugola. FCC called for more network public service programming as a penance, although it was not so characterized. FCC called for minimal public service programming on the networks, rotating in prime time instead of the customary fringe hours. Desperate, the networks announced several new public affairs and documentary shows for the next season. Result of the scandals was new laws (1960) to curb quiz show rigging, payola, and plugola. Stations were required to announce when they had received anything of value for broadcasting content. Secret assistance to contestants in purportedly real contests could draw a maximum punishment of one-year imprisonment and a $10,000 fine. Deceptive programming was no longer merely possible evidence of unfitness for license renewal. In the following years rigged programs did not return, and payola and plugola diminished.

● "Perry Mason," mystery drama based on the Erle Stanley Gardner character. The show, which starred Raymond Burr (1917–), became one of the most successful mystery series on television. After it left the Columbia Broadcasting System in 1966, it had many reruns. An attempt at a revival in 1973 was unsuccessful. In the mid-1980s updated versions aired as special programs, with Burr, now bearded, still playing the attorney Mason.

1959. Section 315 of the Communication Act (1934) amended by Congress (14 September) to exempt news reports from the Federal Communication Commission's equal-time rule; statutorily supported "Fairness Doctrine." Journalists no longer were required to give candidates for public office equal time on news programs. But Congress specified that the exemption did not relieve "broadcasters, in connection with the presentation of newscasts, news interviews, news documentaries and on-the-spot coverage of news events from the obligation imposed upon them under this Act to operate in the public interest and to afford reasonable opportunity for the discussion of conflicting views on issues of public importance." Thus the amendment (Public Law 86-274, 86th Congress) gave the public a legal right to hear different opinions on controversial public issues.

● Television Information Office founded in New York by National Association of Broadcasters to improve the public image of scandal-ridden TV.

● "Bonanza," an adult western. One of the most popular westerns ever on television, the series ran 14 seasons on the National Broadcasting Company network before beginning a long run in syndication. Lorne Greene (1915–) starred.

1960. Selling post-1948 films to television begun by major Hollywood studios.

• Number of UHF television stations at a low of 75 (previous high: 120 in 1954).

• Midwest Program on Airborne Television Instruction transmitting educational programming after 15 years of experimenting and planning. From transmitters in aircraft, MPTI, funded mainly by the Ford Foundation, provided instructional TV to schools in Illinois, Indiana, Kentucky, Michigan, Ohio, and Wisconsin. Airborne transmission was discontinued in 1968 because of financial and scheduling problems.

• Stations' responsibilities in public-interest programming outlined by Federal Communications Commission in its first major policy statement on the subject since its "Blue Book" in 1946. The new statement became the guide to public service programming obligations. Indicating what would be expected of licensees, FCC listed "major elements usually necessary to meet the public interest, needs and desires" of a station's community. Those elements were an opportunity for local self-expression; development and use of local talent; editorials by licensees; market and weather reports; service to minority groups; and agricultural, children's, educational, entertainment, news, political, public affairs, religious, and sports programs. While the FCC emphasized local community needs, it did not specify what class (e.g., prime) or quantity of time stations should devote to what kinds of programs.

• Equal-time requirement for fringe-party candidates for president and vice president suspended by Congress for 1960 campaign to permit Democratic and Republican candidates to debate on TV. Section 315 of the Communication Act (1934) required that broadcasters give candidates for political office equal access.

• Face-to-face debate by Democratic and Republican candidates for president on campaign issues on three national television networks (26 September; 13, 21, 26 October). Many observers thought the "great debates," which gave less known Democrat John Fitzgerald Kennedy (1917–1963) national exposure, strongly influenced the election, which Kennedy won. In the first debate Kennedy appeared confident and energetic, while Vice-President Richard Milhous Nixon (1913–) looked furtive and tired. Nixon performed better in the October debates.

• Television's most important role yet in a presidential campaign. Since 1952 the number of TV stations had quadrupled and the number of home sets had doubled. For the first time TV political revenue passed radio's.

• On election night first use by the major networks of computers to predict winners of political offices. In the early evening National Broadcasting Company predicted Democrat John F. Kennedy would win by a wide margin, while Columbia Broadcasting System predicted Republican Richard M. Nixon would win by a landslide. The thin margin of Kennedy's victory became apparent early the next morning.

• *Harvest of Shame* on CBS television (25 November). The documentary, narrated by Edward (originally Egbert) Roscoe Murrow (1908–1965), described migrant farm workers' problems in the United States.

• End of daytime serials and most other radio network entertainment programming, leaving news and special events programs. Network radio had waned in the 1950s as its advertisers and stars had moved to network TV. Times sales for national radio networks had dropped $133 million from the 1948 high to $35 million (1960), but time sales for all radio had risen as the number of small stations increased. Virtually dead as a national medium, radio became primarily local; typical programming was music, news, and sports, with some public affairs.

1961. Broadcasting by 560 commercial television stations, mostly VHF, and 50 educational TV stations.

• For the first time live radio and television coverage of a presidential news conference (January).

• First TV coverage of a manned space flight (May)—for suborbital flight of Alan Sheppard.

• Characterization of television as a "vast wasteland" by Newton Norman Minnow (1926–), chairman of Federal Communications Commission, in a speech (May) to National Association of Broadcasters. Indicating his displeasure with much broadcast programming, Newton Minnow told NAB members: "I invite you to sit down in front of your television set when your station goes on the air and stay there without a book, magazine, newspaper, profit-and-loss sheet or rating book to distract you—and keep your eyes glued to that set until the station signs off. I can assure you that you will observe a vast wasteland." Appointed by President Kennedy in January 1961, Minnow pushed for more high-quality programming. Frustrated by conservative holdover commissioners, he resigned in 1963.

• Standards for FM stereo broadcasting approved by FCC (April); combined General Electric and Zenith systems. FM expanded with stereo transmission (June–), while storecasting and other multiplexed services continued.

• Of 25 class I-A (clear channel radio) frequencies, 13 discontinued (September) by FCC to allow for more local AM stations. (About 3,600 AM stations existed in early 1961.) As a result, many new daytime or low-power stations were founded. By the early 1970s few clear channel stations broadcast alone day and night.

• "Dr. Kildare," an early medical drama series on television.

• "The Andy Griffith Show," a situation comedy about a folksy small-town sheriff. In the television series Andy Griffith (1926–) was supported by comic actor Don Knotts (1924–).

1962. Suburban Broadcasters application for a radio station license in Elizabeth, New Jersey—adjacent to New York City—denied by Federal Communications Commission because applicant had made no effort to plan service that would fill Elizabeth's needs. Applicant had copied a program schedule used in its proposals for stations in other states. This and similar cases led the FCC to adopt its "suburban policy" requiring applicants for stations adjacent to large markets to show intentions to serve the suburban community for which the license would be issued (not the adjacent metropolitan market).

• Educational Television Facilities Act (May) providing $32 million in grants over five years for ETV station equipment. The act encouraged development of state educational broadcasting systems, which evolved into parts of a national noncommercial radio and TV system.

• Telstar communications satellite launched (10 July) into orbit, making possible live telecasts between Europe and United States. The American Telephone & Telegraph satellite was launched by the U.S. National Aeronautics and Space Administration.

• Three major classes of FM stations and provision for 10-watt noncommercial educational stations established by FCC (July). FCC assigned about 3,000 potential stations to about 1,800 communities and allowed most existing stations to remain in place. The new policy ended several years of consideration and a short freeze on new FM licenses. The thaw, along with the 1961 stereo standards, accelerated FM's growth.

• Section 303 of the Communication Act (1934) amended (September) to require all new television sets to have UHF reception capability by early 1964. Most sets had not been manufactured with UHF channels. Congress hoped the new requirements would improve UHF's competitive position with VHF.

• Communications Satellite Corporation founded by Congress to unify U.S. activities and provide international leadership in space communication.

• "Beverly Hillbillies," a series about a suddenly oil-rich hillbilly family that moved to Beverly Hills, California, but retained its country ways and garb. The show became one of the most popular situation comedies on television. Christian Rudolph "Buddy" Ebsen (1908–) starred.

1963. First public telecast between Europe and United States made with the launching of Telstar II (7 May).

• Live TV from space by astronaut Gordon Cooper to show what earth looked like from orbit.

• Option agreements giving networks control over affiliates' time blocks banned by Federal Communications Commission. The ban had been first proposed in the 1941 *Report on Chain Broadcasting*.

• "Instant replay," using videotape, first used in sports coverage, by American Broadcasting Company. ABC sports head Roone Arledge

(1931–) was credited with the innovation, which became widely used in sports coverage.

● Television newscasts lengthened from 15 minutes to 30 minutes by Columbia Broadcasting System and National Broadcasting Company (September).

● For the first time TV the main source of news for Americans. According to an Elmo Roper poll for the Television Information Office, TV was by far the "most used" and "most believed" news medium, a conclusion newspapers disputed.

● Concentrated 4-day TV coverage of President Kennedy's assassination in Dallas, Texas, and its aftermath. TV reported public and official reaction, funeral preparations, first hours of President Johnson's administration, Jack Ruby's shooting to death of suspected assassin Lee Harvey Oswald (live on camera), the funeral, and the burial at Arlington National Cemetery. According to CBS, 93 percent of U.S. homes were tuned in during the burial; in the average home that day TV was on 13 consecutive hours. Many observers called the reporting, which preempted most other programming, TV's finest hour and reflective of the medium's maturity.

1964–1972

Period of Dissent

Books

1964. A *Quantity of Copies of Books v. Kansas* (378 U.S. 2105). In this case the U.S. Supreme Court found a Kansas obscenity statute unconstitutional. The statute authorized seizure of allegedly obscene publications before judicial determination of their obscenity and their destruction after the determination. Under the law county officials had seized 31 paperback novels at P-K News Service, Junction City. Seized titles included *The Sinning Season*, *Lesbian Love*, *Sin Hotel*, *The Wife Swappers*, and *Sex Circus*. After a hearing, a district court judge ordered the 1,715 copies of the 31 titles destroyed, an order upheld by the Kansas Supreme Court. P-K News Service appealed, saying the procedure was prior restraint on the dissemination of books and thus a violation of the First Amendment. (Obscenity was not an issue.) The U.S. Supreme Court found that the procedures for seizing and impounding the books pending hearing inadequately protected against suppression of nonobscene books. Kansas officials, the Court ruled, should have provided P-K News Service an adversary hearing before seizure.

● Three best sellers—*Candy*, by Terry Southern and Mason Hoffenberg; *Four Days*, historical record of the death of President Kennedy, from assassination to burial, compiled by *American Heritage* magazine and United Press International; and *Profiles in Courage*, by John Fitzgerald Kennedy (1917–1963). The last, originally published in 1956, had won a Pulitzer Prize in 1957. Kennedy (U.S. President, 1961–1963) also wrote *Why England Slept* (1940) and *To Turn the Tide* (1961).

● *The Witnesses: The Highlights of Hearings Before the Warren Commission on the Assassination of President Kennedy*, prepared by the New

York *Times* Washington bureau. Included was testimony by key witnesses and photographs entered as exhibits.

1965. Two best sellers—*How To Be a Jewish Mother*, by Dan Greenberg, and *The Little Drummer Girl*, by John le Carré, pseudonym for David John Moore Cornwell (1931–). Other U.S. best sellers by British author le Carré included *The Spy Who Came in from the Cold* (1963), *The Looking Glass War* (1965), *A Small Town in Germany* (1968), *Tinker, Tailor, Soldier, Spy* (1974), and *The Honourable Schoolboy* (1977).

1966. *A Book Named "John Cleland's Memoirs of a Woman of Pleasure" v. Attorney-general of the Commonwealth of Massachusetts* (383 U.S. 413). In this case the U.S. Supreme Court ruled that the book was not obscene. Lower courts had found that the novel, popularly known as *Fanny Hill*, was obscene and consequently not protected by the First and Fourteenth amendments. The Supreme Court reversed that finding on the basis of the test applied in *Roth v. United States* (1957) and whether the book was "utterly without redeeming social value."

• Four best sellers—*How to Avoid Probate*, by Norman F. Dicey; *Human Sexual Response*, by William H. Masters and Virginia E. Johnson; *In Cold Blood*, by Truman Capote (1924–1984); and *Valley of the Dolls*, by Jacqueline Susann (1921–1974). Other Susann books included *The Love Machine* (1969) and *Once Is Not Enough* (1973). *In Cold Blood*, which Capote called a "nonfiction novel," was one of the most popular works of this period's "new journalism," a genre in which authors applied fiction techniques to presentation of factual material. Other Capote books included *Other Voices, Other Rooms* (1948), *The Grass Harp* (1951), and *Breakfast at Tiffany's* (1958).

1967. *Games People Play*, by Eric Lennard Berne, a best seller.

• *The Fixer*, by Bernard Malamud (1914–), awarded a Pulitzer Prize. Other Malamud novels included *The Natural* (1952), *The Assistant* (1957), *The Magic Barrel* (1958), *A New Life* (1961), and *God's Grace* (1982).

1968. Two best sellers—*Our Crowd: The Great Jewish Families of New York*, by Stephen Birmingham (1931–), and *The Confessions of Nat Turner*, by William Styron (1925–), which won a Pulitzer Prize. Styron's *Sophie's Choice* (1978) was a later best seller. Other Styron novels included *Lie Down in Darkness* (1951) and *The Long March* (1952). Birmingham's other books included *The Towers of Love* (1961), *Jacqueline Bouvier Kennedy Onassis* (1978), and *The Auerbach Will* (1983).

• Reports by two presidential commissions. *Report of the National Advisory Commission on Civil Disorders* was popularly known as the "Kerner Report," after Illinois Governor Otto Kerner, who headed the study of increasing violence among blacks. The commission investigated riots in Cleveland, Detroit, Newark (New Jersey), and Watts (Los

Angeles), finding them rooted in more than 300 years of racial inequities. *Rights in Conflict: The Violent Confrontation of Demonstrators and Police in the Parks and Streets of Chicago During the Week of the Democratic National Convention* was popularly known as the "Walker Report," after Daniel Walker, director of the Chicago Study Team of the National Commission on the Causes and Prevention of Violence. Researchers found that provoked police had often responded with "unrestrained and indiscriminate" violence, sometimes singling out reporters and photographers and deliberately damaging their equipment. Still, media (especially television) emerged with a "tarnished image" for "paying too much attention to the demonstrators" and for "reporting too much violence."

1969. Four best sellers—*Airport*, by Arthur Hailey (1920–); *Couples*, by John Updike (1932–); *The Money Game*, by Adam Smith, pseudonym for George Jerome Waldo Goodman (1930–); and *Myra Breckenridge*, by Gore (Eugene) Vidal (1925–). Other Hailey best sellers included *Wheels* (1971), *The Moneychangers* (1975), and *Strong Medicine* (1984). Other popular Updike books included *Rabbit, Run* (1960), *Rabbit Is Rich* (1981), and *The Witches of Eastwick* (1984). Goodman wrote the novel *The Bubble Makers* (1955) under his own name and *Supermoney* (1972), *Powers of Mind* (1975), and *Paper Money* (1980) as Smith. Gore Vidal's other best sellers included *Washington, D.C.* (1967), *Burr* (1973), *1876* (1976), and *Lincoln* (1984).

• *Them*, by Joyce Carol Oates (1938–), an acclaimed volume of poems. Oates's short stories and novels, including *With Shuddering Fall* (1963) and *Wonderland* (1971), were also praised.

1970. Garland Publishing, Inc., founded by Gavin and Elizabeth Borden chiefly to publish reference books and reprints. In 1985 Garland expanded its legal and textbook departments.

• Four best sellers—*The Godfather*, by Mario Puzo (1920–); *Portnoy's Complaint*, by Philip Milton Roth (1933–); *The Promise*, by Chaim Potok (1929–); and *The Selling of the President*, by Joe McGinniss (1942–). McGinniss's other books included *Heroes* (1976) and *Fatal Vision* (1983). Other Puzo best sellers included *Fools Die* (1978) and *The Sicilian* (1984). Other Philip Roth books included *Goodbye, Columbus* (1959), *Letting Go* (1962), *The Breast* (1972), *The Professor of Desire* (1977), and *The Anatomy Lesson* (1983). Other Potok books included *The Chosen* (1967), *In the Beginning* (1975), and *The Book of Lights* (1981).

1971. Four best sellers—*The Bell Jar*, by Sylvia Plath (1932–1963); *Bury My Heart at Wounded Knee*, by Dee Brown (1908–); *Day of the Jackal*, by Frederick Forsyth (1983–); and *The Pentagon Papers*, by the New York *Times* staff. The last was a purloined Top Secret federal government study of the "History of the U.S. Decision-making Process on Vietnam Policy," which the *Times* had publicized. Newspaper publication of the politically and diplomatically sensitive study led to federal government suits (1971) against the *Times* and Washington *Post*. Other Forsyth best sellers included *The Fourth Protocol* (1984). Other Brown books included *Wave High the Banner* (1942), *Yellowhorse* (1956), *Fort Phil Kearney* (1962), *Tepee Tales* (1979), and *Killdeer Mountain* (1983). Other books by Plath, a leading poet, included the collection *Ariel* (1965).

1972. Two best sellers—*The Boys of Summer*, by Roger Kahn (1927–), and *O Jerusalem!*, by Larry Collins (1929–) and Dominique LaPierre (1931–). Collins and LaPierre also wrote *Is Paris Burning?* (1964) *and The Fifth Horseman* (1980). Kahn's other books included *The Passionate People* (1968) and *The Seventh Game* (1982).

● *The Sunlight Dialogues*, by John Champlin Gardner (1933–1982), published. Other John Gardner novels included *Grendel* (1971) and *October Light* (1976).

Newspapers

1964. *New York Times v. Sullivan* (376 U.S. 254). In this decision the U.S. Supreme Court laid the foundation for a new, national law of libel. On 29 March 1960 the *Times* had published a full-page advertisement, co-sponsored by 64 prominent people, protesting actions by Montgomery, Alabama, police against followers of Martin Luther King, Jr., during civil rights demonstrations. L. B. Sullivan, one of three city commissioners, sued, claiming that false statements concerning Montgomery police defamed him, even though he was not named in the ad, because he had supervisory authority over police. Several statements in the ad were erroneous, and a jury awarded Sullivan $500,000 damages, a judgment upheld by the Alabama Supreme Court. The U.S. Supreme Court unanimously reversed the judgment. Agreeing that news media needed protection, the justices interpreted the First Amendment to protect "uninhibited, robust and wide-open" debate on public issues without "any test of truth." The amendment, Justice William Joseph Brennan, Jr. (1906–), further wrote in the court's opinion, "prohibits a public official from recovering damages for a defamatory falsehood relating to his official conduct unless he proves that the statement was made with 'actual malice'—that is, with knowledge that it was false or with reckless disregard of whether it was false or not." And, the court determined, the errors in the ad were not malicious. The *Times–Sullivan* decision eroded the tradition of leaving civil libel law up to individual states and with the new actual malice rule shifted the burden from defendants to plaintiffs who were public officials. Subsequent cases, affecting both print and electronic media, would broaden and refine the doctrine.

• Los Angeles *Faire Free Press* (May–March 1978) founded by Art Kunkin as a four-page sheet distributed free at the Renaissance Fayre sponsored by radio station KPFK. As the *Free Press* it became the most successful alternative, or underground, paper of the period. The "Freep" served a subculture unreached in southern California by traditional journalists. Culturally and politically radical, the paper soon gained a reputation for attacking "police brutality" and President Johnson's Great Society as well as for pushing rock music, drug use, and sex. Besides "swinging" classified advertisements, it was known for antipolice cartoons, criticism of prominent politicians and social figures, startling language, and serious comment on local and national issues. Aggressive journalistically, it reported on conditions in Watts before the 1965 riots there. Publication of a list of names of undercover narcotics agents angered Los Angeles police, who refused Kunkin a press pass. By 1970 the weekly had grown to 48 pages and had a paid circulation of 95,000. In the changing social climate of the mid-1970s, the *Free Press* unsuccessfully tried different approaches to reach a wider audience. In January 1978 Larry Flynt Publications, Inc., bought the paper.

1965. Three leading alternative, or underground, papers founded. Berkeley *Barb* (1965–1980), founded by Max Scherr during the free-speech movement and student opposition to the University of California administration, became the best-known campus-related antiestablishment paper. The *Barb* reflected the subculture of the university area. It provided a voice for protesters, published Bay-area exposés, was in the vanguard of the sexual revolution, and made money on circulation and blatantly sexual classified advertisements. In 1969 some staff members resigned over disagreements with Scherr and founded the rival *Tribe*. The *Barb*'s influence waned. Detroit *Fifth Estate* (November–), founded by Harvey Ovshinsky, was politically radical. It ran lots of matter from the Liberation News Service (f. 1967) and Underground Press Syndicate (f. 1966). In 1969 Ovshinsky left, and content became more original and cultural. New York *East Village Other* (–1971) was a protest paper more radical than the competing, pioneering *Village Voice* (f. 1955). *East Village Other* was especially known for its innovative art.

1966. *Sheppard v. Maxwell* (384 U.S. 333). In this decision the U.S. Supreme Court specified actions judges should take to avoid prejudicial publicity. On 4 July 1954 Dr. Sam Sheppard's wife, Marilyn, had been murdered at their home in a Cleveland suburb. The case was thoroughly covered and commented upon in the media, especially metropolitan dailies, which ran such headlines as "Why Isn't Sam Sheppard in Jail?"

299

and "Quit Stalling and Bring Him In" even before Sheppard was charged. A headline over a front-page editorial in the Cleveland *Press* read, "Getting Away with Murder." Before the verdict was in, a headline reported "Sam Called a 'Jekyll-Hyde' by Marilyn; Cousin to Testify"; but the cousin did not appear as a witness and no such testimony occurred. Subsequently, *Press* Editor Louis B. Seltzer took credit (in his *The Years Were Good* memoirs) for forcing law enforcement officials to try Sheppard. The courtroom was jammed with media representatives. In 1954 Sheppard was convicted; in 1956 the U.S. Supreme Court refused to review his case. In 1963 the Supreme Court held that in habeas corpus proceedings (which require authorities to justify detention of prisoners) state court convictions could be reviewed in federal district courts. If reasons for detention were insufficient, a prisoner could be freed. Sheppard filed petition for a writ of habeas corpus against E. L. Maxwell, warden of Ohio State Penitentiary, supporting it with five scrapbooks of clippings, mainly from the *Press* and Cleveland *Plain Dealer*. In 1964 Chief Judge Carl Weinman of the U.S. District Court for Southern Ohio found several violations of Sheppard's constitutional rights, including the following: The trial judge had not disqualified himself although his impartiality was in question. He had not granted a change of venue or a continuance because of extensive newspaper publicity before the trial. He had been unable to maintain jurors' impartiality because of that publicity. He had allowed unauthorized communications to the jury during its deliberations. The State of Ohio appealed Weinman's decision in favor of Sheppard, which a U.S. court of appeals reversed. In an 8–1 decision the U.S. Supreme Court reversed the murder conviction on the grounds that pervasive prejudicial newspaper publicity had deprived Sheppard of a fair trial. Justice Tom Campbell Clark (1899–1977) wrote in the majority opinion that the "trial judge did not fulfill his duty to protect Sheppard from the inherently prejudicial publicity which saturated the community and to control disruptive influences in the courtroom." Then the Supreme Court enumerated steps judges must take if necessary to ensure fair trials. Judges must grant a continuance or a change of venue (e.g., to a county with less publicity about a case) whenever it is likely that the pretrial news would prevent a fair trial; prohibit extrajudicial comments by an attorney, witness, or other party who would divulge prejudicial information; insulate prospective witnesses from media; sequester the jury; and adopt strict rules on courtroom use by newspeople. The Supreme Court warned that failure to take such safeguards could lead to reversal of convictions. To avoid infringing on First Amendment rights, the Supreme court did not suggest controls on media outside courtrooms. As a result of this landmark decision, Sheppard was tried again, this time with tight restrictions, including a limit on the number of reporters in the courtroom. On 16 November 1966 a verdict of not guilty was returned.

• "The Reardon Report of the American Bar Association", another result of *Sheppard v. Maxwell* as well as of the report of the Warren Commission on the Assassination of President Kennedy (1964), which questioned whether the suspected assassin could have received a fair trial because of massive publicity, and other free press–fair trial cases. Justice Paul C. Reardon of the Supreme Judicial Court of Massachusetts headed an ABA committee of lawyers and judges who, like the U.S. Supreme Court, favored making judges responsible for curtailing pretrial publicity generated by the defense or prosecution. The committee recommended withholding certain information from the media, including any criminal record of the accused, existence of a confession, speculation on a possible plea, and prospective witnesses' names. Also the "Reardon Report" recommended prohibiting photographs or interviews of suspects without their consent. In February 1968 the ABA adopted the recommendations. Many media people protested the restrictions on release of information before trials and outside of court. By 1969 some local and state press-bar committees had negotiated voluntary "fair trial" provisions that would not jeopardize a free press. Beginning in the late 1960s, many newspaper and television organizations supplemented their verbal coverage of major trials with artists, who sketched courtroom scenes.

• Two suburban dailies founded—the Arlington Heights, Illinois, *Day* (January–), by Field Enterprises, and in Suffolk County, N.Y., the *Sun* (November–October 1969), by Cowles Communications, Inc. The Arlington Heights daily was the first of four *Days* founded by Field's Day Publications, Inc., in Chicago's northwest suburbs. Others were the *Prospect Day* (April–), for Prospect Heights and Mount Prospect; the Des Plaines *Day* (August 1968); and the *Northwest Day* (June 1969). In June 1970 Field's northwest competitor, Paddock Publications, Inc., bought the *Days* and Field's southwest suburban weeklies group. *Northwest Day* was discontinued, and the other three merged with Paddock's counterparts. Cowles's *Sun* had 73,000 subscribers in rapidly growing Long Island but lost money because of circulation and other problems.

• Three alternative media organizations founded—the San Francisco *Oracle* (–1969); Washington, D.C., *Free Press*; and Underground Press Syndicate (–1973?). *Oracle* was originally edited by John Brownson and George Tsongas. Graphically innovative, it became especially known for its sensational psychedelic effects that set standards for other underground papers. *Free Press*, founded by Michael Grossman and Arthur Grosman, was a scatological paper that covered federal government and emphasized radical politics. Underground Press Syndicate was developed by Tom Forcade as more of a cooperative clearing house, library, publishing company, and advertising representative than a news service. Forcade later won the right to cover Congress. In 1972 UPS reported 450 subscribing papers.

1967. Companion cases of *Associated Press v. Walker* and *Curtis Publishing Co. v. Butts* (388 U.S. 130). In these decisions the U.S. Supreme Court clarified and expanded its *New York Times v. Sullivan* doctrine (1964), which required that public officials prove actual malice to win libel suits concerning their official conduct. In the first case, retired Army Major General Edwin A. Walker, who was involved in demonstrations opposing a black's attempt to enroll at the University of Mississippi, filed a chain suit against newspapers and broadcast stations that had carried an allegedly defamatory report about him. AP reported that Walker had taken command of a violent crowd and led a charge against federal marshals. AP also reported that he had encouraged violence and provided demonstrators advice on counteracting tear gas effects. In a Texas court Walker won a $500,000 judgment, upheld by the state supreme court. The U.S. Supreme Court reversed the judgment on the grounds that Walker was a public figure, that he had voluntarily participated in an important public controversy, and that AP had showed no actual malice because it had followed "accepted publishing standards" for the rapid dissemination of "hot news." The second case did not involve breaking news. Wallace Butts, University of Georgia athletic director, sued the *Saturday Evening Post* for an article in which he was accused of participating in an attempt to fix a Georgia-Alabama football game. The article, "The Story of a College Football Fix," accused Butts of giving secrets to Paul Bryant, University of Alabama football coach. (After suing, Bryant settled out of court.) Butts won a $460,000 judgment in trial court after *Saturday Evening Post* attorneys were unable to prove the truth of the accusation. The U.S. Supreme Court affirmed the judgment, finding that Butts was a public figure but that the magazine had showed actual malice. In the opinion, Justice John Marshall Harlan (1899–1971) said the Court found "highly unreasonable conduct constituting an extreme departure from the standards of investigation and reporting ordinarily adhered to by responsible publishers." Harlan distinguished between breaking news and less timely news. Classified as the latter, the football fix story required "thorough investigation of the serious charges." But, the Court found, "elementary precautions were, nevertheless, ignored," thus showing "reckless disregard for the truth." In the two cases the Supreme Court extended, 5–4, First Amendment protection from news stories about public officials to reports about public figures and further defined the test of actual malice with the test of extreme departure (from accepted publishing practices).

• Los Angeles *La Raza* founded, one of many Latino papers founded in this period. *La Raza* advocated improving education and housing and ending police harassment of young Hispanics.

• Six notable alternative, or underground, papers founded. Boston *Avatar* (June–April 1968), founded by Mel Lyman, was a philosophical

16-page tabloid that avoided radical politics. The paper interpreted current issues and featured astrological and occult aspects of the youth movement. It was noted for its sophisticated graphic effects, especially in color. Chicago *Seed* (May–1972), founded by Earl Segal, was published irregularly, usually every two or three weeks. It had a lighter tone than most alternative papers. Known for its imaginative presentation and color psychedelics, *Seed* often used high-quality newsprint. Around the end of the decade 24,000 copies were printed each issue. Milwaukee *Kaleidoscope* (–1973) was founded by John Kois, Bob Deitman, and John Sahli. It was one of the best-edited alternative papers. *Kaleidoscope* used color and contained a wide range of matter, including underground comics and stories on drugs, high school problems, police harassment, and women's liberation. The paper expanded from one edition and 3,500 copies to editions in Milwaukee, Chicago, and Madison, Wisconsin, and 40,000 copies (1969). Oakland, California, *Black Panther* (April–) was founded by Huey Newton and Bobby Seale in reaction to racial injustice. The organ of the Black Panther Party, the weekly campaigned to help blacks and other oppressed peoples in the United States and abroad. Around 1970 the 24-page tabloid had a national circulation of 85,000. Philadelphia *Distant Drummer* (November–1973), founded by Editor Don De Maio, was an unusual alternative paper in that its purpose was survival. In pursuit of economic security it avoided frequent obscenities, subjective reporting, and radical politics. Advertising and editorial emphasized rock music. Other content included cultural subjects, local politics, and theater reviews. In two years *Distant Drummer* went from monthly to bimonthly and its circulation from almost 300 copies per issue to 10,000. San Francisco *Open City Press* (November–March 1969), founded by John Bryan, also emphasized rock music. By May, Bryan had moved the paper to Los Angeles and shortened the title to *Open City*. Bryan made the most of the broadside format with unusual free-form graphics and layouts. Besides continuing emphasis on rock music, *Open City* pushed for sexual freedom and reported on the cultural underground in southern California. The paper was colorful, scatological, uninhibited.

● Liberation News Service (–1973), founded by Marshall Bloom and Ray Mungo, twice a week provided alternative-paper members with packets of essays, news stories, photographs, poems, and underground comics. In 1972 LNS reportedly served about 50 papers plus many other clients.

● Brush-Moore Newspapers, Inc., purchased by Lord Thomson of Fleet for $72 million, the most money involved in a newspaper transaction until then. Brush-Moore consisted of 12 dailies and 6 weeklies, mostly in Ohio. The purchase indicated the accelerating media consolidation trend.

1968. Suburban newspaper growth indicated by more than 9.5

million circulation, an increase of more than 3 million since 1950, which more than offset an almost 2.5 million simultaneously lost in metropolitan daily circulation. Biggest gains were in the Boston, Chicago, Cleveland, Detroit, Los Angeles, New York, Philadelphia, and San Francisco areas.

• Covering the Democratic National Convention and related events in Chicago (August), about two dozen newspaper reporters and photographers beaten by city police.

• New York *Rat* (–1970), founded by Jeff Shero, a politically radical alternative, or underground, paper. Content of the weekly (except biweekly in 1969) included counterculture news; four-page features and center-spreads in color; and a rock music section. For the 1968 Democratic National Convention a special edition of 50,000 was distributed.

1969. *Citizen Publishing Co. et al. v. United States* (89 S. Ct. 927). In this decision the U.S. Supreme Court banned joint operations of daily newspapers. In 1965 the *Arizona Star*, a morning daily, and the Tucson *Daily Citizen*, an afternoon daily, combined all departments except news-editorial. The Justice Department charged that the end of commercial competition was unreasonable restraint of trade in violation of the Sherman and Clayton antitrust acts. A federal district court agreed, and the Supreme Court affirmed, 7–1. The Supreme Court found that the two Tucson papers had entered into the joint operating agreement—which included market allocation, price fixing, and profit pooling—for monopolistic purposes. If the *Citizen* had been failing and contemplating liquidation, which it apparently was not, the formation of Tucson Newspapers, Inc., might have been justifiable; but it would have had to show that the *Arizona Star* was the only purchaser available. The papers were ordered to separate. Affected by the Supreme Court's decision were 44 dailies in 22 cities engaged in joint operating agreements. Such combinations were soon saved by Congress in the Failing Newspaper Act (1970).

• Competition among large general-circulation dailies in urban areas continuing to drop. In New York the number had dropped to three (*Daily News, Post, Times*), down from 15 in 1900. Only two major competing dailies were published in Detroit (*Free Press, News*), Los Angeles (*Herald-Examiner, Times*), and St. Louis (*Globe-Democrat, Post-Dispatch*). Economic difficulties were blamed for the decreases. At the same time, groups expanded holdings, shrinking the number of owners further. For instance, the Los Angeles Times Mirror Company (which had been forced by the federal government to divest its suburban San Bernardino *Sun* in 1967) was involved in two of the largest transactions (1969–1970), which totaled $125 million. It purchased the Dallas *Times Herald*, with its broadcasting interests, and Long Island *Newsday*.

• An estimated combined readership of 3 million for some 600 alternative papers. Although these counterculture papers varied, they usually were thin, cheaply produced, and technically crude outlets for radical political ideas ignored or stifled by the establishment (commercial) press. Commonly, alternative papers espoused racial equality and legalization of marijuana while they opposed the "establishment" (government and social leaders, etc.) and the Vietnam war. Some emphasized radical politics, others rock music, many sexual freedom. Typically, papers were advocative and subjective, often containing obscenities and other shocking language. Most alternative papers carried some advertisements, typically for such products as records and organic foods; obscene classifieds for various varieties of sex were popular.

1970. An estimated 7,610 to 9,400 general-interest weekly newspapers (number depending on the definition) being published.

• Failing Newspaper Act, soon renamed Newspaper Preservation Act, signed into law (15 U.S.C. 1801–1804) by President Richard Milhous Nixon (1913–). The act overturned the U.S. Supreme Court decision in *Citizen Publishing Co. et al. v. United States* (1969), which banned joint operating agreements by local dailies. Under certain conditions the act provided limited exemption from antitrust prosecution to competing newspapers that formed joint operations. One of the two papers had to be in probable danger of financial failure. The commercial and production departments could function jointly but the news-editorial departments had to be operated separately. Also the arrangement must not drive out or prevent competition. The act let the 22 existing joint arrangements stand but required approval by the attorney general of any future arrangement.

• U.S. Suburban Press Inc. founded as a national sales representative for suburban newspapers; represented more than 1,000 papers by the 1980s.

1971. Of the 1,748 dailies, 883 owned by 155 newspaper chains, accounting for about 64 percent of the total circulation. Since 1945 the average number of newspapers per chain had risen from 4.8 to 5.7. Some chains, or groups, had a variety of media and nonmedia interests, a growing trend. The New York Times Company, for instance, in 1971–1972 acquired not only Florida and North Carolina newspapers but also *Family Circle* magazine. Other holdings included the *Times*'s news service and index, large-type and school weekly editions, one-third of the *International Herald Tribune* (Paris), Canadian newsprint operations, and book publishing houses. The company continued to expand in the 1970s.

• The combined cases of *The New York Times Company v. United States* and *United States v. the Washington Post Company* (403 U.S. 713). In these cases the federal executive unsuccessfully tried to stop permanently the publication of a secret Pentagon study, "History of the

U.S. Decision-making Process on Vietnam Policy." The 47 volumes had been prepared by order of Defense Secretary Robert S. McNamara. The *Times* acquired a stolen copy in March 1971. In late spring several staff members, including former United Press International Vietnam correspondent Neil Sheehan, began working on a series about the study, which validated 1961–1965 reporting by the Saigon press corps. Content was diplomatically and politically sensitive. On 13 June the *Times* printed its first installment. President Richard M. Nixon ordered Attorney General John Newton Mitchell (1913–) to stop further publication, but the *Times* refused. The government, claiming the stories threatened national security, then asked Judge Murray Gurfein of the federal district court in New York City for a restraining order. On 15 June Gurfein issued a temporary order, stopping the series after its third installment. On 19 June Gurfein refused to issue a permanent restraining order because the government had failed to prove more than "embarrassment," but he allowed his temporary order to stand. On 23 June the federal court of appeals in New York reversed Gurfein's decision. The Washington *Post*, meanwhile, had begun its own Pentagon Papers series, which the government also tried to stop. Judge Gerhard A. Gesell of the district court in Washington ruled against "a prior restraint on essentially historical data," a decision upheld by the federal court of appeals for the District of Columbia. On 25 June the U.S. Supreme Court, by 5–4, granted a government request for a temporary restraining order while it heard testimony. Shaken by the adverse vote, newspaper attorneys refused to gamble by pleading that the First Amendment outlawed all prior restraint. The attorneys, instead, showed that the government could not prove that publication of the Pentagon Papers threatened national security. In one anonymous *per curiam* (by entire court) and nine separate opinions, the Supreme Court cited its *Near v. Minnesota* (1931) landmark decision, which outlawed prior restraint. The government, according to the Court, had not met the heavy burden of showing justification for enforcing prior restraint. Justices Hugo Lafayette Black (1886–1971) and William Orville Douglas (1898–1980) stated that any attempt to stop publication would violate the First Amendment. Justice William J. Brennan, Jr., argued that even temporary stays were improper. Justice John Marshall Harlan objected to the haste of the decision, made in a week. Chief Justice Warren Earl Burger (1907–) said the *Times* should return the stolen document. Justices Potter Stewart (1915–1985) and Byron Raymond White (1917–) found insufficient damage for an injunction but suggested that publication of the Pentagon Papers might be prosecuted under the Espionage Act (1917). Although the *Times* and the *Post* were allowed to resume publication, the relief was qualified by the prior restraint that had existed for two weeks while courts resolved issues. Many observers feared a possible precedent for such delays, which newspeople felt could be critical in other situations.

● Minnesota Press Council founded by Minnesota Newspaper Association, Newspaper Guild, media leaders, and public officials; first state-wide press council. Its purpose was to "protect the public from press inaccuracy and unfairness, promote quality journalism while protecting the free flow of information, [and] improve understanding between media and the public." Membership was divided between representatives of the public and the media. First chair was C. Donald Peterson, an associate justice of the state supreme court. Support came from associations, foundations, newspapers, and other corporations. Having no enforcement power, MPC depended on the cooperation of the media and public and relied on the impact of publicity. In the beginning MPC considered only complaints involving newspapers. Most complaints in the first six years involved allegations of unfair and inaccurate news reporting. In 1977 MPC began handling complaints against broadcast news operations in Minnesota.

● Suburban Newspapers of America founded with about 50 publishers as a national trade association representing urban and suburban community papers. SNA fostered development of such papers and helped make them more appealing to local and national advertisers. By the 1980s SNA had 850 member papers with a combined 10.5 million circulation.

1972. *Branzburg v. Hayes* (408 U.S. 665). In this decision the U.S. Supreme Court refused to grant newspeople special immunity from testifying before grand juries. The case was a combination of three involving reporters who refused to testify before grand juries because it would jeopardize their relationships with their sources, thus abridging freedom of speech or press. In one case Paul M. Branzburg, Louisville *Courier-Journal* reporter, refused to provide two Kentucky grand juries information beyond what he had written in eyewitness reports of the manufacture and sale of marijuana and hashish. For protection he cited a state law granting newspeople immunity from disclosing identities of confidential sources. The state court of appeals held that the statute did not protect reporters who witnessed their sources commit a crime. In a second case Earl Caldwell, New York *Times* reporter who had reported on the militant Black Panthers in the San Francisco area, refused to testify before a federal grand jury. He was convicted of contempt, but an appeals court ruled that he could not be forced even to appear before the grand jury unless the Justice Department could show "compelling need" for his testimony. A third case involved Paul Pappas, reporter-cameraman for New Bedford, Massachusetts, station WTET-TV. Pappas had visited a Black Panthers headquarters to witness an expected police raid, which did not occur, and kept his promise not to do a story if there was no raid. He refused to tell a grand jury what he had observed. The Massachusetts Supreme Judicial Court ruled against Pappas, holding that no absolute or qualified reporter's privilege allowed him to refuse to appear before a grand jury or a court. In all three cases the U.S. Supreme Court ruled against the reporters. By 5–4 the Court held that reporters must, like any citizen, answer relevant questions in a valid grand jury investigation or criminal trial. This requirement was not abridgment of freedom of the press or speech, Justice Byron R. White said in the majority opinion, rejecting the "compelling need" arguments. Dissenting, Justice William O. Douglas said that without privilege reporters' sources would dry up, thus stifling news flow. Justice Potter Stewart, joined in dissent by Justices William J. Brennan, Jr., and Thurgood Marshall (1908–), wrote that the majority view invited federal and state authorities to "annex the journalistic profession as an investigative arm of the government." While the Supreme Court's decision was a setback for information media, it did leave open the possibility of legislation to protect reporters electing to withhold source identity.

Magazines

1964. *National Catholic Reporter* founded and edited in Kansas City, Missouri, by Catholic lay people as a liberal periodical. Edited by Robert Hoyt until 1971, the weekly supported reform factions in the church. In the early 1970s traditional Catholics became dominant on the publication, and its influence as a liberal organ diminished. In 1985 the *National Catholic Reporter* was published weekly (except alternate weeks in summer) in Kansas City and had 48,000 circulation. Publisher was Jason Petosa; editor, Thomas Fox.

1965. *Tennis* founded; published in Norwalk, Connecticut. In the early 1970s Publisher Asher J. Birnbaum aimed for people interested in such racquet sports as badminton, table tennis, and tennis. Content included authoritative articles on clubs, conditioning, fitness, nutrition, players, and tournaments. The monthly's circulation rose from 70,000 to 500,000 by the mid-1980s. By then editorial policy emphasized information to help tennis players improve their game. Publisher was Mark Adorney; editor, Shepherd Campbell.

1966. *Ginzburg v. United States* (383 U.S. 463). In this decision the U.S. Supreme Court upheld the conviction of a publisher for "pandering." Involved were publisher Ralph Ginzburg and his quarterly magazine *Eros*, biweekly newsletter *Liaison*, and book *The Housewife's Hand-*

book on Selective Promiscuity. After failing to obtain mailing privileges for *Eros* at Blue Ball and Intercourse, Pennsylvania, Ginzburg mailed his magazine from Middlesex, New Jersey. Advertisements indicated that the publications were obscene. In Pennsylvania Ginzburg was convicted on 28 counts of violating the federal obscenity statute and punished with a $28,000 fine and a five-year prison sentence, one of the heaviest in an obscenity case. An appeals court upheld the conviction. The Supreme Court affirmed it not because the publications might have been obscene but because the ads pandered. Eventually Ginzburg's sentence was reduced to three years. He began serving it on 17 February 1972 and was paroled nine months later.

• *American History Illustrated* founded for a general audience interested in well-researched U.S. history presented in a popular style. In the early 1970s the periodical was edited by Robert H. Fowler and published monthly except March and September in Harrisburg, Pennsylvania. The magazine entered the next decade with about 154,000 circulation. In the mid-1980s *American History Illustrated* was edited by Ed Holm and published monthly except July and August. Content included cultural, military, political, and social history, including profiles of interesting personalities, pictorial features on artists and photographers, and articles on restored historical sites.

• *Cat Fancy* founded for exhibitors, breeders, and pet owners. In the early 1970s the magazine was published bimonthly in San Diego and claimed 120,000 circulation. Editor Leslie S. Smith ran articles about breeding, care, grooming, and health of cats as well as short fiction about them. In the mid-1980s *Cat Fancy* was published monthly by Fancy Publications, Inc., in Mission Viejo, California, and claimed 130,000 circulation. Linda W. Lewis was editor.

• *Circus* founded in New York as a rock music biweekly. By the early 1980s the periodical was published monthly and had more than 134,700 circulation, mostly among males from 16 to 26 years old. *Circus* covered contemporary rock and roll personalities and music news. Publisher and editor was Gerald Rothberg; advertising director, Gary Victor. *Circus* in the mid-1980s had a circulation of over 470,000.

• *Runner's World* founded; became leading runners' magazine. In the mid-1970s it was published in Mountain View, California, and edited by Joe Henderson for active runners, running coaches, and others seriously interested in the sport. Most contributors were runners. Content included personality pieces and how-to features, with emphasis on new research results and techniques. Circulation increased from 16,000 in the early 1970s to more than 400,000 in the early 1980s, when Bob Anderson was publisher and editor. Circulation was 350,000 in the mid-1980s, when Rodale Press, Inc., of Emmaus, Pennsylvania, bought the monthly. Editor Robert David Rodale (1930–) aimed for recreational and competitive runners. Content included articles on training, exercises, personalities, new shoes, and diets as well as photo features of races and runners.

• *Southern Living* founded as a large format edition of *Progressive Farmer* (f. 1886) for southern families; published in Birmingham, Alabama. In the early 1970s Gary E. McCalla edited the monthly for middle- and upper-income homeowning southerners. Content included articles about travel, recreation, food, entertainment, homes, gardening, landscaping, and personalities—all with a southern slant. During the 1970s the periodical passed 1,750,000 circulation, and in the early 1980s, in smaller format, passed 1.9 million. Under President-Publisher Emory Cunningham (1921–), McCalla continued the editorial policy that made *Southern Living* an outstanding regional magazine.

1967. Committee of Small Magazine Editors and Publishers founded as an international nonprofit association of more than 1,200 publishers and editors. Members also included librarians, printers, researchers, and writers. The organization conducted conferences and published the monthly *Independent Publisher*.

• *Psychology Today* (May–) founded by Nicholas H. Charney (1914–) and John James Veronis (1923–) to print current research findings in clear, interesting, technically accurate prose without jargon. In the early 1970s the monthly was published in Del Mar, California, for laypeople and social scientists concerned with individual behavior and society. Scholars wrote the articles. Under ownership of Ziff-Davis, *Psychology Today* attained a national circulation of more than 1 million. In the 1980s the American Psychological Association published the magazine in Washington, D.C. Editor Patrice D. Horn continued the successful editorial policy.

• *Rolling Stone* (9 November–) founded in San Francisco by Jann S. Wenner (1947–), editor, as a tabloid emphasizing rock music culture. Wenner ran many articles by Hunter S. Thompson and cover photographs by Annie Leibovitz. By the tenth anniversary issue (15 December 1977) *Rolling Stone* had moved to New York City and acquired a new logo and 140 staff members. Circulation passed 720,000. In the early 1980s Wenner changed the frequency from twice a month to biweekly; moved music coverage to the back, behind articles on issues, personalities, politics, and motion pictures, as well as after reviews; added fiction to widen the audience; reduced size to magazine format; and mixed quality paper with newsprint. In the mid-1980s Wenner stressed contemporary lifestyles and music. Circulation was about 825,700.

1968. *Aero* founded for aircraft owners. In the early 1970s the bimonthly was published in North Hollywood, California, and edited by Wayne Thoms for owners of pleasure and business airplanes; circulation was 97,000. By the end of the 1970s circulation had tapered to 75,000, where it stabilized, and frequency changed to monthly. In the mid-1980s Fancy Publications, Inc., of Mission Viejo, California, published *Aero*. Editor Dennis Shattuck ran reports on aircraft tests, airports, and other matters of interest to owners of private aircraft.

● *New York* (April–), a spinoff of the defunct New York *Herald Tribune*'s Sunday magazine, founded for metropolitan New Yorkers. Founding Editor Clay Felker (1928–) published such name writers as Jimmy Breslin, Judith Crist, Dick Schaap, Gloria Steinem, and Tom Wolfe. Art director was Milton Glaser (1929–); publisher, George A. Hirsch (1934–). *New York* early became a trend setter for city magazines, carrying pieces with both national and local impact. The weekly was a leader in the "new journalism" (using fiction techniques to present facts). Slick and exciting, *New York* captured influential, sophisticated readers, and by 1970 the magazine was making money. As Felker stressed reportage about fresh and important aspects of New York City life, circulation passed 325,000 in the 1970s. In 1977 Rupert Murdoch (1931–) bought the periodical and replaced Felker with James Brady. In 1980 *New York* absorbed the local events-calendar periodical *Cue*, boosting circulation to 400,000. Edward A. Kosner (1937–) took over as president-editor and continued to edit the News Group Publications, Inc., property in the mid-1980s, running exposés, interviews, profiles, and articles on entertainment, health, lifestyle, local politics, and many other fields of interest to its readership. Circulation exceeded 436,000.

● *Official Karate* founded for readers interested in martial arts; outstanding in its field. Published in Derby, Connecticut, by Charlton Publications in the early 1970s, the monthly was edited by Al Weiss, who ran material about unestablished as well as established people in the martial arts, reports on tournaments, and articles on controversial topics. Circulation was 100,000 into the mid-1980s, when Weiss edited the magazine in New York.

1969. *Change* founded as an educational periodical funded by the Ford Foundation. In the early 1970s Editor-in-Chief George W. Bonham aimed for college and university faculty and presidents as well as others involved in higher education. Content included in-depth articles with high intellectual content on academic, cultural, and social problems. A leader in its field, the monthly had 35,000 circulation. In the late 1970s and early 1980s circulation declined by about half, and frequency was reduced to ten, then eight times a year. Content included information about academic leaders, institutions of higher learning, and research projects as well as philosophical pieces.

● *Dog Fancy* founded for dog owners. Published in San Diego in the early 1970s, the periodical carried articles on such topics as grooming and health, and included fiction pieces. Circulation increased to 64,000 by the end of the decade, then rose to 80,000 by the mid-1980s, when the monthly was published by Fancy Publications, Inc., of Mission Viejo, California. Editor was Linda W. Lewis.

• *Interview* founded. Early content included interviews with leading figures of art, fashion, movies, music, society, and stage who talked about their lifestyles. In the early 1980s the monthly was published in New York by Andy Warhol, originally Andrew Warhola (1927–), and edited by Bob Calacello, who ran general entertainment and photo features. Circulation exceeded 95,500.

• *National Wildlife* founded for readers interested in the environment, natural history, and outdoor adventure. The bimonthly emphasized wise use of natural resources, including preservation of wildlife and its habitat. In the early 1970s John Strohm edited the periodical in Milwaukee. By the mid-1980s he and the National Wildlife Federation magazine had moved to Washington, D.C. In the mid-1980s circulation was about 850,000.

• *Penthouse* founded in the United States by Bob Guccione (1930–), who had published it for four years in England. Produced in New York, the monthly was aimed at young, college-educated, upper-income men. In the early 1970s Editor James Goode ran a wide variety of fiction and nonfiction. Article topics included crime, health, money, politics, and sex. Color and black-and-white photographs of nude young women fleshed out content. Circulation, more than 90 percent in newsstand sales, passed 4 million in the early 1980s, as *Penthouse* joined the top ten magazines in total revenue with $162,542,000. As circulation dropped in the mid-1980s to 3.4 million, Editor-in-Chief Guccione strove for more blockbusting features, such as a photo spread of the 1984 Miss America nude, and renovated the advertising policy.

• *Apartment Ideas* founded as an annual by Meredith Publishing Co. of Des Moines. In 1973 the publication became a bimonthly entitled *Apartment Life*; in 1977 it became a monthly. Readers' median age was 29. By the early 1980s circulation had risen to 835,000. In April 1981 a major renovation changed the name to *Metropolitan Home*, the paper to heavier stock, and the readership to urban dwellers in brownstones, condominiums, cooperatives, lofts, townhouses, and rented apartments. Content emphasized urban homes and attractions. Publisher was Harry Myers, editor Dorothy Kalins, and circulation more than 780,000. By the mid-1980s circulation had tapered to 750,000, and offices had moved to New York. Content, for urbanites, included service features about collectibles, equity, interior design, liquor, real estate, and wines.

1970. Postal Reorganization Act raised second-class rates and diminished federal distribution subsidies based on the concept that magazines provided a public service. The series of increases resulted in discontinuance of some periodicals, use of lighter weight paper by others, and reduction of format by many. To avoid a portion of the increases, some magazines turned to alternative delivery systems. The act also created the Postal Rate Commission regulatory agency. PRC functions included reviewing Postal Service rate and service changes, investigating complaints, and publishing the *Consumer's Resource Handbook*.

● *Essence* (May–) founded in New York by Publisher Edward Lewis (1940–), Jonathan Blount, Cecil Hollingsworth, and Clarence (Larry) Smith, with financial support from banks and Playboy Enterprises, Inc., as the first magazine designed exclusively for black women. In the early 1970s Editor-in-Chief Marcia Gillespie ran in-depth articles on careers, child care, consumer affairs, health, politics, shopping, the arts, and other topics of interest to black women aged 18 to 34. Monthly circulation was 200,000 and climbing; in the mid-1970s *Essence* was the fastest growing magazine for women. The typical reader was a college-educated black woman in her late twenties with a higher than average household income. In 1980 Gillespie retired, and was succeeded by Daryl Alexander. By the mid-1980s Susan L. Taylor was editor in chief, and circulation was about 800,000. Taylor strove to inform and inspire readers with provocative topics. She ran features about personal experiences, political issues, relationships, and work. Content also included historical, how-to, humor, and self-help articles; personal opinion pieces; and personality interviews. In the mid-1980s *Essence* was looking for quality fiction.

● *The Mother Earth News* founded by John and Jane Shuttleworth in Ohio for ecology-conscious readers. In the early 1970s the Shuttleworths moved offices to Hendersonville, North Carolina, where Editor John Shuttleworth emphasized such do-it-yourself articles as running a home business and building low-cost housing with natural materials. Alternative energy sources, food, gardening, and home improvements were topics. Bimonthly circulation increased from 147 subscribers in 1970 to 160,000 copies in the mid-1970s to 1 million in the early 1980s to 1.9 million in the mid-1980s. Editor Bruce Woods continued the back-to-basics, how-to formula from Hendersonville, where the publishers had developed a 622-acre model energy community.

● *National Lampoon* founded in New York as a humor magazine. Aimed at a college-educated audience of 18 to 35 years of age, the monthly carried cartoons as well as satirical and humorous articles in a variety of formats. Politics and sex were fair game; the periodical was mildly obscene. In the 1970s and early 1980s circulation seesawed, rising to about 900,000 then dipping to about 500,000. In the 1980s, with circulation at about 521,000, Editor P. J. O'Rourke ran timely humor, parody, and satire. Gerald Taylor was publisher.

● *Pure-Bred Dogs American Kennel Gazette* founded; the official publication of American Kennel Club, Inc., New York. The monthly carried articles for pure-bred dog owners and fiction related to dogs. In the mid-1980s Editor Ms. Pat Beresford emphasized nonfiction in the magazine, which had about 50,000 circulation.

● *Smithsonian* founded by the Smithsonian Institution, Washington, D.C., as a "popular class magazine." Subscribers became associate members of the institution. Edward K. Thompson (1907–), publisher and editor to 1981, aimed for affluent, educated readers interested in the same subjects as the institution: fine and folk arts, hard and natural sciences, history, etc. The monthly became known for its authoritative, thorough reporting; clear, nontechnical writing; quality photography; and crisp layouts. *Smithsonian Magazine* was an outstanding publishing success of the 1970s, as the circulation surge from the original 163,596 to the next decade's 1.9 million demonstrated. In the mid-1980s circulation was about 2 million.

1971. *New Woman* founded in Fort Lauderdale, Florida; founding Publisher-Editor Margaret Harold aimed for achieving "Renaissance" career women. In the early 1970s the monthly took a refined feminist outlook, considering women on a parity with men. Articles covered a variety of topics, such as business, psychology, politics, and sexology. Departments covered finances, new marriage styles, raising children, and problems of divorced, separated, or widowed "new women." During the 1970s circulation climbed to about 1 million. In the early 1980s *New Woman* was published by New Woman, Inc., of Palm Beach, Florida. In mid-decade the magazine was sold to Rupert Murdoch and moved to New York. Editor Pat Miller made it a general-interest magazine for women ages 25 to 35, emphasizing self-help in career and love. Nonfiction subjects included beauty, fashion, food, health, money, and travel. Fiction included novel excerpts and mainstream stories. In 1985 circulation was about 1,150,000.

1972. *Folio:* founded by J. J. Hanson as a controlled (free) circulation bimonthly for magazine executives. From offices in New Canaan, Connecticut, Editor Charles I. Tannen ran how-to articles related to circulation, editing, graphics, management, production, sales, etc. In 1977 frequency was changed to monthly, circulation to paid. In the 1980s Hanson continued as publisher and editor in chief of *The Magazine for Magazine Management* (subtitle). He ran articles on all phases of magazine work and reports on developments in the industry. The magazine was especially known for its "Folio: 400," introduced in 1980, which ranked leading magazines according to their advertising and total revenues and their circulation. Special issues included not only *The Folio: 400* but also *The Folio Annual Directory of Magazine Suppliers.* In the mid-1980s monthly circulation was about 10,000.

● *Gallery* founded by F. Lee Bailey and others as a men's magazine copying many of *Playboy*'s techniques in departments, design, and typography. Published monthly in Chicago during the 1970s, *Gallery* appealed to college-educated young executives interested in contemporary lifestyles, business, sports, movies, etc. Popular subjects were rock music and women of the 1970s. Editor Don L. Pierce, Jr., also ran fiction. Pictorial content included photographs of nude young women. Circulation early hit 1.5 million. By the mid-1980s it had dropped to 500,000 and the monthly was published in New York by Montcalm Publishing Corp. Publisher was Milton J. Cuevas; editor in chief, John Bensink.

• *Money* (October–) founded in New York by Time Inc. as a general business magazine that told readers how to manage their own money. In the early 1970s Managing Editor William Simon Rukeyser (1939–) aimed for well-educated middle- to upper-middle income readers. Topics ran the gamut of personal economics, including insurance, investments, savings, and taxes. In the 1980s the managing editor was Marshall Robert Loeb (1929–), who continued the successful formula.

• *Ms.* (January–) founded in New York by Gloria Steinem (1935–), with financial assistance from *New York*, as a monthly for women who wanted to break down the "sexual caste system." Publisher and Editor-in-Chief Patricia Carbine and Steinem aimed for women in and out of the women's movement. Growing rapidly, Ms. cut loose from *New York* in mid-1972 and soon made a profit. During its first two years 450 contributors, some men, helped the feminist magazine grow. It soon won national recognition for its articles, graphics, and service. By 1975 circulation had passed 400,000. In 1977 advertising revenue was $2,158,550, a large increase from the $517,627 in 1972. Early in the magazine's history the Ms. Foundation for Women, Inc., was created mainly to share revenue with the movement by making grants. Gaining nonprofit status, Ms. received privileged postal rates and was permitted to receive tax-deductible outside grants. (Advertising revenue was taxed.) At the same time, Ms. was required to treat political candidates equally. Later, The Ms. Foundation for Education and Communication, subsidiary of the original foundation, was chartered to operate the periodical. To acquire 25 percent ownership, Warner Communications invested $1 million. Entering the 1980s, Ms. innovated more, became more readable and colorful, and added departments. In the 1980s Carbine and Steinem edited for men as well as women of diverse ages and backgrounds who were "committed to exploring new lifestyles and changes in their roles and society." Content included material on people, politics, and the women's movement. Circulation was 450,000.

• *Oui* (October–) founded in the United States by Playboy Enterprises, Inc., under a licensing agreement with French publisher Daniel Filipacchi, "for the man of the world." Six months after founding, monthly circulation peaked at 1.6 million, then held fairly steady for a while before dropping to about 869,000 by the end of the 1970s. In mid-decade Editor Nat Lehrman aimed for well-educated young urban men, running articles of international interest on popular culture, human behavior, sex, sports, and travel. Content also included photographs of nude young women and a variety of fiction. *Oui*'s tone was frisky, irreverent, witty. Later in the 1970s the monthly was moved from Chicago to Los Angeles and edited by Richard Cramer. Sold to Laurent Publications in the early 1980s, *Oui* was moved to New York, where it was edited by Jeffrey Goodman. He emphasized political exposés, profiles of actresses, travel pieces about exotic locales, and how-to articles designed to help readers cope with their environment, as well as a variety of fiction, mostly with sexual or erotic slant. In the mid-1980s, circulation was about 800,000.

● *The Robb Report* founded for "connoisseurs"; covered leisure activities of wealthy people. Circulation was about 30,000 in the 1970s, and climbed to 50,000 by the mid-1980s, when the monthly was edited in Acton, Massachusetts. Managing Editor M. H. Frakes ran informative, useful articles to help readers spend their high disposable incomes intelligently. Topics included automobiles and boats, collectibles and investments, food and dining, home and office design, wine and liquors.

Motion Pictures

1964. *Jacobellis v. State of Ohio* (378 U.S. 184). In this decision the U.S. Supreme Court broadened the social-importance test in obscenity cases by introducing the social-value test. Nico Jacobellis, manager of a theater in Cleveland Heights, Ohio, had been convicted and fined $2,500 on two counts of possessing and exhibiting an obscene film, *Les Amants* (*The Lovers*). Because the French film was obscene, state courts decided, it was not entitled to First and Fourteenth amendment protection. The Supreme Court found the film not obscene and by a plurality reversed the conviction. The court applied the test from *Roth v. United States* (1957): "whether to the average person, applying contemporary community standards, the dominant theme of the material taken as a whole appeals to prurient interest," and if the material goes "substantially beyond customary limits of candor in description or representation of such matter." Roth excluded only material that was "utterly without redeeming social importance." Praise from several film critics indicated that *Les Amants* had some importance. In *Jacobellis* the social importance test gained force. At the same time, the Supreme Court began the test's reformulation into a broader test of "social value," indicating the latter might be applied in future cases. The social-value test suggested that any value, important or not, might redeem otherwise obscene material. Also Justice William Joseph Brennan, Jr. (1906–), defined the "community" as society at large, the nation, omitting variations for regional and local prejudices.

● *Blow Job*, directed by Andy Warhol, originally Andrew Warhola (1927–), was a 30-minute facial reaction shot of a man apparently receiving one. Like other early Warhol films, this one attacked accepted, normal sexual practices and definitions of motion pictures. Some Warhol films were comical or "camp" burlesques or parodies of standard movies. They included *Tarzan and Jane Regained . . . Sort of* (1963), *Harlot* (1965), *Lonesome Cowboys* (1968), *Heat* (1973), and *Frankenstein* (1974).

1965. *Freedman v. State of Maryland* (380 U.S. 1). In this decision the U.S. Supreme Court held that movie censorship statutes must provide procedural safeguards to be constitutional. Seeking to challenge the constitutionality of Maryland's motion picture censorship statute, appellant Freedman had exhibited the film *Revenge at Daybreak* in his Baltimore theater without first submitting the film to the State Board of Censors as the law required. The state conceded that the picture did not violate statutory standards and if properly submitted would have received a license. But Freedman, who contended that the law abridged his freedom of expression in violation of the First and Fourteenth amendments, was convicted of violating the statute. The state appeals court affirmed the conviction. The U.S. Supreme Court unanimously reversed it. By requiring submission of a film before exhibition, not providing judicial participation in the procedure, and not imposing a time limit for board action, the state did not protect an exhibitor's constitutional rights. The statute permitted unconstitutional prior restraint. Justice William J. Brennan, Jr., wrote in the Court's opinion that the statute lacked "sufficient safeguards for confining the censor's action to judicially determined constitutional limits." Brennan said that "the burden of proving that the film is unprotected expression must rest on the censor." A film could no longer be considered "guilty" until proven "innocent." Brennan added that "while the State may require advance submission of all films, in order to proceed effectively to bar all showings of unprotected films, the requirement cannot be administered in a manner which would lend an effect of finality to the censor's determination whether a film constitutes protected expression." The Supreme Court required the following safeguards for a constitutional censorship statute: the burden of instituting a judicial proceeding must fall on the censorship agency, restraint before judicial review must exist for only a brief period to maintain the status quo, and prompt judicial review must be assured. The legal processes, in short, must be expedited to create only minimum hardship on the exhibitor. While the Supreme Court did not declare the Maryland statute unconstitutional, the justices did remove some teeth from film censorship statutes.

1967. Two important new trends led by *Bonnie and Clyde*, directed by Arthur Heller Penn (1922–), and *The Graduate*, directed by Mike Nichols, originally Michael Igor Peschkowksky (1931–). *Bonnie and Clyde*, starring Faye Dunaway (1941–) and Warren Beatty (1937–), was a major statement of the new cinema's values and influenced later films. The "new cinema" (influenced by the French "new wave") was preoccupied with a blemished American dream and with cinematic style. While the new filmmakers preferred the authenticity and naturalness of location shooting over the artificiality of studio work, their innovations reminded the audience that it was watching a motion picture. Moods were intensified with such visual tricks as freeze frames, jump cuts, slow motion, and mixtures of color with black and white. Visual techniques might be enhanced with music that ran in harmony or in counterpoint with a sequence. Rock scores were introduced. The heroes were deviates, outlaws, or social misfits—like the mythic bank robbers Bonnie and Clyde—and the villains, the respectable, legal defenders of societal standards. The heroes often died in the new obligatory unhappy ending. The new cinema made its greatest impact on youth rebelling against conventional, impersonal societal institutions. As an old-school then new-school director, Arthur Penn made a variety of movies, including *The Left-Handed Gun* (1958), *The Miracle Worker* (1962), *Alice's Restaurant* (1969), *Little Big Man* (1971), *Night Moves* (1975), and *The Missouri Breaks* (1976). *The Graduate*, Nichols's most important film, had probably an even wider impact on young audiences than *Bonnie and Clyde*. This film, set in an upper-middle-class suburb, seemed to speak for the younger generation against stifling adult values. Dustin Hoffman (1937–) starred as a new graduate who fled affluent adult society. Another groundbreaking film by Nichols was *Carnal Knowledge* (1971), a serious comedy that tried to deal candidly and maturely with sex. It was perhaps the outstanding cinematic attempt of this period to probe this publicly sensitive topic in a frank manner without stooping to pornography. Two other notable Nichols films in this period were *Who's Afraid of Virginia Woolf?* (1966) and *Catch-22* (1971).

1969. *Bob and Carol and Ted and Alice*, a "suburb movie" directed by Paul Mazursky (1930–), a comic portrait of sexual infidelity. Other Mazursky films included *Harry and Tonto* (1974), *Next Stop Greenwich Village* (1976), and *An Unmarried Woman* (1978).

● *Easy Rider*, made by Peter Fonda (1939–) and Dennis Hopper (1936–), an influential protest film. This low-budget ($370,000) "new cinema" film starred Fonda, Hopper, Jack Nicholson (1937–), and Karen Black (1942–). Its attack on the American dream and conformity, heightened by a folk-rock score, appealed to rebellious youth. The heroes were nonconformists who searched the country on their motorcycles for some elusive American Eden only to find their freedom on the road halted abruptly by the profane guns of civilization. *Easy Rider* became virtually a cult film for youthful protesters. Such a widely distributed protest movie was made possible by the increased artistic freedom that had emerged with the end of big-studio control of filmmaking.

• *Butch Cassidy and the Sundance Kid*, directed by George Roy Hill (1922–), an innovative "new cinema" western. The heroes, played by Paul Newman (1925–) and Robert Redford (1936–), were charming, good-humored criminals, and the story was deliberately halted for an extraneous, idyllic ride on a bicycle to a pleasant tune that had nothing to do with characterization or plot. The ending, too, was typically new cinema, with the protagonists overwhelmed by the amassed guns of civilization. Other Hill films included *The World of Henry Orient* (1967), *Thoroughly Modern Millie* (1967), *The Sting* (1973), *The Great Waldo Pepper* (1975), and *Slap Shot* (1977).

• *The Wild Bunch*, directed by David Samuel Peckinpah (1925–), also an innovative western in the "new cinema" vein. Other Sam Peckinpah films included *Ride the High Country* (1962), *Straw Dogs* (1971), *Pat Garrett and Billy the Kid* (1973), *Bring Me the Head of Alfredo Garcia* (1974), and *Cross of Iron* (1977).

1970. *Cotton Comes to Harlem*, directed by Ossie Davis (1917–). This movie stimulated the early 1970s movement of films created by blacks for black audiences. Though damned by many critics as "blaxploitation" crime stories, the films were financially successful. Another popular movie in this category was *Shaft* (1971).

• M*A*S*H, directed by Robert Altman (1925–), depicting a group of U.S. Army medics in Korea. Released near the peak of U.S. engagement in Vietnam, the movie explored U.S. attitudes toward war, especially against other races in faraway places. (The film was made into a top-rated TV series.) While M*A*S*H was Altman's first major success, his most respected film in the 1970s was *Nashville* (1975). Altman made 15 feature films in that decade, also including *Brewster McCloud* (1970), *The Long Goodbye* (1973), *California Split* (1974), *Buffalo Bill and the Indians* (1976), *Three Women* (1977), and *A Wedding* (1978).

1971. *Five Easy Pieces*, directed by Bob Rafelson, another "new cinema" film.

• *Patton*, directed by Franklin J. Schaffner (1920–), based on the army career of General George S. Patton, played by George C. Scott (1927–). Academy Awards went to the film and Scott.

• *The Last Picture Show*, directed by Peter Bogdanovich (1939–). The film tried to depict intelligently and honestly a slice of life but idealized romantic love. Bogdanovich was influenced by the *auteur* theory, which eschewed big name actors in favor of the director as "star" (author). He recreated the dusty barrenness of the rural United States in the 1950s for *The Last Picture Show*, in the 1930s for *Paper Moon* (1973). Bogdanovich's first movie was *Targets* (1968). His other films included *What's Up Doc?* (1972), *Daisy Miller* (1974), *At Long Last Love* (1975), and *Nickelodeon* (1976).

1972. *Blazing Saddles*, directed by Melvin Kaminsky Brooks (1928–), a zany parody of westerns. This film and Mel Brooks's *Young Frankenstein* (1974) and *High Anxiety* (1977) parodied the stars, style, and plots of old Hollywood studio-era films.

• *Deep Throat*, starring "Linda Lovelace," one of the most financially successful hard-core pornographic movies in history.

• *The Godfather*, directed by Francis Ford Coppola (1939–), a Mafia story whose outstanding financial success stimulated a series of Mafia movies, including Coppola's own *The Godfather II* (1974). A gangster genre classic, the first *Godfather*, which starred Marlon Brando (1924–), exalted the good old days of masculine men, feminine women, and closely knit families. The second *Godfather* continued the story and confirmed Coppola's cinematic mastery. Coppola's movies tended to be either commercial epics like the *Godfathers*, *Finian's Rainbow* (1968), and *Apocalypse Now* (1979), or style pieces like *You're a Big Boy Now* (1967), *The Rain People* (1969), and *The Conversation* (1974). Other Coppola films included *One from the Heart* (1981), *The Outsiders* (1982), and *Rumble Fish* (1983). Coppola ran his own studio, American Zoetrope, in San Francisco.

Radio and Television

1964. An estimated 1,200 cable television systems serviced about 2 percent of TV homes.

• AM-FM radio station owners in markets of at least 100,000 required (July) by the Federal Communications Commission to offer separate FM programming at least half the time. Since the late 1940s most owners of AM and FM stations in the same market had duplicated programming. As a result of the ruling, FM began to specialize as much as AM, broadcasting country and western, rock, and classical music as well as its traditional "wallpaper" (background or "beautiful") music. In the 1970s the FCC rule was extended to smaller markets.

• Subscription Television debuted (July) in Santa Monica, California, serving about 4,000 subscribers with educational and cultural features, movies, and sports. It was briefly offered in San Francisco. This largest operational pay-TV project transmitted over wires original and off-the-air programs. Movie theater owners and other opponents obtained enough signatures on petitions to force a fall referendum. In November the opponents won by a 2-1 ratio. The referendum was later held unconstitutional, but too late to save Subscription Television.

• Network Election Service, later called News Election Service, founded by the networks and the wire services to coordinate reporting election returns.

• Two debuts on the National Broadcasting Company television network—"Another World," a soap opera still running in the 1980s, and "The Man from U.N.C.L.E.," a tongue-in-cheek spy series. The fantastic action-adventure pitted the fearless agents of an anticrime organization (U.N.C.L.E.) against an international underworld organization (THRUSH). Robert Vaughn (1932–) starred.

1965. Number of commercial stations—4,019 AM, 1,270 FM, and 569 TV; noncommercial stations—about 25 AM, 255 FM, and 99 TV. Ninety-seven percent of U.S. households had AM sets, about 40 percent had FM, and about 93% TV.

• Early Bird the first commercial communications satellite launched (6 April) into synchronous orbit; enabled continuous TV transmission between Europe and the United States.

• *Estes v. State of Texas* (381 U.S. 532). In this decision the U.S. Supreme court reversed a conviction because TV coverage caused distractions during the trial. In a Texas court Billie Sol Estes had been convicted of swindling farmers by selling them nonexistent fertilizer equipment and tanks. Over Estes's objection, the judge permitted TV to cover pretrial hearings and the trial. Cameras, cables, crews, lights, and microphones were present. Estes appealed partly on the grounds that TV in the courtroom had created a carnival atmosphere that denied him due process of law. Overthrowing the conviction 5–4, the Supreme Court ruled that defendants' Fifth Amendment rights to a fair trial superseded TV news teams' First Amendment rights. Appearing on TV, some justices believed, could have adverse psychological effects on the defendant, judge, jurors, and witnesses.

• Home videotape recorders, similar to those used by industrial and educational institutions but less expensive, marketed with little success.

• By late year 1,847 cable TV systems operating, Federal Communications Commission reported; 758 franchised systems not yet operating and 938 franchise applications pending.

• Three debuts on the National Broadcasting Company television network—"Days of Our Lives," a soap opera still running in the 1980s, and two spy series. "I Spy," starring white actor Robert Culp (1930–) and black actor Bill Cosby (1937–) as American undercover agents, was the first TV show with a black star to survive. "Get Smart" was a comedy starring Don Adams (1927–) as a bumbling spy and Barbara Feldon (1941–) as his "sidekick."

1966. In all, 108 educational television stations (up 54 since 1961) operating and 291 educational FM stations (up 105 since 1961).

● Jurisdiction over cable television (15 February) by Federal Communications Commission, which called for CATV systems to carry all local signals and limit importation of distant signals. In August the FCC created a special CATV advisory group to implement rules, expedite processing of applications, and the like.

● *Office of Communication of United Church of Christ v. FCC* (359 F.2d 944). In this decision the U.S. Court of Appeals for the District of Columbia (designated in Communications Act [1934] to hear appeals from FCC decisions) established the principle that citizen groups have a legal right to participate in FCC hearings that affect their interests. FCC had denied the church's Office of Communication, which aided local broadcast consumer groups, permission to participate in the license renewal proceedings for WLBT of Jackson, Mississippi. The citizens group tried to block renewal, alleging that WLBT ignored blacks, who made up a large proportion of the community. FCC followed customary practice, considering itself representative of the public or other broadcasters, and renewed the license. The appeals court, however, reversed the renewal, holding that groups representing the audience were entitled to participate in the proceedings. (The station eventually was sold to a new licensee.) Over the next several years the court ordered the commission to hear other citizen groups, expanding public access to FCC decision-making. License renewals were no longer automatic or routine.

● National Broadcasting Company's "World Premiere" aired. It started a trend of made-for-TV movies; other networks soon followed. Networks had run out of feature films for prime time, as Hollywood production dropped after 1948, so they began shooting their own 90- or 120-minute movies. In the 1971–1972 seasons, 100 made-for-TV films were shown on all three full-service networks. Some movies doubled as series pilots or also ran in theaters abroad.

● Marked expansion of television coverage of the Vietnam war as U.S. involvement expanded and fighting increased. It was TV's first war.

● Overmyer Network to become the fourth commercial TV network, Daniel Overmyer (owner of WDHO-TV, Toledo, Ohio) announced (July); to include two hours of a live show from Las Vegas and two hours of news. In October the network claimed 85 affiliates. In March 1967 a West Coast syndicate took control, and the chain became United Network, which finally went on the air in May. UN fed its two-hour Las Vegas program to 125 stations; most costs were covered by

13 advertisers. In June the United Network was discontinued when it could not pay for American Telephone & Telegraph line interconnections.

● More color than black-and-white TV receivers sold for the first time (December). New studio cameras with improved color quality, definition, and resolution stimulated advances in programming and sales. By 1967 about 16 percent of homes had color sets.

● "Batman," parody of the comic strip. The series on the American Broadcasting Company television network starred Adam West, real name William Anderson (1929–).

● "Mission: Impossible," a serious but fantastic spy series. The international intrigue involved a group of heroes, including black actor Greg Morris (1934–), who played an expert electrical engineer, thus making the program a television leader in casting blacks as major characters. Plot solutions required complicated, sophisticated electronic and mechanical gimmicks. In the standard opening scene the lead character for a particular week picked up in some remote place a cheap, tiny tape player that would deliver instructions then "self-destruct in five seconds."

● "The Newlywed Game," a syndicated television series. Newlyweds were asked to match spouse's answers to silly, intimate questions. Created by Chuck Barris, it ran to 1974, then 1977–1980. It returned in 1985 as "The New Newlywed Game," with long-time host Bob Eubanks.

● "Star Trek," a science-fiction television series. The story involved the voyage of the Starship *Enterprise* and her crew, including an alien executive officer with pointed ears. "Star Trek" became a cult show, with young fans known as "Trekkies." After a three-year run, longer than most sci-fi programs, original episodes were rerun through the mid-1980s. A cartoon version for TV and a film version for theaters also were produced.

1967. Fairness Doctrine required that stations run antismoking spots to balance cigarette advertisements, the Federal Communications Commission ruled, applying the doctrine to commercials for the first time. Origin of the issue dated to January 1964, when the surgeon general released a research report asserting that cigarette smoking might be dangerous to the health of the smoker and linking smoker to cancer. In 1965 the federal Cigarette Labeling and Advertising Act required health warnings on packages and in printed ads. Pressures increased on broadcasters to limit cigarette advertising. When WCBS-TV of New York refused the request of attorney John Banzhaf III for time to air antismoking spots, Banzhaf appealed to the FCC, which found the station violated the Fairness Doctrine. After the FCC ordered stations to broadcast the antismoking point of view, government and voluntary health organizations supplied antismoking spots. Claims for such a right of reply to commercials for other products, including automobiles, flooded broadcasters. In 1968 the U.S. Court of Appeals for the District of Columbia upheld the FCC (405 F.2d 1082). Under pressure from broadcasters the FCC in 1974 issued a *Fairness Report* specifying that the cigarette case had set no precedent and that the Fairness Doctrine excluded regular product commercials.

● Electronic video recorder, invented by Peter Carl Goldmark (1906–1977), introduced by Columbia Broadcasting System. A combination of TV and film, EVR electronically recorded pictures and sound from a TV camera, magnetic tape, or motion picture film on an ultrathin film, then converted that to radio-frequency signals. CBS unsuccessfully marketed EVR for home video recording.

● Public Broadcasting Act (7 November) appropriated $38 million for construction and improvement of noncommercial radio and television and created the Corporation for Public Broadcasting to administer funds. The act was based on the report of the Carnegie Commission on Educational Television, *Public Television: A Program for Action* (January), which had recommended widening the role of public TV, and on congressional hearings, where radio had been added. The Corporation for Public Broadcasting was a quasi-governmental organization directed by a 15-member bipartisan board appointed by the President, subject to the Senate's advice and consent. The act authorized CPB to (1) establish and maintain interconnection among local public stations, (2) underwrite national programming, and (3) raise funds for public stations. Funds came from Congress, corporations, foundations, and other sources. CPB could not operate stations. The Nixon administration (1969–1974) did not strongly support CPB. President Richard Milhous Nixon (1913–) wanted to decentralize the public TV system, giving more power to local stations.

● Of the 51 new TV stations that went on the air in 1967, 26 educational; most UHF.

● "Ironside," a police series on the National Broadcasting Company television network. It starred Raymond Burr (1917–) as a police chief confined to a wheelchair.

● "The Phil Donahue Show," in Dayton, Ohio. Renamed "Donahue," it was telecast nationally from Chicago beginning in 1974, from New York beginning in 1984. Host Phil Donahue (1935–) and his audience interviewed a guest or guests on the topic of the day.

1968. *United States v. Southwestern Cable Co.* and *Midwest Television, Inc. v. Southwestern Cable Co.* (392 U.S. 157). In these cases, the U.S. Supreme Court affirmed Federal Communications Commission authority to regulate cable TV. Southwestern's CATV, Midwest had said, transmitted signals of Los Angeles stations into the San Diego area, adversely affecting Midwest's station there. Bringing in those signals, Midwest added, would fragment the San Diego audience, reduce local stations' advertising revenues, and curtail or end local stations' services in the San Diego area. Saying Southwestern's practice was inconsistent with the public interest, Midwest sought an order limiting the imported signals. FCC so ordered. But an appeals court held that the FCC lacked authority under the Communications Act (1934). That holding was reversed by the Supreme Court, which said that the act gave the FCC authority over interstate commerce and CATV was interstate commerce.

- *St. Amant v. Thompson* (390 U.S. 727). In this decision the U.S. Supreme court clarified what it meant by "reckless disregard" in *New York Times v. Sullivan* (1964). In the heat of a political campaign, appellant St. Amant had read on TV an accusation by J. P. Albin that Herman Thompson had had financial dealings with a man accused of nefarious activities in a labor union. Thompson sued for defamation and won. Upholding the judgment, the Louisiana Supreme Court found sufficient evidence that St. Amant had "recklessly disregarded whether the statements about Thompson were true or false." Reversing the judgment, the U.S. Supreme Court found no evidence that St. Amant had serious doubts about the truth of the statement; Albin had sworn to his statements, some of which St. Amant had verified. Publishing (specifically, broadcasting in this case) with such doubts would have shown reckless disregard for the truth and demonstrated actual malice.

- FCC ruling that in the future a holder of an AM radio license may not acquire a FM or TV license in the same locality.

- Action for Children's Television founded by Boston-area women concerned about excessive advertising directed at children and the glut of violence on the air. ACT became a sophisticated consumer organization and influential national voice. With other groups it helped force the industry and FCC to reduce the amount of violence in children's weekend programming and in prime-time hours. Also ACT campaigned to protect children from commercial exploitation.

- TV coverage of the Democratic National Convention and tumultuous surrounding events in Chicago. Outside convention hotels police and youthful antiwar and antiestablishment demonstrators clashed for consecutive nights. Mayor Richard Daley's supporters charged that the presence of TV cameras and their lights stimulated the rioting. Several cameramen were clubbed by police. Inside the convention hall several reporters were arrested or roughed up as Daley forces tried to control the convention. Afterward TV was criticized for showing too much violence.

- Subscription television (pay-TV) authorized (13 December) by FCC, which delayed putting its rules into effect until Congress could react. Rules limited pay-TV over the air to cities with more than four commercial stations; then operators would have to program at least 28 hours a week. Most restrictions were on content. No commercials were allowed. A maximum 90 percent of content could be sports and motion pictures. Movies had to be newer than two years old, and sports events could not have appeared on free TV in the previous two years. Also pay TV operators could not show any continuing series. Technical standards were announced in fall 1969. By 1977, after challenges, many restrictions had been modified or eliminated by FCC and courts.

• On live TV (24 December), reading by Apollo 8 astronauts from Genesis while in the moon's vicinity; viewers given a close-up of that planet's surface.

• More than $40 million in campaign funds spent by major political parties for television and radio time, up from $14 million spent on broadcasting in 1960 and $2,250,000 spent on radio in 1940.

• "Rowan and Martin's Laugh-In," comedy-variety series on the National Broadcasting Company television network. The program, which starred Dan Rowan (1922–) and Dick Martin (1922–), was imitated by several other shows.

1969. Controversy over ownership of Boston *Herald Traveler*'s WHDG resolved by Federal Communications Commission, which awarded the license to a locally owned, independent consortium. The action ended a controversy that had begun in 1957, when the awarding of the television license to the newspaper, which owned a radio station, had been challenged. The unique 1969 decision stimulated an increase in petitions to deny license renewals; such proceedings were no longer mere formalities. After appeals failed, the *Herald Traveler* surrendered WHDG, then went out of the newspaper business, retaining only its radio station.

• Public Broadcasting Service (April–) founded by Corporation for Public Broadcasting and many noncommercial TV stations primarily to distribute programs. Funded mainly by Congress and foundations, PBS oversaw station interconnections; it did not produce programs. After 1978 satellites facilitated wider distribution, and PBS reorganized to emphasize providing programs. A new Association for Public Broadcasting—later named Association for Public Television—took over PBS' research and lobbying functions for stations.

• *Red Lion Broadcasting Co. v. FCC* (395 U.S. 367). In this decision the U.S. Supreme Court upheld the Fairness Doctrine. In 1964 the FCC had promulgated rules for broadcasting editorials, specifying that the stations would have to seek opposing views; the commission also specified rigid rules for informing persons attacked, for providing texts, and for providing rebuttal opportunities. In November 1964 WGCB of Red Lion, Pennsylvania, broadcast a recorded program in which the conservative Reverend Billy James Hargis attacked Fred J. Cook, author of a book criticizing Arizona conservative Senator Barry Goldwater, 1964 Republican presidential candidate. Cook demanded time to reply from WGCB and the 199 other stations carrying Hargis's broadcast. WGCB offered to sell reply time. After Cook appealed to the FCC, it ordered the station to give him the time. WGCB refused; the case went to court, the station losing all the way to the top. In 1968–1969, meanwhile, the FCC had promulgated regulations on the "personal attack" aspects of the Fairness Doctrine. An appeals court in Chicago had upheld an attempt by the Radio Television News Directors Association to relax the editorializing and personal attack regulations, which RTNDA thought restricted broadcast journalism. The Supreme Court combined the two opposite decisions. In June 1969 it upheld the FCC's public attack and editorializing rules and Fairness Doctrine on the grounds that they were authorized by statute and constitutional. The Supreme Court ruled that, given the scarcity of frequencies, the public's rights of access to information and ideas were more important than broadcasters' rights. The landmark decision gave the fairness concept, previously part of the "public interest" standards, statutory authority.

● Man's first landing on the moon a live telecast (20 July).

● "Sesame Street" produced by the Children's Television Workshop for preschool children; began daily telecasts (fall) on public TV stations. Using commercial techniques, the educational program became a hit among critics and children, continuing into the 1980s as a popular children's program. It was supported by the Carnegie and Ford foundations and U.S. Office of Education. "Sesame Street," which emphasized letters and numbers, soon was followed by "The Electric Company," a program for older children that emphasized spelling and words.

● Cable TV systems with more than 3,500 subscribers required (October) by FCC to make facilities available for local program production and presentation.

● Nixon administration's antimedia campaign launched (November) by Vice President Spiro Theodore Agnew (1918–) in a speech to Republicans in Des Moines, Iowa. Agnew accused TV journalists of liberal bias. He complained that the three major networks controlled the nation's thinking and rhetorically asked who had "elected" the small group of network officials and journalists who made news decisions. The administration's ire had been raised by the networks' "instant analyses" immediately after broadcasting presidential speeches. Viewers who opposed this treatment were not placated to learn that commentators usually had copies of President Nixon's speeches to study hours in advance. The Columbia Broadcasting System did halt its postspeech analyses for a while in 1970–1971. Agnew was joined by other politicians who unleashed their resentments against TV. Prompted by adverse public opinion and implied threats of more government regulation, broadcasters explained their practices, improved some, and strived to increase their professionalism.

• Public Health Cigarette Smoking Act banning cigarette advertising on radio and TV effective 2 January 1971, removing Fairness Doctrine obligation to carry counteradvertising.

1970. Commercial stations totaling 4,267 AM, 2,184 FM, and 677 TV; noncommercial stations, about 25 AM, 413 FM, and 185 TV. Ninety-eight percent of U.S. households had AM sets, 74 percent had FM, and about 95 percent TV.

• Common ownership of AM, FM, and TV stations or of a radio and TV station in the same market prohibited (March) by Federal Communications Commission; existing combinations excepted until sold. Altogether, owners were allowed seven stations of each kind (AM, FM, TV).

• National Public Radio founded to interconnect stations and to produce programs for noncommercial stations. Programming, funded by the Corporation for Public Broadcasting, began in April 1971. That year NPR began "All Things Considered," a late afternoon news and public affairs program that provided more depth than commercial radio news shows. An early "Morning Edition" with a similar depth approach began in 1980. NPR's cultural affairs programming included classical music concerts. In the 1970s a minority of all operating noncommercial stations used NPR programs; in 1979 NPR provided about 20 percent of its member stations' daily programs. In the early 1980s NPR sought to expand its outlets.

• Network prime-time TV programming limited (May) by FCC to three hours nightly, ending network control of syndicated programming. The Prime Time Access Rule restricted programming in the top 50 markets to 7 to 11 P.M. in the Eastern time zone and 6 to 10 P.M. in the Central and Mountain zones. PTAR removed a half-hour that networks had programmed for their affiliates. FCC permitted syndicated off-network shows for PTAR's first year. Subsequently stations were required to fill the half-hour with independently syndicated shows or to produce their own programs. Instead of increasing local public affairs programming, as commissioners had hoped, this requirement led to inexpensive syndicated entertainment fare—travelogues and cheap adventure, variety, and game shows—little different from network fare. PTAR was long debated and occasionally modified.

• UHF-TV channels 69–83 reallocated (May) by FCC to nonbroadcast uses, reducing spectrum waste. Inefficient for broadcasting, the channels were reserved for land mobile, safety, and special radio services, etc. FCC had stopped assigning channels above 69 in 1966.

• Office of Telecommunications Policy (June), a staff agency within the White House to advise the president; Clay Whitehead named first director. OTP's functions, which included long-range policy planning, were less technical than political. OTP worked to get sympathetic news treatment for the Nixon administration. Whitehead tried to drive a wedge between commercial and noncommercial broadcasters, as well as between networks and their affiliates, and tried to swing public opinion against the networks. OTP sought five-year terms for broadcast licenses and limits on the Fairness Doctrine, public broadcasting financing, and program reruns. After President Nixon resigned (1974), OTP faded. President Jimmy (James Earl) Carter, Jr. (1924–), eliminated the agency, transferring most of its functions to the Department of Commerce.

1971. *Rosenbloom v. Metromedia, Inc.* (403 U.S. 29). In this decision the U.S. Supreme Court extended the rule in *New York Times v. Sullivan* (1964), which applied to public figures' public life, to include private persons involved in an event of public interest. In October 1963 Philadelphia police had arrested George A. Rosenbloom, a book and magazine distributor, on a criminal charge of selling obscene material and three days later confiscated some of his allegedly obscene publications. Metromedia's WIP broadcast twice that police had confiscated 3,000 "obscene" works from Rosenbloom; the Philadelphia radio station used no qualifying word such as "allegedly." Rosenbloom was acquitted after the trial judge found the nudist magazines Rosenbloom distributed not obscene. Considering WIP's reports defamatory, as virtually labelling him a criminal, Rosenbloom sued WIP for civil libel. Unable to prove the truth of the news report, WIP tried to convince a jury that the broadcast was protected by qualified privilege because the information had come from a police officer's statement to the media. The jury was unconvinced. Rosenbloom won $275,000 in damages. The Pennsylvania appeals court overturned the judgment, ruling for WIP. By a plurality the U.S. Supreme Court affirmed the appeals court's decision because private citizen Rosenbloom had been involved in an event of public interest and WIP had not recklessly disregarded the truth. The Supreme Court refused to differentiate between a "public" and "private" individual when the public interest was involved and required either one to prove actual malice to recover for damage to his/her reputation.

● "The Selling of the Pentagon" on the Columbia Broadcasting System (23 February). The program criticized spending large amounts of tax monies on military public relations and led to accusations that CBS violated the Fairness Doctrine. Conservatives in Congress and other critics alleged bias and misrepresentations in the television documentary, which criticized the Defense Department for huge spending to drum up support for higher military appropriations. The issue was especially sensitive because of controversial U.S. involvement in the Vietnam war. Objections to "The Selling of the Pentagon" led to hearings that spring by the House Special Subcommittee on Investigations, which concentrated on film editing and other documentary methods. The subcommittee subpoenaed (17 April) CBS to provide "all notes, film, sound tape recordings, scripts, names and addresses of all persons appearing in the telecast, and a statement of all disbursements of money made in connection with the program." CBS President Frank Stanton (1908–) refused to provide any material not broadcast. Citing First Amendment protection, he said that providing outtakes and other nonbroadcast material would make broadcasters afraid to do investigative reporting. The subcommittee tried to have Stanton cited for contempt of Congress but failed when the House of Representatives voted (13 July) 226–181 to return the citation to the subcommittee. As a result of points raised in the hearings, some changes were made in the ways documentaries were produced, including tightening controls on objectivity.

1972. *Television and Growing Up: The Impact of Television Violence* (January) by the Surgeon General's Scientific Advisory Committee on Television and Social Behavior. The report, which was based on laboratory and field research, indicated that TV violence might cause some children to behave aggressively. Results suggested that such behavior appeared in children predisposed to be aggressive and in certain environments. The conclusion that video violence could affect some viewers sometimes was nothing new.

● Definitive rules for cable TV (February) by the Federal Communications Commission, limiting CATV in 100 markets. Rules included requiring stations to offer channels to educational institutions and municipal governments and to provide access to the public. Rules also included limiting importation of signals in smaller markets because adverse effects on local noncable TV stations might be greater than in larger markets. Older systems were exempted from these new, more complex regulations. The rules became effective 31 March.

● First videocassette machine, Sony U-Matic, for business and educational uses; supplanted electronic video recorder of 1967.

● Political campaign expenditures for broadcasting continuing to increase. Parties spent $60 million in 1972, up from $40 million in 1960.

● An estimated 2,841 CATV systems reaching about 9.5 percent of TV homes, increases of more than 1,600 systems and more than 7 percent in this period.

1973–1985

Economic and Legal Challenges

====||●||====

Books

1973. *Miller v. California* (413 U.S. 15). In this decision the U.S. Supreme Court eliminated the broad "utterly without redeeming social value" test of obscenity and replaced the national basis for the test with a local, community standard. Marvin Miller had mass-mailed brochures advertising the "adult" books entitled *Intercourse, Man-Woman, Marital Intercourse,* and *Sex Orgies Illustrated.* He was convicted of mailing unsolicited sexually explicit material in violation of a California statute. A state court upheld the conviction. The U.S. Supreme Court remanded the case for consideration. The Court reaffirmed that hard-core pornography was not protected by the Constitution; patently offensive material could be censored if it lacked "serious literary, artistic, political or scientific value." That determination could be made, the Court said, by local judges or juries. At the same time the Supreme Court handed down similar decisions in *Kaplan v. California* (413 U.S. 115), *Paris Adult Theater I v. Slaton* (413 U.S. 49), *United States v. Orito* (413 U.S. 139), and *United States v. 12,200-Ft. Reels of Super 8mm Film* (413 U.S. 123). The decisions reversed about 15 years of liberal opinions on obscenity.

● *Jonathan Livingston Seagull*, by Richard David Bach (1936–), an allegorical novel, a best seller. Another best seller by Richard Bach was *The Bridge Across Forever* (1984).

● *The Boys on the Bus*, by Timothy Crouse, describing the 1972 presidential campaign. The "boys" were members of the press corps who followed the candidates.

1974. Two best sellers—*All the President's Men*, by Carl Bernstein (1944–) and Robert Upshur Woodward (1943–), and *Jaws*, by Peter

331

Bradford Benchley (1940–). Peter Benchley's other novels included *The Deep* (1976) and *The Island* (1979). Another Robert Woodward and Bernstein best seller was *The Final Days* (1976). Woodward also wrote *The Brethren* (1980), a best seller co-authored with Scott Armstrong, and *Wired: The Short Life & Fast Times of John Belushi* (1984).

• *Time on the Cross: The Economics of Negro Slavery*, by R. W. Fogel and S. L. Engerman, published. The authors analyzed the institution of slavery, combining traditional historical method with quantification.

1975. Three best sellers—*Curtain*, by Agatha Christie, pseudonym for Mary Clarissa Miller (1891–1976); *Looking for Mr. Goodbar*, by Judith Rossner (1935–), and *Ragtime*, by Edgar Laurence Doctorow (1931–). Other fiction by E. L. Doctorow included *World's Fair* (1985). Christie, an English novelist and playwright, wrote more than 80 books, including *The Murder of Roger Ackroyd* (1926). Another of Rossner's books was *Attachments* (1977).

1976. Copyright Act (17 U.S.C. 102), effective 1 January 1978; replaced 1909 statute. Congress's aim was to protect copyright holders fairly without inhibiting development of new communication technologies and preventing their use by the public. Still copyrightable were books, broadcast programs, motion pictures, and musical compositions. The new law also included choreographic notations, computer programs, and sculptures. (Not copyrightable: brand names, ideas, slogans, titles.) For the first time works were protected by statute from the moment of their creation. The creators then could license use of their works to others for royalties. "Use" included displaying, performing, and publishing. The traditional "fair-use" concept was retained, allowing free use of some copyrighted material without permission; however, specific circumstances in which fair use existed remained open to interpretation. Major changes were instituted in the length of copyright. For works created before 1978, the initial 28 year period continued in effect, but in most situations the renewal period was now 47 years. For works created after 1977, a copyright lasted for the life of a work's creator plus 50 years. After that a work entered the public domain, enabling anyone to use it without paying royalty or obtaining permission.

• *Roots*, by Alex Palmer Haley (1921–), a best seller. Alex Haley's novel of Afro-American heritage won a Pulitzer Prize (1977).

1977. *The Simmarillion*, by John Ronald Reuel Tolkien (1892–1973), a best seller. J. R. R. Tolkien's other fiction included *The Hobbit* (1938) and *The Lord of the Rings* trilogy (1954–1956).

1978. *A Distant Mirror*, by Barbara Wertheim Tuchman (1912–), a best seller. Barbara Tuchman's other works included *The Guns of August* (1962) and *Stillwell and the American Experience in China, 1911–1945*

(1971), both Pulitzer Prize winners; and *The March of Folly: From Troy to Vietnam* (1984).

● *Shosha*, by Isaac Bashevis Singer (1904–), published. Other works by Polish-American writer Singer, who won the Nobel Prize for Literature in 1978, included *A Day of Pleasure: Stories of a Boy Growing Up in Warsaw* (1969) and *A Crown of Feathers* (1973).

● *Bells in Winter*, by Czeslaw Milosz (1911–), published. Other works by the Polish-born U.S. poet, who won a Nobel Prize for Literature in 1980, included *Postwar Polish Poetry* (1965).

1979. Three best sellers—*Aunt Erma's Cope Book*, by Erma Louise Bombeck (1927–); *The Complete Scarsdale Medical Diet*, by Herman Tarnower and Samm Sinclair Baker; and *The Matarese Circle*, by Robert Ludlum (1927–). Other best sellers by Ludlum included *The Parsifal Mosaic* (1982) and *The Aquitaine Progression* (1984). Other best sellers by Erma Bombeck included *If Life Is a Bowl of Cherries—What Am I Doing in the Pits?* (1978) and *Motherhood: The Second Oldest Profession* (1983).

● *The Stories of John Cheever*, by John Cheever (1912–1982), a Pulitzer Prize winner. Cheever's works also included *The Brigadier and the Golf Widow* and *The Wapshot Scandal* (1964), *Bullet Park* (1969), *Falconer* (1977), and *Oh What a Paradise It Seems* (1982).

1980. *Jailbird*, by Kurt Vonnegut, Jr. (1922–), a best seller. Vonnegut's other works included *Mother Night* (1961), *Slaughterhouse Five* (1969), *Palm Sunday* (1981), *Deadeye Dick* (1982), and *Galapagos* (1985).

1981. Three best sellers—*The Beverly Hills Diet*, by Judy Mazel; *Remembrances*, by Danielle Steel; and *Noble House*, by James Dumaresq Clavell, also author of *Shogun* (1975).

1982. Five best sellers—*E.T. The Extra-Terrestrial Storybook*, by William Kotzwinkle; *Jane Fonda's Workout Book*, by Jane Fonda (1937–); *Living, Loving and Learning* and *The Fall of Freddie the Leaf*, by Leo Buscaglia; *North and South*, by John Jakes.

1983. Eight best sellers—*The Lonesome Gods*, by Louis L'Amour (1908–); *The Robots of Dawn*, by Isaac Asimov (1920–); *In Search of Excellence: Lessons from America's Best-Run Companies*, by Thomas J. Peters and Robert H. Waterman, Jr.; *Megatrends: Ten New Directions Transforming Our Lives*, by John Naisbitt; *The One Minute Manager*, by Kenneth Blanchard and Spencer Johnson; *Pet Sematary* and *Christine*, by Stephen King (1947–); and *Return of the Jedi Storybook*, adapted by Joan D. Vinge.

1984. Three best sellers—*Dr. Burns' Prescription for Happiness*, by George Burns, originally Nathan Birnbaum (1896–); *Eat to Win: The Sports Nutrition Bible*, by Robert Haas, M.D.; *Iacocca: An Autobiography*, by Lee Iacocca (1924–) with William Novak. *Iacocca* continued a best seller into 1986.

1985. Five best sellers—*The Accidental Tourist*, by Anne Tyler; *Lake Wobegon Days*, by Garrison Keillor; *A Light in the Attic*, by Shel Silverstein; *Webster's Ninth New Collegiate Dictionary*, published by Merriam-Webster; and *Yeager: An Autobiography*, by Chuck Yeager and Leo Janos.

Newspapers

1973. National News Council (–1984) founded "to examine and report on complaints concerning the accuracy and fairness of news reporting in the United States, as well as to initiate studies and report on issues involving the freedom of the press." At first only foundations funded the NNC; by 1979 about 30 media organizations, including newspapers, contributed about 20 percent of the grant funds. From the beginning, some media organizations, including the New York *Times*, refused to cooperate with NNC in any way. The eight media and ten public members met periodically to discuss complaints filed against media and to propose statements of policy about such media issues as restrictions on court coverage. Initially, NNC restricted complaints to national news media; in 1974 it decided to accept complaints about any U.S. broadcast and print media. Having no enforcement power, NNC relied on the power of publicity, public opinion, and media practitioners' sense of responsibility. Accomplishments included getting columnists and syndicates to report their personal conflicts of interests.

• "Watergate" the biggest news story of the year, finally getting wide coverage after sparse coverage in latter 1972. The story, Senate hearings, and trials of the conspirators involved in the Republican break-in of the Democratic national campaign headquarters in the Watergate building, Washington, D.C., led to the resignation of President Nixon on 9 August 1974. The Watergate exposé was led by the Washington *Post*.

• *Cantrell v. Forest City Publishing Co.* (419 U.S. 245). In this decision the U.S. Supreme Court held a newspaper liable for invasion of privacy by one of its reporters. Two employees of the Cleveland *Plain Dealer* (published by Forest City Publishing), reporter Joseph Eszterhas and a photographer, had gone to Point Pleasant, West Virginia, about five months after a bridge over the Ohio River had collapsed. The collapse had killed 44 people, including Melvin Aaron Cantrell, to whose home they went to interview his family. Cantrell's widow was not home when the two journalists entered it. Whether they had been invited into the home was unclear, but no one asked them to leave and the Cantrell children did not object to being photographed. An article appeared in the *Plain Dealer* magazine supplement on 4 August 1968. The five published pictures depicted the home as dirty and the children as poorly clothed, untidy. The story contained inaccuracies, including the implication that Mrs. Cantrell was home when the newsmen were there. The plaintiff alleged that the journalists had portrayed her in a "false light," unreasonably publicized the Cantrell's private lives, and intruded (the last was not presented to the jury). Cantrell filed both invasion of privacy and libel suits. The jury awarded her $60,000 for invasion of privacy. In the *Plain Dealer*'s appeal the appellate judges dismissed an attempt to restore the intrusion part of the original complaint because the damage claim resided in publication, not physical intrusion by the journalists. The appellate court reversed the jury on the grounds that it had been improperly instructed that it must find "actual malice" (reckless disregard for the truth or knowledge of the information's falsity) to award damages. Acting on Mrs. Cantrell's appeal of that decision, the Supreme Court decided, 8–1, that the jury had been properly instructed and ordered reinstatement of the $60,000 award. For the Court, Justice Potter Stewart (1915–1985) concluded that sufficient evidence existed to support the jury's finding of knowing or reckless falsity against the reporter and his publishing company, but not against the photographer. Stewart found "calculated falsehoods" in the article but truthful representations in the photographs. Forest City Publishing was held liable because the reporter was acting as an employee of its newspaper when he prepared the article. The case did not create a definitive standard for false light privacy claims by private persons, according to Stewart, because neither party objected to the trial judge's jury instructions that actual malice had to be found.

• *Miami Herald Publishing Company v. Tornillo* (418 U.S. 241). In this decision the U.S. Supreme Court held that citizens do not have a right to access to newspapers. Pat Tornillo, an unsuccessful candidate for the Florida legislature, had sued the *Herald* for refusing to publish verbatim his replies to two editorials critical of him. Basis of the suit was a state law that required a newspaper to give equal space for a reply by a candidate whose character or political record it had attacked. A Dade County court held that the statute was unconstitutional because a state could not assume the editorial function and tell a newspaper what to print or what not to print. Upon appeal, the Florida Supreme Court reversed the trial court, holding that the statute was constitutional because its purpose was to enhance the flow of ideas and information; therefore, it did not incurse upon First Amendment rights. A right of reply was needed to assure citizens information about all sides of a controversy, the state supreme court suggested. Appealing to the U.S. Supreme Court, the *Herald* argued that the statute placed the government in the editor's chair, allowing the state to control editorial decisions about publishing content critical of political candidates. Censorship in the guise of promoting fairness was, the newspaper contended, still censorship. The U.S. Supreme Court unanimously overturned the state supreme court's decision, holding the statute unconstitutional because it violated the First Amendment by requiring public access to a newspaper. Chief Justice Warren Earl Burger (1907–) agreed that the statute intruded upon editors' functions and that government could not compel editors to publish what they reasonably thought should not be published. "A newspaper is more than a passive receptacle or conduit for news, comment, and advertising," Burger wrote in the court's opinion. "The choice of material to go into a newspaper, and the decisions made as to limitations on the size of the paper, and content, and treatment of public issues and public officials—whether fair or unfair constitutes the exercise of editorial control and judgment. It has yet to be demonstrated how government regulation of this crucial process can be exercised consistent with First Amendment guarantees of a free press as they have evolved to this time." Burger also commented: "A responsible press is an undoubtedly desirable goal, but press responsibility is not mandated by the Constitution and like many other virtues it cannot be legislated."

1974. Merger of the Knight and Ridder groups, indicating a major merger trend. Knight brought to the merger the Akron *Beacon-Journal*, Charlotte *News* and *Observer*, Detroit *Free Press*, Miami *Herald*, and Philadelphia *Inquirer* and *News*. Ridder brought to the merger 11 midwestern dailies, including the St. Paul *Dispatch* and *Pioneer Press*; and 6 California dailies, including the San Jose *Mercury* and *News*. In the late 1970s Knight-Ridder Newspapers owned 34 dailies, 14 weeklies, 2 radio stations, and 1 television station.

1976. Total dailies, 1,756 in 1,550 cities; 39 cities with 2 or more competing dailies, 20 with 2 dailies in joint printing arrangements; 122 with 2 dailies published by 1 owner; and 1,369 with 1 daily.

• *Nebraska Press Association et al. v. Judge Stuart et al.* (427 U.S. 539). In this decision the U.S. Supreme Court struck down a trial judge's restrictions on court coverage. In the Lincoln County preliminary hearing of an accused murderer, the judge ordered news media, including their representatives covering the proceedings in open court, not to report the existence or substance of any confessions or other information "strongly implicative" of the defendant. The 22 October 1975 court order expired when the jury was impaneled. On 30 June 1976 the U.S. Supreme Court declared the "gag order" unconstitutional prior restraint. The Court ruled that the prohibition of "implicative" information was "too vague and too broad," that the media had a right to report events in open court if they did not jeopardize a fair trial, and that no threats to a fair trial were apparent. The media victory was diminished by the

Court's reluctance to make prohibition against prior restraint absolute. In the opinion Chief Justice Warren E. Burger wrote: "We need not rule out the possibility of showing the kind of threat to fair trial rights that would possess the requisite degree of certainty to justify restraint." Further, the victory in Washington came too late: the judiciary had in fact restrained the press in Nebraska until the gag order was set aside.

• Government in the Sunshine Act (Pub. L. No. 94-409) signed (September) by President Gerald Rudolph Ford, Jr. (1913–), to take effect 12 March 1977. The act's purpose was to provide the public with "the fullest practicable information regarding the decision-making processes of the Federal Government . . . while protecting the rights of individuals and the ability of the Government to carry out its responsibilities." The law required that more than 50 federal agencies, boards, and commissions (including the Federal Trade Commission) open their meetings except when discussions might affect the "interests of national defense or foreign policy," might disclose matters specifically exempted by statute, or might disclose trade secrets and confidential commercial or financial information. Also exempted were meetings concerned solely with internal personnel practices and rules. Reasons for closed meetings had to be certified by the legal head of an agency (excluding cabinet departments). The law required agencies to announce a week in advance the date, place, and subject of meetings and if they would be open or closed. Compliance with the law was mixed.

1978. Peak of 167 newspaper groups. These groups owned more than 60 percent of the 1,753 dailies and accounted for 72 percent of the almost 61.5 million daily circulation and about 80 percent of the almost 52.5 million Sunday circulation. The largest 20 groups accounted for half of daily circulation and 56 percent of Sunday circulation. In number of newspapers, Gannett led with 79; it had the most widespread properties, ranging from Guam to the Virgin Islands. Gannett was second in circulation to Knight-Ridder Newspapers, which had almost 3.7 million daily.

1979. An estimated 100,000 people professionally practicing public relations and about 1,500 public relations agencies.

1980. A daily paper being read by 7 out of 10 adults every day, by 9 out of 20 at least once a week. Circulation was 62 million in a population of 226 million (increases since 1930 of 22 million and 104 million respectively). Since 1970 circulation had increased for many newspapers, but in the 20 largest cities it had decreased by 21 percent while population had dropped by 6 percent. Circulation loss was heaviest in major metropolitan areas, where declines kept static the national total.

1981. Total of 1,745 dailies in 1,559 cities; inflation a factor in the 18-paper decline since 1961. Competing dailies were published in 30 cities. The only city with as many as 3 dailies published by three different owners was New York. Among the largest cities, only Baltimore, San Antonio, and San Diego had as many as 3 dailies with two owners. No other large city had more than 2 general circulation dailies. The 12 large cities with 2 dailies published by different owners were Boston, Chicago, Columbus (Ohio), Dallas, Denver, Detroit, Honolulu, Houston, Los Angeles, San Francisco, Seattle, and Washington. In 22 of the 2-paper cities the business and mechanical sides were operated jointly. One owner published the 2 dailies in 103 cities, including Indianapolis, Jacksonville, Milwaukee, Philadelphia, Phoenix, and San Jose. Having only 1 daily were 1,404 cities, including Cleveland, Memphis, and New Orleans. Total daily circulation was 61.4 million.

• Total of 7,666 weeklies, according to the National Newspaper Association. Total circulation was 45 million (21 million increase since 1960). Suburban and county-seat weeklies were most profitable.

• Pioneering experiments made in pagination by Westchester Rockland Newspapers of Harrison, New York. In pagination complete pages were transmitted from computer memory directly to printing plates. Pagination was made possible by the video display terminal, which had replaced the typewriter on many newspapers in the 1970s (and 1980s). A VDT consisted of a televisionlike screen over a typewriterlike keyboard; the terminal was connected to a central computer. A reporter could type and edit a story on the VDT, then store the copy in the computer; an editor could retrieve the copy, edit it, and transfer it to an automatic typesetting machine. Editors also could call up press association copy on VDTs.

1982. Total of 155 newspaper groups (a 12-group decrease since 1978). They controlled 65 percent of the dailies and 72 percent of the total daily circulation. The groups averaged almost 7.5 dailies each; almost half of the groups owned two or three dailies. By circulation the 10 largest groups were (from the top) Gannett and Knight-Ridder (each with 6 percent of the daily circulation), S.I. Newhouse, Chicago Tribune Company, Dow Jones, Times Mirror, Scripps-Howard, New York Times Company, Hearst, and Cox. The 5 largest largest groups controlled 25 percent of the daily circulation. Only 16 groups had circulations of more than 750,000.

• USA Today (15 September–) founded in Arlington, Virginia, by the Gannett Co. Inc. as a national Monday–Friday newspaper. Circulation began in selected metropolitan areas then extended across the country, exceeding 1 million by mid-1983. USA Today used satellites to transmit images to regional printing plants. The daily became recognized for its colorful graphics and concise stories; content included news of national interest, briefs from around the country, and lots of sports and weather information for travelers. USA Today celebrated its third birthday with 1,350,000 circulation, making it the third largest daily (behind the *Wall Street Journal* and New York *Daily News*). In late 1985 Gannett announced the first printing of *USA Today* outside the United States—in Singapore for distribution in Asia. The company planned to print also in Zurich for distribution in Europe and the Middle East by May 1986. Satellite transmission made the international edition feasible. *USA Today* ended 1985 with domestic bureaus in Atlanta, Houston, Los Angeles, San Jose, and New York. Publisher was Cathleen Black; senior vice president for advertising, Valerie B. Salembier; editor, John C. Quinn; and executive editor, Ron Martin. Price per copy was 50 cents, double the original price.

1983. Daily newspaper numbers and competition down while per-copy prices and total circulation up. There were 1,711 dailies, a net loss in just two years of 34 papers, partly because of higher costs for supplies and labor, losses of national advertising to television, and a recession slump in classified and other advertising. The dwindling number of newspapers was partly the result of mergers of evening dailies into their morning affiliates—32 such consolidations since 1978. The consolidated dailies often became all-day papers. For the first time morning dailies led evening dailies in circulation, about 33 million to 29 million. The number of cities with two papers published by one owner had dropped to 95, the number of cities with competing dailies to 29. Many dailies had increased prices to 25 cents per copy, but total circulation was at an all-time high of 62,487,000, the most increases going to medium and small papers, particularly in suburbs.

● About 2,000 suburban newspapers in circulation, 300 of them dailies, and about 2,000 large-city neighborhood newspapers. The greatest growth of suburban and neighborhood papers was in Chicago, Detroit, Los Angeles, New York, and Philadelphia. The foreign-language press included fewer than 40 dailies, reflecting a steady decline in the twentieth century. (Peak year was 1914, with about 1,000 papers, 140 dailies.) There were perhaps no more than 200 nondailies in foreign languages. Most papers were printed in Chinese, German, Italian, Japanese, Lithuanian, Polish, Russian, Yiddish, and Spanish. The 9 Spanish-language dailies included the New York *El Diario-La Prensa* with 69,000 circulation, Miami *Diario de las Americas* with 62,000, Los Angeles *La Opinion* with 51,000, and the Laredo (Texas) *Times* with 20,000.

Magazines

1973. *Texas Monthly* (February–) founded in Austin by Michael Richard Levy (1946–), president and publisher; editor was William

Broyles (1944–). Circulation was concentrated in Austin, Dallas, Fort Worth, Houston, and San Antonio. Content included depth reporting, quality writing, and guides to entertainment and events. Circulation climbed from 41,500 in 1974 to more than 289,000 in 1985, when Gregory Curtis edited it for urban Texans. *Texas Monthly* covered the state's business, culture, lifestyles, politics, and sports.

• *New Times* (October–8 January 1978) founded in New York as a biweekly news magazine. Publisher was George A. Hirsch; editor, Jonathan Z. Larsen. Content included spot news stories, exposés, satire, and features. Most readers were college-educated males about 30 years old. Circulation rose from about 130,000 reported in 1974 to 356,000 in 1978. Less than a year before its discontinuance, *New Times* was sold to MCA, Inc.

• *Viva* (October–1978) founded in New York by Bob Guccione (1930–) as a sexy monthly for women. Editor was Kathy Keeton (1939–). Early issues included totally nude males and lots of advice about sex. *Viva* appealed more to men, including homosexuals, than to women, and very little to magazine distributors. In 1976 Keeton discontinued total male nudity to help improve sales in supermarkets. Circulation was about 360,000 when the periodical was discontinued.

1974. Elmer Gertz v. Robert Welch, Inc. (418 U.S. 323). In this decision the U.S. Supreme Court drew a sharp distinction between public officials or public figures and private individuals in civil libel cases involving an issue of public interest. The case stemmed from the 1968 killing of a Chicago youth by a police officer, who was convicted of second-degree murder. The victim's family retained attorney Elmer Gertz to represent them in a civil suit against the officer. In an article in the March 1969 issue of *American Opinion*, magazine of the John Birch Society (published by Robert Welch, Inc.), Gertz was accused of having a criminal record, of being the "architect" of a "frame-up," and of being a "Communist-fronter." A federal district court judge ruled that the words were libelous per se (in themselves defamatory), and a jury awarded Gertz $50,000 damages. Reconsidering the applicability of *New York Times v. Sullivan* (1964), the judge decided that Gertz would have to prove "actual malice" (knowledge of falsity or reckless disregard for the truth). The court entered a judgment for Welch, sustained by a circuit court of appeals. The U.S. Supreme Court ruled, 5–4, that in events of public interest private citizens such as Gertz could recover proved actual damages without having to prove actual malice if they could show that the false statement was published negligently. For private citizens the actual malice test applied only when seeking punitive damages. Thus the Supreme Court modified its position in *New York Times v. Sullivan*.

• *Hustler* founded in Columbus, Ohio, by Larry Claxton Flynt

(1942–) as a monthly emphasizing sexually explicit fact, fiction, and photographs. In 1976 circulation was 1,960,000. In 1980 the periodical's guarantee was 1.8 million, mostly on newsstands. Early in the decade the publisher claimed 3 million circulation. Content included exposés, interviews, and profiles as well as fiction and photos. In the mid-1980s circulation was down to about 944,000.

• *National Star* founded by Rupert Murdoch (1931–) as a weekly tabloid; later named *The Star*. With editorial color and sensational material, the "new kind of newspaper" (as it initially called itself) soon registered a million circulation but then fell back. After several editors failed to increase circulation, Murdoch modernized content to coincide with the times, playing down crime and scandals and playing up astrological predictions, health news, Hollywood and television celebrities, and service features. By the late 1970s the "newsmagazine for the entire family" (as it now called itself)—whose readership was mostly women—registered more than 3 million circulation. With 3,444,669 circulation in 1980 the "weekly entertainment magazine" (as it also called itself) ranked sixth among weeklies; sales flourished at supermarket checkouts. In 1984 circulation exceeded 3,406,900, mostly newsstand sales, ranking the *Star* nineteenth in circulation among *Folio:*'s 400 leading consumer magazines. In total revenue the periodical ranked twenty-fifth with an estimated $109,395,000. In the mid-1980s the *Star* was published in Tarrytown, New York. Publisher and editor was Ian G. Rae; executive editor, Phil Bunton. Aimed at families, including grandparents, young parents, and teenagers, the *Star* carried exposés, celebrity profiles, health news, how-to's, new product information, photo features, and other general-interest articles.

• *People Weekly* (4 March–) founded in New York by Time Inc. for a mass market interested in "the stars, the important doers, the comers, and . . . ordinary men and women caught up in extraordinary situations." Aiming for 18- to 34-year-old men and women, Managing Editor Richard B. Stolley emphasized newsmakers in short articles and many photographs. *People Weekly* made money within 18 months, unusually soon in the magazine business. In the first five years advertising revenue rose to more than $90 million, circulation to 2,300,000. A pioneer in the use of a variable, or floating, rate base, the magazine charged advertisers only for actual circulation. Metropolitan and regional editions allowed advertisers to target audiences. Publisher Richard J. Durrell operated on a tight budget with minimum personnel, using work by many free-lance writers and photographers. Among *Folio:*'s 400 leading consumer magazines in 1984, *People Weekly* ranked third in total revenue with $387,288,000 and twenty-fourth in circulation with 2,768,105. Publisher was S. Christopher Meigher III; ad director and associate publisher, William S. Meyers.

1975. *Time Inc. v. Firestone* (424 U.S. 448). In this decision the U.S. Supreme Court narrowed the definition of public figures in civil libel cases. In 1967 Russell Firestone had won a divorce from Mary Alice Firestone in a West Palm Beach, Florida, court. *Time* mistakenly reported that adultery and cruelty were the grounds for the divorce, and Mrs. Firestone sued for libel. She was awarded $100,000 in compensatory damages for mental anguish and pain, a court decision reversed by a Florida appeals court then reinstated by the state supreme court. *Time's* attorney argued that Mrs. Firestone was a public figure; she was a prominent social figure in Palm Beach, and she had held news conferences during the trial. The U.S. Supreme Court held that she was not a public figure because she did not have a special role in public affairs. The justices said that to be considered public figures libel plaintiffs must be considered public figures for all purposes, be intimately involved in resolving important public issues, or have thrust themselves into the vortex of public controversy to influence issues. The Supreme Court ruled, 5–3, that publishers could be held liable for reporters' negligently misinterpreting court decisions and remanded the case for evaluation of *Time's* reporting.

• *Mother Jones* founded in San Francisco as a radical periodical in the tradition of Mary Harris "Mother" Jones (1830–1930), an individualist, socialist, and pioneer union organizer. The monthly became known for its excellent graphics, investigative reporting, and lively writing. Topics included consumer and environmental protection as well as contemporary and historical profiles of ecologists, filmmakers, musicians, sociologists, writers, and other activists. Circulation rose to 220,000 in the late 1970s then dropped to about 160,000 in the mid-1980s.

1977. *Heavy Metal* founded in New York as an illustrated science fiction-fantasy monthly for adults. Content included original narrative art and informative features on new art, books, film, and music. Slant was contemporary and futuristic. The periodical entered the 1980s with about 190,000 circulation. Publisher was Leonard Mogel; editor, Julie Simmons-Lynch.

• *Us* (3 May–) founded in New York by the New York Times Company as a pictorial entertainment biweekly. Designed for sophisticated adults 18 to 34 years old, *Us* emphasized events, personalities, and trends. It also carried commentary and features on books, film, music, television, sports, etc. *Us* began with an advertising rate base of 750,000, then cut back to 500,000 as sales dropped below expectations, perhaps because the paper and typography were dull and grey. Around 1980 Peter J. Callahan bought *Us*. In the mid-1980s circulation exceeded 950,000. Publisher was Donald E. Welsh; advertising director, Patricia M. Weeks.

1978. *Omni* (October–) founded in New York by Bob Guccione as a controversial mix of fantasy, science fiction and fact, and the paranormal. Publisher and Editor Guccione and President Kathy Keeton emphasized development and exploration of life and space in the twenty-first century. *Omni* ended 1984 with 842,282 circulation.

1979. *Geo* founded in New York by Gruner + Jahr, who had published successful versions in France and Germany. The general-interest monthly carried beautifully printed and illustrated features about the arts, environment, human behavior, nature, politics, science, and travel. It was not clear, however, if *Geo* was a geography, news, science, or travel magazine. Because of the confusion over its identity, advertisers hesitated to buy space. *Geo* lost millions of dollars. In 1980 the owners retrenched, originating less material in the United States and running more from the German edition. With price per copy at $4 and circulation around 230,000, *Geo* was purchased in 1981 by Knapp Communications Corporation of Los Angeles. The new owner changed the editorial leadership and the design, but circulation rose insignificantly. In 1984, however, advertising pages increased more than 27 percent through November, including a surge in September when *Geo* declared itself a travel magazine. But then ad pages fell back to previous levels. Editor Kevin Buckley ran articles lavishly illustrated with colorful photographs from remote parts of the world and printed on high-quality paper, making the magazine expensive to produce. By 1985 per-copy price was $2.95; but advertising and circulation gains (rate base: 255,000) were insufficient, and costs were too high to expand readership significantly. *Geo*'s last issue was February 1985. Later that year a revival was considered.

● *Self* (January–) founded in New York by Condé-Nast Publications for women concerned with mental and physical fitness. Publisher Peter George Diamandis (1931–) and Editor Phyllis Starr Wilson (1928–) emphasized self-improvement with practical features on such topics as careers, fitness, health, male-female relationships, medicine, and money. By 1982 circulation had passed 1 million; in the mid-1980s it was about 1,029,000.

● *Science 80* founded to narrow the gap between scientists and nonscientists. Content included articles and summaries about advances, controversies, discoveries, ideas, and personalities in contemporary science and technology. In November 1980 frequency shifted from bimonthly to ten times a year. The periodical appealed to an affluent audience, mostly men with a college education. *Science 81*—the name changed with the years—had a 675,000 rate base. *Science 84*'s circulation was more than 700,000. The magazine was published by the nonprofit American Association for the Advancement of Science in Washington, D.C., and edited by Allen L. Hammond. Tod Herberts was managing publisher; Marjorie Weiss, advertising director.

1980. *Discover* (October–) founded in New York by Time Inc. to report news of science and technology for lay readers. Emphasizing developments that affected readers' daily lives, the monthly began with 400,000 circulation. In a few months Time Inc. guaranteed advertisers 600,000. By 1985 circulation exceeded 977,000. Publisher was James B. Hayes.

• *Magazine Age* founded in New York for advertisers and ad agencies. Circulation early exceeded 39,000, then dropped to about 32,000 in the mid-1980s, when the monthly was purchased by MPE, Inc., of New Canaan, Connecticut, and edited by Robert Hogan.

• *Next* (March/April–1981) founded in New York by Carroll Dowden, Al Vogel, and others. The monthly, published by Litton Publications, emphasized the consequences of contemporary developments. Editor John Van Doorn ran features on myriad topics, such as the future of culture, economics, ecology, health, law, lifestyles, military affairs, philosophy, politics, psychology, and technology. Publisher was Stephen M. Blacker.

• *Prime Time* (January–) founded in New York as a monthly for people of 45–65 years of age. Circulation rose from an initial 70,000 to some 179,000 in 1981. Editor Bayard Hooper emphasized articles on food, nostalgia, and travel.

1981. *High Technology* founded in Boston for technical and nontechnical professionals and senior managers in business and government. Content included articles on technological advances and their possible impact on business, as well as departments on government policy, investing in high-tech companies, and microcomputer technology. In 1985 Bernard A. Goldhirsh was publisher and editor in chief; circulation was about 303,000.

• *Shape* founded in Woodland Hills, California, for physically active women. In the first year, Publisher Joseph Weider reported, circulation exceeded 300,000. Editor-in-Chief Christine MacIntyre ran regular features on medicine, nutrition, and sports as well as book excerpts, exposés, how-to's, interviews, etc. Self-described as the monthly of "Merging Mind and Body Fitness," *Shape* ranked among the top five health and fitness magazines in 1984, according to *Folio:*, with $13,407,000 total revenue. Circulation in the mid-1980s exceeded 517,000.

1982. *American Health* founded in New York by American Health Partners to cover both lifestyles and scientific aspects of health, including clinical advances, fitness, holistic healing, laboratory research, and nutrition. Frequency went from bimonthly to nine times a year. Circulation quickly reached 400,000, then rose to more than 680,000 in 1984; in 1985 it was about 850,000. Emphasizing *Fitness of Body and Mind* (subtitle), *American Health* was one of the fastest growing consumer magazines. Publisher was Owen J. Lipstein; editor in chief, T. George Harris; advertising director, John B. Caldwell.

● *Computer Retail News* founded in Manhasset, New York, by CMP Publications, Inc., for dealers, distributors, independent resellers, mass merchandisers, store owners and managers, systems houses, and vendors in computer retailing. Content included information about advertising programs, financing, market strategies, merchandising techniques, personnel management, site selection, store design, and trends. In the mid-1980s, under Publisher Kenneth D. Cron, the weekly had more than 39,000 circulation.

1983. Two new microcomputer periodicals, among many founded in the early 1980s for consumers—the monthlies *COMPUTE!'s Gazette* and *Family Computing*. The former was founded in Greensboro, North Carolina, by Compute! Publications, Inc., for owners and beginning-to-intermediate users of Commodore personal computers. Content included information on computer use and programming, home and educational applications, and new productions. In the mid-1980s, under Publisher Gary R. Ingersoll and Editor Lance Elko, *COMPUTE!'s Gazette* had about 290,000 circulation. *Family Computing* was founded in New York by Scholastic Inc. for prospective, beginning, and intermediate users of personal computers in the home. Content included new-product information, telecomputing tips, and money management techniques. In the mid-1980s, under Publisher Shirrel Rhoades and Editor-in-Chief Claudia Cohl, *Family Computing* had about 383,000 circulation.

● *M* founded in New York by Fairchild Publications division of Capital Cities Media, Inc., for successful, sophisticated men. Featuring successful men's lifestyles, the monthly emphasized excellence and took an international perspective. Associate Publisher and Executive Editor Thomas Moran ran articles about adventure, the arts, fashion, fine dining, grooming, sports, travel, wine, etc. In the mid-1980s circulation exceeded 115,000; publisher was Eugene F. Fahy.

1984. *National Geographic Traveler* founded in Washington, D.C., by the National Geographic Society as a quarterly. In mid-decade Editor Joan Tapper ran text and photographs mainly about popular and accessible off-the-beaten-track destinations. Circulation exceeded 1 million.

● *MBM* founded in New York by George C. Pryce, publisher and editor, for black professional men. The bimonthly had a circulation of about 100,000 in 1985.

● Four new electronics bimonthlies by McGraw-Hill Publications Company—*Communications System Equipment Design, Computer Systems Equipment Design, Industrial Electronics Equipment Design,* and *Military/Space Electronics Design.* Each magazine was aimed at design engineers and covered its industry segment. Circulation for each periodical was 25,000.

1985. *Spin* founded in New York by Bob Guccione, Jr., publisher and editor, for rock music fans. In late 1985 circulation climbed toward 150,000.

● *Bicycle Guide* founded in Allentown, Pennsylvania, by Bike-On-America for recreational bicyclists. The periodical included product reviews, maintenance advice, and training tips. Publisher was Bill Fields; editor, John Schubert. Circulation was 100,000.

Motion Pictures

1973. *American Graffiti*, directed by George Lucas (1944–), a stylistic recreation of the 1950s with a rock and roll sound track; set box office records. Other Lucas films included *THX 1138* (1971) and *Star Wars* (1977), first in a science-fantasy trilogy (others 1980, 1983) set in the future in "another galaxy." This narrative blockbuster used Dolby (stereo) sound and no major U.S. star (best-known actor was Sir Alec Guinness [1914–]).

● *The Exorcist*, directed by William Friedkin (1939–), vividly and terrifyingly brought the devil to the screen. Other Friedkin films included *The Night They Raided Minsky's* (1968), *The Boys in the Band* (1969), *The French Connection* (1971), *Sorcerer* (1977), and *Cruising* (1979).

● *Mean Streets*, directed by Martin Scorsese (1942–), an organized-crime story shot in New York's Little Italy. Other Scorsese films included *Taxi Driver* and *Alice Doesn't Live Here Anymore* (1974), *New York, New York* (1977), and *The Last Waltz* (1978).

● *Sugarland Express*, directed by Steven Spielberg (1947–), a thriller and his first successful feature. Four Spielberg record-setting movies were *Jaws* (1975), *Close Encounters of the Third Kind* (1977), and *E.T.* (1982) for box office grosses; and *1941* for box office losses. His successes also included *Raiders of the Lost Ark* (1981), *Indiana Jones and the Temple of Doom* (1984), and *The Color Purple* (1985).

1974. *Badlands*, directed Terrence Malick (1943–), a modern western in which the automobile replaced the horse on the prairie. Malick's other films included *Days of Heaven* (1978).

● *Jenkins v. State of Georgia* (418 U.S. 153). In this decision the U.S. Supreme Court ruled that the film *Carnal Knowledge* was not obscene under constitutional standards established in *Miller v. California* (1973). Jenkins had been convicted of violating the Georgia obscenity statute for exhibiting the film at an Albany (Georgia) theater. The Supreme Court unanimously reversed the conviction, holding that the film was not the "public portrayal of hard-core sexual conduct for its own sake and for ensuing commercial gain," which the court had held punishable in *Miller*. In the opinion Justice William Hubbs Rehnquist (1924–) said that juries do not have "unbridled discretion" to determine what is "patently offensive."

● *Lenny*, directed by Bob Fosse (1927–), portraying the life of the late comedian Lenny Bruce. Like *Lenny*, Fosse's *Cabaret* (1972), starring Liza Minnelli (1945–), made a social statement; Fosse and Minnelli won Academy Awards. In *All That Jazz* (1979), a departure, Fosse created dazzling dances.

1975. *All the President's Men*, directed by Alan J. Pakula (1928–); depicted the Washington *Post*'s exposure of the Watergate scandal. Robert Redford (1936–) and Dustin Hoffman (1937–) starred. Later Pakula films included *Comes a Horseman* (1978), *Starting Over* (1979), *Rollover* (1981), and *Sophie's Choice* (1982).

1976. *Carrie*, directed by Brian De Palma (1940–), a thriller. Other De Palma films included *Obsession* (1976), *The Fury* (1978), *Dressed To Kill* (1980), *Blow Out* (1981), and *Scarface* (1983).

● *Rocky*, directed by John G. Avildsen (1942–), a low-budget blockbuster about a prizefighter, played by Sylvester Stallone (1946–). Avildsen won an Academy Award. His other films included *Joe* (1970) and *The Karate Kid* (1984).

1977. *Annie Hall*, directed by Woody Allen, originally Allen Konigsberg (1935–), a New York-based comedy. Academy Awards went to Allen (as director), co-star Diane Keaton (1949–), and the film. With *Annie Hall* Allen firmly established himself as the foremost cinematic comedian of his time. His films typically depicted characters out of step with society and grappling with sexual insecurities. Earlier Allen movies included *Take the Money and Run* (1969), *Bananas* (1971), *Everything You Always Wanted To Know About Sex* (1972), *Play It Again, Sam* and *Sleeper* (1973), and *Love and Death* (1975). Later films included *Interiors* (1978), *Manhattan* and *Stardust Memories* (1980), *A Midsummer Night's Sex Comedy* (1982), *Zelig* (1983), and *Broadway Danny Rose* (1984).

1978. *The Deer Hunter* directed by Michael Cimino (1943–), the powerful story of working-class buddies whose lives were critically affected in the Vietnam war. The film and Cimino won Academy Awards. Other Cimino films included *Day of the Dragon* (1985), a crime film criticized by Chinese-Americans for stereotypical depiction of them as gangsters.

● *Heaven Can Wait*, directed by Warren Beatty (1937–) and Buck Henry, a low-budget blockbuster comedy-fantasy about attainment of the American Dream of love, wealth, and eternal life.

1979. *Kramer v. Kramer*, directed by Robert Benton (1932–), starring Dustin Hoffman. The film, director, and actor received Academy Awards. The story was about a father's custody of his child after the mother had deserted them for a career.

1980. *The Empire Strikes Back*, directed by Irvin Kershner, the second film in the science fiction-fantasy Star Wars trilogy (begun in 1977 and completed in 1983).

1981. *Reds*, directed by Warren Beatty, who also starred; depicted Communist John Reed's involvement in the Russian Revolution. Beatty won an Academy Award for his direction.

1982. *Gandhi*, directed by Richard Attenborough (1923–), starring Ben Kingsley (1943–) in the title role. The film, director, and actor received Academy Awards. The movie depicted Gandhi's passive resistance for India's independence. Attenborough's other films included the musical *A Chorus Line* (1985).

1983. *Return of the Jedi*, directed by Richard Marquand, the third installment of the Star Wars trilogy begun in 1977; Academy Award winner for special visual effects.

● *Terms of Endearment*, directed by James L. Brooks (1940–), an emotional story about a mother and adult daughter. Brooks and star Shirley MacLaine, originally Shirley Beatty (1934–), won Academy Awards.

1984. *Amadeus*, directed by Milos Forman (1932–), about a royal court composer's envy of Mozart; an Academy Award winner.

● *Ghostbusters*, directed by Ivan Reitman, a horror film spoof in which three professors battled evil.

● *The Killing Fields*, directed by Roland Joffe, based on the true story of a New York *Times* correspondent's search for the Cambodian assistant he had left behind after a Communist victory in that country.

1985. *Back to the Future*, directed by Robert Zemeckis, a science fiction-fantasy; one of the year's most popular movies.

● *Fast Forward*, directed by Sidney Poitier (1924–), a story about clean-cut Ohio kids who went to New York to break into show business. The flick suffered at the box office when the teenage movie boom went bust.

● *King David*, directed by Bruce Beresford, starring Richard Gere (1950–) in the title role.

Radio and Television

1973. *Columbia Broadcasting System v. Democratic National Committee* and *Federal Communications Commission v. Business Executives' Move* *for Vietnam Peace* (412 U.S. 94). In these decisions the U.S. Supreme Court ruled that broadcasters are not required to sell time for editorial advertisements. During the Vietnam war BEM had tried to buy time for spot announcements that countered Army recruiting spots. WTOP of Washington, D.C., refused, saying as a policy it did not sell time for editorial commercials. BEM went to the FCC, which ruled in favor of the radio station. FCC similarly ruled against DNC, which had asked that stations not be allowed arbitrarily to refuse to sell time to "responsible entities" to solict funds and comment on public issues. FCC said (1971) that the Fairness Doctrine did not require paid access, and that rejoinders to "advertorials" (commercials discussing controversies of public importance) mostly depended on licensees' "good faith" discretion. A circuit court of appeals held that the ruling violated the First Amendment, reversed the FCC, and remanded the cases. The Supreme Court ruled, 7–2, that licensees whose policy is to refuse advertorials are not obligated to sell time for them. Chief Justice Warren Earl Burger (1907–) said in the opinion: "Since it is physically impossible to provide time for all viewpoints . . . the right to exercise editorial judgement was granted [by Congress] to the broadcaster," who "is allowed significant journalistic discretion in deciding how best to fulfill Fairness Doctrine obligations, although that discretion is bounded by rules designed to assure that the public interest in fairness is furthered." The Supreme Court's decision allowed broadcasters to continue exercising their own judgment in selling commercial time.

● Senate Watergate Committee hearings carried on television for several weeks, helping focus national attention on the scandal, which gradually led to uncovering President Nixon's participation. Witnesses told or evaded telling about the conspiracy to assure Nixon's reelection and the coverup of that conspiracy. So viewers could choose between hearings and regular entertainment shows, networks for a while alternated coverage. Watergate TV coverage, which had been weak the year the scandal broke (1972), spread during 1973; news stories and special programs increased.

● Administrative requirements, mainly for radio stations, reduced by FCC, foreshadowing a deregulation trend.

1974. Total of 3,158 cable television systems serving 8.7 million subscribers in 13 percent of the homes with TV (since 1950, increases of 3,088 systems, 8,686,00 subscribers and 12.9 percent homes).

● Watergate impeachment hearings for President Nixon (July), the first television coverage of the House of Representatives. Also TV and radio covered live the last day (8 August) of the Nixon administration, including the first presidential resignation ceremonies and speech, and the first day (9 August) of the new administration, including the swearing in of Vice President Ford as President.

• Westar I launched; first domestic communications satellite. Companies leased channels on the Western Union satellite, then sold access to them at a lower cost than American Telephone & Telegraph land lines. Westars and other "domsats" could relay signals to destinations within a region or country, serving more ground stations than international satellite systems.

• "Mystery Theater," a nightly one-hour original drama on radio. The Columbia Broadcasting System series provided the first radio network vehicle for acting and writing talent in more than 20 years. Host was E. G. Marshall (1910–).

• "Little House on the Prairie," a dramatic series on the National Broadcasting Company television network. It starred Michael Landon, original name Eugene Maurice Orowitz (1937–).

1975. Future cross-media ownership in the same market banned by Federal Communications Commission. The rules restricted newspaper ownership of radio and television stations. FCC let stand existing combinations until changes in ownership and required divestiture within five years in communities where the only daily and only station were under the same ownership. The rules were in reaction to increasing cross-media ownership. Concentration was especially apparent in broadcasting, where three networks dominated and where about 50 percent of the TV stations and 80 percent of the radio stations were owned by companies that owned at least one other broadcast or print outlet. Newspapers owned about 27 percent of TV stations and about 7 percent of radio stations. Group ownership was especially marked in the 100 largest markets (which contained about 87 percent of U.S. TV households), where groups owned about 75 percent of the TV stations.

• Betamax home video cassette recorder ($1,300) introduced by Sony; first on the market. Betamax enabled users to record TV programs and view them any time they chose. Within ten years, with many manufacturers in the market, VCR sales were booming.

• *Cox Broadcasting Corp. v. Martin Cohn* (420 U.S. 469). The U.S. Supreme Court considered a public disclosure case for the first time. WSB-TV of Atlanta had broadcast (1972) the identification, based on public records, of a 17-year-old who had been raped and had choked to death on her vomit. Relying on a Georgia law that prohibited such identification of a victim, the girl's father sued, claiming the broadcast had invaded his privacy. Cohn claimed the right to be free from unwanted publicity about his private affairs. As a person of "ordinary sensibilities," he considered the publicity offensive. The report's accuracy was undisputed. Delivering the decision in favor of WSB-TV for the Supreme Court, Justice Byron Raymond White (1917–) said that the state could not block accurate identification of the rape victim obtained from judicial records open to the public. "At the very least," said White, "the First and Fourteenth Amendments will not allow exposing the press to liability for truthfully publishing information released to the public in official court records. If there are privacy interests to be protected in judicial proceedings, the States must respond by means which avoid public documentation or other exposure of private information . . . must weigh the interests in privacy with the interests of the public to know and of the press to publish."

● Electronic news gathering—use of portable television cameras live or use of videotape rather than news film—expanding rapidly among local stations. Portable color cameras, videotape recorders, and other new ENG equipment allowed TV journalists to cover the news faster, more flexibly, and more economically than possible with film.

● More exemptions to Section 315 of the Communications Act (1934) being permitted by the FCC. Presidential candidates' news conferences and political debates qualifying as bona fide news events were exempted from the equal time provision. The events had to be broadcast in their entirety, and debates had to be conducted by disinterested third parties. (Previous exemptions remained.) The new exemptions led to radio and television debates by the Democratic and Republican presidential candidates under auspices of the nonpartisan League of Women Voters in 1976, 1980, 1984.

1976. Broadcast programs copyrightable under the new Copyright Act (17 U.S.C. 102), effective 1 January 1978. The new law required copyright owners who licensed their works to television stations to grant blanket secondary transmission rights to CATV systems that pick the programs off the air and transmit them to subscribers. CATV paid the Copyright Royalty Tribunal, established to set and handle the fees. Thus cable system operators could legally pick up and transmit signals without getting permission from originating stations.

1977. Christian Broadcasting Network (April–) in operation, providing a video program service by satellite interconnection. By mid-1981 CBN distributed 24 hours per day of programs, including "The 700 Club" and other Christian or family shows, to 2,800 cable systems with a total of 11.8 million subscribers. In the early 1980s CBN's holdings included Portsmouth, Virginia, UHF station WYAH-TV, three other television outlets, and six FM stations.

● *Home Box Office v. Federal Communications Commission* (567 F.2d 9). In this case the Court of Appeals for the District of Columbia Circuit ruled that the FCC had no power to make rules for cable pay-television. FCC had restricted the types of programs that cable pay-TV operators could siphon off the air. Home Box Office (f. 1972), a leading pay-cable company, and other such operators objected, and the federal appeals court consolidated fourteen other cases with HBO to render its *per curiam* (court as a whole) decision. The court held that the FCC had failed to justify its position that cable TV must operate as a supplement to broadcast TV rather than as an equal to it. (Rules pertaining to subscription broadcast TV were unaffected.) The U.S. Supreme Court refused to review the decision. A FCC study of the economic relationship between broadcast and cable led the commission to lift its two rules banning most importation of distant signals and protecting some syndicated programming from free cable competition. Under the new policy the FCC encouraged competition between cable and broadcasting.

• Most chain broadcasting regulations for radio canceled by FCC. Because networks no longer dominated radio, which had become a local medium, the rules had become pointless. FCC did, however, maintain its nonexclusivity rule (prohibiting a network contract from preventing an affiliate from accepting programs from other networks and prohibiting an affiliate from preventing its network from offering rejected programs to other stations in the same market). Also the FCC added news agencies' (e.g., Associated Press and United Press International) audio services, provided by interconnections, to the definition of radio networks. Easing the rules was part of a deregulation trend.

• "Roots" miniseries televised by American Broadcasting Company on eight consecutive nights (January), reaching an unprecedented audienceof as many as 80 million people. The 30 January installment reached 36,380,000 households. The 12-hour serial portrayed the heritage of U.S. blacks, creating strong emotional impact among those in the audience. Alex Haley's *Roots* was one of many novels serialized in four to ten episodes, beginning in 1976, as specials or fill-ins for canceled regular series; new series on TV fell from 39 to 26 or fewer annually.

• QUBE founded by Warner Cable Corporation, subsidiary of Warner Communications, as a unique interactive, off-air cable television system for subscribers. Warner, one of the largest multiple system operators, selected Columbus, Ohio, as the test market because it demographically reflected markets nationally. QUBE offered ten channels including all available commercial and noncommercial stations in the market; ten premium pay cable channels featuring first-run movies, entertainment specials, exclusive sports events, and soft-core pornographic films; and ten channels of locally produced programming. QUBE also offered interactive channels enabling viewers at home to "talk back" to their sets by pushing buttons. At the cable head a computer quickly analyzed viewers' responses, enabling researchers to alter procedures during a test and opening new possibilities for audience research design.

• USA Network (September–) in operation, providing a video program service by satellite interconnection. Content included "Calliope," a children's program, and sports (75 percent). In the early 1980s USA

Network distributed programs ten hours a day to 1,425 CATV systems serving a total of 8 million households.

1978. Showtime (March–) providing a video program service by satellite interconnection. Content included specials, sports, and first-run movies. In 1979 Showtime operator Viacom sold half interest to TelePrompTer, providing more CATV customers and greater financial strength. In the early 1980s the pay-cable service distributed programs 24 hours a day to 1,100 CATV systems serving a total of 2 million households.

● KSL-TV of Salt Lake City broadcasting one of the first teletext services (June–). Content included newspaper advertisements as well as airline and movie schedules. System later adapted for home computer access.

1979. Estimated 79.3 million black-and-white television sets, 71.3 million color sets, and 79.3 million radios in use in the United States. Estimated average TV viewing time: 29 hours per week.

● A *Public Trust* released (January) by the Carnegie Commission. It called for strengthening public broadcasting. The new Carnegie-supported study group had been announced in June 1977 (after a decade of public broadcasting development since the first Carnegie report [1967]). The "Carnegie II" report called for tripling federal funding of public broadcasting, providing more support for new technology, replacing the Corporation for Public Broadcasting with a trust to protect it from political pressures, and improving national radio coverage by adding 250 to 300 public stations. Congress was disinclined to increase public expenditures substantially, but many Carnegie II proposals were later effected.

● Three satellite-delivered video program services launched—Cable Satellite Public Affairs Network (March–), Nickelodeon (April–), and Spanish International Network (September–). The first, C-SPAN, was founded by the House of Representatives to televise fully its proceedings, National Press Club speeches, educational programs, etc. Broadcasters could pick up C-SPAN programs, but most commercial stations used only occasional excerpts. C-SPAN programs were underwritten. (In 1985 the Senate considered televising its proceedings beginning in 1986.) The second service, Nickelodeon, programmed just for children (through teens), providing documentaries, dramas, films, etc. In the early 1980s Nickelodeon distributed 13 hours a day of programs to 1,200 CATV systems serving a total of 4.8 million households. The third service, SIN, distributed Hispanic programming supported by advertisers to both CATV systems and specialized broadcast stations. Programs included drama, news, Spanish-language movies, and sports. In the early 1980s SIN distributed 24 hours a day of programs to 106 CATV systems serving 2.7 million households.

● First network telecast with a fiber-optic link reported. For Columbia Broadcasting System coverage of a National Football League game between the New York Giants and the Tampa Bay Buccaneers, fiber optics connected Tampa Stadium to downtown Tampa (5.6 miles), from where the signal was distributed by nonfiber-optic means to 20 cities. In 1984 American Telephone & Telegraph completed a fiber-optic link in New England. In fiber-optic technology, light waves pass through microscopic glasslike strands, allowing distortionless transmission. Laser beams thus carry information equivalent to that transmitted on thousands of cable channels.

● *Herbert v. Lando* (441 U.S. 169). In this decision the U.S. Supreme Court opened the editorial process to scrutiny in libel suits. Television producer Barry Lando of CBS had investigated former U.S. Army officer Anthony Herbert's claims that the army covered up U.S. atrocities during the Vietnam war. Using those findings, Mike Wallace had videotaped an interview with Herbert for "60 Minutes." Herbert alleged that, among other things, the interview portrayed him as a liar. On this and other grounds he filed suit against Lando for libel. Seeking evidence of "actual malice," Herbert tried to explore Lando's "state of mind" when he prepared the program. Plaintiff wanted to know, for instance, what Lando had thought about his sources' veracity as well as what Lando and Wallace had discussed when selecting material to broadcast. Lando refused to answer, claiming First Amendment protection from probes into the editorial process. He claimed that journalists had the right to keep the editorial process and news sources confidential. He argued that revealing sources' names and reporting notes, including videotapes and internal memoranda, would have a "chilling effect" on gathering and reporting news. A federal appeals court agreed that the editorial process was protected by the First Amendment against probing by public figures such as Herbert who sought evidence of the actual malice they needed to win libel suits. But the U.S. Supreme Court ruled that it could not require a plaintiff to prove actual malice and then "erect an impenetrable barrier" to gathering that essential evidence. Sued for libel, journalists must disclose opinions they held while preparing the report as well as the reasons behind their news judgments. According to the Supreme Court, the doctrine in *New York Times v. Sullivan* (1964) made it necessary that plaintiffs inquire into the state of mind and conduct of defendants who prepared allegedly libelous reports. The Supreme Court rejected the chilling effect argument. *Herbert* thus armed public figures with a new weapon to extract evidence of actual malice.

● *Writers Guild v. Federal Communications Commission* (609 F.2d 355). In this case courts rejected the industry's own "family viewing time" policy. FCC Chairman Richard Wiley had apparently urged the

National Association of Broadcasters and the networks to limit violence in programs telecast 7–9 P.M. Monday–Saturday and 6:30–8:30 P.M. Sunday in the Eastern time zones (one hour later in Central and Mountain zones). CBS President Arthur Taylor supported the policy, and most of the industry followed. Opposition came from the West Coast packaging companies, which created about 80 percent of all programs. Family viewing time kept sex and violence off the air during evening times when children most likely would be viewing. Such policy would take the heat off networks and stations for supposedly adversely influencing children's morals and behavior. The NAB code adjured broadcasters to avoid entertainment programming inappropriate for a family audience during the hour just before prime time and during the first hour of prime time. If an occasional entertainment program during those hours was inappropriate for family viewing, broadcasters should alert viewers with advisories. Challenging the FCC in court, the Writers Guild of America, Screen Actors Guild, producers, and other interested parties claimed that Wiley had violated the First Amendment by strongly encouraging the NAB code provision and that networks had violated antitrust laws by agreeing to abide by it. Because the provision also applied to stations abiding by the code, it also would probably reduce revenues from syndication (non-network programs sold to stations). In 1976 Judge Warren J. Ferguson of the U.S. District Court, Central District, in Los Angeles ruled that because the FCC chairman had pressured, or "jawboned," the industry into imposing the family viewing hours on itself, the policy amounted to censorship, and therefore was unconstitutional. Each licensee, the court said, must make its own final decisions on programming. The U.S. Court of Appeals for the Ninth Circuit overturned (1979) the lower court's decision, but only on jurisdictional grounds, leaving the self-regulatory policy in doubt. As a result, NAB dropped mandatory adherence to its code and rewrote it to prohibit broadcasting indecent, obscene, or profane material—as determined by members.

1980. Three satellite-delivered video program services launched— Black Entertainment Network (January–), The Movie Channel (January–), and Cable News Network (June–). The first, BET, distributed ethnic programming supported by advertisers to both CATV systems and specialized broadcast stations. In the early 1980s BET distributed 15 hours of Sunday programming to 685 cable systems serving 7.1 million households. The Movie Channel distributed movies twenty-four hours a day to 1,175 CATV systems serving 1.1 million households in the early 1980s. The third service, CNN, was a 24-hour news service founded by Robert Edward Turner III (1938–), owner of Atlanta superstation WTBS, CNN headquarters. Ted Turner's CNN provided hard news and feature reports, offering a two-hour prime-time newscast daily and updates hourly. Other programming included interviews. In the early 1980s CNN served 1,270 CATV systems with a total audience of 7 million households.

• National Association of Public Television Stations founded by public TV licensees to coordinate efforts in the three nonprogramming areas of planning, representation, and research.

• Two videotex trials involving daily newspapers. In Columbus, Ohio, the *Dispatch* provided electronic editions with CompuServe time sharing and Associated Press cooperation. QUBE subscribers and personal computer owners could directly access stories in the *Dispatch's* computer. Other newspapers and a magazine joined the experiment. They included the Atlanta *Journal* and *Constitution*, Framingham (Massachusetts) *Middlesex News*, Los Angeles *Times*, Minneapolis *Star* and *Tribune*, Norfolk *Virginian-Pilot* and *Ledger-Star*, San Francisco *Chronicle* and *Examiner*, Washington *Post*, and *Better Homes & Gardens*. In Coral Gables, Florida, Knight-Ridder Newspapers began VIEWTRON, rotating 30 terminals among 160 households. Users with these terminals attached to their receivers could access about 15,000 pages of information provided by the Associated Press, Miami *Herald*, and Universal Press Service. Among VIEWTRON advertisers were Eastern Airlines, J.C. Penney, and Sears, Roebuck. Videotex systems such as these provided two-way communication via cables or telephone lines. Because individuals actively participated in selecting newspaper, magazine, or other information, videotex was more personalized than older mass media. Videotex services matured in the 1980s as more people acquired personal computers, used as access hardware.

1981. INDAX videotex service testing (February–) by Cox Cable Communications, subsidiary of Cox Broadcasting Corporation, for its cable services subscribers. In March 1982 commercial operation began in Cox's Omaha cable system.

• Total of 4,350 CATV systems serving 4.5 million in 1970.

• Maximum term for broadcast station licenses extended in Communications Act amendments from three years to five years for television and to seven for radio. Under another amendment the Federal Communications Commission was to select among contenders for a license by lottery instead of by hearing, thus awarding the license on the basis of chance rather than qualifications.

• Four programming requirements for radio licensing eliminated by the FCC to encourage diversity and thereby best serve the public interest. Eliminated were (1) formal ascertainment for ensuring localism, (2) keeping logs (basis of the composite week for performance assessment), and rules for setting (3) minimum amount of nonentertainment programming and (4) maximum amount of advertising content. Stations were still obligated to keep records (open to public) of their programming dealing with local problems, evidence that might be used in renewal proceedings. A major goal of the FCC's deregulation policy was diversification of ownership and control.

• Three teletext systems tested in Los Angeles involving the Columbia Broadcasting System, National Broadcasting Company, and KCET. The CBS Broadcast Group's EXTRAVISION began as a one-way system with receivers in shopping malls and other public places, later operated as a two-way system and expanded to homes. Content included about 80 pages of information, such as traffic reports, stock prices, sports scores, smog conditions, news updates, airline schedules, and activities and events calendars. NBC's Tempo consisted of information transmitted from a computer at the NBC Teletext Broadcast Center in Burbank to KNBC. Content included such information of local interest as biking and walking tours, gallery and museum listings, restaurant listings, and theater programs. On weekends Tempo ran such features as letters from viewers and ski reports. Through the cooperation of advertisers who received free time and space, NBC experimentally measured viewer reactions to various ad formats and messages. KCET cooperated with the CBS and NBC services, becoming the first public station to experiment with teletext (WETA of Washington, D.C., followed in 1981). KCET's "now!" magazine format included a contents page from which viewers could make selections; financial, national, sports, and weather reports; and cultural, educational, and "Inside L.A." sections.

• Estimated 2 million home videotape recorders sold before 1982.

1982. American Public Radio founded by some public radio stations involved in producing their own programs. APR aimed to assist member stations in distribution, marketing, and scheduling.

• INC Telecommunications announced by National Public Radio as a 24-hour digital technology delivery system using the FM subcarrier frequency of member stations. The stations would transmit data to decoders in subscribers' homes for appearance on a personal computer; data could be stored and converted to hard copy. Potential uses included electronic mail, financial services, and training programs. In the venture with NPR was National Information Utilities of McLean, Virginia; support would come from subscriber fees.

• Mass Media Bureau created in Federal Communications Commission's merger of its Broadcast and Cable Television bureaus. The new bureau assumed control of cable systems and TV and radio stations. Mass Media Bureau had four divisions: (1) Policy and Rules, to handle allocations, international matters, legal aspects, policy analyses, and technical problems; (2) Enforcement, to consider Section 315 and Fairness Doctrine issues, to oversee equal-opportunity employment, and to handle complaints; (3) Video Services, to process applications for cable systems, distribution services, standard TV, and low-power TV; (4) Audio Services, to handle AM, FM, and auxiliary radio services.

1983. Direct broadcast satellite service to central Indiana by United Satellite Communications Inc. In DBS television program signals were beamed via satellites to small antennas at business places and homes.

• Teletext officially approved by Federal Communications Commission; no technical standards specified. Teletext consisted of the one-way transmission of textual information using the vertical blanking interval (unused scanning lines) of a TV signal; transmitted over telephone lines or cables.

1984. INTELSAT V satellite series launched to meet much of the world's communication needs in the rest of the decade. The most sophisticated system available, INTELSAT V consisted of seven satellites and had much larger capacity than previous INTELSAT systems. The synchronous orbit satellites were developed by AeroNutronic Ford. The global system was managed by International Telecommunications Satellite Organization, which had more than 100 member countries.

• Olympic Games teletext service operated by KTTV-TV of Los Angeles in cooperation with Ameritext, British Broadcasting, Harris, Sanyo, Taft, and Zenith corporations. During the summer Los Angeles games, KTTV-TV provided about 100 locations with a 100-page service, including traffic reports supplied by the California Transportation Department and information about the Olympics.

• "The Cosby Show," one of the highest-rated situation comedies in television history. A family show, it starred black actor and comedian Bill Cosby (1937–).

1985. About 5,600 CATV systems served about 10,500 communities.

• General Electric Co. announcement (December) of plans to buy Radio Corporation of America, thus reviving one of the first major corporate relationships in broadcasting. Merger subject to U.S. Justice Department approval.

INDEX

Index

(*Newspapers are listed under their city of publication in alphabetical order.*)

Index

Index

Index

Index

Index

Index

Index

Herald of Truth, 77
Herbert, Anthony, 354
Herbert, B. B., 100
Herbert Hoover: A Reminiscent Biography
    (Irwin), 128
Herberts, Tod, 343
Here Is Your War (Pyle), 233
Hergesheimer, Joseph, 111, 122, 149
Heroes (McGinniss), 297
Herrick, Robert, 112, 117, 127
Herrick, Sophia Bledsoe, 80
Herrold, Charles D. ("Doc"), 147
Hersey, John, 111, 184
Hershey, Laura G., 109
Herter, Christian A., 61
Herzog (Bellow), 250
Hibbs, Ben, 33–34
Hicks, George, 243
Hicks, Granville, 141
Hicks, Wilson, 214
Hidden Hand, The (Southworth), 40
Hidden Persuaders, The (Packard),
    272
Higbee, Arthur, 133
Higginson, Thomas Wentworth, 90
Higgs, John W., 50
High Anxiety, 320
Highlights of Manhattan (Irwin), 128
High Noon, 263
High Sierra, 218
High Technology, 344
Hildreth, Richard, 37
Hilgard, Ferdinand Heinrich Gustav
    (Henry Villard), 78
Hill, E. Trevor, 155
Hill, George Roy, 319
Hill, Isaac, 27
Hillman, Alex L., 237
Hillman Periodicals, Inc., 237, 256
Hill of Summer, The (Drury), 273
Hills Beyond, The (Wolfe), 170
Hilton, James, 202
Hindenburg disaster, 226–227
Hiroshima (Hersey), 184
Hirsch, George A., 311, 340
Hirsch, Sidney D. Mttron, 176
His Girl Friday, 220–221
His Picture in the Papers, 160
History of New England (Winthrop), 17
    see also Journal
History of New York . . . by Diedrich
    Knickerbocker, A, (Irving), 23
History of the Colony of Massachusetts
    Bay, The (Hutchinson), 4

History of the Conquest of Mexico
    (Prescott), 38
History of the Conquest of Peru (Prescott),
    38
History of the Conspiracy of Pontiac
    (Parkman), 39
History of the Plimouth Plantation
    (Bradford), 41
History of the Reign of Charles V
    (Prescott), 38
History of the Reign of Ferdinand and
    Isabella (Prescott), 38
History of the Reign of Philip the Second,
    King of Spain (Prescott), 38
History of the United States (Adams), 150
History of the United States (Bancroft),
    37
"History of the U.S. Decision-making
    Process on Vietnam Policy,"
    297–298, 305–306
Hitchcock, Alfred Joseph, 222
Hobbit, The (Tolkien), 332
Hoberecht, Earnest, 133
Hobson, Laura Z., 247–248
Hodkinson, W. W., 159
Hoe, Richard March, 50
Hoe, R. & Company, 68–69
Hoffenberg, Mason, 295
Hoffman, Dustin, 318, 347, 348
Hogan, Robert, 344
Hokinson, Helen, 183
Holbrook, Eliza, 46
Holden, Liberty E., 48
Holding, Elisabeth Sanxay, 116
Holies Newspapers, 257
Holland, Josiah Gilbert, 82
Holley, Marietta, 88
Hollingsworth, Cecil, 313
Hollywood, 160, 186, 259–260,
    261–262, 283
Hollywood Production Code, 219, 220,
    263, 283
Holm, Ed, 309
Holmes, Mary Jane, 40, 41
Holmes, Oliver Wendell, 41, 150
Holmes, Paul, 280
Holt, Hamilton, 61
Holt, Henry, 65
Holt, John, 13
Holt, Henry, & Co., 65
Holt, Rinehart & Winston, Inc., 65,
    196
Holt & Williams, 65
Holton, Anne, 218

Index

Index

Index

Index

Index

Index

Index

Noah, Mordecai Manuel, 27, 29
Nobel Prize, 169, 171, 201, 204, 212,
    250, 265, 333
Noble, Edward J., 164, 242, 243
Noble House (Clavell), 333
Nock, Albert Jay, 173–174
No Cross, No Crown (Penn), 4
Noel, Frank, 130
Nones (Auden), 248
nonexclusivity rule, 352
Norfolk (Va.)
    Journal and Guide, 136
    Ledger-Star, 356
    Virginian-Pilot, 356
Normand, Mabel, 146
Norris, Frank (Benjamin Franklin
    Norris), 95, 113, 122, 188
Norris, John, 101
Norris, Kathleen Thompson, 86, 111,
    113, 121, 122, 128
North American Newspaper Alliance,
    171
North American Regional Broadcasting
    Agreement, 229
North American Review, 32
North and South (Jakes), 333
North by Northwest, 222
North East, 84
North East Magazine, 41
North Star, The, 63
Northwest Day, 301
Northwood, or Life North and South
    (Hale), 24
Norvell, Joshua, 27–28
Not as a Stranger (Thompson), 271
Nothing Sacred, 221, 240
Nothing So Monstrous (Steinbeck), 204
Notorious, 222
Not Without Laughter (Hughes), 169
Novak, William, 333
Novelist, 87
Novicki, Margaret A., 278
"now," 357
Noyce, Robert Norton, 275
Numismatic News, 257
Nun's Story, The, 263
Oakland (Calif.) *Black Panther*, 303
Oates, Joyce Carol, 297
obscenity, 107, 143, 197, 202–203,
    228
    Alberts v. State of California, 272
    Bantam Books v. Sullivan, 273–274
    *A Book Named "John Cleland's
        Memoirs of a Woman of Pleasure,"*

*v. Attorney-general of the
    Commonwealth of Massachusetts*, 296
*A Quantity of Copies of Books v.
    Kansas*, 295
Butler v. Michigan, 271–272
Ginzberg v. United States, 308, 309
Jacobellis v. State of Ohio, 316, 317
Jenkins v. State of Georgia, 346–347
Joseph Burstyn, Inc. v. Wilson, 284
Kaplan v. California, 331
*Kingsley International Pictures Corp. v.
    Regents of University of State of New
    York*, 284–285
*Manual Enterprises, Inc. v. J. Edward
    Day*, 281–282
Miller v. California, 331, 346–347
Paris Adult Theater I v. Slaton, 331
Rosenbloom v. Metromedia, Inc., 329
Roth test, 316
Roth v. United States, 272, 296, 316
social importance test, 316
"social value" test, 296, 316, 331
Times Film Corp. v. Chicago, 285
United States v. Orito, 331
*United States v. 12,200-Ft. Reels of
    Super 8mm Films*, 331
Obsession, 347
Occasional Reverberator, 10
Ochs, Adolph Simon, 46, 51, 101
Ochs-Oakes, George Washington, 154
O'Connor, Edwin, 63
O'Connor, Edwin Greene, 271
October Light (Gardner), 298
Octopus, The (Norris), 95
O'Dell, Edith, 183
Oestreicher, J. C., 136
Of a Fire on the Moon (Mailer), 248
Office of Censorship, 234, 240
*Office of Communication of United Church
    of Christ v. FCC*, 322
Office of Coordinator of Inter-American
    Affairs, 235
Office of Telecommunications Policy,
    328, 329
Office of War Information, 234–235,
    241, 253
Official Detective Group, 185
Official Karate, 311
Of Men and Women (Buck), 201
Of Mice and Men (Steinbeck), 204
Of Time and the River (Wolfe), 170
O'Feeney, Sean (John Ford), 221
Offers, Jane M., 183
Ogden, Robert Curtis, 122

Index

Index

Index

Index

Runyon, Alfred Damon, 114, 203
rural free delivery, 104
Rural New Yorker, 59
Rush, Benjamin, 15
Rusher, William A., 278
Russell, Benjamin, 18
Russell, Bertrand, 216
Russell, Charles Edward, 111, 138
Russell, John B., 34
Russo-Japanese War, 113
Russwurm, John B., 29
Rutledge (Harris), 41
Ryan, Clendenin J., 181
Sabatini, Rafael, 87, 122
Saboteur, 222
Sabrina, 239
Sacred Wood (Eliot), 168
Saerchinger, Cesar, 195
Safer, Morley, 196
Sagan, Carl, 218
Sahli, John, 303
Sailor on Horseback (Stone), 273
St. Augustine (Fla.) *Florida Gazette*, 28
St. Elmo (Evans), 41
St. Elmo (Wilson), 66
St. Louis
    Democrat, 52
    Dispatch, 69, 74
    Emigrant and Western Advertiser, 28
    Enquirer, 28
    Globe, 52
    Globe-Democrat, 26, 52, 74, 171, 304
    Missouri Gazette, 26
    Missouri Republican, 26
    Post, 69, 74
    Post-Dispatch, 74, 304
    Republic, 26, 52, 101
    Star-Times, 74
    Western Journal, 27–28
St. Nicholas, 85
St. Paul (Minn.)
    Daily Pioneer, 50
    Dispatch, 336
    Minnesota Pioneer, 50
    Pioneer Press, 50, 336
"Saki," 183
Salamander, The (West), 274
Salembier, Valerie B., 339
Salem (Mass.) *Essex Gazette*, 13
Salinger, J.D., 249
Salomon, Erich, 209
Salsberg, Arthur, 277
Salten, Felix (pseud. of Felix Salzmann), 170

Salt Lake City *Deseret News*, 51
Salute, 253–254
Salvation Army, 107
Salzmann, Felix (Felix Salten, pseud.), 170
"Sam 'n' Henry," 199
Samson, Jack, 236
San Bernardino (Calif.) *Sun*, 304
Sanborn, Franklin Benjamin, 76
Sanctuary (Faulkner), 170
Sandburg, Carl, 74, 121, 137, 141, 142, 169, 257
Sanders, Charles L., 238
Sandrich, Mark, 219
San Felipe (Tex.) *Telegraph and Texas Register*, 45
San Francisco
    Alta California, 49, 50
    Bulletin, 52–53
    California Star, 49
    Call, 52, 53
    Call-Bulletin, 52, 53
    Chronicle, 70, 137, 356
    Daily Examiner, 70
    Daily Morning Chronicle, 69–70
    Dramatic Chronicle, 69
    Elevator, 70
    Evening Examiner, 70
    Evening Post, 53
    Examiner, 53, 70, 98, 356
    Illustrated Herald, 171, 172
    News, 53
    News-Call Bulletin, 53
    Open City Press, 303
    Oracle, 301
    Wah Kee, 74
San Francisco Exposition (1915), 147
Sangster, Margaret E., 109
Sanitary and Heating Age, 87
Sanitary and Heating Engineering, 87
Sanitary Plumber, 87
San Jose (Calif.)
    Mercury, 336
    News, 336
San Simeon, 222
Santa Fe (N. Mex.)
    Crepusculo de la Libertad, El, 44
    Republican, 50
Santayana, George, 105
Saratoga Trunk (Ferber), 168
Sarnoff, David, 161, 164
Saroyan, William, 112, 114, 277
satellites, 51, 131, 133, 165, 180, 197,

419

Index